HIT THE TARGET, RATHER
THAN YOUR POCKET WITH CCI

CCI clays have been designed to perfection by shooting men for shooting men. Many years of patient research have gone into making them the best clays available today. They trap without breaking, fly true, and shatter when hit.

This is why CCI have rapidly become Europe's No. 1 clay, chosen for every major event in 1982/1983, 1984 and 1985.

Our targets are available throughout the UK, but should you have any difficulty we will be pleased to help. Just call us on the telephone number below and we will give you our nearest distributor.

So, the next time you shoot clays, choose the best, choose CCI. And, remember, we are just as keen on price as we are on quality. Also, look out for the additions to our range which will be out soon.

CCI International, Priors Haw Road, Corby, Northants, NN17 1JG.
Telephone Corby 60933, or Telex 342420 CCI UK.

Everything you need to prepare a delicious hot meal …anytime, anywhere.

Whether clay shooting, rough shooting or wild fowling, or just out walking for the day, have you ever really fancied a hot meal but dismissed the idea because of all the fuss and bother? If so, Hotcan has the perfect answer with a unique range of self-heating meals in a can designed to keep hunger at bay and the bird in the bag.

Hotcan is the ultimate convenience meal. No preparation, no external heat source, no utensils and no washing up. Simply pierce the can with the spike provided, remove the ring pull top and occasionally stir the contents. The food is piping hot and ready to eat in about 10 minutes.

Described as "Substantial, balanced and nutritious", Hotcan is available in a range of tempting recipes including sausages beans and baconburger, beef casserole, chicken casserole, Irish stew, vegetable curry and turkey curry with rice – just the thing for the Glorious Twelfth or any other date on the shooting calendar for that matter.

In fact, Hotcan is so convenient it can be enjoyed anywhere, anytime, no matter what the occasion.

Try Hotcan today and savour the delicious simplicity of a simply delicious idea.

SELF HEATING HOTCAN MEALS

BEEF CASSEROLE WITH VEGETABLES AND GRAVY

Hotcan Limited, Stadium Court, Parkgate, Rotherham, South Yorkshire S62 6EW. Tel: 0709 69856/9

THE SHOOTING HANDBOOK

Edited by John Humphreys

Sixth Edition

Beacon Publishing
Jubilee House, Billing Brook Road,
Weston Favell, Northampton
Telephone: (0604) 407288
Telex: 312242 MIDTLXG

£5.95
ISBN 0 906358 65 5

SHOOTING CONTENTS

Foreword by John Swift

Director, Conservation and Research
British Association for Shooting & Conservation

In the past twelve months the B.A.S.C. has been growing even faster than before any many people have been asking the reason why. Record numbers of new members have been recruited. The Association's individual membership is now approaching 75,000 with well over 600 affiliated clubs and registered syndicates throughout Britain. The latter have shown a particularly rapid increase. Two new regional offices have been set up and extra staff have been taken on for a growing volume of firearms work, as well as in the education and training and public relations fields.

Why is this happening and why is it so important for shooting. It is happening because people are increasingly recognising their responsibilities to help ensure the future of their sport and that the B.A.S.C. is the only organisation which is in a position to carry that message forward effectively. It is important because it shows that those involved are starting to take their sport's future seriously. It also enables the Association to combat political threats more effectively. It provides the resources for projects which demonstrate on the public stage all that is good and responsible about shooting sports, in particular what is being done in the fields of education, conservation and practical research.

There is no doubt that the general public increasingly recognise that shooting makes a big contribution to the wellbeing of the countryside in a way which cannot be matched by the government funded or voluntary bodies. The public is also increasingly prepared to accept that man's freedom to "hunt" is evermore understandable in a world which is increasingly urban and plastic packed. Many do not, however, perhaps yet appreciate that over 5,000,000 people from all walks of life are actually involved in country sports and who find them immediately rewarding and morally approvable.

The scale of commercial interest outlined in this Shooting Handbook serves to reflect the public support for shooting and, indeed, other country sports. But in an age when tiny, but well organised, minorities comprising the animal rights groups, animal liberation movements, hunt retributionists and so on, are becoming ever shriller and more extreme in their exposition of new ways to break the law and threaten public safety, the sportsman, the businessman, the gamekeeper and their representatives must help each other and work together to keep our house in order and present the truth as it is in a fair and honest way.

The 1985 Shooting Handbook is part of that effort.

Education — The Voluntary System
Gerry Turner

The B.A.S.C. ideal is "that all who shoot conduct themselves according to the law and to the highest standards of safety, sportsmanship and courtesy; with full respect for their quarry and a practical interest in wildlife conservation and the countryside." Sporting shooting has become much more than simply the harvesting of a natural resource for personal pleasure. The sportsman in general, and the wildfowler and rough-shooter in particular, pursue wild and often migratory birds which rely on a wide range of different habitats for survival. In pursuing such quarry the sportsman must become involved in a wide range of issues with which wildlife conservation is concerned.

Sporting shooting cannot take place without affecting the countryside as a whole; those who shoot should be aware of the implications of their actions. They should also be aware of the effects of other pressures such as pollution, afforestation, urbanisation, increasing access to the countryside and an increase in leisure time, all of which will have an effect on the countryside and its wildlife. In consequence it has become necessary to strengthen the sporting ethic by developing well-defined statutory regulations and codes of practice within which the sport can flourish. The sport evolved with a very strong sporting etiquette. A knowledge of the laws relating to the sport, coupled with a knowledge of that code, plus the ability to apply that knowledge in a practical manner, are all essential pre-requisites of sportsmanship. Anyone who takes part in the sport without this basic knowledge is likely to be a danger, not only to himself but also to others, and ill risk bringing the sport into disrepute.

Traditionally the skills and knowledge required by those entering the sport would have been passed down from father to son or even, for a minority, from a gamekeeper down to his employer's sons. Such an apprenticeship is undoubtedly the best way to learn subjects such as gun handling, quarry identification and range judging, all of which require practical application in order to ensure that they are sufficiently ingrained as to be second nature. One of the traditional ways to learn safe gun handling was to let the pupil carry a stick which had to be handled as though it were a loaded shotgun, and when that was carried correctly to progress to an un-loaded shotgun until, ultimately, the great day would arrive when the first cartridge could be loaded into the breech.

The social structure of those who take part in sporting shooting has altered considerably in the last few years. There are many now who wish to take up the sport, or indeed who have entered it, who have no real knowledge of shooting, of the laws and traditions of the countryside, or the quarry species they pursue and the management needs of those species.

The shooting organisations, not least the B.A.S.C., have not been slow to respond to the growing need for education and training of newcomers, and have used many means to provide the necessary guidance. The B.A.S.C. produced a Code of Practice series in the 1970s; programmes of specialist courses on all aspects of shooting are run not only by the B.A.S.C. but also by the Game Conservancy and the British Deer Society. During 1983 the B.A.S.C. introduced the Proficiency Award Scheme for Sporting Shotgun Shooting in order to give everyone, not only newcomers, who shoot, a practical method of achieving a measure of self confidence which they would not otherwise have been able to achieve. Participation in the scheme indicates that those attending have at least taken their sport seriously and are aware of, and can implement, certain prescribed minimum standards of conduct, with particular reference to safety, sportsmanship and courtesy. Regional Education Development Officers, acting in a voluntary capacity, organise courses of instruction and assessment on a county-wide basis throughout the country.

Future

In shooting, as in many other leisure pursuits, it is evident that the behaviour of the vast majority of shooting sportsmen is acceptable. It is a small minority who cause the problems which then reflect on the rest of the shooting community. Recent calls for a system of mandatory tests for all who take part in sporting shooting represent bureaucratic, very expensive and possibly a totally inappropriate means to solve a small problem. Mandatory testing would effectively result in an attempt to needlessly legislate for a standard already being voluntarily practiced by most shooting people in order to simply lift those few at the bottom end of the scale who would probably not conform to any standard voluntary or otherwise.

Given the strong influence which the traditional sporting ethic brings to bear on participants, the voluntary training schemes currently being adopted will be able to maintain satisfactory standards. Not least in importance is the P.A.S. which will, over the next three years, cover every county in England, Wales Scotland and Northern Ireland. The B.A.S.C. has committed itself to provide the necessary resources for a programme of voluntary education; all that is required is for committed volunteers to come forward in order to be trained to run the courses. Further details of the Proficiency Award Scheme for Sporting Shotgun Shooting are available from Gerry D Turner, Development Education Officer, B.A.S.C., Marford Mill, Rossett, Wrexham, Clwyd.

Conclusion

Much of the criticism which is levelled against shooting sports is as a direct result of misunderstanding, or of bad behaviour being witnessed in the field. The rights and privileges of sportsmen to continue to enjoy their sport, and the satisfaction of conserving the countryside and wildlife, depend very much on the behaviour of all sportsmen. We will be judged by our attitude and behaviour. We must, all of us, ask ourselves whether or not we need to learn more about the sport or indeed attend a ''refresher course''.

The Shooting Sportsmans' Responsibilities in the Future

Pamela Brogan

The C.L.A. theme for the 1985 GAME FAIR at Stoneleigh Abbey — "Living together in the Countryside" suggested the important role both urban and rural communities must play if Britain's countryside and its fieldsports are to be enjoyed by future generations. Increased focus on the "in-vogue" conservation programmes by the press and media, coupled with the misunderstanding generated by the word, 'preservation' has resulted in only widening the gap between town and country. Given these present times, this is very unfortunate when the direct opposite could be so powerful, and thus more mutually beneficial.

Facets of country living, hitherto either ignored or taken for granted have now become political issues, like the recent Curlew and Redshank controversy. Victory will be won more and more at Parliamentary level which poses interesting questions for the shooting sportsman. What are his responsibilities in the future? To help understand the background to this question and the necessity to ask it, one should be aware of the effects that civilization, and the insidious path of progress has wrought on nature's original structures.

To explain very simply and briefly how the interest in fieldsports developed, one has to return to earliest man, whose survival relied on his purveyance of food by fleetness of foot, bow, and spear. As Ice age became Stone age, and Iron became the Bronze age, Man had learned to cultivate the land, tame the wild beast, and domesticate the wild dog, to a role more satisfying as a companion on his hunting pursuits, now developed to a science of sport.

Significant events occurred during the 14th and 16th centuries that not only laid the foundation stone but also shaped the outlines of modern fieldsports.

It is interesting to relate the first act restricting shooting with guns was passed in 1496, and Henry VIII is credited with issuing the first game licences in 1533. In the pure sense of hunting, this must have been the heyday of hawking, coursing, stalking, fowling, game hunting and fishing.

A major step forward for the sport of shooting was made in 1860 with the introduction of the Breech loading shotgun, initiating the concept of driven game, which nowadays encompasses not only gainful employment for thousands, but also pays a healthy dividend to the exchequer while conserving the natural asset, and its habitat.

Land used changed dramatically in the 19th and 20th centuries affecting it biologically and economically — precipitating several of the problems facing the shooting sportsman in 1986:- mechanization, modernization, the development of and increased usage of chemical sprays for agricultural use, massive cultivation of pastureland, afforestation, drainage, pollution, hedgerow removal, urbanization, motorways, and the dramatic rise in the number of motor cars, and by no means least, the increase in leisure time now available to the working man. So what used to be a large pond with few fish had become a small pond with seemingly too many fish. The landowner and shooting man's response to this difficult situation was a reasonable one. For example they undertook the task of breeding thousands of pheasants (an expensive project) not only for their ground but, benefiting local fieldsportsmen. Also, thus removing stress from the over-pressurised "wild bird".

Large areas of Britain's nationally and internationally important wetlands owe their conservation and preservation to wildfowling clubs, who not only manage shooting levels but also set aside unshot areas for feeding and roosting refuges. They are also actively involved in wardening and habitat management. The ultimate concern of wildfowlers is the long term protection of wetland habitats, and the Kent Wildfowling and Conservation Association displayed both financial and creative initiative by purchasing 750 acres of prime salt marsh in the Medway.

The growth of organisations like B.A.S.C. and the Game Conservancy endorse the shooting sportsman's committment to the future of his sport by the conservation of it.

The work 'Balance' is defined as, "any condition of equilibrium" which if achieved, undoubtedly results in success. The balance of nature has been restored quite effectively, in the past couple of decades but particularly over the last five years by responsible, like-minded people who conserve, preserve, and shoot. Much has yet to be done if the scales are to be kept balanced. Some pointers to the shooting sportsmans' responsibilities:

1. Sportsmen need to respond to changing land use, farming and afforestation problems.
How?
Landowners, farmers and foresters ought to plan and design wildlife conservation features on their land. The Government should encourage this.

2. Everyone (urban and rural) must respect the countryside, its ways, and lores, as well as those who live and work there.

3. It should be incumbent on all those who shoot to join the B.A.S.C.; to have a powerful and influential, unified voice in present and future developments on conservation, quarry lists, firearms, and their use, and in particular, legislation affecting present and future situations.

4. More than ever, it is incumbent on the shooter to behave in a responsible manner, at all times, from the security and handling of his personal fire-arms, to the foreshore and the country estate. Education is part of this responsibility, nowadays ignorance on any subject is unforgivable.

B.A.S.C. provides advice, practical help and training courses, to achieve standards of conduct for sporting shots. It also provides individual and third party insurance against accidents.

Are field sports going to survive in the future? Attempts orchestrated at two levels, are seeking to undermine this future.

1. The restriction from Europe on firearms possession is a real THREAT, so it is therefore essential for all who shoot to lend their maximum political weight, to the shooting lobby's voice in Parliament and elsewhere, to stand up for their rights to own and use sporting guns.

The small, but politically organised Anti-groups have gained some ground, simply because they are more single minded. If they are allowed to continue unopposed, the balance of nature's scales will be tipped destructively. No one will win in this circumstance. It is up to you — THE SHOOTING SPORTSMAN OF TODAY TO SECURE THE FUTURE FOR CONTINUING GENERATIONS.

Editor's Preface

— JOHN HUMPHREYS —

I have been associated with *The Shooting Handbook* first as a contributor and, for the last three years as Editor, and it never fails to delight me that such a high calibre of sportsman/writer is prepared to submit copy for what has, admittedly, become an established institution in the shooting world. Sportsmen tend to be either good communicators or knowledgeable practitioners: all too rarely do the two talents merge in one individual but the 1985-6 Handbook has gathered together a high proportion of them.

For example, few men in Britian know more about stalking than Arthur Cadman and Edgar James, names which are household words among stalkers not only throughout the UK but on the Continent. Both have the knack of communicating and can do so from the position of strength due to experience in their subject which few may surpass. By the same token, Alan Murray is a professional wildfowler; shooting geese and helping others to shoot them is how he makes his living and he writes of what he knows as one of the top goose shooters in the country.

Trevor Norfield captures the essence of basic gundog training and the simple problems of the early work which are too often neglected by the experts who may have become more preoccupied with advanced training. Trevor writes from experience of his early trials and errors, but do not be deceived by his modesty; he knows as much about practical gundog work as many and more than most. Sam Grice, founder, inspiration, organiser and CPSA coach of the Public Schools clayshooting world maintains our 1986 themes of serving youth, how to do it and what to buy. Sam writes from his unchallenged position in the world of clays and youngsters. The increasingly popular air rifle is covered with similar expertise by John Fletcher and who could be better qualified than the Editor of *Airgun World* to write with authority on the subject? By the same token, Richard Atkins is Editor of *Target Gun*, the premier magazine in its field, so that specialised aspect of gunmanship is also expertly covered.

The four wheel drive vehicle is an ever popular section as well as a subject for debate, and Rodney Tibbs, who makes his living from being an expert on motor vehicles, has taken a shrewd look at the increasingly complex world of the cross country, dual purpose wheels for the shooting man.

The woods, fields and their birds are not neglected but dealt with by John Richards who looks at the shooting scene in Spain, Mike Swann of the Game Conservancy concentrates on the mysteries of the most exciting game bird, the red grouse, while I, happy to be in such illustrious company, permit myself a few thoughts on modern pigeon tactics and controlling vermin on the shoot.

The future of our shooting lies in the hands of our children and Brian Martin of *Shooting Times* tells youngsters how to make a modest entry into the shooting world by starting at the bottom, while Des Wilson of *Sporting Gun* reveals some of the snags and offers tips on buying a second hand shotgun and also takes a look at that hardy annual, shotgun cleaning and maintenance. David Garrard's theme of ammunition for the small bore shotgun also implies an interest in the young entry.

These and other pieces of expert and interesting opinion, anecdote, advice and up to date news of equipment, written by a first eleven of modern sportsmen, comprise a package with which I am proud to be associated.

The Buyers' Guide section, a comprehensive directory of the goods and services available to the shooting man, incorporates an enhanced and updated 'Where to Shoot' in response to reader requests for more of such information.

The Buyers' Guide will be found on the counter or near the telephone of all the gunshops and dealers listed here; the traders have already expressed their delight with the supplement and left us in no doubt how invaluable it has proved to them.

The whole book is for you, the reader, and not for us who produced it. The accuracy of the entries is monitored and updated carefully, but it can be only as good as the information we receive from the traders and readers themselves and their response to our mail 'shots'. Please let Beacon Publishing know as soon as possible if your business has changed its address, telephone number or status so that our record for accuracy may be maintained. It seems a pity if customers are obliged to look elsewhere just because you did not spend the price of a phone call or a stamp to keep the information 100% accurate, which is our aim.

In the meantime, may I wish all good fortune to UK sportsmen, especially shooters. Support your organisations, keep your feet, backsides and powder dry, and good reading.

Clays for Youngsters

SAM GRICE

Sam Grice is a schoolmaster at The Leys School, Cambridge and holds a life long interest in guns and shooting. In 1976 he founded The Leys Clay Pigeon Shooting Club and after arranging informal competitions against neighbouring schools, went on to organise the first Public Schools Eastern Area Championship in 1977. The logical extension of this was a National Championship the following year, an event which grows annually as more Independent Schools become organised and involved in Clay Pigeon Shooting. Over 400 Junior Competitors participated in last year's Championship.

To improve the standard of his own coaching, Sam qualified as a C.P.S.A. Club Coach and as well as coaching some thirty-five young shots twice weekly at his own School Club, he is also Senior Coach at the Cambridge Shooting Grounds. Always keen to expand the sport, he has recently accepted the appointment of Coach to the Cambridge University Clay Shooting Club.

Sam firmly believes that success with youngsters is built primarily on patience, safe gun handling, a properly fitted gun and a thorough grounding in the elementary techniques.

There are few youngsters who do not relish the prospect of firing a weapon at a target, especially a target which flies through the air. Therefore, in terms of raw, enthusiastic material our Schools would seem to be the obvious place to recruit young blood into Clay Shooting.

I discovered when I formed my own School Club an understandable ignorance of the sport amongst the teaching profession. However, having worked out costs, explained the Safety Rules and blueprinted a format for the Club, I invited the Headmaster to "have a go" one afternoon. Since then, I have received every support from the School, both financial and otherwise.

But how I envied the highly organised Rifle Shooting set-up at Schools level - their National Championship at Bisley, the prestigious position they held, their facilities and coaching and their ability to bestow status by awarding School Colours. All this, surely, was something to emulate and perhaps one day Clay Shooting in schools might achieve some parity.

Although our two hundred or so Public Schools contain large numbers of boys who shoot game and who have access to guns, I found that no really serious attempt had ever been made to organise the sport as more than a one-off activity having no real status. It seemed, initially, that the only way to build up a proper organisation would be by inter-Schools, then Area and ultimately a National Competition if the sport were to achieve the necessary purpose and required status. Schools Clay Shooting could only gain recognition by the number of pupils involved and by success at a high level. This has now come

about, thanks to the help of many benefactors, not least Eley cartridges, who from the start have continued to support and generously sponsor all our events.

Our young shots are the future of the Sport - its very lifeblood in fact. They need the enthusiasm of adults, both teachers and parents to take charge of and establish Clay Shooting in the sports curriculum using either a local club or, if viable, a distant and safe part of the School grounds.

Here, I must stress that my propositions are idealistic. They can never be realised on a large scale for a wide and obvious variety of reasons, but, where local facilities exist, it should be possible for a small but significant proportion of schools to promote Clay Shooting as a regular activity. Happily this is the case for some thirty Public Schools plus several Prep

A study in concentration. Jamie Garland prepares for a shoot-off.

Schools who are now fully committed to, and equipped for, Clay Shooting and their number grows each year. This means that at least five hundred young shots are being properly educated in safe gun handling, behaviour on the shooting ground and the correct and skilful use of a shotgun. Hence the vital importance of educating young people by practical and exciting involvement in shooting and field sports. Where better to start than by learning to shoot clays safely and successfully? Indeed at Seaford College in Sussex every new boy tries Clay Shooting as part of his first year basic skills programme. Little wonder that they have a Clay Club of over eighty pupils plus an enviable sporting layout and a Skeet range in their extensive School grounds. In contrast, here at The Leys we make frequent use of the nearby Cambridge Shooting Grounds.

And so, on to the coaching of beginners. Using a 12 bore O/U with a light one ounce load, a simple going away bird provides an ideal first target for the novice. With the stock properly bedded into the shoulder pocket and cheek placed correctly on the comb, the Coach can help the pupil point accurately and the clay is smashed, so fixing the correct sight picture in the pupil's mind from the very first shot. A normal sized fourteen year old can support a 12 bore and by using a light cartridge will receive less recoil than from a light 20 bore. The heavier gun is also steadier on the target and therefore less likely to wobble about especially with the Coach supporting under the foreend. Remember that youngsters tire more quickly than adults and care must be taken not to overdo things. When coaching a group one should rotate their shooting, giving each of them several goes of perhaps five shots at a time.

Young pupils vary in their first approaches to shooting a gun, but all are nervous, excited and desperate to succeed. Tensions can be alleviated by chatting about their various interests, hobbies, sport or T.V. programmes! The pupil then usually begins to relax and enjoy his first successes with the appropriate amount of praise from the Coach. Hence the need for good coaching from the outset. It is a wise investment to learn any new skill correctly from the very beginning and none more so than in shooting.

A really worthwhile gift to any young shot would be perhaps three or even five lessons with a good Coach. Faults regularly observed in adults would be eradicated before developing. If to practise any

The fruits of success. Sam grice with the Leys school 'A' team 1984 British Public Schools Champions.

skill perfectly and correctly means improvement and success then, conversely, to practise incorrectly means deterioration, lack of success and demoralisation. If any fault is assiduously practised anyone can become brilliantly bad at it! A good Coach will pinpoint potential faults even before a shot has been fired and cartridges wasted.

Talking of cartridges, one ounce of No.7 shot will shatter most sporting clays, cause less fatigue and give more comfortable shooting too. A bruised shoulder and flinching from heavy loads are the very things a novice can well do without. There are several excellent brands available in one ounce loads. Maionchi make a very impressive trainer cartridge. Eley Impax and Winchester G.B. 7s are ideal for normal range sporting birds. Eley also produce a very good short 2" cartridge which is very light indeed. It is a pity that these and several other reputable light loads are generally more expensive than the regular 1 1/8 ounce cartridge. Jimmy Ling of Hoxne, Diss has excellent 1 oz. loads specially made up at a very reasonable price and can provide a first rate 7/8 oz. cartridge with shot size as required. Given the choice, I would opt for 8 or 9 shot every time.

Everything purchased in bulk is cheaper and ordinary black clays are no exception, the coloured ones costing a little more but proving very useful against a dark background. The 90 mm midi makes a fine target and is available in yellow, white, orange and black from Hepworth Refractories. It is sensible to 'phone around for the lowest prices. Here in Cambridge I am fortunate enough to have delivery included in the price of my clays from John Eastaff of Bedford.

A School's first expenditure is likely to be that very vital piece of equipment - a trap. All the well known makes on the market are well engineered and competitively priced - they have to be to survive. Don't forget that a base or stand will be needed to anchor the trap. The Farey double arm Levermatic is a superbly built trap, safe and easy to operate. Priced at around £200 they are well worth the expense. Lower priced Farey traps are available. The Bowman Sledge double arm 'Super Two' is easy for a junior to operate and retails around £90. Newboult and Thorpe's range starts at £45 and the Stuart Double Teal Mk. 2 is priced at £95 with the single arm at £84. All these traps are well made and represent good value. A double arm trap is, of course, a more versatile piece of equipment.

Safety in the use of traps is of paramount importance, as a wrongly handled trap could inflict serious injury or worse, kill a careless or inexperienced trapper. A trap should always be loaded with the left hand, the right remaining clear of the arm. For optimum safety it is advisable to purchase a trap which locks when cocked and is released by a lever, rather than an arm over centre trap, which can be released by an accidental nudge. All young trappers should be fully trained to operate a trap safely and correctly.

Ear muffs or plugs should be mandatory, as damage to the ears and consequent loss of the upper partials has been proved conclusively when the ears are exposed to regular percussive vibrations - shooting! Bilsom manufacture a wide range of muffs but some products can be a little too bulky. I personally favour the slimline Silenta Mil, finished in olive green. It folds away easily and is light and effective and is becoming increasingly popular on shooting grounds.

Very useful is a cap with a good peak to shield the eyes from clay fragments and the head from flying shards. Of complementary benefit is a good pair of shatterproof glasses such as Optix Cormorants, retailing at around £18.

Any jacket worn should never be baggy enough to catch the butt nor have a right hand breast pocket to snag when mounting. A properly fitting skeet vest is a good investment with capacious pockets for cartridges. There are many styles available from about £25 upwards.

Guns for young clay shots should not be so light as to produce excessive recoil, nor so heavy that they cause fatigue. Remember, that an O/U is used only on the stand itself and then in short bursts. It usually spends a fair amount of time in its gunslip, in a gun rack, or held rested. So a gun which can be swung and pointed easily but which is heavier than a game gun is ideal. Take the Coach's advice and buy the best gun you can, making sure that it is properly fitted.

There are several well tested, new, imported makes available at the lower end of the market. Prices would start at about £260 for an E.Rizzini ejector. Parker Hale offer their Midland 502 model at £281 and the 503 at £326. The Spanish Lanber Field ejector retails at £250 and the extensive Lincoln range is excellent value. Models obviously increase in price according to finish, woodwork and better quality materials. Such is the Beretta 686 Special Sporting - outstanding value at £575.

Regarding chokes, most O/U guns are too tightly choked for novices and extra expense may be incurred by having it removed, therefore Skeet borings would be of more benefit to a young shot, or improved cylinder and ¼ choke. Using a trap cartridge very good patterns will be thrown too. I would hope that parents would buy the best they could afford and I have found that they generally do. It is always a source of great pleasure and pride for parents to see their offspring achieving success and enjoying it too. I know - I'm one myself.

With the advice of his Coach the young shot is now set up to enjoy and, I hope, excel at his new sport and, surely, the finest accolade he can give his Coach is when he says "you make it so simple". And so it should be, because that is the Coach's job well done, precisely because it has been done well.

The coach must be in control of the gun at all times.

Wild Goose Chase

ALAN MURRAY

Alan Murray shot his first goose in December, 1969, and from then on was smitten.

He set out to learn all about geese; the species, habits, food, calls and the arts of decoying. After 11 years he had shot nearly every goose marsh in Britain and decoyed in all the major goose counties in Scotland from Dumfries to the Hebrides. In August 1980 redundancy was imminent so he decided to become a Wildfowling Guide, and moved to Scotland which resulted in an ambition fulfilled. Five years later he is a well established guide with regular clients and a first class reputation, taking five guns per week, and specialising in goose shooting.

Inland goose shooting is a form of fowling different from foreshore gunning, as you are decoying the feeding ground and not flighting, so the gun and ammunition vary a little from those used for foreshore shooting. I recommend my shooters to use the gun they use regularly, as the intention is to get the geese within range. An ideal gun is 2¾ inch chambered 12 bore, ¼ and ½ choke using 1 ¼ ounce or 1 ½ ounce of No. 3 shot, the reason being that your shooting is done within 40 yards maximum range and the combination I have recommended throws an excellent pattern at that distance. The trick is to get the geese within range, and this is done by means of a combination of decoys and a call used properly. The variety of calls and decoys on the market at the moment can leave you stuck for choice, but I use 15 shell decoys, (from Shooting Developments, Fife), and 4 full bodied decoys as sold by Ralph Grant. I have been using this combination for 5 years and found it very effective, mainly because I have the sighting value of the full bodied bird and the movement of the shells.

As for laying out the pattern, I have tried out most methods; the horse shoe pattern is favoured by American goose shooters, the idea being to persuade the

geese to land in the opening. Books recommend that you have all your decoys facing into the wind, because it was always thought the geese fed or stood head to wind. In my opinion this makes the picture look too artificial: you must always try and make your decoys appear natural and you can only do this by watching a field of geese feeding, not for 10 minutes from a car, but from a hide for an hour or two without you gun. This is two hours well spent, as you will be rewarded with in-depth knowledge about feeding geese you did not think existed. So your decoy plan should be set with your birds in random positions with 3 or 4 placed away from the main pattern Then stop, look and ask yourself if it looks natural; if you have watched the geese you will know. Once you have got your pattern right, stick to the same number of decoys and you will eventually find that you have no problem in laying them out in the dark. I find that about 20 decoys are enough, as putting large numbers out can tend to lead to mistakes. I also use the magnum goose decoy, a bird approximately 4 times bigger than a normal full

bodied decoy. I do not recommend the beginner to use these unless he intends to have many blank flights as it takes a deal of trial and error to handle them properly. Once you have done so, they can produce decoying at its best.

It is not essential to decoy a feed, but you may decoy under flight paths or on any favourable field which the geese pass. If you are using magnums, the bigger the field the better, as there is no background against which the geese can relate to the size of your decoys.

Now you have your decoys laid out you need to supplement them with a call. The geese will be greylags or pinkfeet, and I use two calls, the OLT L22 and the OLT 600. In my opinion these are the best, the L 22 for pinkfeet and 600 for greylags.

The actual calling takes a long time to learn but if you combine your watching visits with the arrival of the geese, you can listen to them and pick out the main calls you will need. Firstly you must master the call of the geese on the ground seeing a skein of passing or incoming birds. This is an intermittent call. When the geese turn towards you the call

Greylags on an Autumn stubble.

The knack is to decoy the geese within easy range.

becomes more continuous without a break and, as they actually come in, they burst out chattering excitedly. One important thing to remember is to stop calling when the birds have set their wings to land.

Once you have got the decoys and the calling right and the geese are coming in to you, wait until they are over your killing area or between you and your decoys, as then you minimise the risk of wounded birds — and do not move until the last minute.

Once you are in a goose area the fields you seek are early season stubbles, mid-season potato fields, and late season grass or winter cereal. You will find that grey geese go to the same area season after season, providing they are not over-shot. Remember this when they are coming in to your decoys: do not over kill, but think of another day and above all respect your quarry. They are too noble birds to be slaughtered or abused.

It was a November morning with a howling gale and pouring rain, what I call "a sit in the Landrover morning". When we arrived at the farm, dawn was a long way off and the geese would still be sheltering on St. Serfs waiting to battle through the storm to their feeding grounds. I knew the geese would be late moving so I told the lads to "Get in the Landrover and have a cuppa, we've plenty of time yet". The old hands jumped in the motor and relaxed. The two novices sat in their car fidgeting and bursting with enthusiasm. Every two minutes they were at my window, "should we not be getting ready now Mr.Murray?". Being a guide you get used to soakings, ditch baths and cold feet so you tend to husband your enthusiasm and cherish every warm dry moment. So they all started to get ready and I sat in the motor, already dressed,

waiting. Five minutes later someone called "Come and look at this!". So I got out and looked across the field — I thought I had seen it all — but there, in the cold, grey dawn, walking across the field, were my two elderly novices in full regalia of waxproofs and wellies, bala-calvas and carrying *black city umbrellas.*

As a wildfowling guide I meet shooters from all walks fo life from surgeons to miners, all with one thing in mind, the wild geese. When my guns are with me I treat them all the same, no matters how important they are, as I like a friendly, relaxed atmosphere but I make it clear that they are there on a goose shooting holiday, not a concentrated kill. We have many interesting little daily happenings, some amusing, some sad, but they all form part of a goose shooting holiday. Once I had a gentleman and his wife out at the end of September, not goose shooting weather, but shirt sleeve and waistcoat order. We were out on two mornings and shot eleven geese.

The first balmy morning we were walking down the lane to the fields; dawn was breaking and a goose called. I did not take much notice because if I had to stop and listen to every goose calling in the pre-dawn gloom, I would never make it to where I wanted to set up before daylight. We were nearly at our destination when another goose called, a mature gander, and the whisper came, "I can see it! I can see it!". So amid the flurry of bags dropping and guns clicking I spotted the goose against a pale crack in the sky but goose fever had struck my guns. "Call it, Alan, see if we can get it". I started to call; he answered, I could not see him as he had vanished in the black, but we chattered away; he was getting closer and I knew we had him, for he suddenly appeared 20 yards out 10 feet off the ground. "Take him", a slight pause and the gun stabbed fire into the

The writer, with two in the bag, uses his call.

night. The goose turned a back somersault and dropped stone dead on the stubble. The guns shot another five that morning and returned in high spirits for breakfast with the first geese of the season in the bag.

The next morning we did manage to get to our chosen ditch without interruption; I put out the decoys and sat down with my flask, but it was full daylight before the geese left the loch. A skein of 20 came along the valley; I called to them, they spotted the decoys and started their excited chatter, turned and came in on set wings. They were over the decoys when the guns shot two nice right and lefts. Next, a single bird came in on silent wings without calling. If we had not spotted him early, he would have landed amongst the decoys. One shot dropped him amongst the shells. He was still lying there when I spotted another single bird. I called him, and this one decided to do a couple of circles round the decoys. It did not make much difference as he was already in range, right above the gentleman, but no shot. I thought, "He's not sure of the range", so I shouted along the ditch, "Take him next time round". He came round again, but still no shot. "What the hell are you doing?" I shouted. Came the reply, "Would you call so that it flies over my wife, as I would like her to shoot the last goose of the morning". His wife was 50 yards down the ditch from me. Directional calling! "That's new", I thought. "Does he think I'm that good, or is it just a severe case of goose fever?"

On another occasion I had with me John and Ernie, brothers from Cheshire, good lads who come with me every season. We set up on a 'tatty' field waiting for greylags. What happened that morning I have never seen before and I do not think I shall ever see again. The geese came and were decoying very nicely and the lads had shot 2 or 3, when a little skein came in from the front. They overshot the decoys and passed about 30 yards above us. John singled out a bird and fired; it folded up dead in the air so he swung onto the next. As he fired at his second bird, the first one dropped between it and his muzzles. His shot struck the falling goose at about 6 feet range blowing a gaping hole through its middle and embedding the plaswad in its chest. The odds on that happening must be very long indeed.

Magnum decoys, four times life size, but not easy to deploy.

Then there was the morning when I had four first-timers, keen lads, all looking forward to their first goose. The night before I gave them a pep talk about the morning's foray. Morning came and we set up on a grass field that pinks had been using for a couple of days. I had the boys in the ditch, two on each side of me, closer than I would do with experienced goose shooters, so that I could keep an eye on them and tell them when to shoot. The geese were 'acting-up' that morning and the decent sized bunches would not come in, but I managed to get singles and twos or threes over the decoys. 14 shots later we had not got a goose so I called

A mixture of Shell and full-bodied decoys which the writer finds most effective.

the boys together. I told them to try and select a bird even if it took two barrels for the one goose. We waited a while longer but nothing came so I got out of the ditch ready for packing up, when I spotted 5 geese. I called and they answered, so I jumped back into hiding. I kept calling and the geese reacted perfectly, in that they came to the decoys, "Give 'em it", I shouted. The boys jumped up and four geese dropped, the fifth one flying away unscathed, calling in the plaintive manner only a lost goose can.

I answered and he turned and came straight back to the decoys. The boys were so excited about their first goose they had forgotten to reload, so I shot him, a first year bird. With that I collected the decoys and the five dead geese. The boys were all excitedly discussing their first goose and all their adventures. One of them asked, "Why did that one come back after all the shooting?". I laid out the five birds, an adult pair and three immature ones and said, "It's a family party; the single bird I shot was one of the young ones. He had lost the rest when you shot and he came back to my call thinking it was one of the family calling".

When I had finished there were no questions, just a silence and the look on their faces told me all I wanted to know. They had pangs of regret and felt a little sad. I have seen it so many times and they had learned in one morning what some shooters never learn, namely respect for the geese. That was three years ago and those same boys still come to stay with me, and first class goose shooters they have become.

Beginners Gundog
TREVOR NORFIELD

In 1975, Trevor Norfield went shopping for a lurcher and returned with an English Springer Spaniel! With a 75% working pedigree, steeped in mythical names of great dogs from the past, young Moss soon showed a natural inclination to work in preference to play. As a direct result, his somewhat bemused owners decided he had better revive his dormant boyhood fanaticism for shooting, and get himself a gun! With a little rough shooting and considerably more beating on some reputable Yorkshire estates, the bug had truly bitten.

In the lifetime of the original dog, involvement is now close to saturation point, with Trevor now shooting in a Cambridgeshire syndicate and with business interests in the manufacture of shooting accessories and local gun retailing at The Cambridgeshire Gun Centre.

One ambition remains; to own and train a dog with a chance of taking it's owner through a Field Trial!

'A dog is for life, not just for Christmas' is the worthy sentiment expressed on the odd car sticker that I've spotted recently. It serves to remind one that a gundog is for twelve months a year and not merely a 'tool' for use during a comparatively short shooting season. For the novice or experienced shooter contemplating his first dog, it must be remembered that, like it or not, the animal must be allowed to become part of the family and can then, in ill-considered circumstances, become a considerable 'tie'. As an example, our family 'kennel' now consists of three spaniels and a West Highland White terrier, so with little hope of paying expensive boarding fees, we now only take holidays where the 'pack' can be included!

So, after the requisite amount of thought, discussion, threats of divorce etc; you've concluded that a dog is essential. I will now stick my neck out further and say that providing you have the right type of canine material; undertake lessons at the correct pace and in the correct order, then training is the EASY BIT. MAINTAINING that training at its finished level is the tricky part. There are no hidden mysteries to gundog training, but you must have the correct temperament yourself and the inherent ability to 'think dog' at times, in order to be one jump ahead. I know a thankfully small number of shooting folk, some of them dog owners, who will never train a dog; who could be apprenticed to the best professional for fifty years and still be unable to train a dog.

CHOICE

Assuming then that the fighting has died down, and the decision been taken in favour of acquiring a puppy or young dog, how do we go about choosing the right one? If you've no idea how to go about it, try to find someone who does; preferably a friend or acquaintance with at least a basic knowledge of dogs who is willing to accompany you whilst searching. That way, you always have them to blame if things go wrong later on! Scour the Dogs for Sale columns in the sporting press and especially the local newspaper to give you a current idea of what is available nationally and close to home. As a general guide, if your shooting is static ie. driven game or hide shooting, go for a retriever breed which will take more kindly to sitting and waiting. The thing I love most about a spaniel is it's constant inquisitiveness. You can have superb sport with a spaniel without shooting a thing, but it will always want to be 'on the go'. If this fits your requirements, then a spaniel it must be.

If the bank balance will run to the asking price of a six month old animal, then see a selection at exercise and make a considered choice. Choosing from a

The writer "en famille" with his pack.

squeaking litter of ten week-olds rather increases the element of luck. I am, at best, described as a 'noisy' handler and generally follow the old adage of picking what appears to be the boldest of the litter. My last attempt at this rather contradicts that theory as the chosen bold pup matured minus several of its 'marbles', whereas her fat, docile litter mate, taken along really as a stable companion, has turned out to be a real cracker! Whatever you decide to do, try to get to see one, or preferably both, parents working. Delve into their pedigrees even if it makes little sense to you at the time, avoid show bloodlines, and best of all, try to view or get information on any previous progeny of the same parentage. I do not subscribe to the theory that bitches are gentler and more easily trained than dogs, though do bear in mind that bitches come 'into season' occasionally, and usually at the most inconvenient time! It is just an extra burden one has to learn to live with, and I am always loathe to tamper with their 'parts' as you may well regret at a later date being unable to breed from a super bitch that you had rendered sterile for your own convenience. Healthwise, no breeder, 'backyard' or otherwise, of any reputation, will object to a veterinary 'once-over'. Price, frankly, is of little consequence; just rest assured that in terms of pleasure and extra game before the guns and in the bag, an efficient dog will pay for its' keep a hundredfold.

HOUSING

It was a matter for debate whether to write the housing section first, as there would be little point in bringing home your new charge without it having somewhere to go! I would always come down in favour of an outdoor kennel. It need not be elaborate but should be secure, dry and free from direct draughts. It rather stings the memory to say that even if your new dog whines or barks during his first few days and/or nights in his new home, you MUST stick at it until he accepts it as his sanctuary. Easier said than done when surrounded by close neighbours of the non-doggy variety! Your dog will benefit from outdoor life, developing a substantially thicker coat to keep out the elements, plus the fact that the kennel itself may well prove to be a valuable training aid in the future. Don't expect him to enjoy prolonged solitary confinement, but let him out regularly or even join him inside as he builds up his familiarity and trust of you and your

family. I have converted old outside toilets into kennels and have built others from scratch. In retrospect I would build housing now in ¾ inch exterior ply with a substantial wood floor, well supported away from any source of rising damp. 2×2 rough-sawn softwood is ideal for posts and frames, wired across in the ever-useful 'weld mesh' galvanised netting. Elaborate design instructions are unnecessary; just use common sense and a little pre-planning of the space available to you, always bearing in mind that you will need easy access for regular cleaning. My own current kennelling consists of basic pent-roof sheds with linking runs, all on a sound base of concrete slabs. Inside I provide a 4ft × 3ft sleeping box where the dog's own body heat provides adequate warmth.

FEEDING

The daily menu for my first pup consisted of biscuit meal and tins of ultra-expensive tinned 'meat'. On opening a tin one morning, my brother, home from University and presumably feeling suicidal, dug in and promptly at a juicy looking lump from the top! 'Mmm … T.V.P.'!! There was I, cheerfully paying an arm and a leg for Texturised Vegetable Protein plus 75% water! All-in dried dogfoods were rapidly gaining in popularity at the time so we quickly joined the throng, experimenting with many different brands along the way. Moss is now ten years young and the only meat he has seen since puppyhood is on the occasional marrowbone and even more occasional table scraps. Shop around with care for these cereal foods as some are quite obviously manufacturers mill-waste. I have fed both meal and pelleted forms from Centrepoint Feeds Services for several years, knowing it to be purpose manufactured, extremely economical, ultra-convenient and, above all, highly nutritious.

EARLY TRAINING

Assuming our young dog or puppy has been given really adequate time to get to know you and his new surroundings, it is no detriment to begin encouraging his learning through play. Take any training very slowly, step by step and for short periods only, well before the novelty of any new 'game' wears thin. By all means let the young dog play with the kids and other dogs, but when it comes to training play it must be just him and you, with as few distractions as possible. I've successfully employed the tarmac quadrangle

Daily exercise should be fun: the dog is not aware that it is being trained.

between blocks of lock-up garages as an early learning centre — so boring for a dog's sensitive nose that all his attention is focused on you, and that is just what you're after! Most animals will comply with commands when food is involved, so encourage patience and steadiness by making the pup wait at a 'sit' for a few moments before diving into his bowl. The same empty bowl dropped with a clang on the floor of the run will prepare the youngster for sudden noises (at a later stage, gunfire), whilst associated with something pleasureable.

As soon as his immunisation programme is completed, you will doubtless want to get him used to walking out on a lead. Don't go all soft-hearted when you have to drag him along on his bum, or he does his utmost to dislocate your arm; a softly spoken 'Heel', and make sure that he does just that. Short journeys of maybe a few yards will suffice with a young pup, then as his confidence grows you can hiss the command to 'Sit'. A doleful stare is all the response you may get at first, but ALWAYS make him comply as with any command and press his haunches firmly to the ground. If the dog doesn't appear to comprehend, then it is probably your fault for not showing him precisely what is required. Barbara Woodhouse invites a good deal of 'mickey taking', but she is quite obviously in the business of training people as well as their pets. Keep both commands and words of praise short and succint — 'What a naughty boy, why don't you ever do as you're told?' is utter rubbish to a dumb animal and will never be answered or understood!

Whistle signals must be equally clear and concise; introduced in conjunction with the appropriate command and/or hand signal. A repetitive triple note for return, a long blast for stop and short pip for turning to the opposite 'tack' whilst quartering. A single tone, high-pitch stag or buffalo horn whistle is fine for all commands, though I have used a 'thunderer' or referee's whistle as a stop. 'Silent' whistles seem fine in theory, but I prefer to hear what I'm up to, even if the dog chooses to ignore it!

Any retrieving practice should be strictly in fun, with anything the dog likes to carry used as his first dummy. A narrow, fenced footpath is an ideal place to start retrieving, to restrict any deviation from a straight gallop back to you. Tuck yourself into a fence corner if the pup shows a tendency to run past you. One or two enthusiastic retrieves is ample. Avoid like the plague your natural tendency to keep flogging away until your aim is achieved. If you or the dog are unhappy about a particular exercise, put him on his lead, take him home, then sit and 'mull-over' the problem. 99.9% of the time it will have been YOU at fault, not the dog.

Well into the training programme of my first dog, he had begun to take hand signals at a distance without a hitch. One evening he consistently went in the opposite direction to that which I indicated. Two sleepless nights later, I suddenly 'twigged'. I had been signalling with my back to the setting sun and poor Moss had been unable to even see me, let along my wild gesticulations, being blinded by the dazzle. The biggest 'clanger' dropped with this dog was my eager acquisition of the ubiquitous 'dummy launcher' — the best thing since sliced bread but only when used in moderation and in the correct situation. As he proved to be a keen and efficient retriever, there was I, happily sending him for 150 yard retrieves, time after time, with no apparent lethargy on his part. Then we came to 'quartering' or hunting the ground in front of, and well in range of, the gun. He merrily proceeded to do what he knew and loved best; getting his nose down 150 yards from his handler! This was an entirely self-imposed problem that I've never

All-in-one dried foods are better than tinned meat.

really overcome with him, so hopefully you will appreciate what I mean by getting things in the correct order!

Follow you manual of instruction, be it book, magazine series or video very slowly and step by step. A thorough grounding in obedience is essential before the dog has any concept of hunting, live game or guns. The intricacies of advanced training are too involved to reproduce here, but I hope we have an idea now of how and where to make a start.

THE SHOOTING FIELD

I would say that more potentially good dogs are spoiled by hasty introduction to 'the real thing' than by any other means. It is much easier said than done, but for however long it takes, leave your gun at home for the novice dog's first few outings and let your friends do the shooting. It is impossible to concentrate both on your 'keyed-up' dog and the high cock pheasant heading straight for you. The least lapse in your canine concentration and there is every chance the dog will take full advantage of his new found freedom and please himself. September 1984 brought my first kind invitation to shoot walked-up grouse in Yorkshire. I think the other guns probably questioned my sanity in having a trio of spaniels at heel but by now I knew the youngsters' idiosyncracies and was confident that they would not spoil anyone's sport. You can generally depend on someone else's dog being less well-behaved anyway! Everything went as well as one could expect; game was scarce and conse-

quently the spaniels came into their own. Walking a line through high heather meant one virtually always had the questing dog in sight and therefore under control. Into the wind young Rowan quartered her ground like an expert, dropped at the flush of our first bird, and stayed dropped as it fell. Another spaniel from way up the line ran-in to pick it! Despite this interruption I was well pleased and able to work the three dogs in rotation; one questing whilst the other two remained at heel, which is always good practice to overcome their competitive jealousies.

Two months later, and back on our Fenland pheasant shoot, the comparison was quite devastating. I was expecting the same two young dogs, still early in their first season, to sit at a peg whilst the birds came thick and fast. DISASTER! My shooting suffered even more than usual and worse, in no time at all the dogs were developing some very bad habits. Unlike the pheasants, I was brought back to earth with a resounding thump. Months of training and careful introduction to game were disappearing fast. I didn't practice what I preach and put my gun away, or even revert to using one dog at a time; and now have the doubly difficult task of trying to rectify matters for next season. Suddenly spare time is at a premium, there are Summer working tests to prepare for, and then your Editor asks me to write an article on gundog training; good grief!

Perhaps I should have gone for a lurcher........?

Four Wheels for the Shooter

RODNEY TIBBS

Rodney Tibbs has been motoring correspondent of the Cambridge Evening News for over 25 years and during that time claims he has driven the majority of vehicles ever to have appeared on the public road. He has taken a particular interest in the emergence of the four wheel drive machine in both utilitarian and luxury car forms. Most owners, he says, have little idea of their vehicle's true capabilities. Here he tries to indicate what can be done with 4WD and takes a comprehensive look at what is currently available.

There was a time when four wheel drive meant either Jeep or a little later, Land Rover. Anyone contemplating four wheel drive found himself faced with a massive vehicle, rugged, uncompromising and one which was very definitely engineered for all terrain work and not for shopping in the High Street.

All that has changed and go-anywhere machines have even divided into two distinct lines of development — the descendant of the Jeep and Land Rover in the form of comfortable machines which remain He-Man vehicles — and very ordinary looking road going cars which have a full four wheel drive capability.

In a sense this has not helped the shooting man. I can recall when a days shooting meant hauling the gear in an early form of estate car. It would have been trimmed in wood rather like a country cottage and would rejoice under the name of shooting brake. Often such machines were ugly, not very practical and suited more on paper to the shooting man than to actual conditions in the field.

But at least the choice was simple. Now the choice is so wide and so good that the entire market becomes very bewildering, so mystifying in fact that it is more important than ever to have a very clear idea of just what you want to do with your four wheel drive set of shooters wheels.

Rodney Tibbs.

If for example you are going to need a very respectable vehicle which is going to form your basic transport throughout the year and take you on the occasional shooting expedition, then a car with four wheel drive is clearly going to be on your shopping list.

If you are fortunate enough to be able to run more than one vehicle then clearly you will have in mind something which can be set aside for your hobby and which can be tailored to cross the sort of countryside and conditions over which you might habitually shoot.

In the first category, that of the car which can take you most places, the choice has never been wider. Fiat's little 4 × 4 Panda, for example, gave me a series of startling surprises when I drove it in the wilds of Scotland on land specially provided by the Forestry Commission for test purposes. This tiny machine with an engine of 965 c.c. and massively reinforced underbody is the world's first four wheel drive machine with transverse engine layout.

Not only this but if possesses the ability to change in and out of four wheel drive at speeds up to 30 miles an hour which means that one can retain momentum when approaching a diabolical section of forest track while bringing much needed extra grip into play. There is good rear end accessibility and rear folding seats so in spite of its modest measurements it is still capable of taking a small shooting party across snow, slush, slime or bog, depending upon their quarry.

At exactly the other end of the scale must stand the Audi Quattros. Quattro versions are now available on the entire Audi range and these are luxurious machines which not only provide the advantages of a permanent four wheel drive layout but which also offer the driver selectable differential locks for both the centre differential and the rear differential. Turning electric switches brings the various locks into play and by intelligent use of them the driver can obtain far superior grip in poor conditions than even that provided by a straight four wheel drive system.

It is with such machines as the Quattro that one has to consider rather more than simply the terrain one is to cover and the gear to be carried. The man who lives some distance from what the Point-to-Pointers call "fair hunting country" will have to consider the time he has available to get himself there. Should he be fortunate enough to live on the doorstep of the grouse, for example, then speed is not important. But if he is hauling himself up from East Anglia than a fast car with four wheel drive is clearly the answer.

From the top Quattro at around £21,000 and the little Fiat at just over £4,000 there is fortunately still a useful choice in the car category. Subaru manage to pitch their prices neatly between these extremes with some very useful machines. There is the 1800 DL estate and GL estate at around £7500 to £8500 and the 1800 GLF hatchback at around £5,900.

Fiat Panda 4 × 4.

Audi 90 Quattro.

The Subaru's might easily have been designed exclusively for the shooting man. With the estate versions one gets a cavernous interior, quite capable of taking a couple of gun dogs with a clip in division at the rear, and there is even a sort of "sub boot" under the floor for valuable odds and ends — cartridge packs perhaps. There is even a "hill holder" device for taking off uphill without hanging on to the handbrake and on the optional automatic transmission version four wheel drive is automatically engaged whenever wheelspin is detected.

I once found myself in the middle of a very slimy and muddy farmyard indeed, more by accident than design whilst driving a Subaru. It romped out of trouble in conditions which would have easily beaten a traditional two wheel system yet the cars are stylish and just as much at home shopping in the High Street as hacking their way through the glens.

Another car in this category which is certainly worth considering is the Toyota Tercel estate car at about £6,800. I had the pleasure of trying out this vehicle on Lord Brockett's estate near Hatfield where some very slimy woodland tracks lead into perfect pheasant shooting. The Toyota has recently been given extra torque and some improved gearbox ratios and it was able to cope very well indeed with some exceptionally sticky going through some long bracken.

I have purposely dwelled a little on the 'car' side of the four wheel drive market because it is newer and less familiar than traditional 4WD types and for this reason is less likely to be familiar to the shooting man.

However there remains a substantial number of customers who wont be tempted away from Land Rover and its subsequent family of vehicles under any circumstances and for them the field remains as comprehensive and as impressive as ever. Remaining with Toyota just for a moment we could go on to look at the Land Cruiser which is a Japanese copy of the Range Rover if ever there was one. Unlike Range Rover it does offer a diesel engine in standard form and it also features lots of room at a price around £13,500.

But the real thing in both Land Rover form and Range Rover form is both British and impressive, much copied and thus flattered but never bettered in my opinion. I am prepared to say that the average owner of either of these classes of four wheel drive machine has neither the nerve nor the knowledge to exhaust their capabilities. At Solihull near Birmingham Land Rover have a savage test track which offers everything from one in three gradients (it is rather like driving up a vertical wall) to forested areas deep in swamp.

I have taken both Land Rover and Range Rover round these test grounds, often with water and mud sliding round the top of the bonnet and still the vehicle has kept going. Their cross country capabilities are quite phenomenal with the driver's nerve failing long before the vehicle gives up. Land Rovers run from the 110 hardtop at around £9,300 to the 110 V8 County at around £12,000. The County offers a high degree of comfort not found before in Land Rover and is really a down market version of the Range Rover which hovers around

Subaru 1800 4WD.

Land Rover Ninety off road.

£16,131 for the four door to £17,916 for the Range Rover Vogue. Automatic transmission is around £900 extra. Finally if neither the 110 nor the Range Rover fit your requirements there is always the ubiquitous Land Rover 90 which at £7,600 is probably the best known of all four wheel drive vehicles and is still as tough and bouncy as ever.

Mercedes Benz are well able to compete in the luxury end of the market with their 230 GE (£14,600), the 280 GE (£16,250) and their 300 GD (£15,560) which at first sight seem competitively priced until one realises these figures are for short wheelbase models. However they have commanded a substantial amount of interest in the face of rugged machines from other makers at much lower cost. I can only assume that the cachet which goes with the name still give Mercedes an edge in what is known in the business as "niche" marketing.

One can move a substantial way down market from Mercedes and still get a highly satisfactory vehicle for one's hunting expeditions at much easier prices. I am thinking in particular of the Lada Niva which believe it or not is highly popular in Germany, right under the Mercedes' nose! There it is the hunting fraternity who provide a substantial number of the sales although over in the French Alps I notice it is very popular not for hunting but simply because it provides a very cheap means of going anywhere on a mountain.

The Lada Niva is not the most handsome vehicle one could wish for but it does sell for £5,500 or so, an astonishingly low price for a big, he-man sort of machine which can give a very good account of itself with permanent four wheel drive. It employs coil springs to very good advantage and I always think that another point in its favour is the extensive waterproofing of the electrics, air intake and exhaust, for river crossings. Don't expect lots of luxury but do be impressed with its massive rear loading door.

That leaves me with just a few machines with which to wrap up this survey of four wheel drive on the British market. The first is the Daihatsu Fourtrak at around £7,000 and its attendant Estate Car at around £8,800. These jointly cover both ends of the market with an essentially two seat vehicle in the Fourtrak and a roomy five seat affair in the estate car. The latter incidentally has a diesel turbo option which makes it well worth considering.

Mitsubishi Colt's Shogun has provided me with many a happy hour and I would commend its ability to offer quite startling acceleration and speed on the open road. If you have to travel some distance to your venue yet need the use of a true cross country machine then I think the Shogun should certainly be on your trialling list. Prices are around £9,500 depending on your choice of engine and extras not to mention the various types of body.

Finally there is the Dacia Duster (must be one of the oddest names in the field) and the Trans Cat. The Dacia Duster GLX costs a modest £6,000 or so but is much more Jeeplike in size than say the similarly priced Niva. It uses Renault running gear and engine of only 1397 c.c.'s but does offer a range of smart body styles.

Transterrain Ltd of Littleport near Ely are the importers of the Trans Cat which is produced in Portugal using Peugeot direct injection diesel engine. There is no petrol version and the machine is workmanlike and substantial. The station wagon costs around £8,600 and there are other versions including a pick up at around £7,325.

All I have been able to do here is to set out a shopping list with some hints to guide the shooter in the best direction for his requirements. Don't forget, always think hard about what you want to do with your shooters wheels, study the terrain over which you intend to travel and look closely at the loads, both human, mechanical and canine you may wish to carry.

Then ensure that your choice meets these requirements. Happy shooting — and four wheeling.

Mitsubishi Colt Shogun.

Shooting in Spain

JOHN RICHARDS

For the past fifteen years John Richards has lived in North Wales, where he has been able to enjoy his favourite pastime all forms of shooting and in particular — wildfowling — on the Dee and Mersey Marshes.

John studied agriculture at The Royal Agricultural College, Cirencester, where he gained a National Diploma in Agriculture. He then chose to work in East Africa for three years and, on his return, entered the University College of North Wales and studied and gained a Degree in Economics.

Professional involvement with field sports started in 1972, when he joined The Wildfowlers' Association of Great British and Ireland as Assistant Development Officer. Later he was to become Director — Development for The British Association for Shooting and Conservation (formerly WAGBI) until the time he left in 1984. John is a regular contributor to Field and Foreshore (Shooting Times and Country Magazine).

S pain is a vast country, occupying most of the Iberian Peninsula. Some 195,000 square miles. Imagine a rocky plateau, sloping slightly to the southwest, crossed by several mountain ranges. The south is bounded by the Sierra Nevada and the north by the Pyrenes and the Cantabrian Mountains. The interior has extremes of temperatures, in summer much of the country is very dry — particularly in the extreme south where the countryside is semi-arid. In comparison with our own country very little of Spain is urbanised or heavily populated.

Spain may be synonymous with bullfighting but it also has a less well publicised tradition of shooting sports which are followed by dedicated and knowledgeable sportsmen and women in breathtaking countryside, often in the remoter parts of the country.

Spanish sportsmen take their sport very seriously and there are now 36 National Parks and 3,600 private reserves for game, plus a further 60 reserves which have been designated within the high mountainous regions.

Hunters are well informed and they understand the importance of flora and fauna management. I well recall when I visited Spain, seeing the controlled hunting zone notices which were signposted and the gamekeepers who were responsible for ensuring that poaching was kept to a minimum and it was also obvious that every effort was made to control vermin.

In Britain Spain has become synonymous with red-leg partridge shooting over the rich lowland farms that grow sunflowers, maize, sugar-cane and wheat. Moving between the crop rows it is common to see coveys of twelve or more red-leg partridges. As a driven sporting quarry there are few birds which are as elusive and, undoubtedly, the rolling landscape and warm stiff levantine wind makes the shooting extremely exciting and very testing for even the most experienced shot. Realistically, it is estimated that 500 partridges could quite easily be bagged by ten or twelve average shots who, in one day would shoot five drives with double guns. Lines of wattle and stone butts are constructed in some areas where regular flight-lines have been established. In other areas guns are placed strategically where folds in the ground provide adequate safe cover.

Much has been written about red-leg partridge shooting in Spain but rather less on the traditional way that red deer and wild boar are hunted. Stalking as we know it in the traditional Scottish sense is practised in some areas. On the large keepered estates excellent trophies of red and fallow deer, wild boar and even moufflon are to be found. The sporting agency brochures stress the physical strength which is needed to negotiate the mountain terrain and from what I saw of one area, known as the Sierra de San

Spanish Partridge, now sought after by the U.K. sportsman.

You can pay up to £15.00 per bird to shoot partridge in Spain.

Pedro, stalking in this countryside would never be easy. One brochure I recently read suggested that "for those that do not have good legs, mountain goat and chamois are in almost all the reserves"!

By far and away the most common method of hunting is the 'Monteria'. The origin of this method of hunting springs from the thirteenth century, when it was recognised that it was necessary to control deer and wild boar. Due to the huge areas involved in the mountainous country it was decided that the only way in which the area could be sensibly hunted was with the help of hunting dogs and organised deer drives. The size of the operation is difficult to imagine. Between thirty and forty hunters, sometimes more, meet early in the morning and after having drawn a peg number are placed approximately 400 yards apart, within the hunting area, each hunter having with him a rifle .270, 7 mm or .300 being the preferred calibres. I was assured that it was not dangerous as each gun is

placed very carefully in the rugged landscape and generally speaking shooting is permissible in any direction, except when the beaters are in close proximity. Huntsmen assemble, each with perhaps 20 to 30 hounds. The huntsman is known as a 'perrero' and carries a horn which is blown at frequent intervals, so he can keep in touch with his own particular hounds, (prodencos and mastines). The co-ordination and positioning of the hunters is of paramount importance, nowadays this is often done with the help of short-wave radios.

Once the 'Monteria' starts it is essential that the hunter remains absolutely still while he waits for stags and hinds to be driven to him. It is not hard to imagine the excitement as the huntsmen with their dogs commence the drive, which may be started several miles from the line of guns. The dogs move through the Mediterranean thickets, sticky leaved shrubs which grow to shoulder height, and between the Ilex, cork oak and alder.

The thorn and Eucalyptus trees are everywhere and hunters and beaters are dressed in leather skirts called 'Zajones', strong leather boots are also essential.

Only red deer stags are shot but all wild boar are fair game. With the number of rifles and the huge areas that are covered by the hounds it is not uncommon to have at least one beast accounted for by each member of the party, very often some of the guns in the centre of the lines are successful in shooting four or five animals. The luck of the draw plays an important part in how much opportunity an individual sportsman might have to shoot in any one day. The 'Monteria' is also a social occasion to be shared with ones friends and, like all field sports in Brit iin, to be in the field, to hear the dogs working and to share the spirit of the day with your colleagues is a never to be forgotten experience.

In certain parts of Spain, wild boar are hunted with a pack of dogs, but the

Spanish partridges are all wild stock.

also interesting to note that visitors to Spain who are over twenty-one can purchase up to five guns which can be taken out of the country.

The formalities for obtaining the necessary documents which I have mentioned are all normally dealt with through Agencies and I am confident should not cause the visiting sportsman any inconvenience.

If I have whet your appetite for sport in Spain then let me make it clear that the cost of all forms of shooting is not cheap, partridge shooting is on a par with the cost you would expect to pay in Britain, i.e. between £12 and £15 per bird bagged. The 'Monteria' shooting, for an all-in cost which would perhaps include hotel, guides, tips, etc. might be as much as £300 to £400 per day per person. In this instance trophy costs would also be covered. For stalking the costs would be considerably higher and trophy charges would be made separately.

hunter is allowed only a knife to despatch the animal when it is eventually at bay. Imagine the excitement of hunting in this manner when it is well-known that the tusks of a boar are like sharp knives, capable of slitting the fiercest dog or the most careful hunter!

To shoot in Spain you must have a hunting and shooting licence, which is issued by the Provincial Head Office of the National Nature Preservation Institute, which is associated with the Ministry of Agriculture, Fisheries and Food. This Licence is necessary before anyone is able to hunt or shoot in any part of Spain. Visitors will be asked to show their passport but under normal circumstances the Agency through which the shooting holiday has been booked will arrange all such licences. In addition you will need a Special Arms Licence which will most likely be valid for two months. This is issued by the Head Police Commissioner for the area where you intend to hunt and when applying you will be asked to present your Firearm or Shotgun Certificate to verify ownership of the weapon. Remembering that Spain has a fine tradition of gun making it is

Red stag, shot in Spain by the traditional MONTERIA method.

Wonderful Grouse

MIKE SWANN

Mike Swann is Technical Information Officer of The Game Conservancy, the premier orginsation which seeks to reconcile the world of game birds with the often conflicting needs of farming and modern use of the countryside. Thanks to The Game Conservancy we are finding out more about the requirements of our game birds, especially the red grouse and the grey partridge, both of which are causing concern due to their waning populations. In this thoughtful and erudite article, he focusses on the red grouse, that expensive but most exciting game bird, tries to identify some reasons for its decline and hints at what might be done to restore it to something approaching its former glory.

The grouse is a bird which captures a place in the sportsman's heart, which is perhaps second to none. Why should this be so? Undoubtedly the fact that one can only shoot a red grouse in Britain is a contributory factor, for this particular race of gamebird is found in no other part of the world. Also, and perhaps more significant, there is that feeling of being "on top of the world" on the moors in August for the first game shooting after the long summer lay-off, with the coveys skimming fast over the heather to the waiting Guns.

Sad news then, that the grouse is in decline in many parts of its range, for while the populations in Northern England seem generally to be holding their own, there has undoubtedly been a decline in Scotland, Wales and Ireland. Many possible causes have been suggested, and indeed exhaustively discussed, but no single factor has been identified as being responsible.

Hence the initiation of the Game Conservancy's Scottish Grouse Project which, following a highly successful appeal for funding, has started to assess the situation. In the first instance, a thorough and exhaustive survey of bag records has been undertaken, not only for grouse, but also blackcock and capercaillie. This has revealed a fascinating pattern which is common to all three species, of stable but periodically fluctuating populations until the First World War, when a drop occured. In the years which followed, the situation was restored until another major decline occured during the Second War. This time the recovery was only partial, with the pre-war levels not being attained in many cases, although a reasonable stable population was achieved until the mid 1970's, when a new and accelerating decline set in. This decline is still continuing at an alarming rate.

Perhaps most interesting of all, however, is that this has been patchy in distribution, with some estates maintaining generally high bags throughout the period. Also, in the northwest Highlands, where densities have never been so high, the situation still seems fairly satisfactory, with sufficient grouse still being present to provide sport for the traditional method of walking-up or shooting over setters or pointers.

It is, of course, well known that the red grouse requires heather as its main food source. Thus, where heather has been lost, either through excessive burning and grazing which produces poor grassland (or "white moor") or to afforestation, it is inevitable that grouse will be lost. This cannot, however explain a decline in areas where the traditional well-managed heather moorland remains.

It is also true that the number of hill keepers has fallen, and this may well

Red grouse are in serious decline in many areas.

have been a significant factor, particularly when one bears in mind the increasing population of foxes and other predators which have occured over much of Britain. With fewer keepers to control them, and vast safe havens in the form of huge conifer forests, it is not surprising that there has been a dramatic increase in fox numbers in many parts of Scotland.

Similarly, reduced numbers of keepers inevitably means reduced heather management, so that it may well be that the quality of much of the grouse habitat has fallen too. Other factors have been mooted, notably the increase in some areas both of ticks and the associated problem of Louping Ill — a disease which can be fatal when contracted by grouse.

For its first season of research the Scottish Grouse Project will carefully monitor events on the moors, and will attempt to elucidate at what stage in the life cycle problems arise, whether it be at egg laying, during incubation, during the rearing of chicks or over winter. Intensive experiments will then commence aimed at reversing the tide and ensuring that grouse numbers rise again.

In spite of the decline, the demand for grouse shooting, both from British sportsmen, and from visitors from overseas continued to increase, to the extent that top quality driven grouse shooting on the most densely populated moors has now become very expensive, with shooting being let at prices of £40 per brace of birds or more. This is good news indeed for those remoter parts of Britain where the flagging rural economy needs every penny it can get. Not only is the income from shooting directly beneficial to the local people, but there is also the money spent on accommodation, for both the sportsmen and their friends.

Where does all this leave the less wealthy of British shooters, who could not possibly afford to take driven shooting on this scale but who would like to enjoy some grouse shooting? Fortunately there are many other options available so that almost anyone can find something to suit his pocket.

For Guns who prefer driven birds, but who would be satisfied with more modest bags, there are many moors which just do not produce enough birds to command premium prices, but where excellent shooting can neverthless be obtained. Similarly, after the main days of August and early September, bag ex-pectation will be inclined to fall away on most estates, with rentals following suit. By this time in the season the birds will also be stronger on the wing, and thus all the more exciting when they come streaking down on the wind.

Walking-up grouse is less testing in terms of marksmanship and is therefore scorned by a minority of shots. Nevertheless a covey of birds bursting up from the heather can be very disconcerting for the inexperienced — it is so easy to fail to pick one's bird, consequently shooting a large hole into fresh air! Also for many people, the real magic of the whole event is in the dog work and fieldcraft needed to get to terms with the game. While spaniels and retrievers can often prove excellent workers on the moor for grouse, showing endless drive and enthusiasm, it is surely the sight of well trained setters or pointers which traditionally arouses the greatest excitement for the walking sportsman. These dogs, by their very nature of having long legs, and working on air scent rather than ground scent,

People on shoot.

A spaniel retrieving a blackcock.

also have the advantage of usually being better able to cover the huge areas of ground needed on the less populated moors. Even if a spaniel or retriever could cover the ground, it would inevitably flush the majority of the birds out of shot of the gun, while the pointing or setting dog freezes the moment it catches scent of its quarry, waiting for the Guns to move in before the birds are flushed.

Large estates often have some marginal ground, outside the main keepered areas, where the lower populations of grouse are perfectly suited to walking-up in this way, areas which, were they not walked-up would probably be ignored completely. These places can produce thoroughly exciting shooting at really very modest cost — usually with the services of a keeper or guide of some sort included, to ensure that the visiting guns do have a good day. Similarly, as one moves further north and west, there are vast areas of wetter moorland where the main interest is in deer, but where good walked-up shooting can be available.

Perhaps most exciting of all for the visitor, with a week's shooting in mind, is one of the many estates where mixed sport can be obtained. For these Guns there can be the delights of a couple of days walking grouse, another in the woods after blackgame and pheasants, some driven snipe on the bogs and marshes, and a duck flight or two to round things off — a veritable feast of variety that will be remembered for a lifetime, long after many a day of more ordinary shooting had merged into the jumble of half recollections of the past.

With so many driven grouse shoots today having trouble in finding good teams of beaters, now that there are fewer people living in the remote parts of Britain, there is another way to join in the grouse scene for the enthusiast who lives reasonably close. This, of course, is if you are prepared to devote some time to helping the hard pressed keeper on his main days, by beating or picking-up, and maybe also by giving up a day or two in the spring when he can use all the help he can get for the heather-burning. Those who prove sound and reliable will not only discover the enjoyment to be had in doing this work, but may well be invited to carry a gun on the keepers' days, when they too may have the privilege of standing in the best butt for a spectacular drive.

In the future, all sportsmen will wish to see a recovery of grouse populations to this former glory, with the results of research by the Game Conservancy and the other organisations in the field combining to give us a greater understanding of the problems faced by this unique bird which is so much a part of the British scene.

Heather burning is an important part of grouse management.

Shooting and Europe

GRAHAM DOWNING

Graham Downing has recently joined the Country Landowners Association as Press and Information Officer and, as such, he will doubtless be playing a significant role in the running of that most prestigious sporting and social highlight of the calendar, the CLA Game Fair.

Prior to that, he was Information Officer for the BASC, a post he occupied with distinction, spending some of his time dealing with the EEC sporting policy matters and, more than most, has been made aware that UK shooting may no longer be considered in isolation from field sports in Europe as a whole.

In this article he highlights some of the issues with which, like it or not, the UK shooting man needs must come to terms.

The British have something of a reputation overseas for their independant mentality. Their insularity in matters European is well known, and whatever the result of that infamous plebiscite on EEC entry, one suspects that the bulk of the British population were still dragged kicking and screaming into the Community. But whatever the feelings of a nation which has for a thousand years sat comfortably inside its moat and cocked a snook at any country which has tried to dictate terms to it from across the channel, there is simply no standing in the way of history. In these days of superpowers to east and to west, Europe and its various international institutions is increasingly becoming a political unit rather than a group of nations which simply co-operate, or not as the case may be, on matters of trade and economics. And international politics today affect, and will increasingly do so in the future, every aspect of our way of life.

To understand how all of this involves shooting it is first of all necessary to distinguish between the principal European institutions, and the influence which they can have on those of us who take our recreation in the countryside. The oldest of the institutions which affects us is the

Council of Europe. Founded as long ago as 1949, the Council was formed in order to achieve a greater degree of harmony between the European Parliamentary democracies. It has 21 member states, stretching from the Atlantic seaboard to the Eastern Mediterranean, encompassing an enormous range of ethnic groups and attitudes.

Since the 1960's the Council of Europe has become increasingly involved in environmental issues and in particular has taken an interest in matters such as European nature conservation and national parks. Any examination of Europe's wildlife habitats inevitably impinges upon shooting, and sure enough, the Council's committee on the environment and natural resources has recently come to examine the possibility of increasing the uniformity of conditions

within which European sportsmen are able to participate in shooting. In particular, the committee has looked at the establishement of a statutory hunting examination for all those who shoot.

It may come as a bit of a shock to some British shooters to learn that mandatory examinations prior to the acquisition of a hunting permit are commonplace in continental Europe. Indeed, among our EEC partners, eight out of ten already have some form of statutory test. Although tests may well serve a useful purpose in other countries though, it is generally recognised that the traditions behind sporting shooting in Britain, and especially the strict control of shooting rights by private landowners and the strong social pressures upon those who shoot to behave safely and responsibly, have led to some of the best regulated, safest and most highly sought after sport

The U.K. shooter has expressed himself overwhelmingly against tests.

being found with the U.K. Moreover, British sportsmen have shown overwhelmingly that they do not want mandatory tests. In a recent B.A.S.C. survey, more than 70% of respondents rejected government intervention in this area. Although any recommendation which the Council of Europe might make regarding shooting tests will not be binding upon the British Government, such recommendations do place considerable moral pressure upon member states to conform with the view of the majority.

One institution which does of course enact legislation which is binding upon Britain is the European Economic Community, and nowhere can the power of EEC influence upon field sports in Britain

be seen more clearly than in the framing of the Wildlife and Countryside Act 1981. This piece of legislation which now forms the main framework within which the shooting of wild birds can take place in this country, has its roots in the 1979 EEC Directive on the Conservation of Wild Birds. The directive made a series of regulations concerning the protection of birds and their habitats with which member states were obliged to comply. In particular it created schedules of quarry and non quarry species, to be used as the basis for individual state legislation, and made provision for the protection of internationally important waterfowl habitats.

To the British sportsman, the changes incorporated in the 1981 Act as a result

of the Directive were fundamental. Not only was the list of quarry species substantially reduced, but new statutory pressures were placed particularly upon the wildfowler, who found his rights to shoot over important wetland sites coming under close scrutiny.

It is true that every effort is being made by the shooting organisations to modify some aspects of the 1981 Act. The B.A.S.C. is, for example spearheading attempts to have the curlew, redshank and stock dove reinstated on the quarry list.

These species at least fall within the EEC schedule of birds which may be shot within Europe. The brent goose, however, does not, and any attempt to reinstate it upon the British quarry list will

Brent geese — Europe will have a say as to whether they will be reinstated as a quarry species.

first of all mean having the appropriate schedule of the Birds Directive altered accordingly. In this way the EEC imposes yet another tier of administration upon the sportsman.

One of the problems associated with European directives is that they are administered by government agencies, often alongside other legislation of a purely national nature.

When in early 1984 wildfowlers woke up to find that their shooting grounds were not only being designated Sites of Special Scientific Interest under our own Wildlife and Countryside Act, but also Special Protection Areas under the Birds Directive, their own deep concern for the future of their shooting was heightened by the fact that the Nature Conservancy Council, the government's advisor on conservation matters, was unable to say whether SPA designation would in future restrict wildfowling activity.

Although much discussion had taken place during the framing of the EEC Birds Directive, and the duty of governments to take steps to conserve certain important wetland sites had been established, it was and is still not resolved whether or not SPA designations will affect shooting rights, and if so, then to what extent. So even when wide ranging and loosely worded policy documents are agreed at International level, it is still often difficult to say exactly how they will affect the individual sportsman going about his traditional business.

What is clear, though, is that field sports interests need to make their voice heard loud and clear at European level. There are almost as many field sportsmen in the EEC, for example, as there are farmers, yet the influence of the sporting compared to the agricultural lobby is small indeed.

International problems require international solutions, and the voice of field sports in Brussels is F.A.C.E., the Federation of Field Sports organisations of the EEC. Supported by Sportsmens' organisations throughout the community, including B.A.S.C., B.F.S.S. and the Game Conservancy, F.A.C.E. ensures that issues which threaten to adversely affect field sports are swiftly tackled.

But even with an exceptional full time Secretary General in the shape of Yves Lecocq, F.A.C.E. is hampered by lack of funds. It relies entirely upon finance supplied by the national organisations,

In 1979 the EEC passed a directive about the protection of habitats.

The powers of Brussels now take an interest in the practices of the U.K. wildfowler.

and in Britain these sadly command the support of but a fraction of the sporting community.

For decades field sports organisations have addressed their attention to our own parliament at Westminster. Now there is a new potential source of danger, indirect maybe, but no less threatening. Issues such as SPA designation and mandatory tests must surely stand as a warning to field sports bodies that Europe has to be taken seriously, and to individual sportsmen that those bodies must be granted greatly increased support to enable them to fund the safeguarding of our shooting at a new international level.

Target Shooting Today

RICHARD ATKINS

Richard Atkins is the Editor of Target Gun magazine, a monthly magazine specialising in all forms of pistol, rifle and shotgun target shooting and hand loading.

Richard gives a brief insight into some areas of the world of Target Shooting.

It is not possible to elaborate fully on the diversity of sport and competition available under this heading in a short article of this type but I will endeavour to convey a broad outline to illustrate the subject.

Three basic categories exist by virtue of the ammunition used. These are: Airweapons, where high grade pistols and rifles are used to compete at 6 yards and 10 metres, accuracy potential can be judged by the fact that the 10 metre air rifle target 'bull' measures one millimetre in diameter! Great skill is required due to the low velocity of the pellet hence a longer barrel time, resulting in more time for error. Added to this, airweapon events are almost entirely 'standing only', the most difficult position to master.

Airweapon shooting is increasingly popular, partly due to costs as pellets are cheap (though the better rifles and pistols are not!) and a British Championship event is held in Cardiff each year, run by the NSRA. European and World Championships are also held and do not forget the Olympics, in which Barry Dagger won a bronze medal in the Air Rifle event for Britain in 1984.

Many shooters whose main interest lies in other branches of target shooting use airweapons as a means of regular, convenient practice, especially as the degree of difficulty makes it extra beneficial.

Top among the makes of target quality airweapons are Anschutz, Feinwerkbau and Walther rifles and for pistols Air Match, FAS, Feinwerkbau, Pardini-Fiocchi and Walther.

100 yard outdoor range provides a real test of .22 marksmanship.

SMALLBORE

The natural progression from airweapons is to smallbore shooting. This is based on the use of .22 calibre rim fire ammunition in both pistol and rifle. i.e. diminutive .22 Long Rifle round may be but a bare inch in length but it is capable of tremendous accuracy and consistency. Top grade ammunition such as Eley Tenex or RWS R50 can hold groups of below ¾ inch at 100 yards, which may surprise those not familiar with this ammunition.

When one considers this potential, the joy to be had from using ones skill to achieve this performance using a small bore rifle on an outdoor range becomes more easily understood. The comment is sometimes heard, "What is the fun in punching holes in a piece of paper?" The person asking has little perception of the degree of precision involved and skill which must be developed to wring this potential out of the gun/ammunition combintion.

The most demanding form of small bore pistol shooting is the Free Pistol event, here a highly developed pistol, with few restraints upon design, as the name implies, is used at 50 metres. The bull measures just 2inches in diameter. Such precision is hard to comprehend in a pistol, but there it is, an Olympic event too. Free Pistol is a minority discipline due to a combination of the degree of difficulty, the cost of specialised guns such as those by Hammerli, Toz and Pardini, (which are only suited to this one discipline) and lack of 50 metre pistol ranges.

SMALLBORE RIFLE

Shooting with the smallbore rifle is tremendously popular in the UK. Many take up the sport from early introduction connected with their schools, the cadets

Anschütz 1813 Super Match.

or company club. Much of the shooting takes place indoors at 20 and 25 yards range. This is considered a basic training facility and allows all year round practice whatever the weather. Club and postal competitions are also shot under these circumstances.

However, for many the real test and enjoyment of small bore rifle shooting is on outdoor ranges at 50 metres and 100 yards. Major competitions usually involve shooting at both distances such as the 'English Match' consisting of 30 shots at each distance for a score ex 600. It was in this event that Mike Sullivan won a bronze medal in Los Angeles, the first medal by any British competitor in LA hence shooting became worthy of television coverage, for a few fleeting moments.

The rifle shooting mentioned so far is shot from the prone position but the most demanding discipline is the 'Three Positional'. This involves shooting from prone, kneeling and standing positions bringing different problems to overcome at each position, to achieve a good total performance. Standing is the most difficult, providing the least stable support. Britain again won a medal in the '3P' at Los Angeles, when Malcolm Cooper, probably the best known shooter in the country, won a gold medal with 1173 points ex 1200 under sweltering conditions.

Again the NSRA, of whom details can be found elsewhere in this book, are the responsible body for small bore rifle shooting and details of clubs can be obtained from them. Alternatively your local gunsmith, police station or perhaps library, may be able to provide details of your nearest club.

There is no need to own your own rifle, most clubs have several for use by members. You will in any case need to already belong to a club to obtain a Firearms Certificate (FAC), enabling you to own a smallbore target rifle. Once you become reasonably proficient you will want to buy your own rifle so that you can become totally familiar with it. You should purchase your own ear defenders as soon as you decide to attend the club regularly and accessories such as a 'spotting' scope, shooting mat, ammunition box and shooting jacket, will all come later.

Shooting Jackets can prove very beneficial and excellent quality can be obtained from English made brands such as Tucker, Buttstop and Michael Clothing, at very competitive rates.

Imported jackets such as those by Anschutz are very high quality but rather expensive.

A new match rifle will cost in the region of from £500 upwards, for one of the better known makes such as the BSA Mk5, the only British offering. Based on the Martini action which is easy to use whilst in the prone position.

German rifles dominate the world scene with names like Anschutz, Walther and more recently Feinwerkbau being the best known. Anschutz has by far the greatest market penetration. All these makes use the bolt-action system. Left and right handed models are available.

As prone shooting is most prevalent a 'Prone' rifle is the best choice for a beginner as a rule, in addition to which a 'Free' rifle will cost around £100 more. The added adjustments and refinements can serve to confuse the beginner, so are probably best avoided until more expertise is gained.

One reason for the popularity of small bore rifle shooting is that it is reasonably inexpensive to participate in. Ammunition ranges from around £2.50/100 rounds for practice ammunition to around £5.50/100 for the best match ammunition available such as Eley Tenex or RWS R50. No major outlay need occur until purchasing a rifle.

FULL BORE

The term full bore applies to all centre-fire cartridge pistols and rifles where calibres exceed the .22 inch rimfire

(Long range pistol) 300 yards with a Pisol? Yes, thats one use for a Ruger .44 Magnum.

round. The most popular calibre for target pistols and revolvers are .32 Smith and Wesson and .38 Special. For target rifles 7,62 Nato ('308 Winchester) is the almost universal round, barring for 300 metre shooting.

Full bore rifle shooting takes place at greater distances and hence there are fewer ranges to be found, most of which are connected with the MoD. Two basic categories exist 'short range' which means from 200 to 600 yards and long range from 600 yards to 900 yards.

A smaller number of enthusiasts continue on to 1000 and even 1200 yards, these being the Match Rifle men, very few ranges exist for this distance, Stickledown at Bisley being the best known.

A number of rifles are available, amongst the better known are Grunig and Elmiger, Swing, Parker Hale and a number of specials built up on military actions. If both distances are to be shot competitively, two rifles will be required, a stiff actioned one for up to 600 yards and one using the No 4 Enfield which gives good compensation over the greater ranges, particularly when a less consistent batch of ammunition is encountered, ammunition being supplied for many Target Rifle competitions, usually Radway Green (RG). Commercial ammunition such as Norma or Federal may only be used in certain specified competitions. Match riflemen usually use homeloaded ammunition as little factory

ammunition is made to perform well at such long ranges.

300 metre shooting is the up and coming discipline, popular in Europe but just getting under way here. It uses three positions too, as in the 3P small bore. It is also the only full bore rifle discipline shot from a covered firing point. All others are shot on the open range.

The NRA are the governing body for fullbore rifle shooting in the UK, more information can be had from them.

PISTOL SHOOTING

By far the greatest growth in target shooting in recent years has been in pistol shooting. Many choose it for pure recreation whilst others take it more seriously. It can be seen from the fact that 33 events were included at 'Pistol 85' organised by the National Pistol Association, that choice is vast. From high precision events like Free Pistol and Centrefire Precision to Rapid-Fire where five turning targets must be shot in rapid succession, with UIT Centrefire in between combining elements of both.

Other events cater for Classic revolvers, pocket pistols and Service Pistol where only the 'as issued' 9mm Browning Hi-Power may be used. Long range events are gaining in popularity, here pistols are stretched to their limits with shooting taking place at 100, 200 and 300 yards. Again, 'homeloads' are essential for these

longer ranges. The ILRPSA (International Long Range Pistol Shooting Association) can provide details of this form of shooting.

For many, recreational shooting and the pleasure of shooting a 357 or 44 Magnum revolver, Colt 45 ACP Pistol or classic military piece, such as a Luger is sufficient reward, without the need of competition.

I cannot conclude this piece without a brief mention of the two disciplines which have shown such growth, that several specialist gunsmiths have built a business around supplying their needs and competitions are sometimes over subscribed. These are Police Pistol and Practical Pistol.

The former is shot 'precision' at 25 metres, with speed elements involved with single shots in 2 (two) seconds at 15 metres in two strings of six shots, plus a further six shots at 7 metres where two shots are put on the turning targets in two seconds, repeated three times. This is evolved from Police training methods, as the name implies and is an exciting but manageable discipline.

Practical Pistol is based on Power, Speed and Accuracy, this being the motto of the UKPSA (United Kingdom Practical Shooting Association) who control the sport in the UK.

Smith & Wesson Model 639, 9-shot, 9mm.

The essence being multiple shots in minimal time on varied and sometimes moving targets, from a variety of body positions sometimes involving other restrictions such as barricades and grilles etc. In addition, strong and weak hand shooting is involved, plus correct use of holsters and enforced reloads.

As centrefire ammunition is used for both the above and useage can be high factory ammunition at £12-£15/100 rounds is less often used and reloads at less than half price become the 'norm' but that's another story in itself!

Woodland Stalking

EDGAR JAMES

Edgar James
Born in Cornwall 1926.

On leaving school served an apprenticeship in Engineering. Always interested in country pursuits as is to be expected living in country district. Shot clays seriously for some years before becoming interested in deer after seeing roe in Dorset whilst holidaying with a wartime friend who supplied the first opportunities to stalk roe.

Raced motor-cycles in the fifties but roe stalking and later fallow deer in Devon, were always the main hobby.

Turned professional stalker in 1970.

Has to date hunted in U.S.A., Canada, Germany, Belgium and France.

Which is the best calibre for British deer? How often have I been asked that question! To be quite honest I do not think that it can really be answered. Any legal calibre bullet and smaller, not legal bullets will kill deer, we all know this.

The law demands a minimum of .240 calibre and the modern range starts at .243 (6 mm) and goes on up. In my opinion it is a matter of personal choice and although some stalkers will argue that their choice is the only one to consider, there is more to the subject than that.

Probably the four most popular calibres are .243, .270, 7 mm and .308, all excellent cartridges depending on where they are used. I think the .243, even when using the 100 grain bullet has its limitations in woodland stalking, also when used on large woodland red stags. The .270 loaded with 130 grain bullets is a superb cartridge but one has to be very careful in woodland — it takes very little to upset the 130 grain bullet at around three thousand feet per second.

My choice for many years and hundreds of deer has been the .308 hand-loaded with 150 grain bullet but this is only what I prefer and does not answer the original question. Stick to any of the legal cartridges and you will not go far wrong. Take no heed of the "experts" who tell you that the heavy .30 calibre bullets excessively damage venison — so will small calibres if not properly placed — often more so.

The sub calibre .22 centre fires are not at all suitable for general stalking and should be left to the "Verminters" for whom they were designed. Unfortunately, there are some people who should know better, actually advocating the making legal of these cartridges for roe. They should realize that once in the hands of a budding stalker they would be used on any species as opportunities presented themselves. I must point out that over the last thirty-seven odd years I have mistakenly used, almost everything from the 'Hornet' up! Enough said!

A word on scopes and rifles. Buy the best scope that you can afford and avoid all gimmicks. For general stalking a good fixed power scope of 4× — 6× is all that you will ever require. Most modern rifles shoot well; if they do not they can almost always be made to. Remember a 'best' scope on a cheaper rifle is by far the better choice than the other way round. The same advice is offered on the choice of binoculars. If you cannot see well enough you cannot identify or shoot!

The fitting of scopes to rifles is a fairly straight-forward operation but I would normally recommend that it be left to a competent rifleman. I say normally, but after seeing some pretty awful work carried out by so called experts, perhaps it is just as well for a sensible stalker to fit his own scope. Probably the most important thing to watch out for is that you use the correct size rings. For instance a one inch ring will not fit a continental 26 mm scope tube. Have a care when you fit your scope.

Even in the open, a deer is well camouflaged.

Woodland stalking is a wonderful hobby and profession, if you are of the right temperament; Stalking does not suit everyone. If you hope to fire a lot of shots forget stalking, you will be extremely lucky if you shoot once in three of four outings. Have a few outings with a professional stalker. If you are still with us after a week of 3.00 a.m. risings in Spring or the same number of days in Winter in sub zero weather, — welcome, but shoot or not, it is really wonderful to be out and about just after dawn especially in Spring, to see the countryside and its inhabitants as few people ever see it. I never, even after all these years, tire of it and I am sure that Bracken — my spaniel and ever eager stalking companion, enjoys it as much as I do. Bracken has accompanied me throughout the years and he is often instrumental in my getting a shot that I would not have got had I been alone. He senses deer that I am not aware of and lets me know by going 'on point'.

One morning last December I remember well; I was not having much luck on that cold morning, numb feet and fingers kept me thinking of the fire and hot breakfast that would be waiting for me when I got home. Suddenly Bracken stopped, never more than a single pace in front of me — I froze. Bracken was rigid and looking into a nine or ten year old unbrashed douglas plantation, the lower branches starting about two feet from the ground. I dropped slowly to my knee, rifle at the ready; quickly I picked out the two roe that were standing some way into the plantation. A doe and doe fawn. Five minutes later I was 'gralloching' both of them on the grass ride. Bracken was lying close-by watching me, I am sure that old dog smiles when a deer is grassed, especially when he knows that he had a hand in it. Sometimes when I fail to pick out a beast that he can see or smell he becomes impatient, and quietly whines and raises his ears but never does he do anything to spoil things.

Stalking, unless as a professional you are accompanying a client, can be a rather lonely pastime but with a companion like Bracken one is never lonely. Train your dog, if you are fortunate enough to own one, to stalk with you and do not worry if it has a lot of white markings. Several times I have had deer in view but been unable to shoot because of obstruction or some other reason, I

A roe stepped out from behind a tree...

then leave the dog sitting in full view of the beasts and ease off to a better position. Usually the deer will stand like statues watching the dog thus allowing me time for a shot from a better position. They seem to be fascinated by the motionless dog.

While on the subject of dogs, in my opinion everyone who stalks deer, be it for a hobby or profession, should have a suitable dog or at least have one on call for the inevitable occasion when a deer dashes off at the shot, hopefully to drop dead nearby perhaps in thick cover or unfortunately, goes off wounded. In either case a dog will be needed. Do not commence your search too soon; wait at least twenty minutes, even if you are sure it was a good shot. Many "dead" beasts have run off at the approach of a human being. Obviously a dog who will find a

dead deer and pull down a runner is ideal; unfortunately all dogs will not do both. My spaniel, despite all my praise will not; he is excellent at finding the dead beast but is not belligerent enought to attack a live deer. Two years ago on a Spring morning I shot, from a high seat, a yearling buck that I was sure had fallen dead to the shot but, as it had been standing in low cover, it had dropped out of my sight. However, I was quite confident so decided to stay where I was for a while in hope of another shot. I glanced down to the foot of the seat, Bracken was lying perfectly still; as always, he never runs into the rifle shot — if only he was that steady on the pheasant shoot!

Eventually I decided to stalk but first collect the buck. After walking very carefully the hundred and twenty or so yards I realized that the tree stump that I had used to mark the position of the fallen buck was not the only one, so I sent Bracken off to 'find'. He quartered the ground in front of me, then disappeared from my view and did not reappear. Good, I thought and the familiar picture came to mind, namely Bracken standing over the dead beast, tail wagging violently and licking the bullet wound.

I was soon disillusioned for, on stepping a yard or two to the side to pick up sight of the dog who was behind a stump, I saw to my great consternation that he was standing alongside, but nose to tail to the buck. Both stood with heads down, "Bracken's" tail at full droop and with a look of sheer dejection on his face — he was completely baffled, so was I for the moment. However I eased my rifle to 'high port' and breathed "Heel", fortunately the dog obeyed immediately the one command. He was probably glad to hear it anyway. Seconds later, before it had time to react the buck was felled by the neck shot, the first shot was too far back. I have two terriers that are used on runners, they would have certainly known what to do in the above circumstances; they are characters in their own way, but that's another story.

Fired from a rifle held at about fifty degrees, any of the previously mentioned cartridges will send their bullets up to about five miles before dropping to the ground and would you believe that I have come across stalkers who had been using the skyline to silhouette deer at night to obtain a shot, and this in the heavily populated south! None of them realized the tremendous distance a rifle bullet can travel, even after passing through a deer. The only backstop for a high power, centre fire bullet is the ground and every endeavour must be made to use it; there is little fear of a ricochet from a soft point hunting bullet but the possibility must always be taken into consideration.

If your hunting grounds are very flat, use high seats especially for roe. The continental stalkers (hunters) have a saying "stalk a stag, wait for a buck". You will not go far wrong if you abide by this. We are, of course, talking about woodland deer and I am sure that you will enjoy every session in a high seat on deer ground. Perhaps it is fair to admit that I prefer to stalk my deer and 90% of my animals are taken by this method. I know every yard of my areas and this is a tremendous advantage. When I have to use a high seat in the interests of safety or better viewing, such as over and into young plantation, I am quite happy if my only company is the odd pheasant, hare or rabbit, not forgetting Bracken —

Model 70F.XTR. 'Featherweight' a high power rifle will send a bullet up to five miles.

dozing under the seat. However if nothing moves, though I must admit this is rare in the lovely Wessex woodland where I stalk, I do become rather restless and wonder what is around the corner. More than once I have been caught out by an emerging deer when climbing down the ladder.

Well-remembered is one Winter evening many years ago, a freezing February and one of the worst Winters I can remember. I had stuck it for some time sitting in the high seat overlooking a field of frozen Winter wheat. It looked most uninviting but the farmer had seen six or seven roe on it the previous evening. After an hour I called a halt and started to climb down. Two rungs from the top, and to my consternation, out came a roe not sixty yards away, then another and yet another. There was I not daring to move; I just hung on with half frozen fingers until they settled down to pick at the white growth. I felt a little sorry for them as they had been having a hard time for several weeks. Moving very carefully I put one leg between the two top rungs and hooked the toe of my boot behind the lower rung, thus leaving both hands free. Two of the three deer were does; one dropped to the first shot, the other ran towards the edge of the field but made the mistake of pausing for a moment, as roe often do. Then to my surprise another roe came out of the wood almost at the sound of the second shot, a doe fawn, which fell to the third shot. I felt no elation on that foul evening.

If all this talk of early mornings and cold Winters has not deterred you and you are still with us, I wish you 'Wiedmanteiel'. As our Continental hunters greet one another. Wiedmantiel — Good Hunting!

Roebuck, unconscious of the human presence.

Airguns are not Toys

JOHN FLETCHER

With a break of just over a year in 1983/84, John Fletcher has been involved with airgun shooting since 1977. Helped with the launch of 'Airgun World', Britain's first airgun magazine, in July of that year, and is now the magazine's Editor.

He was involved in the first ever field target shoot in 1980, and instigated the first Airgun Fair at Packington Park in April 1985.

Here John assesses the many changes in the airgun scene over the past few years — and gives a general review of the situation today.

Handle one of today's top quality airguns and you know immediately that you are dealing with a serious sporting weapon — and certainly not with a toy. Deeply blued metalwork, oil finished, hand chequered walnut and a weight of well over 8 lbs make it quite clear that today's sporting air rifle is not to be dismissed as a mere plaything.

This has not always been the case. Until the last few years most airguns were more closely related to pop-guns than to "serious" rifles — although there have always been honourable exceptions — and they were used for shooting at targets and tin cans in the back garden rather than for anything more ambitious.

Now that has all changed. Whereas the serious sporting weapon was once the exception, now it is the rule. Modern air rifles develop power right up to the 12ft lbs. muzzle energy legal limit — or considerably over for those who possess a firearms certificate — and they are superbly consistent.

Coupled with the latest ammunition, made to high standards and to one of an astonishing number of new designs, they are quite capable of producing one inch groups and smaller at ranges of 30 yards or more. That has led to airguns being used on an ever increasing scale for vermin control and hunting species such as rabbits and woodpigeon for the pot — and to the growth of an all-new sport.

FIELD TARGET SHOOTING

Back in the 1980 Britain's first airgun magazine, *Airgun World*, joined forces with the now defunct Sussex Armoury company to organise and sponsor the first ever Field Target Championship. In this, metal silhouettes of rats, rabbits, pigeon, crows and squirrels were marked with 'kill areas', at which competitors fired from ranges between 10 and 50 yards.

The target area was a circle no more than 1½ inches in diameter — and the event was a tremendous success. It gave all those shooters who had invested in expensive air rifles and telescopic sights something in which their top quality hardware really came into its own.

From such small beginnings, the sport has grown so that there are now dozens of field target clubs throughout the country, as well as a number of major national events.

The British Association for Shooting and Conservation (BASC) runs a series of field target events at country fairs which regularly attract entries of 200 or more competitors.

The leading makes of rifle in the early days of the sport were Feinwerkbau, Weihrauch, Webley and BSA, with the more expensive German guns just tending to have an edge. But field target shooting has been partly responsible for one of the most notable airgunning trends of recent years — the tendency to modify and customise standard air weapons.

CUSTOM AIR RIFLES

Customising started in a fairly small way with a select band of airgun retailers offering rifles which they had 'tuned' — which, in the case of air weapons, involves polishing and lubricating the action to make it smoother and more efficient.

From this it was a small step to improving the woodwork — by adding chequering, improving the quality of the finish or fitting a butt plate. Now there are a vast number of firms offering some form of customising.

Market leaders are undoubtedly Venom Arms, who offer a bewildering array of heavily modified Weihrauchs, Webleys and other rifles. They tune the action, offer a range of attractive Tyrolean, Sporter or thumb-hole stocks and generally do all they can to offer the ultimate spring air rifle. Prices are well over £200 — but there are queues of people eager to buy these exceptionally fine, precision made sporting weapons.

BRITISH BOUNCE BACK

During the 1980s much of the emphasis in the airgun market has been on German

A fully customised version of the Weihrauch HW77.

The Theoben Sirocco has been a great success.

weapons, which have enjoyed a reputation for power, accuracy and reliability. British weapons, often for no good reason, have tended to be ignored.

Now that has all changed, with traditional leaders Webley and BSA being joined in the battle against foreign importers by newer names such as Air Arms, Theoben and Saxby Palmer.

Webley is a household name, of course, and the company produces a full range of guns from the familiar, world beating Webley pistols, through the Victor, Vulcan and Viscount rifles, to the latest Omega rifle. This last design was produced after extensive research to find out exactly what airgunners want — and it has been accepted immediately as a competitive top of the range air rifle.

BSA is another household name — and their Scorpion pistol and Meteor, Mercury and Airsporter rifles have given thousands of shooters a good deal of pleasure over the years.

The company changed ownership in the first quarter of 1985, however, and it has now adopted a far more positive and progressive attitude than had previously been the case. Within weeks of the change of ownership, BSA announced the introduction of three dramatic new rifles.

One — the VS2000 — features a revolutionary nine pellet rotary magazine. Another — the Airsporter Stutzen — has an elegant full length fore-end, similar to BSA's top-of-the-range centre fire rifles. The third, known as the Challenger, is a re-stocked Mercury, which has been extensively modified to make it more acceptable to field target shooters.

The last two of these rifles feature an all-new style of insulated scope ramp, designed to eliminate movement of the scope caused by recoil. In all, these changes have given BSA products a dynamic new look for the second half of the 1980s.

Air Arms are a Sussex based company producing a range of sidelever cocking rifles. With their elegant Camargue, Mistral and Bora models, Air Arms have established themselves as front runners on the domestic air weapons front. They, too, have a 'magazine' device as an option on their rifles, and have earned a reputation in the last few years as a company that is prepared to learn from experience and improve its products whenever the opportunity presents itself.

Rather different is the story of Theoben Engineering. Formed by Dave Theobald and Ben Taylor three or four years ago, the company uses a revolutionary power source in its much acclaimed Sirocco rifle.

Whereas virtually all other British air rifles use a spring driven piston to compress the air which propels the pellet up the barrel, Theoben use an inert gas to perform the same function. This gives a smoother action, with less recoil and noise. The Sirocco has proved to be very popular with the most discerning airgunners, only its price preventing it becoming a favourite in terms of sheer numbers.

Finally, Saxby Palmer have evolved a range of air cartridge powered rifles and revolvers. These use rechargeable compressed air cartridges as a power source, and offer the advantage of a completely recoilless action coupled with the satisfaction of a bolt action rifle or a genuine air revolver.

The company's Orion 6 and Model 54 revolvers offer remarkable accuracy, together with the ability to fire six shots literally as fast as you can pull the trigger.

A field target shooter in action. Note the customised rifle.

This kind of technical innovation is typical of the spirit which should ensure that Britain's airgun industry does not go the same way as its motorcycle or shotgun industries. Until the past year or so it had seemed that German manufacturers — with Weihrauch in their van — would sweep the British trade before them. They certainly still pose a threat — but there is no doubt that British airgunners can now buy British without losing out.

AMMUNITION

Until the 1980s airgun pellets were all much the same — featuring a waisted 'diabolo' shape and a round nose. They were all made of lead.

Now that has all changed. Scarcely a month passes without some new type of lead pellet being introduced, and these may now have flat or pointed noses and any number of 'driving rings' to complicate their shape.

The Silver Jet was one of the first 'unconventional' pellet designs.

How effective many of these innovations are is doubtful, but there is no denying the will to experiment among today's airgunners. Recent years have also seen the introduction of a variety of non-lead types of ammunition — fuelled partly by the environmentalist objections to the use of lead, and partly by the search for harder ammunition. Leading names here are Prometheus, Titan Black, Sussex Sabo and Saxby Palmer.

TELESCOPIC SIGHTS

BSA were the first to introduce telescopic sights on air rifle in the 1960s, but it is only in the past five or six years that their use has become almost universal among serious — and not so serious — airgunners. Look through any of the airgun magazines and you'll see page after page of advertisements listing rifle/scope combinations in which the scope is given very nearly as much prominence as the rifle.

Even at the relatively short ranges at which air rifles are used scopes can offer real advantages — especially when it comes to picking out the partially obscured, 1 ½ inch diameter kill area of a field target.

The basic airgunning scope has come to be regarded as the 4 × 32 (which means it has a magnification of 4 times and an objective lens 32 mm. in diameter), but top field target shooters and dedicated airgun hunters will pay up to £100 for a variable magnification, parallax adjustable sight.

TARGET SHOOTING

Paper target shooting at 10 metres and six yards is still a popular sport — and is the most specialised form of airgun shooting. The recoilless rifles and pistols used for this form of shooting are heavy, low powered and virtually useless for anything other than the purpose for which they were designed.

They again are expensive — costing up to £500 — and target shooters take great care to select the best possible ammunition. All target shooting is carried out with .177 (4.5 mm) calibre weapons and ammunition, rather than the .22 (5.5 mm) calibre which has traditionally been more popular in this country for general use.

PLINKING

Plinking gets its name from the noise an airgun pellet makes when it hits a tin can — and quite simply it involves any form of airgun shooting that you practise "just for fun".

Any air weapon is suitable, from the most humble pistol or imported Russian air rifle upwards. Air pistols, which are restricted by law to a muzzle energy of 6 ft. lbs. unless you have a firearms certificate — are in their element for this form of shooting. Webley, with their Tempest and Hurricane, and BSA, with their Scorpion, have always been very strong in this field.

But with the exception of plinking, it is quite clear that modern airguns are not toys. They are used in rigorously demanding competitive sports, and many airgunners spend well over £200 on their basic equipment. Some indeed, may spend close to £1,000. And that, let's face it, is serious money!

Just some of the many scopes available.

Getting with the Beat

BRIAN MARTIN

Brian Martin has been Assistant Editor at Shooting Times since 1977, for which magazine he has written the Country Scene page under the pen-name Rusticus since 1979. He has written extensively on fieldsports, natural history and other subjects for various magazines and newspapers, and has written chapters for several important shooting books.

His first major book, "Sporting Birds of the British Isles", was published by David & Charles in July, 1984 and he is co-author of "Game Cook — from field to table", published by Burlington Publishing Co in November, 1984. He is currently researching two books, one of which is on the great shooting estates. Aged 37 and married, with two children, Brian now lives in Surrey.

Brian Martin advises the beginner who must start "at the bottom" in game shooting and be prepared to go beating.

Much has changed since 'driving' gamebirds for sport became popular towards the end of the 19th Century. Whereas such activity was once synonymous with wealth and privilege, today it is fair to say that anyone with the will and dedication can participate. Lack of finance does not necessarily mean being confined to a largely supportive role while the man with the fat wallet has all the fun.

While money certainly can buy instant access to 'live' shooting, it cannot necessarily guarantee satisfaction in the sport. On the contrary, for a sporting father to place his inexperienced child in a standing line of Guns is to invite the rapid onset of boredom.

Just as the best manager and practitioner in any walk of life is the one who is totally familiar with and fully understands the work of each and every employee, so the most satisfied and accomplished Gun is the one who recognises the importance and co-operation of everyone in the shooting field. Thus starting "at the bottom" is useful not only

in making initial contact with shooters but also in providing a thorough grounding which should result in long-term satisfaction in the sport. Little wonder then that DIY shoots, in which the Guns are also the beaters and gamekeepers, have become increasingly popular in recent years.

Irrespective of the type of shooting hankered after, usually it is necessary to establish 'contacts' and to win their confidence in sport where safety and reliability always come first.

Shooting certainly does tend to run in families and anyone with a shooting father is obviously off to a good start. Others will have a shooting friend prepared to show one the ropes, or employment connected with farming or land management might provide an introduction. But what of the lad with no contacts, especially the one further isolated through living in an urban area? Fortunately, all with sufficient motivation can succeed.

A good start is to realise that most branches of 'live' shooting are linked, not only in that they shelter under the same national organisations such as the BASC,

Attending clay shoots will often introduce you to gameshooters.

but also because most shooters have interests in several branches of the sport. For example, most gameshooters have at least a passing interest in clayshooting, if only to sharpen up their skills: thus regular attendance at a clay club or shooting school frequently brings introductions to and subsequent friendships with gameshooters. Invitations frequently follow.

You might be tempted by an advert to buy pigeon shooting at, say, £20 per day, but the advertiser will not care a jot whether you be expert or novice: he only wants your money and you are likely to be disappointed. On the other hand, it is worth studying *local* farms with pigeon problems. Of course, you will get many refusals: so many people are after the shooting nowadays, but a polite approach at a sensible time of day, and perhaps leaving your telephone number for later reference, should pay dividends in the long run. And one day, when you have shown the farmer that you are safe, reliable and conscientious, and care for his stock, crops and the countryside, you might even be able to broach the subject of shooting the game on his land or perhaps paying him a small rent to enable you to put down a few gamebirds. But always an introduction through an experienced friend is best and once you have a good name it is often easy to extend your boundaries onto neighbouring properties.

If you want to take up wildfowling then you should write to the BASC for details of your nearest club. But you will need to be both hardy and dedicated, for the coast is a tough place subject to great pressures and club entry requirements today are generally exacting. In most cases you will need to serve a year's associate membership, during which time you will be allowed to shoot only with one of the members who have proposed you, and you must satisfy committee members that you are aware of relevant law and etiquette and can identify all the quarry species. Yet wildfowling is a rewarding sport and this too might bring an introduction to game-shooting for many wildfowlers are also gameshooters or regularly beat or pick-up for game shoots.

You are most unlikely to see an advertisement asking for beaters. Today there is almost always an army of volunteers at the ready and their inclusion is usually through being in the right place at the right time, though their motivation might vary.

It is not only potential gameshooters who wish to go beating. Today, when so many people are utterly frustrated by life cut off from the great outdoors, a surprisingly large number of people will go beating simply to get out into the countryside. Very often they have no desire to shoot but are quite happy to bring pleasure to others. They may not be as proficient as seasoned, regular beaters, but they can usually be 'knocked into shape' by a competent keeper or shoot captain. Some will even beat for no reward, though a pheasant or two to take home is always appreciated.

For other people the financial rewards are paramount. There have always been those prepared to put in a very tiring day's work for a modest £5-10, and perhaps lunch or a beer thrown in, and in recent decades this has included university students as well as the poorer members of the community. And some, especially since the recession left so many people on the dole, have made beating and picking-up almost a profession. The unemployed especially are able to get to the many shoots which are held on weekdays and some people make a reasonable income through regular attendance at three or four or even more shoots in one week. Others are self-employed, with flexi-hours, and are no doubt tempted by potentially tax-free income!

Despite this competition, with patience you will get the chance to beat and this is the area in which the professional keeper is most likely to want help. A few people, however, usually through personal introduction, do get the opportunity to help a keeper with his other duties such as rearing and vermin control. This is usually done with no cash reward but such volunteers will obviously get the first option of any pigeon shooting going and others will be after the work experience to help secure keepering employment later.

BEFORE YOU GO

Once you have fixed yourself up with some beating then, if closer involvement with shooting is your ambition, there is quite a lot for you to consider before the first day arrives.

Read as much as you can about the sport for, though nothing will ever replace practical experience, you can save yourself a great deal of embarrassment, time and trouble. And behaving incorrectly might also mean that you are not invited back a second time.

For a start you should know the law, shooting etiquette and all safety procedures, and in this respect the BASC produces a useful series of Codes of Practice. You don't want to look "green around the gills" in front of "weather-beaten professionals" and should know, for example, how to 'despatch' a wounded bird humanely if the opportunity comes your way. A sharp blow to the back of the head is most popular and, while your beating stick might have the weight, a special 'priest', designed for the purpose and popped in your pocket, is better. Always try to acquire the reputation for being generally useful and willing.

Make sure that you know exactly where the meeting place will be and what time you should be there. Always ask before taking anyone else or a dog along. A badly behaved dog will win you no friends. Also find out if lunch is to be provided — probably not.

Careful consideration of what to wear is also important for not only will suitable clothing make you more effective as a beater but also make your day a great deal more tolerable. Obviously pay close attention to the weather forecast but always be prepared for the worst and take waterproofs even if the day starts off dry. You will need these on your legs even when it is not raining for much of the cover, such as kale, will be drenched with dew. Wellington boots are always advisable, though on grouse moors strong, leather walking boots will be better to support the ankles and minimise perspiration.

Obviously most shooting days, being in mid-winter, will be cold and keeping warm is a priority. There are many good outdoor jackets available now which are both waterproof and windproof but it is worthwhile trying to find one which reduces condensation through perspiration as walking through thick scrub always works up quite a sweat. Recently introduced 'Goretex' coats are said to overcome this problem while keeping the rain out, but they are considerably more expensive than those of the perennial, waxed, Barbour type. A neat appearance is obviously desirable, but practicality is most important and in any line of beaters you will see some amusing sights string and all! And don't forget your hat.

Don't keep the rest of the group waiting.

ON THE DAY

Arrive in good time. Pay close attention to the orders for the day and for goodness sake ask if you don't understand anything. Don't stand around talking between drives but hurry to the next assembly point or else you will get left behind.

As the line of beaters proceeds pay special attention to the instructions of the keeper in charge. Keep up when he tells you; go faster when he directs, in order to hasten the shooting, or go slower when he wants to avoid a flush of birds over the Guns. Sometimes you will be directed to stop and then you should keep tapping to stop birds running back, especially through thick cover. Very often you will be in woodland or dense scrub and then you will need to keep in touch with your neighbours. Keep in line and pass the keeper's instructions down the way. He will sometimes let one end of the line advance more rapidly in order to counteract the effect of a strong cross-wind, so consider this before trying to compensate and straighten up.

There is no need to bellow repeatedly. Keep calm and by all means call as well as tap but do keep quiet when driving partridges. Sometimes, as on a grouse moor, you may also be given a white flag to wave and this is as much for your own safety when nearing the Guns as it is to move the birds. Some, especially partridges, will never be dissuaded from altering their flightlines.

A good beater will not pass thick cover such as bramble for the sake of an easy life. He will attempt to tramp through it for this is far more effective in moving birds on than shouting and poking about with a stick ever is. The distance between each beater will be determined by the thickness and extend of cover but do avoid bunching up to make conversation while being inattentive.

Occasionally you may be asked to act as a 'flanker', when you will proceed slightly ahead of the line at the side in

If you are not sure where to go next always ask.

A white flag helps to ensure your safety.

order to prevent birds running or flying out. Overall, the line will be 'shaped' by the keeper to funnel the birds towards the waiting Guns.

Another important position is of a wood or end of hedgerow where birds, especially the wily customers later in the season, may slip away unnoticed. The stops must be in position before the line even begins to move or call. The stop will tap continuously to warn Guns where he is and to avoid a build-up of birds and a subsequent flush. Always the aim is steady shooting.

As you walk through regimented crops or down drills, occasionally side-step a few paces so that sharp-eyed birds will be flushed by your surprise manoeuvre rather than sit tight.

As you get within hailing distance of the Guns it is always helpful to them if you give warning of birds getting up, especially where thick cover gives little notice. "Forward" or "Over" will suffice for pheasants but when a woodcock gets up then one should call the bird's name so that the Guns can prepare themselves for this testing target. Sometimes there will be walking Guns in or near the line and they too will appreciate your warnings of birds getting up as they are allowed to shoot those going back which might otherwise be lost.

Along the way, and especially away from the main shooting, you may pick up a shot bird, but do remember to tell the keeper or official pickers-up so that they avoid wasting time. Also try to 'mark' birds down by remembering landmarks such as rocks and trees as this will all help to make the day run smoothly. Sometimes you might be able to leave marker sticks.

On a 'cocks only' day call "cock" or "hen", but never criticise the Gun who makes a mistake for it is not always easy and it might be you one day. "Good shot sir" will be appreciated but never attempt to tell anyone other than a good friend where he went wrong! Help any Guns negotiating fences or other obstacles by holding their kit and be polite to any farm staff encountered along the way. Always close gates and avoid trampling crops.

Remember this advice and you will succeed. Everyone makes the occasional mistake in the beginning and all, except those relating to safety, should be forgiven as shooters are among the friendliest group of people in the sporting world. The rewards are great, and it is customary for the loyal, regular beaters to be invited to shoot on the 'Keeper's Day' at the end of the season!

Buying a Second~hand Gun
Gun Care DESMOND MILLS

Desmond Mills started his working life as an apprentice Gunmaker with the House of Purdey. Bound apprentice for seven years working under the great Gunmakers of the day, Mr Ernie Laverence who designed and built the Purdey over & under and Mr Ben Delay senior actioner of side by side shotguns and big game rifles. Received the Freedom of the City of London for Gunmaking. After completion of National Service returned to Purdeys and subsequently offered a position with E.J. Churchill Gunmakers to be responsible for building his 'Best' Premier sidelocks and his famous 'Zenith' over & under. In addition he was responsible for the training of apprentices in the art of Gunmaking.

Left to become self employed making guns for the trade: has been connected with the Gun Trade for the past thirty five years.

Much of his spare time is spent demonstrating at country fairs. Talking on shotguns and safety to various clubs and organizations. Inolved with the B.A.S.C. in North Yorkshire as an honarary Education Officer in their educational scheme. Regular contributor to Sporting Gun Magazine, an avid game shot and member of two shoots.

The purchase of a second hand shotgun involves a certain amount of risk to the purchaser. For the layman it is most difficult to detect every defect or weakness. Frequently guns are offered for sale from persons who know little or nothing about the mechanism, safety aspects of the weapon or more importantly what the law demands. Guns can be purchased from auctions held in small village halls or from a member of ones local clay pigeon club, apart from being advertised in shooting magazines or the local newspaper. Guns purchased in this manner can often turn out to be highly dangerous and in some cases worthless. Guns need to be viewed by a qualified person preferably a practical gunsmith. That is someone who has been trained in the making or repairing of a variety of different makes and models. There are however a number of more obvious points for which one can look out for.

Regardless of the makers name that has been engraved on the top rib and the condition that the gun has been presented in the same detailed checks and inspection need to be made. The barrels require removing from the action to establish that they bear valid proof marks. Under the Gun Barrel Proof Act it is an offence to sell or offer for sale a weapon i.e. shotgun, rifle, revolver or pistol unless it bears lawfully impressed and valid proof marks. Many second hand guns appear to be properly proofed and marked but in fact have been weakened due to the enlargement of the bore. This has been in many cases due to removing deep pitting, rust and dents, hence the proof marks are rendered invalid. Special equipment is required to measure the bore size and determine whether proof marks are valid or not. Contrary to belief there are no provisions in the proof regulations that allows the sale of an unproofed arm as an ornament or "wall hanger". Inspection of the proof marks will indicate whether it is the guns first or second proof and if second proof then it will greatly effect the guns value.

Check the barrels for bulges, dents and pitting. Pitting is very serious depending upon its depth and position in the tubes. Hold the barrels in both hands and approximately fourteen inches away from ones face. Keep both eyes open and position the barrels into the light so as a cone of light is formed from the nose end to the breech end. This will enable you to more easily determine the condition of

A handsome Action does not automatically mean a sound gun.

the barrels, both on the inside of the bore and the exterior of the tubes including the rib. Examine the chambers for depth for its is not unknown to find that deepening has taken place. Choke is another area that needs to be viewed for the barrels could have been cut down in length thus removing the choke cones. Next, check that the barrel lumps are not loose. Look for the tell tale signs of hammer marks on the bite. This is an old dodge to make the gun appear tight in the jointing and on the face, but place the barrels back onto the action without the fore-end and try for any movement between the two. At the same time take note of any play in the stock especially around the head, that is where the metal of the action has been let into the wood. Any movement experienced is commonly referred to as Headache. When carrying out this test hold the gun by the hand or small of the stock with both hands. Place the heel of the stock in the groin and point the barrels upwards and at an angle. The reasons for not placing the fore-end on the gun is that the fore-end pushes the cross pin into the hook of the barrels and the action onto the face thus preventing any movement that may be felt. The barrels can now be removed and the action and stock examined. If the action has been presented in the popular silver brush finish look closely at the crispness of the engraving. Has it been polished in an endeavour to enhance its appearance? Examine the face of the action for pitting around the striker holes. Inspect the slots and flats of the action body for any tell tale signs of having been squeezed in. The root of the action is where the flats meet the face, the most critical part of the action body, as it is possibly the weakest, cracks if any are most likely to appear in this area. The wood work needs to be viewed for cracks and deep dents. Stocks are most vulnerable around the head and the hand. If any repairs have been carried out in these two areas then I would not consider the purchase of the gun, for in my opinion they are never very successful.

Oil saturation is another fault in old guns and in some instances rots the wood. Breech pin, hand pin, trigger plate pin in fact all pins should have crisp slots free from mutilation. The general appearance of the gun should be one of crispness. Having put the gun together place snap caps in the chambers of the barrels. It is always a good idea to test the gun to see if the ejector work functions

Paradox gun cleaner — ideal for "inner cleanliness".

correctly, don't be in a hurry to open the gun to see how far you can fling the snap caps out. Partially open the gun holding it by the fore-end in the left hand and very gently with the heel of the right hand tap the stock at the heel. Listen carefully for the sound of a little click, this is known as primary ejection. The slower you can open the gun by tapping the heel the better. Proceed carefully opening the gun and at the same time watching the extractors until the gun is finally open to its full extent. The conclusion arrived at will be a) The gun has been regulated correctly. b) One side is slower in ejecting thant the other. c) The snaps caps hit the face of the action or d) The gun will not eject. Most people when testing the gun for extraction are too

eager to open the gun as quickly as possible and in so doing one tends to help throw the snap caps out. Hence the faults mentioned do not become apparent.

The operation of the safety calls for a sensitive touch. Push the safety thumbpiece forward slowly using just sufficient pressure of the thumb to enable you to feel the slide moving forwards. Now push the top lever open very slowly and watch the thumbpiece return to the 'safe' position. Immediately it will be seen if the safety work is functioning correctly of needs timing.

Trigger pulls are normally tested with the aid of a spring balance, although you should be able to feel if they have drag or very light or heavy poundage. Again it is a question of positive touch with ones finger and pulling the trigger off very slowly. The operation needs to be repeated several times before a decision can be made.

The final test is to note the amount of drop the gun has. Open the gun fully and look to see if the fore-end iron is coming into contact with the bottom of the action. Tell tale signs of the drop needing attention are a mark on the bottom of the action and the edge of the fore-end iron burred over. Having carried out your examination of your prospective buy consideration has to be given to work necessary to rectify some of the faults you may have found. This can be expensive depending on the fault, type of action and make of gun. What one considers to be a bargain and cheap could well prove to be expensive in the long run. Consider all the facts and don't rush into buying the first gun offered.

If contemplating the purchase from a shooting friend or advertisement in the Shooting Press, then I would strongly recommend that you ask for written proof by a qualified Gunsmith be obtained by the vendor. Insist that bore sizes and barrel wall thickness are measured and recorded in the report. This can prevent any misunderstanding once the gun has been purchased. If the vendor is not agreeable to producing written confirmation of his gun then my advice is to leave well alone.

GUN CARE

Over one million people are the legal owners of shotguns in this country. A large percentage of gun owners fail in my mind to give their guns the care and attention needed, for the average shooting man often neglects the basic cleaning and maintenance of his gun. Regardless of whether the gun is an expensive model or not it is the responsibility of the owner to ensure that his gun is well maintained. Generally speaking a well maintained gun is a SAFE gun. Next to ignorance and careless handling the worst enemy of any gun is rust, for without protection it will quickly oxidise. If your gun has been serviced regularly then its re-sale value is greatly enhanced. Uncleaned guns deteriorate rapidly and consequently lose value and even become beyond repair with a couple of years. Correct gun care is simply a matter of finding time and cleaning the gun in a logical sequence and applying the right amount

of lubricant. I stress the right amount of lubricant because so often guns arrive at my workshop for their annual strip and clean covered in oil. I often see shooters at the end of a days shooting feverishly squirting a well known brand of solvent, that can be used for almost anything or so the advertisement would have us believe, into the slots of the action and every conceivable hole in the gun including the striker holes and down the barrels, in the firm belief that they are doing a first class job of gun cleaning. They are wasting their time and in fact doing far more harm than good. Oil rots wood and dirt adheres to oil. The secret

Some of what you will need to look after your gun.

of good cleaning is to use lubricants very sparingly, only a thin film is required after having first thoroughly cleaned the part.

Misuse of ones gun is often attributed to the type of gun slip or cover we use. Guns transported in the back of Landrovers and Range Rovers need protection. I much prefer the padded or simulated sheepskin type of gun cover. Guns placed in webbing or plain material slip and are subjected to the barrels being rubbed and in time this removes some of the blueing. If the gun slip is fully un zipped it allows for ease of drying after having used ones gun on a wet day.

To enable your gun to be cleaned properly you must have suitable cleaning materials. Many of the firms who distribute guns, market excellent gun cleaning kits which contain cleaning rod, phospher bronze brushes, lambs wool mops oils and greases, or they can be purchased separately. Parker-Hale have for many years marketed a wide range of cleaning accessories from a moderately

priced cleaning rod to a deluxe presentation set beautifully presented in a hard wood case. Their current catalogue is well worth purchasing for within its pages is a wealth of information. Gunmark have recently introduced gun care products including cleaning rods and a variety of accessories. At last years Game Fair they demonstrated a stock polishing kit for the do-it-yourself shooter. One can achieve excellent results by following the instructions carefully. Another well known gun importer David Nickerson has had great success with his Phillips gun care products, many of which I have used on my demonstrations at various

country fairs. Abbey Chemical Co. have for many years produced a wide range of oils and lubricants for both air guns and shotguns which include stock oil, gun lube, grease and blue-gel to name but a few. The most recent firm to launch into the gun care market are Dan Arms UK. Ltd. who supply brushes and rods in 12.16.20. gauge sizes together with a suitable gun oil. Birchwood Casey the well known American gun care products firm manufacture a comprehensive range of stock polishes, sealers, stains and waxes. These are available through Gowers. An excellent booklet can also be obtained with detailed instructions on using the various products.

A very useful aid to keep in ones gun case is the 'Paradox' gun cleaner, now made in two pieces which screw together. Stored within its handle is an oil bob which simply hooks onto the rod and can be drawn back through the barrels. Marketed by Cambrian Fly Fishers who inform me that it can be washed when dirty in soap and water and it is then like new again.

Having the necessary cleaning equipment we can now proceed to clean our gun in a logical sequence.

BARRELS

Using the phospher bronze brush attached to the cleaning rod commence to scrub the inside of the barrels. Prior to starting with the brush it does help if a bore cleaning solvent is used. Simply apply to a cleaning patch and push through the barrels two or three times. After having scrubbed with the brush, another cleaning patch should be pushed through the barrels. The final operation is to apply a thin film of oil to the tubes by means of a wool mop.

The extractors and extractor bed are a trap for water and dirt. On most guns it is a simple operation to remove them, lift both halves out and wipe clean. Proceed to wipe the bed with the aid of a clean cloth placed over a small file. The easiest method of cleaning the extractor holes is to use a feather. Having made sure that all is clean apply a light film of grease on both the inside of the legs as well as the outside and replace them. Using a clean piece of cloth on a knife blade run it down each side of the rib. It is surprising how much water and dirt can accumulate in this area. A most critical part of the barrels are the lumps for they are subjected to a great deal of wear especially in the hook, this is where the cross pin pivots and the circle for this pulls the action onto the face. These need to be kept spotlessly clean and always have a thin film of grease on the surfaces. Finally wipe the barrels over using a silicone impregnated cloth or apply a thin film of oil with a clean cloth. A very important point to remember is that blood and salt water are prime causes of rusting on barrels, if either touch the metal try and clean immediately.

ACTION

This is the most difficult part of the gun to clean. Many shooters believe that the more oil they apply to the slots and hole the more it will prevent rusting and corrosion.

This is not true, for both dirt and grit adhere to oil and where two surfaces come into contact with each other problems arise. It is not unknown for the gun to seize and become extremely difficult to open. It is essential therefore to make absolutely sure that the slots of the action are kept spotlessly clean. The ideal method is to use a small file, having

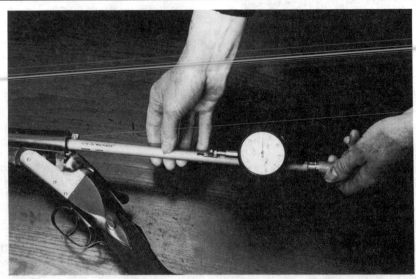

The internal diameter of the bores must be checked for wear and enlargement.

first placed a piece of clean cloth around it prior to inserting it into the slots. The same can apply to those difficult areas of the fore-end. For very small holes and narrow slots I would recommend the use of a feather, having first made sure they are both clean and dry. A clean feather can be used together with a little oil to ensure they are lubricated. Finally wipe the action over with an oiled cloth and include the top lever, trigger guard and triggers. I always carry an impregnated silicone cloth in my gun case. Kept in its plastic bag it will give years of service. These can be purchased from Parker-Hale, Abbey Supply Co. or David Nickerson and they can also be used to wipe the barrels over.

Water will penetrate into the working parts of your gun and can if left over a period of time cause many problems and possibly result in costly repairs. Bearing this in mind you would be wise to have your gun completely stripped and cleaned at least every two years. This work is best undertaken by a practical Gunsmith who will examine every part for wear and advise you on any work that may be required. This is not a particularly costly service and a minor adjustment or repair can often save embarrassment in the shooting field.

THE WOODWORK

Care of your stock is most important. The woodwork on your particular gun could have been treated to one of the many different types of finishes that are on the market. Among the most popular being polyurathene or the conventional

oil finished stock. If your stock has been given a high gloss polyurathene finish then simply wipe dry with a cloth and polish with a little furniture polish, preferably the wax type.

Oil finished stocks when wet appear lifeless and dowdy. To renew life back into your stock does not mean that you have to ply it with gallons of linseed oil. If you do then in time the wood will become oil bound and eventually rot. Excellent do-it-yourself kits are available on the market which will enable you to restore your stock to its former glory. The chequering of both stock and fore-end is best cleaned with the aid of a nail brush, the bristle type not the plastic variety.

Finally the storage of guns is most critical, consider very carefully where you intend keeping your guns. Many problems result when guns have been stored in wet or damp cases or damp rooms etc. If storing until the following day make sure that the case or slip is absolutely dry. If the gun is being cased for long periods of time make sure that you inspect it on a regular basis. It is not sufficient to lift the lid of your case and look in. Take out the gun and thoroughly inspect it, also check the case. It is better to be safe than sorry.

Never put the gun on a wall over a fireplace or close to central heating radiators. Always store in an aired space and preferably under lock and key. If at any time when cleaning your gun you discover a dent or bruise in the barrels then consult a competent gunsmith for his advice.

Pigeon 85~86

— JOHN HUMPHREYS —

The gradual evolution of a new set of feeding and behavioural patterns of Columba Palumbus have been so often observed and commented upon that they require no further confirmation from me. The reasons for the change — more oil-seed rape, heavy shooting over many years, and development of a new instinct of survival in a bird already well-equipped in that department — the explanations are legion, equally thoroughly reported and all of them, in some degree, probably true. The plain fact of the matter is that pigeon shooting is not as easy as it was twenty five years ago: even then, mind you, it was rarely a doddle, but if you found a good feeding field and could shoot it within the next day or two, a bag was almost certain. It was the premise on which most pigeon shooting forays was based, but once that basic assumption appeared to be no longer infallible, there were important implications for the decoyer.

The last two decades have seen the change, a very short period in the evolutionary development of a single species but the woodpigeon, something of a rara avis in the early nineteenth century, possesses the essential quality required for success, adaptability. It changed its habits and waxed in numbers as agriculture developed and by keeping one step ahead was able to ensure its survival. The latest trick is to feed in small hit squads to dodge from field to field, never lingering long in any one place, feeding at unpredictable times of day and thus reducing the risk of being shot and making life hard for the humble decoyer lurking in his bales.

In spite of these new unwelcome trends, it is still possible to make bags which match the best of the old days. Only last season, a certain famous Cambridgeshire pigeon man killed 264 in an afternoon on beans and had a number of other bags around the hundred mark. In late November, a friend shot 72 pigeon on beech mast, one of those freak crops, very attractive to the birds and a fleeting harvest on which to capitalise if you have the chance.

What of the pigeon now that the second half of the decade approaches? The bird may have changed, but the pigeon shooters also have changed. Ever an inventive breed, they too have been quick to adapt some of the old dodges for the modern pigeon. Decoys nowadays need to be very lifelike and ideally incorporate the facility to tilt and rock on the breeze. The answer seems to be a set of the Shell type of decoy (from Shooting Developments) or the hollowed out, home

A good flock of woodpigeons over a corn drill.

made, preserved dead birds pickled in formalin and set in a comfortable, feeding shape and posture. The rubber, full-bodied decoys or even the whole polymer birds tend to be less effective than either of these options. My correspondent Mr Richardson of the Market Deeping Woodpigeon Club has taken the full-frame preserved pigeon to an advanced stage, preferring now, he tells me, the head down, feeding posture to the traditional head-up. A flock of pigeon with all the heads poking up and white collar flashes well displayed, is not a flock at peace but one faintly uneasy and ready to spring at any moment. Such a picture is not an obvious draw for a decoyed bird.

Good decoys are essential but it is important to display them in a natural pattern while leaving a suitable 'killing area', as Archie Coats calls it within easy range of the hide. Pigeons are notoriously difficult to decoy on rape as they are on all greens, so why do not the decoyers seek out the bald, unsown patches, elevate the decoys on twiggy branches propped up in the crop or, better still, assess the flightline and decoy on the easier field next door? It calls for only a little thought to adapt in these sorts of ways: in the old days of rigid thinking

and predictable pigeons, without much thought the decoyer set his pattern in the thick of the crop and hoped for the best. No longer will such primitive tactics pass muster.

Other useful equipment is a wing flapper; I recall from the Game Fair, (and how long ago *that* seems) that there was great demand for the BASC/Semark, hand-operated model, showing that some pigeon men were alive to the implication of changing times. A flick of wing movement can, on its day, be a good draw. A dead bird is best to use on the cradle, as it is still the best static decoy, but a fresh bird should have its wings broken near the body or have been kept in the freezer and thawed out, in which case, rigor mortis will not be a problem.

Lofting poles do not seem to be quite as popular as they were — a pity, for this technique can also turn a poor day into a good one, especially if you have identified correctly the 'sitty tree', (Coats again), often a solitary hedgerow ash or oak which invariably holds a bird or two when you glass the field. It may be that the extra bulk of the poles and the tricky and time-consuming job of manipulating the decoy into just the right position have been obstacles which have been felt,

The hide must be well-made and the decoyer should sit still.

wrongly, I believe, to make the exercise not worth the trouble.

Hides too are lightweight and easily portable; clothing is high quality kammo gear (good ones from Sporting Developments and Pirahana), combining to make the modern pigeon man more mobile, lightly laden and adaptable than he was, nowadays conducting his campaign to suit the altered habits of the quarry. No longer is he committed to one field for the whole day, but must be prepared to move his whole operation, possibly two or three times in the course of one session, his lightweight and easily portable equipment making this possible. I sense that the pigeon shooter of today who can make a bag has not only the old and still essential advantages of the man with access to a great deal of land who can watch it daily and take note of a local build-up, but also one who can remain flexible, both in his thinking and in his equipment. To take that approach is to do no more than any sensible shooting man would do to put himself on terms with his quarry. What applied twenty years ago may not be the right approach today and the case of the wily woodpigeon proves the point.

Use imagination to display decoys effectively.

Ammunition for Small Bore Shotguns

DAVID GARRARD

David Garrard is currently leading a retired life in Norfolk having spent the previous 36 years as an advisor to farmers. His interest in the technical side of shooting started in the 1930's when he assisted a fellow student to pattern a shotgun on a length of wall-paper! A life long commitment to cartridge loading was initiated shortly afterwards when he inherited a set of loading tools. He contributes regularly to the shooting press and is the author of 'The Shooting Times Guide to Cartridge Loading'. He is a keen game and wildfowl shooter being a founder member of the South Lincolnshire Wildfowlers Club, a member of the Wells-on-Sea Wildfowlers Club, the Game Conservancy, BASC, BFSS, and the Salmon & Trout Association, In the close season for shooting and when not engaged in loading and testing ammunition he occupies his time in fly fishing for trout.

A 'small bore' can be described as any gun smaller than 12 bore in barrel diameter. Thus, 16, 20, 28. and .410 guns all fall into this category which in the past extended to such obsolete gauges as .360, 32 and 24 bore. Maionchi alone maintain a small reserve of ammunition for the 2 latter small bores of which 60 guns are thought to be in existence. It is reassuring thus to know that grandad's old favourite can still have an occasional airing.

This article will perforce concentrate very largely on ammunition for 20 bore guns, a slant which reflects the increasing popularity of guns of this gauge for shooting in the field. In USA clay competitions for small bore guns are well established and the popularity of trap competitions for 20 bores is increasing in Continental Europe. Parallel developments in this country could further increase the interest in 20 bore guns and their ammunition. The other small bores are of limited significance on the shooting scene and this is reflected in the restricted range of ammunition available for them.

Prominent among these is that "Cinderella" of guns the elegant 16 bore, now "sandwiched" between lightweight 12 bore guns and a proliferation of 20 bores capable of firing the standard 16 bore load of 15/16--1 oz. of shot. Lacking the versatility of the former and being heavier than the latter the 16 bore tends to "fall between two stools" — could it be that it is doomed to follow the 14 bore into obsolescence? The paucity of the available ammunition certainly suggests that cartridge loaders see little scope for sales.

16 BORE AMMUNITION

Eley offer a single 16 bore cartridge for 2 ½" guns, their 'Grand Prix'. It utilises fibre (Kleena) wadding with 15/16 ozs. of shot in a very wide range of sizes. It is a proven sweet shooting performer for normal game shooting. Eley no longer market their 1.1/8 ozs. "Maximum version of the 16 bore cartridge. Two other excellent "all round" 16 bore cartridges are the Maionchi 1 oz. load (all shot sizes) and the Winchester 'Ranger' (15/16 oz.) in 5, 6 or 7 shot. Both these loads employ a protected charge of hard shot and produce correspondingly hard hitting patterns well suited to the rough shooter or 'fowler'.

Rottweil market the widest choice of 16 bore ammunition. In their 'Tiger' series is a 15/16 oz. load (6 ½ shot only7 which should prove a powerful game load on a par with the Maionchi and Winchester loadings, all for 2 ½" guns. The 'Club' (15/16 oz.) load in No.7 shot is designed for clay shooting but should prove an excellent game getter. Both the Tiger and Club loads are contained in a 67 ½ mm plastic case with the Rottweil patent plastic wad and a pretty hard sample of shot. The 'Wadmannsheil' 16 bore load of 1.1/8 ozs. is designed for 2 ¾ guns and is presumably intended for 'fowling' and similar long range work. Shot size is restricted to 6 ½, 4 and BB. The latter is far too large to maintain effective patterns with 1.1/8 ozs of shot, a

better choice would be No.5. This slight criticism apart the 16 bore Wadmannsheil is a very 'punchy' 16 bore load and the most powerful of it's kind currently available in this country.

20 BORE AMMUNITION

In contrast to the rather limited range of 16 bore cartridges those in 20 bore have proliferated in recent years with a really extensive variety of imported loads becoming available to the devotees of this light, fast handling yet powerful little weapon. The 'original' 2 ½" 20 gauge shot load was ¾ ozs. but for many years now the lightest standard load has been 13/16 ozs. with many loaders marketing a 7/8 ozs. load as their standard offering. Both loads shoot sweetly enough in game guns of a normal weight of around 5 ½ lbs. and have an increasing following among those enthusiasts who find that they provide all the performance that they require in the field.

A youngster will find the lighter gun easier to handle than a twelve bore.

The descriptions that follow should be read in conjunction with the concluding Data Table which presents in a concise form the figures on which the assessments of the individual cartridges are based. The 'action' in a 20 bore cartridge is confined to a proportionally smaller volume than in 12 bore ammunition. It is thus difficult to achieve full velocity, say 1050 ft./sec. within normal Service limits and the velocity of much 20 bore ammunition lies somewhat below this level. The quoted pellet counts emphasise the advantage conferred by using shot not larger than No.7 in size, particularly in the lighter 13/16 and 7/8 ozs. loads. No.6 shot can be used for the larger quarry but pattern densities are bound to fall towards the minimum required levels if larger shot is used, an important point to consider when buying 20 bore cartridges.

CARTRIDGES FOR 2½" CHAMBERED GUNS

Let us first take a look at a couple of old established 'native' loads.

ELEY 20 BORE 'GRAND PRIX' 7.

This widely used cartridge is specifically designed for game shooting with light 2½" guns on the same lines as the well known 12 bore 'GP'. It thus employs Kleena wadding in a yellow plastic case with the Fiocchi 615 primer, 13/16 ozs. of rather soft No.7 shot propelled by 19½ grains of A.1. powder. Normal patterns were well spread with a minimum of central concentration making this cartridge a very useful game getter at average ranges. Pattern quality was enhanced and recoil minimised by modest pressures and velocities.

HULL CARTRIDGE CO. 'THREE CROWNS'

This is another standard cartridge for game shooting loaded into the Fiocchi Tipo 1 plastic case indentical with the 'GP' above. The hotter 615(209) primer ignites 20.5 grains of Nobel 82 powder. 13/16 ozs. of fairly soft shot backed by a card/fibre wadding column produced nicely distributed patterns very much on a par with those of the 'GP'. This is another utterly dependable cartridge for game shooting that develops normal sweet shooting ballistics.

THE GAMEBORE CARTRIDGE CO.

The Gamebore Cartridge Co. market three 20 bore cartridges. 7/8 ozs. and 1

This shooter is overgunned with a twelve bore at this poor quality pheasant.

oz., both in a green 67½mm plastic case (6 & 7 shot) and a 1 oz. skeet load in a 70mm orange plastic high brass case. The 1 oz. game load was examined in detail. The shot load ran a exact 1 oz. of No.7 of average hardness propelled by 17½ grains of A.1. powder. Breech pressures were at the upper limit for 2½" guns with velocity on the low side. The patterns were consistently well distributed without much central concentration and, reflecting the heavy 1 oz. charge were denser than the 'GP' or 'Three Crowns'. and were very effective for game shooting. The modest velocity kept recoil at an acceptable level for lightweight guns. 50 rounds of this load were used for pigeon shooting in the summer months. Results in terms of kills to cartridges were above expectations in confirmation of the findings above.

Maionchi enjoy an enviable reputation in the 12 bore game, clay and wildfowl shooting field. Their range of 20 bore ammunition fully upheld this reputation. Of the 5 cartridges examined 2 were designed for game shooting in 2½" guns.

Special Game (6) Med. Shooting Supplies.

SPECIAL GAME (6) MED. SHOOTING SUPPLIES:

A detailed examination revealed that the 65mm green plastic case contained exactly 13/16 ozs. of No.6 shot propelled by 17½ grains of grey 'flake' powder. Nos. 7 & 9 shot are also available. Petterns were dense and uniform with some central concentration. This is a hard hitting cartridge which would, in my opinion be most effective when loaded with No.7 shot and used in lightly choked guns. Well balanced ballistics were comfortably within 2½" limits.

'M' SPEED 7

Another game' load contained in a 67½mm green plastic case. 7/8 ozs. of hard No.7 shot (No.6 is also available) was loaded ahead of 16½ grains of what appeared to be a Nobel powder. Patterns were denser than the Special Game reflecting the heavier shot charge and the smaller sized shot. This, again is a very effective load that should kill to the limit of practicable range. Guns would need to be only lightly choked for optimum results.

Both the SMI 20 bore cartridges were examined. The 'Standard' cartridge, packed in 10's was based on a 70mm red plastic case which contained 7/8 ozs. of fairly hard shot stated to be No.7 (2.5mm) in size but, which at 400 pellets/oz. was exactly No.7½. A 'G' wad provided obturation and shot protection. 22.0 grains of a grey flake powder imparted a genuinely high velocity to the charge at a pressure nicely within 2½" limits. Patterns were uniform and very well distributed the high pellet counts reflecting the small shot size. A predicted first class field performance is confirmed by a friend's success when using the SMI Standard on everything from pheasants to woodcock.

CARTRIDGES FOR 2¾" GUNS

These usually contain 15/16 ozs. or a full 1oz. of shot and require guns weighing close to 6 lbs. to keep recoil within acceptable bounds. These loads approach the lighter 12 bore loadings in performance and are the obvious choice for rough shooting or the occasional foray onto the salt-marshes. All 3 Rottweil cartridges were examined. Although the two 7/8 ozs. loads are intended for game shooting the pressures developed are high enough to require the use of 2¾" guns.

DATA TABLE

Loads for 2½ inch guns

| Cartridge | Shot | | Ballistics | | | Patterns | |
	Weight (ozs)	Size	% crush	Obvs. Vel. (Ft./sec.)	1in. press. (Tons/sq.in.)	%age	Pellet count in 30in. circle
Eley GP	13/16	7	45	1000	2.28	52	148
Hull C.C.	13/16	7	46	980	2.00	52	151
Gamebore	1	7	41	934	3.02	49	178
Maionchi							
Special Game	13/16	6	29	1020	2.64	63	149
Maionchi							
M Speed	7/8	7	29	980	2.75	62	176
SMI Standard	7/8	7½	32	1117	2.71	52	181
Loads for 2¾ inch guns							
Rottweil Club*	7/8	6½	32	990	3.56	56	154
Rottweil Tiger	7/8	6½	29	1100	3.25	57	157
Rotweil							
Wadmannsheil	15/16	5½	24	1020	2.78	64	141
Winchester							
Ranger	15/16	6½	26	1020	3.06	74	209
Winchester							
Super Speed 28	1	4	19	1090	3.03	61	100
Maionchi							
Special Trap*	15/16	7½	28	1116	3.50	61	223
Maionchi							
Trap 3*	15/16	7½	35	1110	3.55	58	215
SMI**	1	6	23	1042	3.95	54	143
Loads for 3inch guns							
Maionchi							
Magnum 5	1	4	20	1024	3.81	56	128

* Guns should be proved M M. S. P. 3½ tons/sq. in. = 1000 kg/sq.cm.
**Guns should be proved M. M. S. P. 4.0 tons/sq.in. = 1200 kg/sq.cm.

Velocities are Observed Velocities over 20 yards and are derived from Proof House figures.
Patterns were recorded with the nominal half choke barrel of a Berretta U/O gun.

Acknowledgement
The writer wishes to thank Mike Barnes, Editor of 'Sporting Gun' for his kind permission to reproduce the information shown in the DATA TABLE.

ROTTWEIL CLUB (7) 2.5mm

Is the cheapest of the range. The load of 7/8 ozs. of No.63 shot propelled by 21.0 grains of grey flake powder is contained in a 67½mm black plastic case fitted with a 8mm tinned head. The shot was of excellent uniform quality and quite hard. Patterns were of very good uniform quality with less central concentration than might be expected from ammunition of this type. The use of smaller shot, say No.7 would make for greater all round effectiveness. This cartridge could be used with every confidence for game shooting but in view of the fairly high breech pressure developed should be confined to use in guns proved to M.M.S.P. 3½ tons/sq. in. =1000kg./sq. cm.

ROTTWEIL 20 'TIGER' 7.(2.5mm)

This is basically an 'up market' high velocity version of the Club cartridge. A red plastic case with a brassed 12mm head is employed. The shot charge of 7/8 ozs. of No.6½ was excellent stuff in every way. The powder was a wondrous product, 20.5 grains imparting a well above average velocity to the charge at just within 2¾" pressure limits. Pattern density and quality were on a par with the Club cartridge but the significantly higher velocity should ensure ample striking velocity at the longest range. A first class load with great potential in the field.

ROTTWEIL 20 WADMANNSHEIL 6.(2.7mm)

A 70mm black plastic case with a tinned 12mm metal head is employed. 21.0 grains of powder lies behind exactly 15/16 ozs. of high quality extremely hard shot, size 5½. Patterns were dense with marked central concentration and reflect ballistics which combine good velocity with very modest 1" pressures. At ordinary ranges very little choke would give all the pattern necessary for clean kills. The relatively large shot size resulted in rather low pellet counts suitable only for ground game or the larger flying quarry. Loaded with No.7 or 6½ this cartridge would hold it's own with many of the 1 oz. 12 bore loads. A most impressive product.

Winchester list 2, 20 bore cartridges

THE RANGER 20

This load was originally loaded into a compression-formed case but the latest version utilised a plastic tubed case (65mm) with an integral plastic base-wad. 19½ grains of a ball powder provides the power behind a Winchester plastic Handicap wad and 15/16 ozs. of very high quality, very hard No.6½ shot. The ballistics developed were ideal for ammunition of this type. Patterns were uniform and exceptionally dense with a good deal of central concentration. At game ranges only a whisper of choke would be needed for the most effective shooting. A close shooting load, typical of the marque.

THE SUPER SPEED '28'

This is available in 10's. A yellow 70mm plastic tubed case with a 15mm metal head contained 1 oz. of very hard, high quality shot. The shot size was exactly No.4, 3.1mm. It was propelled by 25.5 grains of a progressive ball powder, probably 540. The plastic wad was of typical Winchester design with a really deep o/p cup. Ballistics were first class. Patterns, as could be predicted, were pretty close though rather more variable than average. Possibly the barrel used did not handle the rather large shot to best advantage. The pellet counts were lower than is desirable for all-round shooting but if loaded with No.6 or 7 shot the Super Speed 28 would be another runner in the hard hitting stakes, ideal for fowling or wherever command of extra range is essential.

The two **Maionchi cartridges** in the 2¾ category are designed specifically for competitive Trap shooting and parallel the maker's 12 bore loads intended for this purpose.

'M' SPEED AZ/20 'SPECIAL TRAP AND 'M' SPEED TRAP 3

Both these cartridges shared an identical 70mm orange case and both contained 15/16 ozs. of high quality No.7½ shot that in the AZ/20 being marginally harder than in the Trap 3. Both powder charges were again identical. Patterns were dense and of excellent quality that should ensure a consistent performance on the most difficult targets. Velocity and pressures were high, indicating the need to use full weight guns proved to 3½ tons/sq. in. Both are really first class clay cartridges that could compare well with many full weight 12 bore loadings.

The SMI 1 oz. load is loaded into a 70 mm orange plastic case, very well finished with a first class crimp. The shot lies ahead of a 20 bore 'G' wad and is powered by 18.0 grains of flake powder. The 1 oz. shot charge was exactly No.6 in size and very hard indeed. The quality of this particular batch was, however, rather disappointing with an undue proportion of mishapen 'oval' pellets. This factor, allied with a very high breech pressure probably accounted for the patterns, though quite satisfactory being rather more open than would be anticipated. Pellet counts were adequate but I would prefer No.7 shot as being a better killing size. The high pressures developed by this cartridge require the use of guns M.M.S.P. = 4.0 tons/sq. in. = 1200 kg./sq. cm.

CARTRIDGES FOR 3" CHAMBERED GUNS

MAIONCHI 'MAGNUM' 5.

This is the ultimate in heavyweight 20 gauge ammunition containing 1¼ ozs. of shot running 180 pellets/oz., very close to British No.4. It is a high quality sample, well polished, uniform in shape and size and really hard. The latter character enables the shot charge to stand up to the very high breech pressure, patterns being denser than might be expected and of good 'duck killing' quality. The shot is propelled by 32.0 grains of grey-bronze flake powder, the whole charge being contained in a dark green plastic 76mm Fiocchi case fitted with their 359 primer and a 16mm metal head. Some shooters may share my difficulty in understanding the purpose of a 3" magnum 20 bore gun firing, as it does, the normal 2¾" 12 bore charge at much higher pressure and with all the disadvantages that this incurs. However the Maionchi 'Magnum' cartridge shows how good design can offset such handicaps and maximise the performance of these unusual weapons.

28 BORE AMMUNITION

This is about the smallest gauge gun with which it is possible to come to terms with game in the field. I have had no personal experience of shooting with a 28 bore gun but, on two occasions was present when a young shot in his early 'teens made good practice on average driven pheasants. At both shoots the ammunition in use was Eley's 28 bore 'Grand Prix', a standard load for 2½" guns containing 7/16 ozs. of No.6 shot - the only size available. The birds were killed cleanly and the young sportsmen reported very little perceived recoil. This cartridge, within it's limits, is clearly an effective load ideal for the novice shooter.

The other 28 bore ammunition currently available is Maionchi's offering of a ¾ ozs. shot charge in a load designed apparently for 2¾" guns. It, like the Eley cartridge is crimp finished which, combined with a plastic wad provides a rather harder hitting load than the 'native' product. Whether this is of much consequence at the short ranges to which the 28 gun is constrained may be debated. The Maionchi cartridge is available in shot sizes 6, 8, &9 - a pretty wide choice for a 'minority' product.

Fiocchi's standard 28 bore cartridge is occasionally available. It contains 5/8 ozs. of shot in all sizes up to No.4 in a 65mm plastic case with a rolled turn-over closure. This cartridge can be considered very much on a par with Eley 'GP' and is a good choice for ordinary game shooting.

Few driven pheasants fly above 20 bore range of the ground.

.410 AMMUNITION

The .410 gun is, in my view, far from being a suitable weapon for the young shooter to make his entry into the sport. The tiny charges demand exceptionally accurate pointing if they are to kill effectively and further require the self control that only comes with experience if out-of-range shooting is to be avoided. A gun for the expert rather than the beginner. There is an exception here. The .410 can be used to accustom a really young shot to the sensation of presenting and firing a gun at an inanimate target - a clay 'bird' propped up facing the shooter serves very well. For this purpose the 'pee wee' 2" cartridge is ideal producing negligible report and recoil even in the little single barreled guns with which youngsters are so often furnished. Apart from this elementary training the minute shot charge is best restricted to small pest control at short range. Eley (Fourten), Fiocchi and Maionchi all market a 2" cartridge containing 5/16 ozs. of shot in a plastic tubed case with a rolled turn-over closure. There is really nothing to choose between them, in fact the Eley and Fiocchi cartridges appear identical in all respects. Eley and Maionchi offer No.6 shot only whereas Fiocchi advertise quite a wide range of shot sizes. If available No.8 or 9 would seem a logical choice for this very close range work. The 'bread and butter' .410 cartridge is the 2½"

version. Eley and Fiocchi again market a very similar cartridge containing 7/16 ozs. of shot in a plastic tubed case with a rolled closure. Both are available in a wide range of shot sizes. Maionchi also produce a 2½" cartridge of similar construction shot sizes 5, 6, & 9 being available.

Patterns from all three cartridges were very similar and confirmed that the use of small shot is essential if pattern density is to remain at a lethad level.

The Winchester 'SuperX .410 cartridge (loaded in a compression-formed case) yielded rather denser patterns which must be attributed to the heavier shot charge (½ ozs.) and to crimp closure. This cartridge in the hands of a good clay shot certainly broke the targets with great regularity at 20–25 yards range– quite an impressive performance.

By the time that this article appears in print a 2½" .410 cartridge from the Gamebore Cartridge Co. should be on the market. It contains 7/16 ozs. of shot propelled by A.1. powder in a plastic tubed case using a plastic wad. Pending pattern tests it is possible to write that the loading combination should give results on a par with it's competitors and uphold the high reputation of this company.

As with the 3" 20 bore it is hard to understand the thinking behind such a 'ballistic abortion' as the 3" .410 bore

gun. To propel what infact is a 28 bore charge from this small diameter barrel involves breech pressures in excess of 4.0 tons/sq. in. (M.M.S.P. of 3" .410 guns is no less than 5.0 tons/sq. in.) Pressures of this order combined with an inordinately long shot column may make for poor quality, erratic patterns. For owners of 3 chambered guns who are determined to extract the last iota of performance from them there exist the Eley 3" cartridge containing 5/8 ozs. of No.6 shot in a P.T. case with a rolled closure. The Winchester 3" version is in a compression-formed case loaded with 11/16 ozs. of shot and finished with a crimp closure. Too much should not be expected from either of these cartridges and comparison with 2½" cartridges may reveal only a marginal advantage.

SUMMARY

The 20 gauge gun reigns supreme in the small bore world. The needs of the game, clay and wildfowl shooter are all comprehensively catered for by a wide 'spectrum' of first class modern ammunition. By comparison all the other small bores–16, 28 & .410 are hardly in the race. Ammunition is available that will enable all of them to realise their limited potential but developments here are constrained by the lack of prospective sales.

A Shoot of Your Own

JOHN HUMPHREYS

Formal shooting has changed radically during the past 20 years. The traditional, keepered covert shoot, which the British have made into an art form and where a blend of careful organisation, some orchestration and a whiff of ritual, with a bag well in excess of three figures, are the main elements, is becoming more infrequent by the year. Its roots lay in the great shooting estates of Edwardian days, where the noblest and the most single-minded competed at Six Mile Bottom, at Holkham and at Elveden, with their pairs, trios and even quartets of guns to see if Lord Walsingham could beat Sir Harry Stoner and to establish which shoot could amass the greatest mountain of the slain.

The news that one estate had topped the thousand head put the next door keepers and their master on their mettle to ensure that, at the earliest opportunity, the record was beaten. The houseparties, high jinks and the amazing standards of marksmanship, by guns who spent all their winters in the shooting field, have become part of the folklore of the sport. It was not unknown for a covey of eight partridges to fly between two pegs and every bird fall, with each gun unerringly picking his own four birds and killing two in front and two behind.

Two appalling World Wars gave even the most hard-bitten bag-filler a new slant on ritual mass slaughter, and he came to appreciate the difference between quantity and quality. Many of the birds in the old days has been testing ones, but the constant straining for the biggest bag betrayed too many nouveau-riche landowners to shovel tame pheasants over closely ranked guns standing far too close to the covert. Such lunatic competition carried within it the seeds of its own destruction.

The great estates were gradually broken up, and driven game shooting fell more into the hands of tenant farmers, business men and the new middle classes. Shoot managers and syndicates appeared, employing the skills of the old keepers, injecting funds into a form of shooting which was already threatened with decline. That decline was arrested, but only temporarily; for the costs of large-scale rearing, despite the development of new foods and methods, of employing a keeper, and the hundred and one incidentals of equipping and running a driven shoot, escalated at the same time as the long recession began to bite. The market was swamped with game so that, at the start of one season, the European cold stores still held thousands of birds from the year before. The best shoots began to let days to paying guns in order to offset their astronomical costs.

Thus, a new approach and a whole new philosophy began to creep in. It was based on the old and good belief that a pheasant driven was a far more challenging and exciting proposition that a pheasant kicked out of a long stubble and ignominiously shot up the backside.

A waxing of general interest in the countryside and conservation, coupled with more leisure time, brought with them an appreciation of the keeper's way of life. Shooting men realised that trapping vermin, planting cover, winter feeding and shooting rabbits, all coupled with a modest, back-lawm rearing programme, could be fun and provide an excellent and fulfilling spare-time occupation.

More practically, it dispensed with the services of the full-time keeper. Few teams of amateurs could hope to match the input or expertise of the regular man on the ground but, alas, few could afford to employ him. That the great profession of gamekeeping should have fallen into decline is sad: every advertised post attracts an average of 150 applicants, many of them first-class men, but the trend is merely one of changing times.

Family and friends can be pressed in as beaters.

KEEN TEAM

I have the shooting on a 1,000 acre Fen Farm, and I have assembled a keen team of DIY shooters to run it, build up their own sport, enhance the ground and stand or fall in direct relationship to the amount of time they put into it. Choosing the guns for such a team is a matter or great care. The qualifications are spare time, enthusiasm, access to tail corn, transport (for shoot days), some keepering expertise and basic practical skills. They should also be cheerful, be prepared to "muck in" and share your own approach to the problem. It is essential that they are all safe and reliable shots. In due course, I assembled just such a group and, under my benevolent dictatorship, they pay enough for the rent, which is by far our biggest expense, and enough pellets, poults and a few incidentals to see us through. Money is what we lack; and we compensate for the shortage by enthusiasm and the vital skills of scrounging, re-cycling, begging, making-do and stretching our meagre funds with parsimonious care.

The farmer of the land is one gun, and a most useful member as he drills and maintains our cover crops and follows an enlightened policy of conservation and habitat improvement on his farm. He also provides a tractor and a covered waggon to transport the beaters. Another strong member is already a part-time keeper, who directs our efforts, obtains poults at favourable rates from his contacts and generally keeps us on the right lines. Another is in sole charge of vermin control and throughout the spring he runs a trapping line of Fenn Mk IV vermin traps and cage mink traps. A fourth has access to surplus corn, dresser gleanings and unthreshed ears; a fifth organises the very important après-shoot refreshments, and shooting suppers which are cooked by the wife of another gun; the next is skilled in wood and metal work, and so it goes on.

Myself? Unskilled in most things, I am organiser, treasurer, letter writer, morale booster, worrier and anything else which it is difficult to categorise. We all assemble at regular intervals to erect or dismantle our rearing pens, plant a few trees, apply the creosote brush or carry out some other major operation. The system "wobbles" from time to time, as is only to be expected, but by and large the operation hangs together.

The shooting days are as carefully planned as are any of the best shoots, with everything driven, in order to be shown to maximum advantage. To save money, each gun provides his own beater, sometimes more than one; and many of these helpers have good dogs. One of them is promoted to head beater, and he will organise the drives. Guns are taken round in the converted body of a baker's van (also made by a member), which is towed behind one of the land-rovers. Our friendly farmer provides beaters' transport so that, apart from a token payment for the three-course hot supper, eaten in the farm centre and cooked at cost, no money need change hands on a shooting day.

The result is that, in six years, bags have risen from 120 head in year one to a few short of 800 now. All the guns feel personally involved in improving the shoot and, given the limitations imposed by time, money and the farming policy, there is no reason why that should not be maintained. The shoot is certainly more fun and each bird is produced at a sixth of the cost of a more traditional set-up.

Someone to look after the game is an essential part of the team.

The three basic elements of building up a shoot are: improving and maintaining the habitat; feeding in winter; and controlling predators.

If this vital triumvirate is maintained, it is impossible not to increase game stocks. The time may come when we might consider taking on a part-time keeper in return for some shooting but, at the moment, it is all too much fun and we begrudge a stranger our pleasures of building something from nothing and watching it grow. Having said as much, we are not tainted with the "numbers" bug, and we feel that 100 head in a day is quite enough to give everyone a good day.

SINGLE INCIDENT

The essence of our shoot can be encapsulated by a single incident, one of many, last season. We were beating one of our strips of kale (which we ourselves had sown) with beaters and dogs (which we had provided), when a glorious cock pheasant sprang from our feet. We had protected that bird from its enemies, provided it with cover and fed it in the January snows and generally seen to its wellbeing. Up and up it climbed to become a splendid bird by any standards, rocketing and curling over George who stood, a distant speck, on the corner of the next field. He raised his gun, and the pheasant plummeted down, suddenly shapeless and aimless and bounced,

quite dead on the frozen plough. When retrieved, the bird was found to be carrying a wing tag, placed there by George himeself, three years before, on one chick from a brood which he had reared from an abandoned clutch and brought down and released from a shoe box as part of his contribution.

The net result is more people enjoying shooting and enjoying the countryside, putting back into the landscape some of the things they take out. The bags might not have satisfied Lord Walsingham, but each bird is carefully appreciated and, most important, shooting may be seen to be contributing to what I believe to be the steadily improving picture of the rural landscape.

All driven shoots should have at least one picker up.

Spring on the Shoot

JOHN HUMPHREYS

Pests, plagues, vermin, varmints, predators or even black-hearted villains — I have heard all those terms and others far too earthy for the gentle readers of this book used to describe the enemies of game. The more thoughtful do not care for the commonly used but opprobrious "vermin" on the grounds that all creatures are things of instinct which eat to live and that to label them by such a derogatory term is to be less than just. Fleas, lice and rats, maybe, but stoats, weasels and crows we place higher up the scale of villainy for such is our curiously ambivalent attitude to animals. Otters, yes, the closely related stoat, no; squirrels, yes, rats, no; butterflies yes, spiders, no. In sort, we are in a mess about the whole business. To unravel the gordian knot is not the purpose of this article but, in passing, I point out its existence as yet a further example of the perversity of that unclassifiable super predator and pest, homo sapiens.

Sapiens or not, we have our value judgements and prejudices comfortably and firmly seated, the shooting man, farmer and gamekeeper being clearer than most in their assessment of what is good or bad in the fauna department. In short, those birds and beasts which conflict with our interests receive an unequivocal thumbs down, those nuisances which prey on the nests, eggs chicks and persons of our precious game birds. We over-populate a wood with pheasants to a degree quite abhorrent to Nature and wonder why nuisances, (I choose the word to offend no-one) move in. We seek to build up numbers of ground nesting species which lay many eggs especially in order that the predatory chain may be fuelled by the spare chicks and eggs, and then we grow apoplectic with indignation when Nature send us the nuisances to cull the surplus. In this, as in so many other ways, man seeks to improve, adapt, restrict and redirect nature for his own ends. I am not complaining, just making the observation.

More birds means a greater shootable surplus and any keeper from any age will tell you that vermin, (sorry, nuisance), control is an essential factor of the equation. A wild pheasant costs a twentieth the price of a reared one, so every nuisance removed, every successful hatch achieved and seen to maturity is a minor triumph, a promise of better sport in the Winter, a considerable financial saving and a superior end product to boot.

Ground nuisances include the feral cat, mink, stoat, weasel, rat and hedgehog. Badgers take an odd nest — you can always tell which by the finely crushed egg shells, but a badger on an estate is worth a deal of pheasants and anyway, like the hedgehog, it enjoys the full protection of the law. I would not dream of touching a badger no matter what he did: he was an English country gentleman before the Normans landed and has a right both to his place and his onniverous diet. Many of the most famous shooting estates support ancient populations and numerous setts. As for the hedgehog, I am rather less certain, for he is a noted hen killer and nest robber and by no means uncommon now that he has learned to avoid the Michelin X's and the awful fate of his forebears of becoming embossed into the tarmac.

The fox is the other problem, undoubtedly a nest robber and decidedly bad news in a release pen, but he represents another man's sport and if you extend the courtesy of your land to the hounds, then the foxes should be left alone. He is a self-regulating nuisance; there will never be a population explosion to exceed the food supply and, equally truly you will never eliminate the last one. A farm without a fox is a poor sort of place and there are enough estates which harbour foxes and run excellent pheasant shoots in the same woods to establish a case for the two sports operating side by side in perfect harmony. A farm with no local hunt, large fox population and a modest game rearing programme might be justified in reducing the foxes. In such cases the lamp and squeaker at night (a rifle or

Every rat killed may mean a wild bird's nest saved.

large shot at close range to avoid wounding, please) or the snare checked at least once a day are the answer. The self-locking snare is now outlawed so all snares must be free running.

On no account should poisoned baits be used for any nuisances. Eggs or rabbit carcases laced with alpha chlorolose, phosdrin or strychnine are non-selective, highly dangerous and illegal. If your man tenant sets them on your land with or without your knowledge, the law will still hold you responsible. A poisoned bait may be carried off by a crow and dropped in a centre of human population, may attract a rare falcon or harrier, may be eaten by a family dog, may be picked up and taken home by a child or, in the case of doctored eggs, suffer the rare irony of being eaten by a pheasant. Leave it!

Stoats, weasels and rats are best caught in the Ministry approved Fenn Mk.4 vermin traps set in natural or man-made tunnels, ie, not open to the sky placed along field headlands, by gateposts, piles of farm debris, in hedge bottoms or anywhere where the little inkers have worn a path. A wise man sets a trap in a place near a track or road; no point in walking quarter of a mile up a field just to confirm that it is empty, but not at the very end of a hedge. A stoat will work along a hedge bottom but, 30 yards short of the end will take a short cut across the corner of the land to the next hedge. There are "Sphagetti junctions" in the nuisance world: find and exploit them. Conceal the trap carefully and leave the run looking natural with lumps of wood, stones or turves blending it with the background. In our Fen fields we cut a miniature layby along a headland and leave two porous land drainage pipes and freshly turned earth to direct the stoat into the tunnel. This protects the Fenn from various violent and devastating agricultural operations which can ruin your traps at a cost of almost a fiver a time. Ideally, a Fenn to every ten acres is about right.

The law demands that traps are checked daily, so if you have to leave home for some reason and cannot arrange for a substitute checker, then all traps must be sprung until your return. Old keepers, keen to show their prowess as vermin men, hung their victims on trees or wires, keepers' gibbets as they were called. This practice has properly fallen from favour since the field sportsman has become more conscious of his public image. The innocent and uncomprehending country walker with children at heel encountering the grisly line of decomposing carcases on a Summer's morning will not automatically espouse the shooting cause as a result of the experience. All your victims should be quickly and discreetly buried but keep a careful note of each catch in your vermin book.

After each success reset the trap carefully, sprinkle fine soil on the pan and rake up fresh earth in the entrances, for no ground nuisance can resist freshly turned soil while a dark hole looks very promising to them. Wear old gloves rather than taint the trap and surrounding earth with tobacco or toilet soap scent. Watch your fingers and, if you anticipate a career as a concert pianist, remove the safety catch with a twig for, in order to catch the scampering, light-footed weasel or rat, your trap must be finely set. To prevent pheasant or partridge blundering in, jab stout twigs in the entrance tunnel to deny them access but leave them wide enough apart to allow your proper clients to proceed with confidence. Spring and reset any trap which has not caught. Little owls, hares and even kestrels have been accidentally caught in the deepest, darkest tunnel traps, so have a care.

Feral cats and mink are easily caught in cage traps available from Gilbertson and Page, Ltd., Place the trap in a likely place, hang an appetising fish head inside and await results. Check daily and dispatch your victims with an airgun at close range. Mink and feral cats are fierce poachers and should be shown no mercy but they deserve a clean and painless death.

The rifle and shotgun are handy tools in the Spring and many an inquisitive stoat or weasel may be 'squeaked' out to show his little nose. They are curious creatures and if, having seen one cross the road, you suck on the back of your hand or purse your lips to produce a thin, kissing sound, he is more than likely to peep out and give you the chance of a shot.

The corvids are the black-hearted villains of the winged nuisance world. All hawks, falcons and every owl, even the little owl, are strictly protected. To kill one might cause you to spend a holiday courtesy of the taxpayer at Her Majesty's pleasure for six months, so

Foxes need controlling where there is no local hunt to keep them down.

again, take care. Rooks are partridge egg experts, but I forgive them. They take early broods but kill so many wire worms and pests and dammit — the old irrationality again — I love them. Crows too take early eggs before the ground cover is up; not much harm there, for early broods have much against them, not least the weather, and the hen will lay again when the weeds have grown high enough to conceal her.

However, crows will also kill chicks: that pickaxe beak was not designed for shelling field peas, so they need to be kept in check. National reports of an explosion in the corvid population are alarming, but ambush them at the nest, keep the rifle with you at all times and be hard on them. Legend has it that crows can count to two so, it you are setting up a nest ambush, take a human decoy with you and send him conspicuously home when you are well hidden. He will fool the watching parent birds. A crow call, crow decoy and a dead rabbit belly up will often attract a bird into range, but you need to keep stock still for a crow has needle sharp eyes and is no fool. The crow trap can work well (design from the Game Conservancy) and trapped birds decoy fresh ones.

Magpies and jays also take eggs, more

Pheasant poults of this age are vulnerable to rats, stoats and weasels.

often those of song birds. Give magpies the full treatment at nesting time but jays are less of a worry so use your discretion. They are useful as watch dogs in the woods, warning of intruders as vociferously as the famous geese on the citadel in ancient Rome.

Time spent on nuisance control is well passed. You are helping song birds as well as game; you will never eliminate the last pest but are playing a vital role in helping nature to balance herself. Without your help, nuisances would quickly outnumber those creatures whose presence we prefer, so your conscience is clear. In its own right, nuisance control is one of the great challenges arts and skills of countryside management and curiously, one with which the general public find it hard to come to terms. Every crow, stoat, weasel, cat or mink you bring to book means a few nests saved, and early Spring is the very time to make a real effort in this direction.

Many an amateur keeper rejoices as much in a rogue cat brought to book as he does a good day at pheasants. Adopt a proper sporting attitude for, after all, you are trying to beat a crafty creature at its own game and employing considerable country craft if you are to be successful.

My last word: have a care with cats and make sure they are feral. Years ago I caught a poaching cat miles from the nearest house, red-toothed with a pheasant poult in its mouth at night. I shot it fair and square with a .22 rifle and a hollow point bullet. It managed to struggle home to die on the hearthrug in front of its agonised owners. Try explaining that away on the grounds of conservation.

The carrion crow is a noted egg and chick stealer.

Rifles for Deer

— ARTHUR CADMAN —

Arthur Cadman would not, I hope, object to my referring to him as one of the grand old men of British shooting. As a wild-fowler, his knowledge is encyclopaedic, while his book, "Tales of a Wildfowler", recently reprinted by Tideline Books, has achieved the status of a classic. He is a famous goose man and has written in Shooting Times of many a memorable flight. He is a respected member of the Council of the BASC.

He is also an accomplished and know-edgeable deer stalker, one of the top flight in the country. In this article he examines some of the complexities of weaponry for deer, the intricacies of the law and other aspects of that fascinating and specialised sport. The subject, Arthur tells me, needs a whole book to itself and in one article he can do his subject only passing justice and identify the key points.

B efore one considers what rifle to use for shooting deer, there are two major considerations which affect the choice. The first is the law. At the time of writing the law in Scotland is being revised but it may be assumed that the proposals will become law by the time this article is published. In England and Wales there are slight differences from the Scottish law. The second considera-tion is the quarry itself. What species of deer will be the main object of any one person's stalking sorties?

The law controls the bullet perfor-mance: the muzzle velocity in feet per second, the power in ft. lbs. and the bullet weight in grains. Solid non-expanding bullets are illegal.

In England and Wales the minimum legal figures are muzzle power 1700ft.lbs. and minimum bullet weight 100 grains.

In Scotland the law differentiates between roe deer and other deer. The proposals are:

Roe deer.
Minimum muzzle velocity 2450 ft/sec.

Minimum muzzle power 1000 ft.lbs.
Minimum bullet weight 50 grains.

Red deer
Minimum muzzle velocity 2450 ft/sec.
Sika and Fallow.

Minimum muzzle power 1750 ft.lbs.
Minimum bullet weight 100 grains.

The calibre of a rifle is not controlled, but in effect the bullet specifications mean that the minimum rifle calibre in England is the .240inch and in Scotland, for roe deer, the .222inch, and for other deer the .240inch.

Now as to the quarry: because in most deer species there is a large difference in size and weight between the sexes it is necessary to consider primarily the male deer, body weight and bullet perfor-mance being the two main factors. So we have red deer stags, sika stags, fallow bucks and roe bucks, (Muntjac and Chinese water deer being much smaller than roe does need not be considered in this connection).

Red and sika hinds, and fallow does weigh much less than the males, but roe does do not need treating separately from roe bucks.

In three localities in Britain red deer stags may weigh 30 stone (420lbs), but few people will ever see a stag of this size. A good Scottish stag will weigh 20 stone (280lbs), but the average stage is

about 200lbs., or less. Good sika stags and fallow bucks approach this category.

A male deer during the rut has a high level of adrenalin and this gives the animal an extra resistance to wounds that are not instantly fatal.

The practical implication of this fact is that the average stalker, shooting the average male deer, must use sufficient striking and bullet power to ensure that the animal is immobilised, if the bullet is somewhat misplaced. This is especially necessary at the time of the rut.

It is in making the right choice that the beginner can become very confused and as every stalker has his own preferences, so often based on his own skill with that particular weapon/bullet, rather than an experience with many different calibres/bullets, personal recommendations may confuse the novice even more.

Let us now consider the confusing nomenclature. In Britain and America the rifle cartridge is designated by calibre expressed in decimal fractions of an inch, for example .222inch, .270inch, .303inch. (the First World War standard) and so on. But in America the year of first production is added, thus the American .30/06 means a calibre of .300inch first used in 1906.

But on the Continent all the figures are in millimetres, the first figure being the calibre (e.g. the very popular 7mm) and the second figure being the cartridge length, the greater length being the more

CF2 Hunting rifle.

powerful. 7×57 means a calibre of 7mm and a cartridge of 57mm.

The range of rifle calibres available for shooting deer is:-

Small Calibres
.222inch Rem
.223inch Rem
Only for use in Scotland on roe deer. (Rem is Remington)

Medium calibres
.243 W (W is Winchester)
.256inch M-S (M-S is Mannlicher-Schönaur)
6.5 × 54mm
6.5 × 57mm
.270W
7 × 57mm.

Heavy Calibres
7mm Rem Magnum (Rem is Remington)
30.06 Springfield
These are too powerful for roe deer (but good for boar on the continent)

Generally speaking the smaller the calibre/bullet the faster the bullet and the flatter the trajectory.

Very high velocity, light bullets are likely to break up within the live target and that produces the maximum killing effect. But there are three main snags. This type of bullet may disintegrate if it hits a twig, frond of bracken, or even a blade of coarse grass: if it does not disintegrate it is more easily deflected than a heavier bullet: and if it does not 'exit' from the live target, without causing immediate death, there will be no blood trail left. Sometimes a too rapid expansion will cause unnecessary damage to venison.

A heavier slower bullet becomes more desirable the heavier the live target. The ideal bullet will 'mushroom' to two and half times its diameter within the animal and leave an exit hole. A point soft point bullet design is to be recommended and it is readily available in most calibres.

The ideal choice is to own two rifles, one light weapon for roe in Scotland (.222 or .223), or a .243 suitable for roe in England (and Wales where roe have just started to colonise) and also in Scotland, as well as for all female deer, and a heavier calibre for heavy stags and big fallow bucks.

But many people who stalk deer cannot afford two rifles and if both roe and red deer are to be shot with the same rifle, the best compromise is a rifle chosen from the mid-range of calibres, say .270inch or 6.5mm. It is worth recording that the Red Deer Commission stalkers who have to shoot marauding red deer use a .270 or 7mm. calibre rifle.

Many stalkers use a .243 rifle for red deer, its lightness and flat trajectory being of considerable advantage, especially in the hands of a first class rifle shot. My own opinion is that a rather heavier rifle is better for a beginner or for an average rifle shot. Once I lost a very large Sika stag. I was certain that my aim at his heart was accurate. The animal stumbled and made off obviously hurt.

A very intensive search the next day was unsuccessful. The animal was lost. Two years later the same stag was seen. He had a star shaped hairless scar on his side outside his heart. Obviously the bullet had disintegrated upon impact. Alas, he was never brought to the larder, so the full extent of the injury was never diagnosed. Had I used my .270 that stag would have died when I shot at him.

The next consideration is the type of iron sights. A wide V and a clear bead are the best, because the point of aim can be found quickly and there is slightly more light with a wide V than with a narrow target type of sight.

However it is now normal for rifles to be fitted with telescopic sights. With increasing age it becomes more difficult to see iron sights clearly. That is one reason for the use of telescopic sights. A telescope will add a few minutes of shooting as the evening light fails and so often an old buck will come out at the last light. Greater accuracy is possible with the use of telescopic sights and that reduces the risk of wounding. But the object of using a telescopic sight is not to increase the range.

Telescopic sights are not standardised. The markings on the scope define magnification 2X, 4X etc. and the diameter of the object lens, measured in millimeters. The larger the diameter of the object lens so far as it is not cumbersome, the better the light gathering ability. Too powerful a magnification is a handicap and there is but little advantage in a variable scope. The larger magnifications tend to emphasise unsteadiness, and greater than 4× is unnecessary. I recommend 4×40.

The graticule of the scope is important. Many variations are available. Thin lines tend to disappear in a bad light. I recommend a bold post and similar crossbar and a thin vertical line on the topside. This last can be used to avoid 'canting' the rifle.

The mounts for the scope must be absolutely rigid and most never be affected by recoil. Fitting proper mounts is a matter

TIKKA stalking rifle from Gunmark.

for an expert gunsmith. There is a great advantage in having a side mounted scope so that the iron sights can be seen underneath the scope. There is nothing more frustrating than to have the scope obscured by rain, or by a snowflake or two, at the very moment when *the* deer is standing "exactly right".

The last piece of equipment for a rifle is the sling. It is important that this should not be smooth or slippery. Rubber reins which have very small protrubances are ideal.

The trigger pull is important. A hair trigger is dangerous. Too heavy a pull is difficult and leads to inaccuracy. This is a matter to be dealt with between the purchaser and his gunsmith, but the vital thing is that a stalker must become so used to the trigger pull of his rifle that his subconscious mind knows exactly when the shot will go off. If he has to think about it, accurate shooting is impaired. Somewhere between 2¼lbs. and 4lbs is ideal.

It is necessary to know how to zero a rifle and any un-explained miss must result in a thorough test of the scope (or iron sights). A rough check is possible in the field and this becomes even easier if the scope mountings allow one to see the iron sights. The bolt is removed and then the rifle must be held absolutely steady. To do this at home, I have an oblong box with a U at one end to hold the barrel and a U or V at the other to hold the stock, just behind the trigger guard. The box is placed on a level table or other solid object. Then the telescopic sights are lined up on some definite item, such as a fence post top. I use a round disc cut for the purpose and hung on a nail at 25 yards or so. The disc should have a clear

M.81 Stalking rifle.

cross, upright and horizontal. After the scope has been lined up, then look through the barrel. The centre of the barrel should be the centre of the cross. An added check (with a suitably mounted scope) is the use of the iron sights which should also be the centre of the cross on the disc. If there is any evidence of an error, then the rifle must be re-zeroed. Also if a bullet of different weight or powder load to the one used for the last zeroing is to be fired, the rifle must be re-zeroed for this bullet.

The object of zeroing, or sighting in, is that every bullet should hit the aiming mark if the rifle is aligned properly. An average standard of performance of the man behind the rifle (or of the accurate rifling of the rifle) is that 5 shots at 100 yards should lie within a 4inch circle.

When zeroing, an accurate shot is taken at 25 yards. The rifle is then clamped in a portable vice with the graticule on the original aiming mark, then the adjustable knobs on the scope are turned to line up on the shot hole. After

this, the rifle is unclamped and another shot is taken at 25 yards to confirm that the bullet is on the aiming mark. It should be noted that a bullet from a scope mounted rifle crosses the line of sight at about 25 yards and then a second time at the zeroing distance required, say 100/150 yards for roe or 200 yards for red deer. Final zeroing should be done at the further distance in accordance with the ballistics for the bullet concerned.

Any gunsmith will provide a ballistic table which will show the different calibres of rifle and details of the bullet used at different ranges.

Oil should be removed from the barrel of the rifle before firing or an erratic shot may result.

Before a beginner takes his rifle for a shot at a live beast, he must have become thoroughly proficient with that rifle on the range. Constant practice is necessary.

He must become familiar with his stalking ground and especially in the case of roe bucks, he should know which buck he intends to shoot before he leaves

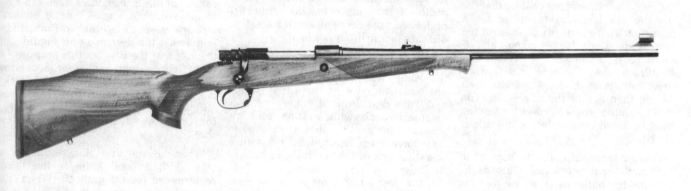

Parker Hale Lightweight stalking rifle.

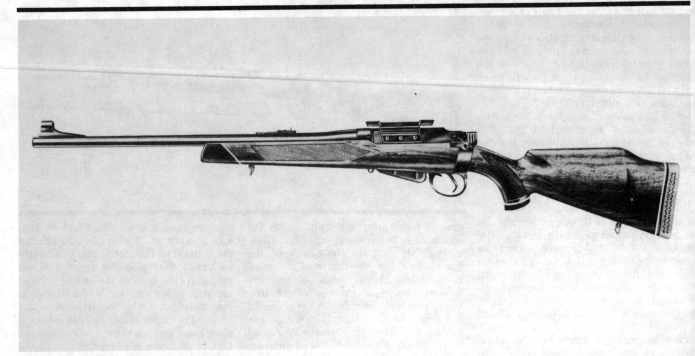

Parker-Hale custom No. 4 .303 Lee Enfield Sporter.

his house. There must be an acceptable reason for shooting that animal — and in the first instance it is desirable to start with an obvious cull animal and, as yearlings are the most numerous culls, and the easiest to stalk, he should start with a poor yearling.

It is a fact that in the excitement of the first encounter with a live deer — especially *the* deer that one intends to shoot — the best target shot on the range may go "all to pieces". The most important things are often forgotten and, of those, a safe background for the bullet is absolutely essential, *under all circumstances.*

I recommend, where possible, that the first shot at a deer should be taken from a high seat. There is plenty of time for the correct decisions to be taken, and if excitement, or 'buck fever', causes unsteadiness, then the rifle must not be fired. Rest, even smoke a cigarette, wait — and then mount the rifle again. The exact position where the deer is standing must be noted always, before the rifle is aimed.

A beginner should take the heart shot. Wait until the deer is standing broadside. Imagine the bullet as an arrow piercing the deer. Mount the rifle slowly (quick movements may alert the deer) taking care not to rest the barrel on a hard object (elbow or wrist may be steadied on a firm rest), and bring the sight up behind the foreleg, until it is between one third and half way up the width of the body. That is the point of aim. Hold steady in both breathing and aim, do not dwell too long, and squeeze the trigger. If the rifle is zeroed correctly and the shot is taken properly, the bullet *must* go where it is aimed.

The report of a high velocity rifle will cause the novice to blink. If the bullet has cut the arteries at the top of the heart, the deer will drop stone dead but he may not see this. If the bullet takes the centre of the heart, the beast is likely to rush off for some 40 yards, and the novice should see this. If the bullet enters the bottom tip of the heart the deer will run the greatest distance before dropping dead.

The importance of memorising the precise spot where the deer stood when the shot was taken now becomes obvious. One must go there first of all, and if the deer dropped to the shot, one must approach with caution and be prepared for another shot (*if safe*) as it may have been stunned by the bullet 'creasing' one of the vertebrae or cutting an antler.

If the deer has run off one must look for 'pins and paint' (hair and blood), which will indicate where the deer was hit. Dark blood is likely to be from the heart. Pale frothy blood indicates a lung shot. A broken leg usually leaves a splinter of bone. If the animal is hit too far back it will move off slowly, hunched up. Particles of guts may be left on the ground where the bullet exited. It is best not to try to follow a deer so wounded until some time has elapsed, otherwise its reserve of adrenalin may result in the animal travelling a long way.

Of course it is preferable for a novice to take his first shot in the presence of an expert. But that does not absolve him from carrying out the necessary proceedures.

Although stalking equipment is not the subject of this article, three items must be mentioned. First a good pair of binoculars are essential in order to find, study and assess the deer. No one should use the scope of the rifle for this purpose — that is very sloppy behaviour. Second a thumbstick, preferably with a wide fork, is a great aid for steadying field glasses and, when a standing shot is necessary, for resting the left wrist, when taking the shot.

When all the foregoing results in a clean kill, a good knife is the third requirement for the gralloch. When the novice becomes expert, then he will find that a dog is a most useful companion when stalking.

Today's Lurcher Scene
Tony Diprose

Todays Lurcher is very different from those used by drovers on their long trips from Norfolk to Smithfield Market in the hard days of the early nineteenth century. No longer do the majority of owners rely on their dogs to provide for meat for the family.

The modern Lurcher is more of a sporting and show dog, the Collie cross giving way to many exotic types.

Lurchers are very good pets and companions, their gentle nature and willingness to please making them ideal family dogs.

No other breed offers so much variety as the Lurcher. What other dog can course rabbits and hares, compete in racing, showing, jumping and obedience trials, and yet be gentle and quiet in the house?

Walk down the road with a Lurcher at your side and its odds on that someone will stop and talk to you. Lurcher folk are the most friendly and genuine people I've ever met, but because of the stigma of the Lurcher's past they are generally shunned by the majority of field sports enthusiasts.

Of course there are a few black sheep in the Lurcher fold, but they are a minority, and until the majority of Lurcher owners are given the chance to prove themselves, the few bad ones will continue to make the headlines and the rest be tarred with the same brush.

The Thames Valley Lurcher Rescue

At the end of 1983, John Corson and myself formed the Thames Valley Lurcher Society. Our intention was to organise shows throughout the summer to raise funds to put back into improving the Lurcher image. We were aware that Lurchers, as well as many other breeds, were by their very popularity finding themselves in dogs homes. To rehome a Lurcher is not quite as simple as it may seem, the new owner has to understand

that if a dog has always been worked by a previous owner, then that dog will expect a similar lifestyle. When you own a dog that has been bred from a running dog and a working strain then it must be offered the opportunity of plenty of exercise, and not just a quick walk on a lead.

With our many contacts from attending shows across the country we knew that there were others who shared our love of the Lurcher and who, like us, hated the thought of a Lurcher being put to sleep because no suitable home could be found.

Hence the Lurcher Rescue Society was born. Many friends who could not perhaps offer a permanent home were willing to temporarily take in a dog, giving us breathing space to find a suitable new owner.

After eighteen months in existence, there is now an excellent register comprising of those requiring a dog and those requiring homes for their dogs. Approximately 300 dogs have been rehomed since the rescue society was formed.

Anyone who would like to know more about the rescue society can contact John Corson on 01 427 8469.

Lurcher Clubs

With Lurcher shows becoming so popular, groups of people all over the country joined together to form Lurcher clubs, some of the more active of these clubs held a combined meeting to discuss the possibility of working together to provide a group of responsible people who could offer advice and practical help to new clubs starting up.

From this meeting was formed the Federation of Lurcher Clubs, the committee being formed from the club representatives in attendance. There would then be a well organised group of people to deal with any press enquiries, club enquiries and individual help that was needed, offering a combined wealth of

experience to anybody who required it.

The president of the Federation of Lurcher Clubs is Colonel Ted Walsh and the secretary is Mrs Gwen Riley. Anyone who wishes to know more about the Federation and who their nearest Federation member is should contact Mrs Riley in the first instance on 0203 317462.

Lurcher Magazine

Most sporting magazines can only offer the odd page or two for Lurcher owners and there was no publication solely for Lurcher enthusiasts. Lurcher magazine was first published in April 1984 and it consists of news, articles, club and show reports, photographs and general information. It is published quartely and is available from Tony Diprose, 13 Battle Close, Speen, Newbury, Berks. The cost is 50p per issue plus 20p postage and package, or £2.50 per annual subscription.

Summary

To summarise, the Lurcher is at last beginning to gain the respect due. Many people who once regarded the Lurcher as "Poachers Companions" are now, not only seeing them in a different light, but are also owning them.

A few words of advice to would be owners. Please do not buy a Lurcher because it is fashionable, they are not objects to reject after the novelty has worn off.

Lurchers, in spite of popular belief, are not "super dogs" they do need training, feeding and caring for. They are also subject to the ills of all canines, especially the killer Parvo Virus. Do get your Lurcher injected as a pup and annually, especially if you visit shows. With care and affection you will find your Lurcher is a loyal and faithful companion that will serve you for many years.

But be warned, once you have obtained a Lurcher, not only will no other breed match up to it, you will very soon also want another and another.......

An Introduction to the Jack Russell Terrier

Formation

The Jack Russell Terrier Club of Great Britain was formed by a few of the breeds enthusiasts in 1975 and from those small beginnings a very strong club has been established. Before you read on, it is not the Club's aim to see the Jack Russell Terrier recognized as a pedigree by the Kennel Club, but to retain the working qualities that has made it internationally famous.

Why a "Jack Russell"

This British Terrier that has worldwide fame is still known in many parts of this country as a Hunt or Working Terrier was given the name Jack Russell as a tribute to the well known hunting parson the Rev. John Russell who lived in the village of Swymbridge in Devon for the majority of his life. Parson John Russell hunted fox and otters and found a great need for a terrier suitable to go to ground. Hence he bred a type predominately white terrier with tan, black or tri coloured markings suitable to run with hounds over difficult Devon countryside. Looks took a back seat to courage, stamina and intelligence. We are now trying to breed a terrier with the same qualities which is also attractive to the eye.

The Jack Russell

You will find that most terriers have the natural urge and ability to hunt and if kept as family pets, which they often are, should be given plenty of exercise; in fact, they are almost impossible to tire. They make excellent house dogs and are very possessive of their family. Kept on a correct diet they will often remain fit and active up to 14-16 years of age. They are not interbred like many pedigree breeds and are therefore, less prone to bouts of hysteria and excitability often found in other breeds.

Breed Standard

Characteristics

The terrier must present a lively, active and alert appearance. It should impress with its fearless and happy disposition. It should be remembered that the Jack Russell is a working terrier and should retain these instincts. Nervousness, cowardice or over aggression should be discouraged and it should always appear confident.

General Appearance

A sturdy, tough terrier, very much on its toes all the time, measuring between 10ins and 15ins at the withers. The body length must be in proportion to the height and it should present a compact, balanced image, always being in a solid, hard condition.

Please Note

For showing purposes terriers are classified in two groups — 10ins to 12ins — over 12ins and up to 15ins.

Old scars or injuries, the result of work or accident, should not be allowed to prejudice a terrier's chance in the show ring unless they interfere with its movement or with its utility for work or stud. All terriers should be entire and capable of breeding.

A Jack Russell Terrier should not show any strong characteristics of another breed.

Breed Register

A breed register is a basic requirement of any breed improvement programme. It provides the only proof of an animal's identity, and, as the years go by, of its ancestry and thus, of its pure breeding. As Registration Cards are filed in the central office, a quick source of reference becomes available to any member seeking to purchase a particular type of terrier or looking for a suitable mating. An application form for registration allows details of the terrier, and a diagram on which to sketch its colour markings for identification. On acceptance, by the Breeds Records Office, a Registration card is issued to the owner giving his name and address, details of the terrier and a copy of the colour markings. Terriers may be registered at any age.

Further Information

For further information, contact:
The Jack Russell Terrier Club of Great Britain. Addresses and telephone numbers of officials will be found in the Associations listings in the Buyer's Guide.

WHERE TO SHOOT

CONTENTS

WHERE TO SHOOT/ ENGLAND

Ⓡ Any kind of non-formal rough shooting including rabbiting, pigeon shooting, walked up grouse and walked up game shooting.

Ⓖ Organised driven game shooting including grouse, pheasants and partridges.

Ⓢ Deer stalking

Ⓦ Wildfowling

AVON

Forestry Commission
South West England
Conservatory, Flowers Hill,
Brislington, Bristol, Tel: 0272
713471

BERKSHIRE

SHOOTING TO LET

Pennsport Ltd
Thames Valley Shooting Ground,
Tomb Farm, Upper Basildon, Nr
Pangbourne, Tel: 0491 671703

Roxton Sporting Agency

10 Bridge Street, Hungerford, Tel:
0488 83222
Ⓖ - *Organise shooting for single guns
or teams. 70 to 700 birds per day.*

BUCKINGHAMSHIRE

HOTELS

Ridgebarn Farm
Cuddington, Nr. Aylesbury, Tel:
0844 291281
Ⓡ Ⓖ Ⓦ - *Ridge Barn lies in the vale of
Aylesbury on 3/4 mile of the River
Thames. Pheasants, Partridges and
Mallards released. Driven days
throughout the season. Inclusive
weekends are our speciality. Excellent
accommodation and dining facilities
and a health club. Also open during
close season for Fishing/Rough/
Vermin shooting weekends.*

SHOOTING TO LET

Stowe School of Sport
Buckingham, MK18 5EH, Tel:
0280 813650

CAMBRIDGESHIRE

SHOOTING TO LET

Greenend Shooting Grounds

Greenend, Primrose Hall, Three
Holes, Wisbech, Cambridgeshire. ,
Tel: 03548 335
Ⓡ Ⓦ - *Parties of four to twelve in self
catering holiday lodge. 1,200 acres
excellent inland duck flighting by
arrangement throughout the season.
Walk up shoot for eight guns every
other weekend. Clay pigeon range for
use of hotel guests.*

Melrose Hotel
Seafront, Weston-Super-Mare,
Somerset., Tel: 0934 20739
Ⓡ - *Low cost mixed walking/driving
days for parties of 7/8 guns.*

CORNWALL

SHOOTING TO LET

Mr. D. Vanstone
Pixieland, West Street, Kilkhampton,,
Bude, Tel: 0288 82255

Ta-Mill Holidays
St Clether, Nr. Launceston,
Cornwall, P15 8PS, Tel: 08406 381
*One of Cornwall's best self-catering
accommodation in traditional stone
cottages, situated in unspoiled valley
of great beauty. Offering rough and
clay pigeon shooting over approx 600*
acres of farmland. Please phone for
brochure and bookings.

Tremaine Green
Pelynt Looe, Cornwall, Tel: 0503
20333

CUMBRIA

HOTELS

Leeming House Hotel
Ullswater, CA11 OJJ, Tel: 08536
444
Ⓖ - *Walked up pheasant grouse.
Driven Grouse.*
Ⓢ - *Roe Deer Stalking up to 2 rifles.
Red Deer stalking.*

Queen Head Inn
Askham, Nr. Penrith, Tel: 09312 225

SHOOTING TO LET

Bracken Bank Lodge Ltd.
Lazonby, Penrith, Tel: 076 883 241
*Grouse driving, pheasant and rough
shooting. Salmon and trout fishing on
River Eden. Bracken Brank Kennels,
Labradors and English Springer
Spaniel puppies and fully trained dogs.*

Mr. K. Dawes
Mungeon Farm, Backbarrow, Newby
Bridge, Tel: 0448 31361

Earl of Lonsdales Estates
Estates Office, Lowther, Penrith, Tel:
09312 392
*Driven Pheasant and Grouse shooting.
Rough shooting in season. Duck
flighting regularly organised in
September, October, November. Roe
stalking over 12,000 acres of
woodland and excellent Red deer
stalking. Trout and salmon fishing is
also arranged.*

Edwin Thompson & Co
42 St.Johns Street, Keswick, Tel: 0596
72988

Holker Estate Co. Ltd.,
Holker, Nr.Grange Over Sands, Tel:
Flookburgh 313/4

DEVON

HOTELS

Arundell Arms Hotel
Lifton, Devon, PL16 OAA, Tel:
0566 84666
*Premier Sporting Hotel. Driven snipe
(4 days, 10 guns) in November,
December and January. Some rough
shooting and driven pheasant.
Salmon, sea trout and brown trout
fishing (private beats, 20 miles) April
to October. Professional fly fishing
tuition and beginners courses.*

R *Early November to late January.
Rough shooting for mainly pheasants,
some duck for a maximum of 8 guns.
Days be arrangement.*

G *Driven snipe shooting from the
end of November to late January.
Four day shoots held weekly for a
maximum of 10 guns. Driven
phheasant shooting - days by
arrangement for maximum of 8
guns. Expected bags 80 to 330
pheasant per day.*

S *Red deer stalking in West Devon.
1 or 2 rifles. Stags from August to*

*end of April. Hinds November to
end of February. Roe Deer - Bucks
May-September, Does November to
February.*

Coombe House Hotel
Gittisham, Nr Honiton, Tel: 0404 2756

Dedes Hotel & Restaurant
1 & 2 The Promenade, Ilfracombe,
Tel: 0271 62545

Lee Bay Hotel
Lee, Nr Ilfracombe, Tel: 0271 63503
*Devon's sporting hotel provides clay school
and CPSA coach facilities all year - special
instruction weekends throughout the year.
Game shooting from October. Deep sea
fishing parties particularly for bass and ray
plus shark. Fly fishing for trout and coarse
fishing.*

R *Late October to end of March.
Pheasant-Pigeon-Woodcock and duck
shooting over 1700 acres.*

G *Walked up and driven pheasant
shooting 6000 pheasants released. Days
with gamekeeper available.*

W *Duck flighting*

Salston Hotel
Ottery St Mary, Nr Exeter, EX11
1RQ, Tel: 040 481 2310
*Well established gundog seminars.
April and September. Shooting
arranged as required at Bicton and
Gittisham.*

SHOOTING TO LET

Nethercott Manor
Rosh Ash, South Molton, Tel: 07697
483

Mr D Vanstone
Pixieland, West Street, Kilkhampton,
Bude

Lovaton Farm
Whiddon Down, Okehampton, Tel:
064723 225 Mr & Mrs Darch S.A.E.
for terms

North Devon Shooting School
139 High Street, Ilfracombe, Tel:
0271 64546
R G *Rough and game shooting
arranged in season. Clay pigeon
shooting by appointment.
Accommodation available if required.
Contact John Hemming.*

**Terry Cowley Shooting
Associates**
Cree Cottage, Woodland Head,
Yeoford, Crediton, Tel: 064 724
380
R *Range of shooting from 1 gun and
dog escorted by gamekeeper to parties
of 8 or 9 guns. Shooting in Devon. Bags
include Duck, Pheasant, Partridge,
Pigeon and Woodcock.*

G *Offer full or half guns in
syndicated shoots in Devon. Also
days driven Pheasant shooting for
parties. Bags from 60 to 100 to 250
per head per day.*

S *Roe deer stalking in Devon or Roe
and Red Deer through co-operating
clients in Scotland.*

DORSET

Milton Lodge Hotel
Milton on Stour, Gillingham, Tel: 074
76 2262

SHOOTING TO LET

Cranborne Game Farm
Wedge Hill, Woodlands, Wimborne,
Tel: 0202 824561 (PROP:MR
CHADWICK)
*Number of days driven pheasant and
partridge shooting to let for parties of
up to 10 guns. Individuals taken to
make up parties.*

W O Harrison
Beacon Hill Cottage, West Morden,
Wareham, Tel: 092445 364 Mr W
Harrison

Severn Sporting Agency
Forthampton, GH19 4NF, Tel:
0684 297904

HAMPSHIRE & ISLE OF WIGHT

Roger Buss Consultant Stalker
1 Oaks Tree, Mark Anthony Court,,
Hayling Island, Hampshire., PO11
OAE, Tel: 0705 463952
S - *Deer stalking on a let day basis -
Hampshire, We t ex, Kent, Surrey
and Dorset. Roe and red deer. Zeroing,
complete outfitting, training and
trophy preparation arranged.*

Whitehouse Farm
Rotherwick, Nr. Basington, Tel:
025672 3700 (daytime)
R - *Rough and pigeon shooting over
500 acres. Day tickets available.
Please phone for details office hours
only.*

HEREFORD & WORCESTERSHIRE

HOTELS

The Cottage in the Woods Hotel
Holywell Road, Malvern Wells, Tel:
06845 3487

The Lygon Arms
Broadway, Worcs., Tel: 0386 852255

KENT

Roundwood Hall
Lyminge, Nr. Folkestone, Tel: 0303
862260 MR J BOOT

LANCASHIRE

SHOOTING TO LET

Kelbrook Shooting Lodge
Kelbrook Moor, Foulridge, Nr. Colne,
Tel: 0254 663547 Day 0282 861632
Evening

Leeming House Hotel
Ullswater, Cumbria,
CA11 0JJ

Tel: (08536 622) Leeming

Leeming House, a member of the Prestige Group offers a high standard of cuisine and accommodation. Built in 1837, this Georgian Manor House, lies in 20 acres of Natural Woodland with Gardens extending to Lake Ullswater. Shooting Breaks for small parties of guns, Driven Grouse and Pheasant, walked up pheasant, Red Deer and Roe Deer stalking is available. Please send for details.

SHOOTING AVAILABLE

Driven pheasant, duck and partridge. Enjoy 1st class high pheasant shooting in the West Country with the specialists in arranging shoot holidays to suit.

Single guns or full parties of 8 or 9 can take advantage of the long week-end shoots and the winter breaks of up to 6 days shooting in the week.

The shooting grounds are all within easy reach of Exeter and with the ground in hand, includes some days on approved estates nearby.

The criteria of approval is for quality and presentation as much as reasonable quantity of game.

The choice of comfortable accommodation includes, bed & breakfast at the local pub, or luxury hotels with sauna and swimming pool. Currently, 6 hotels are used by our guests to suit their needs. These are selected for their expertise with shooting parties and their high regard for service.

Send for your shooting lists for the remaining dates available for this season from

Terry Cowley, Cree Cottage, Woodland Head, Yeoford, Crediton, Devon   Tel: (064724) 380

---

day.

S Roe deer and some Sika and Fallow deer stalking over 24,000 acres of estates in Wiltshire Somerset and Dorset. Seasonal weekly and weekend licenses for 1 to 3 rifles.

D & F Roskell Sporting Services
Trasha Hill Kennels, Pilling, PR3 6BD, Tel: 09952 2761
S G W Driven grouse shooting from 12th August, (8 or 9 guns) to December. Driven Pheasant shooting from November to January. 100 to 200 heads per day, 8 guns Roe Buck stalking from high seats from May 1.

LEICESTERSHIRE

HOTELS

Hambleton Hall
Hambleton, Oakham, LE15 8TH, Tel: 0572 56991 T HART

NORFOLK

SHOOTING TO LET

Noble Sporting Services
82 High Street South, Dunstable

NORTHUMBERLAND

HOTELS

Percy Arms Hotel
Otterburn, Northumberland, Tel: 0830 20261 Carl Shirley

Northumberland Pheasantries
Netherwitton, Morpeth, Tel; 0670 72219

Tweedswood Enterprises
Ray Estate Office, Kirkwhelpington, NE19 2RG, Tel: 0830 40341 Mrs Coxon
Shooting over 13,000 acres in Northumberland.

R Walked up Grouse and mixed shooting August onwards. Parties of 10 guns

G A Number of days driven grouse, Pheasant and partridge shooting for 8 guns. Bags 50-250 a day.

S Roe deer stalking

W Duck and Geese flighting in association with driven pheasant shooting.

OXFORDSHIRE

HOTELS

The Bell at Charlbury Hotel
Church Street, Charlbury, Tel: 0608 810278

SHROPSHIRE

HOTELS

Peter Howe Ltd. (Sporting)

Shooting in Shropshire, Staffordshire and Clwyd. 3 Shoots in hand within easy reach of M6. From Sept—Jan.
Driven partridge days — 9 guns.
Driven pheasant days — 9 guns.
Walked up days — parties of 4/6 guns.
Duck flighting. Beautiful countryside. Ample game reared. Personally supervised by Nigel Howe and Peter Howe

SUTTON CAMP GAME FARM Stoke Heath, Market Drayton, Shropshire.
Telephone: 063 083 - 236

Brookside House Hotel & Country Club
Brookside House, Bronygarth, Nr. Oswestry, Shropshire., Tel: 0691 773288

SHOOTING TO LET

Peter Howe Ltd (Sporting)

Peter Howe Ltd. (Sporting)

Leaton Knolls Estate, Shrewsbury,
Tel: 063 083 236
Mainly shot by syndicate, 4 miles north of Shrewsbury. 2,200 acres, including beautiful Shropshire woodland. 4,000 birds keepered by Steve Brown who produces possibly some of the highest driven pheasant in Shropshire. Saturday shooting syndicate gun 2,000 pounds per annum. Gun available. Personally supervised by Peter or Nigel Howe.

SOMERSET

HOTELS

Tarr Steps Hotel
Hawkridge, Dulverton, Tel: 064385 293 Mr D H Keane

The White Horse Inn
Exford, Somerset, Tel: 064383 229

SHOOTING TO LET

Kittisford Farm
Bathealton, Taunton
Holiday cottage sleeps 5/6. Up to 2 guns rough shooting over 120 acres, mainly rabbit.

Kingstonwell Game & Sporting Services
Coultings Farm, Fiddington , Nr Bridgewater, TEL: 0278 652272
Keepered shoots with all shooting sold by the day. Large numbers of pheasant and duck being released.

Melrose Hotel
Seafront, Weston Super Mare, Tel: 0934 20739

Game Finders Ltd

Game Finders Ltd

Tyning Wood, Gare Hill, Nr. Frome, BA11 5EY, Tel: 09853 317
G Driven pheasant shooting for parties of 8 guns. Bags 75 to 150 birds per

---

STAFFORDSHIRE

SHOOTING TO LET

Peter Howe Ltd (Sporting)

Peter Howe Ltd. (Sporting)

Wood Eaton, Gnossall, Tel: 063 083
236
*Our main shoot lies approximately 8
miles due West of M6 junction 12 and
comprises of 4,600 acres of arable
amd well wooded land. Fully keepered
by George Clarke, who has been keeper
on this shoot for 34 years. We rear 400
partridges, 4000 pheasant and 500
mallard. Our main driven day is
Wednesday, with rough walk up days
on Thursday, but any day can be
arranged. We also have a good stock of
Wild Grey partridges. Personally
supervised by Peter or Nigel Howe.*

Sandon Shoot
The Moathouse, Sandon, Tel: 08897
417

SUSSEX

Priory Country House Hotel
Rushlake Green, Heathfield, Tel:
0435 8302330
*R - Guests welcomed to walk up
selected areas alone or with
gamekeeper.
G - Rear 1,500 pheasants a year and
can beat to a maximum of 10 guns.
Clay pigeon shooting all year round. [
BASC]N*

SHOOTING TO LET

John K Johnson
21 Pearson Road, Pound Hill, Crawley,
Tel: 0293 32634

Oakwood Game Farm
Chichester, W. Sussex, Tel: 0243
786701/775089

Sussex Game Group Ltd
Kirdford, Billingshurst, Tel: 040377 456
Mr T G Crouch

Wappingthorn Farm
Steyning, Sussex, Tel: 0903 813236

WARWICKSHIRE

SHOOTING TO LET

Park Farm House
Ettington Park, Stratford-upon-Avon,
Tel: 0789 740316

WILTSHIRE

SHOOTING TO LET

Avon & Airlie Sporting Ltd
Avon, Chippenham, Tel: 024974
225
*G   Driven grouse, pheasant and
partridge shooting. 3,4,5, or 6
consecutive days shooting each week
throught the season. Shooting is for
complete parties of 8-10 guns but
normally*

Barbury Guns Ltd
44/45 High Street, Marlborough,
Wiltshire, SN8 1HQ, Tel:0672
52862
*First class sporting game shooting
available by the day or season.*

YORKSHIRE

HOTELS

Black Swan Hotel
Helmsle, North Yorkshire, Tel: 0439
70466

The Fairfield Manor Hotel
Shipton Road, Skelton, York, Tel:
0904 25621

Milburn Arms Hotel
Rosedale Abbey, Pickering, Tel: 07515
312

SHOOTING TO LET

E R D Johnson
(Stags Fell Shoot, Simonstone, Nr
Hawes)The Firs, Caperby, Leyburn,
Tel: 09693 347

WHERE TO SHOOT/ SCOTLAND

BORDERS

The Crook Inn
Tweedsmuir, Tel: 08997 272

Lauderdale Hotel
1 Edinburgh Road, Lauder,
Berwickshire, Tel: 05782 231

Sunlaws Hotel
Kelso, Roxburghshire, Tel: 05735
331
*G S Sporting hotel. Driven pheasant
shooting (15 days, 8 guns) in
November, December and January.
Some duck and pigeon shooting. Some
roe stalking. Clay pigeon by
arangement*

Tweed Valley Hotel
Walkerburn, Tel: 089 687 220

**Deer Management & Shooting
Sports**
Oxnam, Jedburgh, Tel: 08354 203
*Deer stalking holidays in South
Scotland covering 44,000 acres.
Firearms certificates arranged for
approved clients. Rifles, telescopes,
binoculars, knives etc for sale. Free
Roe-doe stalking, details on request.
Experienced stalkers or beginners
welcome.*

Lothian Estates
Jedburgh, Roxburghshire, Tel: 0835
62201
*R G Quality driven and walked up
days. Duck and Pigeon shooting
available*

Roxburgh Estate
Kelso, Roxburghshire, Tel: 0573 23333

CENTRAL

Lochearnhead Hotel
Lochearnhead, Tel: 056 73 2290

DUMFRIES & GALLOWAY

'Beechgrove'
Annan, Dumfriesshire, Tel: 04612 2220
[BAS]N

Blackaddie House Hotel
Sanquhar, Dumfriesshire, DG4 6JJ,
Tel: 06592 270

Blue Peter Hotel
Kirkolm, Wigtownshire, Tel: 077685
221

The Boathouse
Creetown, Newton Stewart,
Wigtownshire, Tel: 067182 335

Castlewig Hotel
Nr Whithorn, Wigtownshire, Tel: 098
85 213

Mrs Campbell
6 Ellerslie, Powfoot, Annan,
Dumfriesshire, Tel: 04617 347
*W - Wildfowling, situated right next
to the estuary. Goose flights from
September to February. Bed,
breakfast, evening meal at reasonable
rates.*

Mrs Cavaghan
4 Lakeview, Powfoot, Annan,
Dumfriesshire, Tel: 04617 342

Corsbie Villa Guest House
Corsbie Road, Newton Stewart,
Wigtownshire
Tel: 0671 2124 Mrs E.D. Graham

Corsemalzie House Hotel

Fort William, Newton Stewart, Tel:
098 886 254 Mr P McDougall
*R - Rough shooting on Clugston
Estate, (5,000 acres). Walking up and
driving of game including pheasant,
partridge, woodcock, hare, rabbit,
pigeon, snipe, duck, geese and some
grouse and blackgame on the moors.*

*W - Three duck flighting ponds
providing good sport especially in
September and October.*

Craighlaw Arms Hotel
Kirkcowan, Wigtownshire, Tel:
067183 283
*R - 1 or 2 day rough shoots with keeper
for parties of 4 to 8 guns. October
onwards.*

*W - Wildfowling on Solway. Inland
geese and duck.*

Downshire Arms Hotel
King Street, Newton Stewart, Tel: 0671
2001 Cowie, Gulline and Murdoch

Drury House
Bruce Street,Lochmaben, Lockerbie,
Tel: 038781 295
*R W - Wildfowling on the Solway
Estate. Permits arranged for B.A.S.C.
members. Some rough shooting over
local farms. Information fishing &
shooting. Caravans information - 874.*

Duncree House Hotel
King Street, Newton Stewart, Tel:
0671 2001
*W - Very good goose inland flighting
plus free foreshore shooting for duck
and geese.*

Forestry Commission
Forestry Management Section 231,
Corstophine Road, Edinburgh, Tel:
031334 0303

Galloway Arms Hotel
Newton Stewart, DG8 6DB, Tel:
0671 2282 Mr R. Scott
*R - Shooting over 2,200 acre shoot.
Rough shoot with some pheasant, duck
and snipe.*

Hartfell House Hotel
Hartfell Cres. Moffat, Dumfriesshire,
Tel: 0683 20153
*S   -   Arranged with Forestry
Commission. Prior notification of
dates and requirements essential. Gun
licences arranged for oversea visitors.*

Deer stalking needn't be expensive

The Forestry Commission in Scotland offers some of the finest deer stalking in Britain.

But because it's first class, don't think it costs the earth. For instance a day's stalking could cost as little as £60. Naturally trophy fees are additional and will be assessed on the quality of the head.

Stalking facilities are for Roe bucks, Red stags, Sikka stags and mixed does and hinds. The Forestry Commission also offers excellent rough shooting for grouse, pheasant, blackgame and capercaillie in some forests.

If you'd like to know more contact the area you're interested in for a fully detailed information pack of conditions and charges.

Forestry Commission

North Scotland
21 Church Street, Inverness IV1 1EL (0463 232 811)
Mid Scotland
Portcullis House, 21 India Street, Glasgow G2 4PL
(041-248 3931)
South Scotland
Greystone Park, Moffat Road, Dumfries DG10 9ED
(0387 69171)

Hart Manor Hotel
Eskdalemuir By Langholm, Dumfriesshire, Tel: 05416 217
Most rooms have private facilities.

R *- Walked up pheasant shooting. Small parties by arrangement.*

S *- Roe deer weekend stalking for 1 or 2 guns in private forest.*

Knocknassie House Hotel
Erive by Stranraer, Tel: 077 688 217

Ladyhall Farm
Ruthwell, Dumfriesshire, Tel: 038787 241

Lochanhead House Hotel
By Dumfries, Tel: 038773 378

Millburn Guest House
King Street, Newton Stewart, Wigtownshire, Tel: 0671 2039

Moonflight Cottage
Brow Well, Ruthwell, Dumfries, Tel: Clarencefield 677

Nith Hotel
Glencaple, Nr Dumfries, Tel: 038777 213 Mr K. Houliston

Squires Hotel
Collin, Dumfries, Tel: 038775 696

Summerson Country Holidays
Castlewig Hotel, Nr. Whithorn, Wigtownshire, Tel: Whithorn 213

Torwood House Hotel
Glenluce, Newton Stewart, Wigtownshire, Tel: 05813 469

Kenloch House
Cross Michael, Nr Castle Douglas, Kirkcudbrightshire, Tel: 055667 452 Bob White

Balmaghie & Hensol Estates
South West Scotland, c/o Mr Paul Withington 4 Finney Close, , Wilmslow, Cheshire, Tel: 0625 524519

Balannan Farm
Ringford, Castle Douglas, Tel: 055 722 221
R *- Excellent rabbit shooting over 440 acres for 2 guns. Modern self catering cottage - sleeps six.*

Barncrosh Farm
Castle Douglas, Kirkcudbrightshire, DG7 1TX, Tel: 055668 216

Buccleuch Estates Ltd
Drumlanrig Mains, Thornhill, Dumfriesshire, Tel: 08486 283
G *- Driven pheasant shooting Nov/Jan bags of up to 225 per day. Parties and individuals to make up parties, shooting programme to suit.*

Caldow Lodge
Corsock Lodge, Corsock, Castle
Douglas, Tel: 06444 286
R - *Excellent rough shooting over farm
forest and moors.*

S - *Deer stalking by prior
arrangement. Accommodation in 6
self catering cottages (sleeps up to 3
each)*

W - *Limited Wildfowling*

Comlongen Castle
Clarencefield, Dumfriesshire, Tel:
038787 283

Craigeilea Guest House
Kirkcowen, Wigtownshire, DGH
0HG, Tel: 067183 276
*Rough shooting, wildfowling
occasionally available.*

Forestry Commission
South Scotland Conservancy Office,
55 Moffat Road, Dumfries
S - *Woodland stalking. Roebucks and
does. Accompanied day permit
stalking*

Ladyhall Farm
Ruthwell, Dumfriesshire, Tel: 09884
2307
W - *Excellent wildfowling on main
flight path. Holidays on 150 acre farm
on the Solway Coast. Fully equipped
caravans (excluding Linen). Pigeon
shooting also available.*

Peter Blackburn
7 Lakeview, Powfoot, Annan, Tel:
04617 208
R W - *Shooting holidays over 10,000
acres in Scotland. Game, duck, geese,
rough shooting. Full board
accommodation inclusive price £230
per gun. Six days.*

Mrs C. Pickup
Craigadam, Castle Douglas, Tel:
055665 233
*7,000 acres rough shooting, duck,
geese, stalking, salmon fishing.
Comfortable cottage.*

**Pinebank Shooting & Sporting
Developments**
Corsock, Castle Douglas,
Kirkcudbrightshire

White Hill Sporting Estate Ltd
Bankside, Lockerbie, Dumfriesshire,
Tel: 05765 210
G W - *12 days driven shooting
available each year for 8 guns at a
time. Guests stay in owner's house.
Duck flighting Sept/Nov*

Mr Wickenden
Shennan Creek, Barnbarroch,
Dalbeattie, Kirkcudbrightshire, Tel:
055662 659

FIFE

Rescobie Hotel
Leslie, Fife, Tel: 0592 742143
AA *** RAC *** BTA

W - *Goose shooting and duck
flighting with Alan Murray.
Superb local golf in the summer at St.
Andrews, Gleneagles and Carnoustie.
Starting times booked in advance.*

GRAMPIAN

Kylnadrochit Lodge
Tomintaul, Tel: 08074 230/306
R - *November to January. 3 to 8 guns
in one party. Possibility to shoot
grouse, blackgame, rabbits, white and
brown hare, partridge, pheasant,
snipe, woodcock, duck*

G -*Driven grouse in August and
September in party of 8 guns. Driven
pheasants in November in party of 8
guns*

S - *Roebuck stalking from May to
12th August with 4 rifles per week
maximum. Doe stalking in January.
Red deer (stags) from mid September
to 20th October with 2 rifles per
week maximum*

W - *Duck shooting from September
to December in party of up to 8
guns, one day a week is included in
the mixed game shooting.*

Raemoir House Hotel
Raemoir, Banchory, Tel: 03302 4884

Scottish Highland Field Sports
An Halle, Kellas, Elgin, Moray, Tel:
0343 59387/59354

Ramsay Arms Hotel
Fettercairn, Kincardineshire, Tel: 05614
334

Tor Na Coille Hotel
Inchmarlo Road, Banchory,
Kincardineshire, Tel: 03302 2242

Udny Arms Hotel
Newburgh, Ellon, Aberdeenshire,
Tel: 03586 444
R G -*Atmosphere, antique furnished,
shooting and fishing hotel 12 miles
from Aberdeen. Excellent Cordon
Bleu cuisine, choice of dining room or
informal bistro. Cocktail and cafe
bars. 1st class accommodation*

R G - *Rough shooting including
rabbits and pigeons. Organised
driven game shooting including
pheasants and partridges. The hotel
organises days on a variety of local
estates*

W - *Estuary and inlaid shooting for
duck and geese*

Mr Travers Cosgrove
Station Cottage, Gartly, Huntly, Tel:
046688 277 and: Reading 0734 472524

Glenfiddich Estate
Nr. Dufftown, Banffshire, Tel: 01
623 2801
G - *High quality driven grouse shooting
from late August for max 9 guns. Days
by arrangement*

S -*Red and roe deer stalking by
arrangement*

Orton Management Co Ltd
Croftcroy, Orton, Fochabers, Moray,
Tel: 034388 240, Mr A F Smith

HIGHLANDS &
ISLANDS

Bridgend Hotel
Islay House, Bridgend, Islay, Argyll,
Tel: 049681 212
W -*Goose shooting*

S -*Roe and red deer stalking*

Bruce Hotel
Harbour Street, Tarbert, Argyll, Tel:
08802 577
S -*Red sika and roe. Max of 3 guns.
Over 9,000 acres of mixed woodland
and forestry plantations. All within
reach of Tarbert. Excellent
accommodation at hotel.*

Fearann Eilean Iarmain
Eilean Iarmain, An t Eilean,
Sgitheanach, Isle of Skye, IV43 8QR,
Tel: 047 134 266

Forestry Commission
Forestry Management Section 231,
Corstophine Road, Edinburgh, Tel:
031334 0303

Forsinard Hotel
Forsinard, Tel: 064 17 221
R - *Grouse over dogs*

S -*Red Deer*

Harlosh Hotel
By Dunvegan, Isle of Skye,
Inverness-shire, Tel: 047022 367
*Full a la carte menu including game
and speciality seafoods.*

R - *3 to 5 guns shooting over 5,000
acres of predominately heather
moorland. Also sea, burn and loch
fishing available to residents.*

Invereshie House Hotel
Kincraig, Kingussie, Inverness-shire,
Tel: 054 04 332

Kinlock Ewe Hotel
Kinlock Ewe, Ross-shire, Tel: 044584
253

Knockie Lodge Hotel
Whitebridge, Tel: 04563 276

Letterfinlay Lodge Hotel
Spean Bridge, Inverness-shire, Tel:
039784 222

Rovie Farm Guest House
Rogart, Sutherland, Tel: 04084 209
R -*Accomodation for up to 12 persons. Bed and Breakfast, evening meal. Individuals and small parties welcome*

R - *Mainly rabbit and pigeon with a little pheasant*

S - *Roe deer stalking*

Shieldaig Lodge Hotel
Gairloch, Tel: 0445 83 250
S - *Red deer stags available September to October. Red deer hinds January until middle of February. 1 rifle per day*

G - *Grouse and woodcock*

Taversoe Hotel
Rousay, Orkney, Tel: 085 682 325
R - *Rough shooting package including hotel accommodation. Rabbits, pigeon flighting, some grouse, snipe. Dogs and ferrets welcome.*

Ulbster Arms Hotel
Halkirk, Caithness, Tel: 084783 206

Uiginish Lodge
By Dunveygan, Isle of Skye, Tel: 047022 445
Self catering sporting holidays in 18th century hunting lodge. Twin-bedded rooms, communal kitchen/living area. 5 guns over 5,000 acres. Fishing on stocked lochs. Sea angling - tackle room on premises.

Ullinish Lodge Hotel
Struan, Isle of Skye, Tel: 047072 214

Alladale Lodge
Arday, Ross-shire, Tel: 08633 366

Boondatoon
Stronsay, Orkney Islands, Tel: 08576 248
W - *Self catering cottage on the beautiful island of Stronsay. Sleeps up to 5. Excellent offshore and inland duck and goose shooting available by an arrangement with local estates.*

Findon Mill Ltd
Findon Mill, Culbokie, Ross-shire, Tel: 034987 255

Forestry Commission
North Scotland Conservancy, 21 Church Street, Inverness
S - *Woodland stalking. Red Sika roe deer. Stags/Bucks, hinds/does. Accompanied weekly permits*

Highland Hunting
45 Gordon Street, Aberdeen, Tel: 0224 25228

Kilmartin Farm
Glenurquhart, Inverness, Tel: 04564268

Leckmelm Estate
Leckmelm, Ullapool, Ross-shire, Tel: 0854 2471

Rhidorroch Lodge
Ullapool, Ross & Cromarty, Tel: 0584 2548

Trumland House
Rousay, Orkney, Tel: 085682 263

STRATHCLYDE

Craig Lodge
Dalmally, Argyllshire, PA33 1AR, Tel: 08382 216

Forestry Commission
Forestry Management Section 231, Corstophine Road, Edinburgh, Tel: 031334 0303

Gigha Hotel
Isle of Gigha, Argyll, Tel: 05835 254

Port Charlotte Hotel
Isle of Islay, Argyll, Tel: 044685 312/219
R S W - *Rough shooting, roe stalking and wildfowling in season*

Portsonachan Hotel
By Dalmally, Argyll, Tel: 086 63 224

Ardfin Estate
Isle of Jura c/o The Shooting Lodge, 28-30 Victoria Street, Skipton, North Yorks., BD23 1JE, Tel: 0756 5825

Ardtornish Estate
Estate Office, Morvern, By Oban, Argyll, Tel: 096784 288

Argyll Estates Office
Cherry Park, Inveraray, Argyll, Tel: 0499 2203

Isle of Arran Estate Office
Brodick, Isle of Arran, Tel: 0770 2203

Claonaig Estate
Tarbert, Argyll, PA29 6XG, Tel: 088 06 209

Craigengillan Estates Co Ltd
Craigengillan, Dalmellington, Ayrshire, Tel: 0292 550 366

Cassillis Estate
Estate Office, The Castle, Maybole, Ayrshire, Tel: 0655 82103

Forestry Commission
West Scotland Conservancy, Portcullis House, 21 India Street, Glasgow
S - *Woodland and hill stalking. Red, Sika and roe deer. Stags/bucks, hinds/does. Accompanied weekly and day permit stalking*

Mr P Sinclair
Resipole Farm, Loch Sunart, Acharacle, Argyll, Tel: 096785 235

Skipness Estate
Tarbert, Argyll, PA29 6XU, Tel: 08806 207

Tarbert Lodge
Isle of Jura c/o The Shooting Lodge, 28-30 Victoria Street, Skipton, N. Yorks, Tel: 0756 5825

West Highland Estates Office
7 Agryll Street, Oban, Argyll, PA34 5SG, Tel: 0631 63617

West Highlands Gamekeeper Service
Kirrin Lodge, Eredine by Dalmally, Argyll, Tel: 08664 241

TAYSIDE

Angus Hotel
Blairgowrie, Tel: 0250 2838
G R W S -*Local lochs and rivers provide geese shooting. Grouse, Deer, Pheasant, Blackcock, White Hare, Rabbit. Special hotel rates for shooting groups.*

Ardeonaig Hotel
By Killin, South Loch, Tayside, Perthshire, Tel: 056 72 400

Ballathie House Hotel
Kinclaven By Stanley,, Perthshire, Tel: 025083 268, David Assent, Manager

The Bein Inn
Glenfarg, Perthshire, PH29 9PY, Tel: 057 73216
Coaching Inn, modern accommodation, all rooms with private facilities. A la carte restaurant.

R - *Mixed and rough shooting arranged by the day or longer. Parties for 2 or more guns*

G - *driven pheasant arranged on 3 major estates. Parties of 8 or more guns*

W - *Estuary or inland goose and duck flighting and other decoys*

S - *Roe deer stalking arranged on application*

Dunalastair Hotel
Kinloch Rannoch, Perthshire, Tel: 0882 323 Mr R Fenwick

Foulford Inn
By Crieff, Perthshire, Tel: 0764 2407

Garry Guest House
Killiecrankie, Pitlochry, PH16 5LW, Tel: 0796 3219

Huntingtower Hotel

huntingtower hotel

Crieff Road, Perth, Tel: 073883 241
R G *The hotel and restaurant is well known for its high standard and caters for fishing and shooting groups. Shooting organised through agent, Duncan Clark of Safari Scotland.*

Kirkside House Hotel
Glenisla, By Blairgowrie, Perthshire, Tel: 057582 278

Kings of Kinloch Hotel
Meigle, Perthshire, Tel: 08284 273
R G W S *Shooting by arrangement with local agencies. Self catering lodge with hotel grounds available. The ideal area for the perfect shooting holiday. Overseas parties especially welcome*

Kinloch House Hotel
Dunkeld Road, By Blairgowrie, Perthshire, Tel: 025084 237
R *- Rough shooting in conjunction with local estates. Up to 8 guns shooting pheasant, blackgame, hare etc*

W *- Flighting on local loch for up to 6 guns*

S *-Red, roe and fallow in conjunction with local estates. Driven grouse, pheasant and partridge on local sporting estate*

Lands of Loyal Hotel
Alyth, Perthshire, Tel: 08283 2481
R S *- Shooting by arrangement*

Loch Tummel Hotel
Strathtummel, PH16 5RP, Tel: 08824 272
R *- Rough shooting throughout the season*

S *- Stalking July throughe February*

Lomond Country Inn
Kinnesswood, By Kinross, Tel: 059 284 317/253
R *- Ranging from farm shooting (mixed bag) to keepered walk ups*

G *- Arranged through local landlords and organisations*

W *- Shooting on 9 farms in Loch Leven Area*

S *- Roe deer. Can be arranged if given notice*

The Log Cabin Hotel
Kirkmichael, Perthshire, Tel: 025081 288

Muirton House Hotel
Essendy Road, Blairgowrie, Perthshire, Tel: 0250 2113, Mr Allen J.A.R.
R G S W *Working with the Arran Game Services, who can offer all types of shooting over 7 estates in Perthshire (in excess of 30,000 acres) Prior arrangement necessary*

The Old Station House
Farnell, Brechin, Tayside

Rosebank Hotel
Millar Street, Crieff, Perthside, Tayside, Tel: 0764 3843

Royal Jubilee Arms Hotel
Cortachy, Kirrimuir, Tel: 05754 225

West Tempar House
Kinloch Rannoch, Perthshire, Tel: 08822 338

SHOOTING TO LET

Airlie Estate Office
Cortachy By Kirrimuir, Angus, Tayside, Tel: 05754 222
R G S *We can offer driven pheasant shooting for parties of 8 guns throughout the season. 100 bird days. Rough shooting for 5-6 guns. Weekly programmes. Good mixed shooting and red deer stalking on a weekly basis for 2/3 rifles. Accommodation available at Rottall Lodge.*

Dalmunzie Estate
Glenshee, Blairgowrie, Perthshire, Tel: 025085 226 Evenings
R *- Dalmunzie highland cottages on 6,000 acre estate. Self catering accommodation for 2 to 8 people. Walked up shooting for grouse, blackgame and ptarmigan. Red deer stalking season. Also hares and pigeon*

J & G Harris
Lochan Lodge, Amulrea, By Dunkeld, Perthshire, Tel: 03505 243

J M Morson & Son
Newmiln, Guildtown, Perth, Tel: 0738 51132

Rottal Lodge
Rottal, Glen Clova, Kirriemuir, Angus, Tel: 05755 224/242

WHERE TO SHOOT/ WALES

CLWYD

HOTELS

Golden Pheasant Hotel
Llwynmawr, Nr Llangollen, Clwyd, Tel: 0691 72281
R -G -W - *Shooting available September through January. Single and double driven pheasant days for parties or single guns. Several rough days available weekly. Ducks grouse and pheasant*

Peter Howe Ltd (Sporting)

Peter Howe Ltd. (Sporting)

Bryn-Y-Pys, Shoot, Overton on Dee, Clwyd, Tel: 063 083 236
A typical North Wales Valley through pleasant countryside. The shoot has the beautiful River Dee flowing for three miles through the centre. 4,000 pheasants reared, 400 partridges, 200 mallard. Shooting is syndicated at £1800 per gun. Personally supervised by Peter or Nigel Howe.

SHOOTING TO LET

Halkyn Shoot

Halkyn, Nr Mold, Tel: 0948 840415

DYFED

HOTELS

Hafod Wen
Coedmore Estates, Llechryd, Tel: 0239 87538

Hafod Wen is a particularly delightful secluded fishing/shooting cottage which sleeps 6 and is set in 120 acres of its own outstandingly beautiful woodland and pastureland with its own exclusive fishing on the River Teifi and approx 800 acres of rough shooting. Accomodation: Living room

with Inglenook fireplace, dining room, kitchen, bathroom and 2 triple bedrooms.

The Red House
Llawhaden Nr. Narberth, Dyfed, Tel: 0991 4252
R - *Excellent accommodation for up to 8/10 guests in farmhouse. Pheasant, woodcock, duck and rough shooting available for 1 gun or parties up to 8/10 guns. Walking, riding, flying and salmon fishing by arrangements.*

SHOOTING TO LET

Carmarthenshire & Wales Game Farm
Llanfynydd, Carmarthen, Tel: 05584 491
Shooting available on three estates.

Dyfed Game Farm
Banc Farm, Croff Inn, Llanon, Tel: 09746 634
Superb duck shooting - Also pheasant and partridges.
Charles Grisdale, Banc Farm, Croff Inn, Llanon, Wales. 09746 634.

GWYNEDD

HOTELS

Craig y Dderrwen Country House Hotel
Betws-y-Coed, Gwynedd, Tel: 06902 293

Plas Hall Hotel
Pont-y-Pant, Nr. Betws-y-Coed, Tel: 06906 206

SHOOTING TO LET

Glasfryn Shoot
Tyddn Bach, Pencaenewydd, Pwllheli, Tel: 076688 399
R G - *Driven pheasant and duck shooting. Some rough shooting days.*

POWYS

HOTELS

The Lake Country House Hotel
Llangammarch Wells, Tel: 05912 202
AA***RAC
Enjoy superb cuisine and relax by log fires. Set in 50 acres of beautiful grounds with some of the finest salmon and trout fishing in Wales. Golf, bird watching, tennis and billiards. Mini breaks from £28.50 per day.

Lake Vyrnwy Hotel
Llanwddyn (Mid Wales), Via Oswestry, SY10 OLY, Tel: 069 173 244

Llugwy Hall Country House Hotel
Pennal, Machynlleth, Tel: 065475 228/ 622

Maesmawr Hall Hotel
Caersws, Powys, Tel: 068684 255

SHOOTING TO LET

Haimwood Farm
Llandrinio, Llanymynech, Powys, SY22 6SQ, Tel: 0691 830764
R Serviced farmhouse accommodation. Rough shooting over 900 acres of arable land bordered by River Severn. Some duck, partridge, hare and pheasants in season as well as pigeon and rabbit. High & Low Bird Clay pigeon practice.

W G Lewis
Tynpistyll, Rhayader, Powys, Tel: 0597 810398

Lower Penygelly Farm
Kerry, Newtown, Powys, Tel: 068688 610

WHERE TO SHOOT/ IRELAND

There is a wide variety of shooting available in Ireland, whether it be the rough walk-up over moors and countryside or the more organised driven shoots of the Great Country Houses and Hotels.

A visitor wishing to shoot wild birds which are subject to an open season must be in possession of:
a) A current Irish firearm certificate in respect of each shotgun carried and
b) An Irish hunting licence which authorises the hunting of game species during the open seasons.
Application for both of these documents should be made by post to the Forest and Wildlife Service, Leason Lane, Dublin 2 at least one month prior to arrival in Ireland.

The fee for a firearm certificate is IR£13(£11 sterling) and for a second gun a supplement certificate is required. For this the fee is IR£3(£2.50 sterling).

Ballymaloe House & Restaurant
Shanagarry, Co. Cork, Tel: 01035321 652531, Telex: 75208 BHI

Cedar Lodge Hotel
Carrick Byrne, New Bawn, Co. Wexford, Tel: 01035351 24386

Clare Lakelands Hotel
Scariff, Co. Clare, Tel: Scariff 18

Devonshire Arms Hotel
Pearse Square, Youghal, Co. Cork, Tel: 024 92827/92409

P G Hickey
Ballylane, New Ross, Co. Wexford, Tel: 010 35351 21315

Killoskehane Castle
Borrisoleigh, Tipperary, Tel: 0504 51126

A R H Perceval
Temple House. Ballymotee, Co. Sligo, Tel: 010 35371 83329

Portland House Shoot
Portland House Hotel, Nr Portumna, Co. Galway, Tel: Portumna 171

Seamus Treacy
Moynoe Lodge, Scariff, Co. Clare, Tel: Scariff 271
R - *Rough shooting for snipe, woodcock, pheasant, duck and unlimited pigeon.*

Shooting Days-Youghall
Youghall, Co. Cork, Tel: 010 35324 92157

SPORTING & LAND AGENTS/ENGLAND

Avon & Airlie Sporting Ltd
Avon, Chippenham, Wilts, Tel: 024974 225

A & C Sporting Services
Hornby Castle Estate Office, Hornby, Nr Lancaster, Lancs, Tel: 0468 21291 Mrs S. Battersby

Bernard Thorpe & Partners
Thorpe House, Broad Street, Hereford, Tel: 0432 276202 P.B.Segrott.
R G - *Driven pheasants and rough shooting available for parties of 8. Single days.*

Best in Britain Ltd
48 Epple Road, Fulham, London, SW6 DH, Tel: 01 731 1733 Ms Ashton.

Cowley Shooting Associates Ltd
Tree Cottage, Woodland Head, Yeoford, Crediton, Devon, Tel: 064724 380
R - *Range of shooting from 1 gun and dog escorted by gamekeeper to parties of 8 or 9 guns. Shooting in Devon, Wales and Suffolk. Bags include duck, pheasant, partridge, pigeon and woodcock.*

G - *Offer full or half guns in syndicated shoots in Devon and Wales. Also days driven pheasant shooting for parties. Bags from 60 to 100 to 250 per head per day.*

S - *Roe deer stalking in Devon or roe and red deer through co-operating clients in Scotland.*

Dacre Son & Hartley
The Estate Office, Station Road, Otley, LS21 3DR, Tel: 0943 463321
Sale, lettings and valuations of sporting rights and agricultural properties. Farm and estate management in the North of England.

David Patmore Ltd
High Petergate, York, Tel: 0904 642881

Davis & Bowring
6-9 Main Street, Kirby Lonsdale, Carnforth, LA6 2AF, Tel: 0468 71711
Letting agents for quality driven grouse and pheasant shooting in the North of England.

Edwin Thompson & Co
St Johns Street, Keswick, Cumbria, Tel: 0596 72988 P.W.D. Roberts and N.I. Mason

Gamekeepa Feeds Ltd
Southerly Park, Binton, Stratford upon Avon, Warks, CV37 9TU, Tel: 0789 772429 Mr R. Atkins

Game Finders Ltd
Tyning Wood, Gare Hill, Frome, Somerset, Tel: 09853 317 Mr C. Oliver

Hawkeye Sporting Agency
Contact; Mike Hanley, Hamble House, Meadrow, Godalming, Surrey, Tel: 04868 23411
All forms of shooting to let in UK & Abroad. Other sporting holidays arranged to highest standard.

R - *Rabbiting and pigeon shooting in Oxon, Berks, Hants and other Southern counties. Walked up grouse and game in Yorks, Lancs and Scotland*

G - *Driven grouse, partridge and pheasant.*

S - *Stalking in Southern Counties and Scotland.*

W - *Duck and goose shooting in various parts of the country.*

R E Heathcote-Walker
The Cottage, Gomersal House, Lower Lane, Gomersal, BD19 4HY, Tel: 0274 877498
R - *Rough shooting programme for parties of four to eight guns in North Yorkshire. Pigeon shooting throughout Yorkshire and surrounding counties on day release or season basis.*

G - *Walked up grouse. Driven grouse for eight or ten guns. Accommodation can be arranged. Driven partridge and pheasant on alternative days.*

S - *Limited amount of roe deer stalking available during late April/ May and early June.*

W - *Wildfowling for individuals and small parties. Inland duck shooting. Shooting on the Solway and Central Scotland.*

[SS] - *Overseas shooting holidays and clay pigeon shooting from aboard ship booked on twice yearly trips.*

Hunting UK Ltd
Shell Buildings, Malt Hill Lane, Halesowen, W. Midlands, B62 8JD, Tel: 021 559 9676

John German
Estate Offices, Ashby-de-la-Zouch, Leicestershire, Tel: 0530 412821 Mr Pitts.

John Sale & Partners
18-20 Glendale Road, Wooler, Northumberland, Tel: 0668 81611 M. Cuddigan, ACRIS.

Knight Frank & Rutley
14 Broad Street, Hereford, Tel: 0432 273087

Macsport Ltd
P O Box 2, Banchory, Kincardineshire, Tel: 03302 3302/ 2855
R G S -*Sporting letting agents operating mainly in NE Scotland. Offer the complete service for grouse and pheasant shooting, roe and red stalking.*

Michael C. Litton
Grange Farm, Honingham, Norwich, Norfolk, Tel: 0603 880043

Michael Miller Arms
The Lamb, 8 Cuckfield Road, Hurstpierpoint, Sussex, BN6 9RU, Tel: 0273 834567, Telex: 87515 WISCO

Northern Stalking Ltd
Mill Place, Irton, Holmrook, Cumbria, Tel: 0946 4818 or 09406 276(evenings)

P & G Keeper Supplies

Heathwood Road, Higher Heath, Whitchurch, Shropshire, Tel: 0948 840994 (Day) 0948 840604 (Evening)
Well organised shoot on good country estates

Peter Howe Ltd (Sporting)
Sutton Camp Game Farm, Stoke Heath, Market Drayton, Shropshire, Tel: 063 083 236
Shooting in Shropshire, Staffordshire and Clwyd. 3 shoots in hand within easy reach of M6 - 9 guns. Driven pheasant days - 9 guns. Walked up days - parties of 4/6 guns. Duck flighting beautiful countryside, ample game reared personally supervised by Nigel or Peter Howe.

Roger Buss
Hampshire, Tel: 0705 467236/463952

Roxton Sporting Agency

10 Bridge Street, Hungerford,
Berkshire, Tel: 0488 83222 C.
Orssich or Mark Firth
*Main agents for famous North Devon
Shoots. Days organised to clients
requirements. Also partridges,
pheasants on top quality estates
countrywide. for parties or
individuals.*

Savills
Rolfes House, 60 Milford Street,
Salisbury, Wiltshire, Tel: 0722 20422

Severn Sporting Agency
Forthampton, Gloucester, GL19
4NF, Tel: 0684 297904

Smiths Gore Sporting Agency

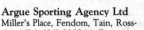

Eastgate House, Eastgate Street,
Winchester, Hants, SO23 8DZ, Tel:
0962 51203
*All venues and types of Game, Deer,
Wildfowl shooting and fishing
available*

Smith-Woolley
27/28 Bridge Street, Cambridge,
CB2 1UJ, Tel: 0223 352566 Mr
R.F.G. Gillington
R G - *Good quality rough pheasant
and partridge shoots available in
various parts of the country. Advise on
buying and selling sporting rights.*

Sportselect Ltd., Sporting Agents
and Consultants
Christopher Egerton, Great Edstone
House, Kirkbymoorside, York, Tel:
0751 31591
G S - *Specialise in organising shooting
holidays with personal attention.
Grouse, pheasant, red deer.*

Strutt & Parker
13 Hill Street, Berkeley Square,
London, W1, Tel: 01 629 7282 Mr
J.H.H. Illingworth.
G S - *Sporting Agency - specialising in
the letting of grouse, pheasant and
partridge shooting and deer stalking,
as well as salmon and sea trout fishing
throughout the UK*

R.B. Taylor & Sons
Southern Cheap Street, Sherborne,
Dorset
TLTel: 0935 813577

SPORTING & LAND
AGENTS/SCOTLAND

Airlie Estates Office
Cortachy by Kimmuir, Angus, Tel:
05754 223

Avon & Airlie Sporting Ltd
Little Kenny, Lintrathen, Kiriemuir,
Angus, Tayside, Tel: 057 56 235 or 202

Argue Sporting Agency Ltd
Miller's Place, Fendom, Tain, Ross-
shire, Tel: 0862 2337 Mr Derry Argue

Bob Sport Scotland Ltd
10/11 Atholl Place, Edinburgh, Tel:
031 229 9999
*We can arrange the following shooting
holidays:-
Grouse, pigeon, ptarmigan, woodcock,
capercaillie, partridge, geese, duck,
blackcock, pheasant, snipe, rabbit,
hare, sika-roe-fallow deer and goats.
Also arrange golf, ski and salmon
fishing holidays.*

John Birth Sporting
Organisation
Greenlawalls Lodge, Duddo, Berwick
on Tweed, Tel: 089082 261

Bell Ingram
Durn, Isla Road, Perth, Tel: 0738
21121

Eskdale Shooting Services
1 Edinburgh Road, Lauder,
Berwickshire, Tel: 05782 231

Fairway Tours
8D Roseberry Place, Gullane, East
Lothian, EH31 2AN, Tel: 0629
842349, Telex: 727862 UK GOLF
G
S - *Stalking for roe and red deer.
Grouse, pheasant and rough shooting
arranged throughout Scotland,
Northumberland and N.Wales.*

Forestry Commission
North Scotland-21 Church Street,
Inverness, IV1 1EL
R S - *The Forestry Commission in
Scotland offers stalking facilities for
Roe bucks, Red stags, Sika stags and
mixed does and hinds. Also excellent
rough shooting for grouse, pheasant,
blackgame and capercaillie.*

Forestry Commission
East Scotland-6 Queens Gate,
Aberdeen, AB9 2NQ

Forestry Commission
South Scotland-Greystone Park,
Moffat Road, Dumfries, DG10 9ED

Forestry Commission
West Scotland-Portcullis House, 21
India Street, Glasgow, G2 4PL

John Dye
Glenkilrie Lodge, Blacklunans,
Perthshire, Tel: 0382 646371

Stewart Henry
Garry Guest House, Killiecrankie,
Perthshire, PH16 5LN, Tel: 0796 3219

Macsport Ltd
PO Box 2, Banchory,
Kincardineshire, Tel: 03302 3022
K Ritchie & M Stewart-Richardson.
R G S - *Sporting letting agents
operating mainly in N.E. Scotland.
Offer the complete service for grouse
and pheasant shooting, roe and red
deer stalking.*

Major Neil Ramsay & Co
Farleyer, By Aberfeldy, Perthshire,
Tel: 0887 20540/20523, Telex:
76371
*Sporting organisers and letting agents
representing estates throughout the
whole of Scotland.
Driven and walked up grouse, also
shooting grouse over dogs. Driven
pheasant shoots and mixed winter
shooting. Deer stalking throughout the
Scottish Highlands. Roe deer stalking.
Letting of furnished self-catering
lodges.
Letting of driven partridge shoots in
Spain and driven pheasant shoots in
Hungary.
Letting of fishing in British Columbia.*

Peter Readman
Sporting Agent, Hirsel Law, By
Coldstream, Berwickshire, TD12 4HX,
Tel: 0890 2139

Safari Scotland
Ardagie Hotel, Pass of Coadie, Forgan
Denny, Bridge of Earn, Perth, Tel:
073881 2995 Mr Duncan Clarke

Safaris Scotland
55 North Methven Street, Perth, Tel:
0738 23679

Scottish Highland Field Sports
'An halle', Kellas, Elgin, Moray, Tel:
03097 6057
*We are professional sportsmen offering
a full shooting and fishing service for
the individual or parties. Everything
organised for your individual
requirements. Offer deer stalking - red,
roe, sika, fallow deer and wild goats.
During winter months, hind and doe
stalking. Shooting - pheasants, grouse,
woodcock, duck and geese. Fishing -
salmon on famous rivers. Trout on
many lochs.*

Sport in Scotland Ltd
22 Market Brae, Inverness, Tel: 0463
222757

Sportselect Ltd
Col. C Egerton, Great Edstone House, Kirbymoorside, York, Tel: 0751 31591
Specialise in organising high quality shooting holidays with personal attention. Grouse, pheasant, red deer.

South of Scotland Sporting Agents
Kirkwood, Dalron, Lockerbie, Dumfrieshire, Tel: 05765 2121277

Travel Scotland Ltd
10 Rutland Square, Edinburgh, Tel: 031 229 7366

SHOOTING HOLIDAY ORGANISERS

A&C Sporting Services
Hornby Castle, Estate Office, Hornby, Nr. Lancaster, Lancs, Tel: 0468 21291

Belvedere Shooting
Naemoor, Rambling Bridge, Kinross, Banffshire, Tel: 025981 330

Bob Sport Scotland Ltd
17 Rutland Street, Edinburgh, Tel: 031 229 9999
We can arrange the following shooting holidays:- Grouse, pigeon, ptarmigan, woodcock, Capercaillie, partridge, geese, duck, black cock, pheasant, snipe, rabbit, hare, sika-roe-red-fallow deer and goats. Also arrange golf ski and salmon fishing holidays.

Caisson Supplies Ltd
91-95 Notting Hill Gate, London, W11, Tel: 01 727 0530
Agents for Lt Col Jeff Cooper's (Arizona) Gunsite courses. Guaranteed Bear Hunts in North America, Big/Dangerous Game worldwide, shooting training courses etc

Safaris
146 Gloucester Road, London, SW7 4SZ, Tel: 01 370 5032/3

Gametrek
Glantre, Pontshaen, Dyfed, Tel: 054 55 376

Hedley Wood Caravan Park & Shooting Ground
Bridgerule, Holsworthy, Devon, Tel: 028881 404

Hippenscombe Farm
Fosbury, Wilts, Tel: 026470 374

Kasimir Swiderski
24 Brechin Place, London, SW7, Tel: 01 373 0493

A Myers Gunmaker, Ballistic Products UK
6 Whitewell Close, Catterall, , Garstang, Lancashire, PR3 1XQ., Tel: 099 52 4251
Bookings now welcomed from old and new clients and friends to enjoy a five day holiday in Perthshire, excellent hotel and cuisine. Goose shooting morning/evening flights or mixed sport, pheasant, grouse, golf, duck flighting, pigeon, ground game, stalking arranged also. Three fully equipped Safari 4WD vehicles, decoys, hides etc all supplied. A bag limit is imposed of 5 geese per gun per flight (greylag and pinkfeet)

Worktown International Travel Services Ltd, Inc MTS Safaris
37 Maddox Street, London, W1R 9LD

Michael Miller, Arms, Armour & Militaria Sporting Agents
The Lamb, 8 Cuckfield Road, Hurstpierpoint, BN6 9RU, Tel: 0273 834567, Telex: 87515 WISCO

Safari Consultants
83 Gloucester Place, London, W1H 3PG, Tel: 01 486 4774, Telex: 8813271 GECOMS G
Traditional hunting safaris throughout Africa, individually planned for the discerning sportsman

Safari Scotland
Ardagie Hotel, Pass of Condie, Forgan Denny, Bridge of Earn, Perth, PH2 9ED, Tel: 073881 2995

Selous Hunters
Horsted Keynes, Sussex, Tel: 0825 790834
Professional African Hunters, offering Big Game Hunting in Botswana, South Africa, Namibia, Sudan, Zambia, Zimbabwe, Alaska, Canada, USA, Australasia. Wild boar in North Africa and Europe. Superb hunting and shooting in Spain on private estates.

Trophy Tours Ltd
Portcullis House, Wooburn Industrial Park, Wooburn Green, Bucks, Tel: 06285 25575

Mr D Vanstone
Pixieland, West Street, Kilhampton, Bude, Cornwall, Tel: 0288 8255
Packages

SHOOTING HOLIDAYS ABROAD

Ecosafaris
146 Gloucester Road, London, SW7 4SZ, Tel: 01 370 5032/373 0473

The Hawkeye Sporting Agency
Hamble House, Meadrow, Godalming, Surrey, Tel: 04868 24311
Specialists in high quality sporting holidays

Kasimir Swiderski
24 Brechin Place, London, SW7, Tel: 01 373 0443

Major Neil Ramsay & Co
Farleyer, Aberfeldy, Perthshire, Tel: 0887 20523/20540, Telex: 76371 RAMSAY G
Shooting organisers in Hungary and Spain

Sport Link (Worldwide) Ltd
19 Quarry Street, Guildford, Surrey, GU1 3UY, Tel: 0483 33771
In association with Shooting Times. Specialists in overseas shooting tours. Wild boar, driven partridges, snipe, duck, etc also big game stalking. First class game to trophy standards. Contact above address for brochure.

M T S Safaris Ltd
6 Bank Street, Malvern, Worcs, Tel: 06845 64550

Trophy Tours Ltd
Portcullis House, Wooburn Industrial Park, Wooburn Green, Bucks, Tel: 06285 25575

PRACTICE & TUITION GROUNDS ENGLAND

AVON

Avon Shooting Ground
Stowey Quarry, Bishops Sutton, Nr Bristol, Tel: 0761 33167

I M Crudgington
Spa Shooting School, 37 Broad Street, Bath, BA1 5LT, Tel: 0225 64928/66325

Lady's Wood Shooting School
Maple Ridge Lane, Horton, Chipping Sodbury, Tel: 045 424 546
Facilities - Instruction and gunfitting for game and sporting clay shots, under natural wooded conditions. For appointments and brochure telephone the Manager, Nigel Teague on Fairfield 260226

BEDFORDSHIRE

Broomhills Gun Ground

14 Church Street, Dunstable, Tel: 0582 64649

23 acres of woodland layed out to provide natural birds. Club shoot every Sunday. Duck flush every Tuesday evening. Private parties catered for. Tuition by appointment. Gunfitting. Clubhouse. Refreshments

Facilities - Sporting D.T.L. Skeet

Flitwick Gun Club

Folly Farm, Maulden Road, Flitwick, Tel: Flitwick 713099

BERKSHIRE

Pennsport Ltd

Thames Valley Shooting Ground, Tomb Farm, Upper Basildon, Nr. Pangbourne, Tel: 049 162 703

Facilities Tuition practice, gunfitting. Guns available. In excess of 70 traps and 5 towers one of which throws a clay over 50 yards high. Also a skeet and ABT layout

CAMBRIDGESHIRE

Cambridge Shooting Grounds

Madingley, Cambridge, Tel: 0954 60249/80032

Facilities - Sporting targets on 14 acres close to Cambridge. (M11 ex 13, take A1303 west. Ground 1/2 mile on right). Regular weekend open shoots plus tuition, private parties and business shoots.

Crowland Gun Club

Crowland Wash, Low Wash Road, Crowland, Nr. Peterborough, Tel: 0733 62971

Greenend Shooting Ground
Primrose Hall, Three Holes, Wisbech, Tel: 03548 335

Facilities - cater for all types of shooting. Clay. Game and wildfowling. Walk up game on 1,200 acres. A.B.T. skeet and complete shooting layout with tower. Self catering accommodation for parties from 2 to 16, 2 fixed towers, 45 feet and 25 feet

Peterborough Gun Club

East of England Showground, Peterborough, Tel: 0733 237057

CORNWALL

Lower Lake Shooting Grounds
Upton Cross, Liskeard, Tel: 0579 62319

West Cornwall Shooting Grounds
Orchard-Lea, Cucurrian Farm, Ludgvan, Penzance, Tel: 0736 740275

CHANNEL ISLANDS

Crabbe Range
St Mary's, Jersey, Tel: 0534 54022
Facilities - skeet, DTL, ball trap, sporting layouts. Three qualified coaches. Large club house. Every Sunday from 10 a.m. and from 6 p.m. Thursday evenings open to non members and visitors

Lecq Gun Club
Lecq Farm, St. Quen, Jersey, Tel: 0534 77266
Facilities - ISU, Skeet, ABT, DLT, Sporting. Small clubhouse. Light refreshments. Qualified coach available. Clubshoots every Sunday from 10.a.m. Open to non members

CHESHIRE

Blakelow Clay Shooting Club
Higher Blakelow Farm, off Buxton Old Road, Macclesfield, Tel: 0625 32191

Little Mill Shooting Grounds
Rowarth, Stockport, Tel: 0663 43273

CLEVELAND

Oaklea Shooting Ground
Whinney Hill, Stockton on Tees, TS21 1BL, Tel: 0642 607060

CUMBRIA

Penrith & District Gun Club
Bowscar, Penrith, Tel: Penrith 62256

DERBYSHIRE

Charlesworth Gun Club
Tanyard Farm, Mossy Lea, Old Glossop, Tel: 0663 43236

Derbyshire Skeet & Trap Club
Jack Hill Farm, Tansley,, Nr Matlock, Tel: 629 2859
Offer facilities for practice and tuition for all types of competitive shooting including Game. Joe Neville (Member of 3 olympic shooting teams) For appointment please contact above.

Harpur Hill Gun Club
Barlow Road, Harpur Hill, Buxton, Tel: 0298 5227
Facilities - skeet, DTL, sporting

Little Mill Shooting Ground (D E Sinclair)
Rowarth, Via. Stockport (Nr New Mills), Tel: 0663 43273

Melbourne Gun Club
c/o The Butts, Cockshut Lane, Melbourne, Tel: 03316 2834

Yeaveley Shooting Ground
Yeaveley, Ashbourne, DE6 2DT, Tel: 033 523 247

DEVON

Dedes Hotel & Restaurant
1 & 2 The Promenade, Ilfracombe, Tel: 0271 62545

Meltor Gun Club
Ashburton, Newton Abbot, Tel: 0364 52644

North Devon Shooting School
139 High Street, Ilfracombe, Tel: 0271 64546

Sid Vale Gun Club
White Cross, Sidbury, Sidmouth, Tel: Sidmouth 3094

Devon & Exeter Gun Club
Thorns Cross Airfield, Between Exeter & Newton Abbot, Tel: Newton St Cyres 602

Hedley Wood Shooting Ground
Bridgerule, Holsworthy, Tel: 028881 404

The Sportsman
Nr Park Hill, Cross Ippledon, Nr. Newton Abbot, Tel: 0803 558142
Facilities - A wide variety of sporting clays. Practice guns available. Gun fitting facilities

DORSET

Broadwindsor Shooting Ground
Broadwindsor, Beaminster, Tel: 0308 68666

Blandford & Dorchester Shooting Ground
Clay Pigeon Cafe, Wardon Hall, Nr. Dochester, Tel: 093583 368

CO DURHAM

Woodlands Close Gun Club
Woodlands Close Farm, Station Town, Wingate, Tel: Hartlepool 61127

Teesdale Shooting Ground
40 Horsemarket, Barnard Castle, Tel: 0833 31118/40358

ESSEX

Ingrebourne Clay Pigeon Club
White Bear Public House, Stamford Rivers,, Ongar, Tel: 01 595 8343
Facilities - Skeet, DTL, Sporting practice stand always available.

Basildon & District Gun Club
Courtaulds Road, Basildon, Tel: 0277
233468

Essex Shooting Grounds
Fyfield Hall, Fyfield, Nr. Ongar, Tel:
027785 404 (day) 0277 86310 (evenings)

Highwood Gun Club
102 Shepherds Hill, Harold Wood,
Romford, Tel: Ingrebourne 49257

**Newland Hall Shooting Ground
& Field Sports Centre**
Newland Hall, Roxwell, Chelmsford,
Tel: 024531 463

Radcliffe Shooting School
Abberton, Nr. Colchester, Tel: 0206
572758
*Address for bookings - 150 High
Street, Colchester. Facilities. Sporting
practice guns available on request.
Gun fitting facilities. Private tuition.
Private parties welcome. Shooting
parties arranged for company
entertainment. Guns for sale.*

South East Essex Gun Club
Tickerds Farm, Watery Lane, Nr
Battlesbridge, Tel: 0277 233468

Windsmoor Clay Shooting Club
Purfleet Shooting Ranges, Purfleet,
Grays, Tel: 04022 20807

GLOUCESTERSHIRE

Forest of Dean Armoury
'Canberra', New Road, Coalway,
Coleford, Tel: 0594 33908
*Coaching and clay shooting. Sporting
layout*

Ridgeway Shooting Ground
Mersey Hampton, Cirencester, Tel:
0793 47455

Stroud & District Gun Club
Water Lane, Bisley, Tel: Stroud 3804

GREATER LONDON

**Holland & Holland Shooting
School**
Ducks Hill Road, Northwood,
Middlesex, Tel: 092 74 25349,
Manager:FLG Griffith-Jones

Regent Shooting Ground
Rowley Green, Barnet by Pass, Tel: 01
449 3287

**West London Shooting Grounds
Ltd**
West End, Northolt, Middlesex, Tel:
01 845 1377

HAMPSHIRE

Apsley Shooting Grounds
Apsley Estate, Andover, Tel: 0264
2403

BBC Sporting Gun Club
Petersfield Road, Whitehill, Bordon,
Hampshire, Tel: Bordon 2573
*Facilities:-Sporting shoots in natural
surroundings, DTL, Sporting, Flush,
practice stand and club shoots locally.*

**Brockenhurst (New Forest) Gun
Club**
New Park Farm Equestrian Centre,
New Forest, Tel: Lymington 75508

**Gosport & Fareham, Sporting
Gun Club**
4 Queens Road, Fareham, Tel:
Fareham 286084

Herriard Sporting Club
Alton Road, Herriard, Nr. Basingstoke,
Tel: 025 683 277

**Marchwood Park Clay Pigeon
Club**
Marchwood Park, Marchwood, Tel:
0703 844359

HEREFORD & WORCESTER

Ian Butler Shooting Ground
c/o Astwood Guns, 4 High Street,
Studley, Warwickshire, Tel: 052 785
4963

Clay Farm
Clows Top, Nr Kidderminster, Tel:
02993 2212, or Clows Top 421

Teme Valley Gun Club
Berrow Hill, Martley, Tel: 0905 611586

HERTFORDSHIRE

Cupid Green Skeet Club
48 Knightsbridge Way, Hemel
Hempstead, Tel: 0442 66313

Regent Shooting Ground
Rowley Green, Barnet, Tel: 01 449
3287

HUMBERSIDE NORTH

Bygot Wood Shooting Ground
Bygot Wood, Cherry Burton, Beverley,
Tel: 0696 4244

Humberside Shooting Ground
Catwick Lane, Brandesburton,
Beverley, Tel: 0482 445284

HUMBERSIDE SOUTH

**Ancholme Valley Shooting
Ground**
Kirton in Lindsey Airfield, South
Humberside, Tel: 0652 52502

ISLE OF MAN

Santon Shooting Centre
Ballacorris, Santon, Tel: 0624
74392
*Facilities - ISU and English skeet,
DTL, ABT. Individual shooters or
small parties preferred. Practice guns
and gun fitting facilities available.
Browning, Miroku dealer for the Isle of
Man*

KENT

Aylesham Gun Club
71 Stuart Road, Aylsham, NR11 6HW,
Tel: 0263 733998

**Biggin Hill Clay Pigeon
Shooting Club**
Stud Farm, 368 Main Road,
Westerham Hill, Tel: Biggin Hill 73089
Facilities - Sporting

Charing Gun Club
Charing Hill, Charing to Canterbury
Road, Tel: Charing 2978

Greenfields Shooting School
Sturry Hill, Sturry, Nr. Canterbury,
Tel: 0227 456959

Mid Kent Shooting Grounds
Langley, Nr. Maidstone, Tel: 0622
861901

Robin Hood Gun Club
Robin Hood Public House, Common
Road, Off Blue Bell Hill, A229,
Chatham, Tel: 0732 823611

Saddlery & Gun Room
368 Main Road, Biggin Hill, Tel: 0959
73089

West Kent Shooting School
Elm Court Estate, Lidsing, Nr.
Maidstone, Tel: 0622 813230

Woodchurch Gun Club
Boulderwall Farm, Lydd, Tel: 0797
222144

LANCASHIRE

S Entwistle (Preston) Ltd
The Cattle Market, Brook Street,
Preston, Tel: 0772 718048

Fluke Hall Shooting Ground
Fluke Hall Lane, Pilling, Preston, Tel:
Pilling 830745 or Lytham 733192

Kelbrook Shooting School
The Shooting Lodge, Kelbrook Moor,
Foulridge, Nr. Colne, Tel: 0254 663547
Day. 0282 861632 Evening.

The Lancashire Gun Club
The Bowers Hotel, Longmoor Lane,
Nateby, Nr. Garstang, Tel: Garstang
4251

**North East Lancashire Gun Club
& Shooting Ground**
Foxendale Lane, Hisham, Tel: Nelson
692440

Newdrop Inn Shooting Ground
Longbridge, Nr. Preston, Tel: 0772
718048

LEICESTERSHIRE

**Aylerton GC Shooting School &
Pistol Range**
Shearsby Spar, Leicester, Tel: 0533
832828

**Aylestone Gun Co Shooting
Ground**
Shearsby Spa, Leicestershire, Tel: 0533
832828

**Melton Mowbray & District
Gun Club**
Wycomb Road, Scalford, , Melton
Mowbray, Tel: Scalford 615

Nevill Holt Gun Club
Between Drayton & Nevill Holt, Nr
Market Harborough, Tel: 0536 770516

Scalford Shooting Grounds
Wycombe Road, Scalford, Tel: 0664
76615

Springwood Shooting Ground
c/o The Butts, Cockshut Lane,
Melbourne, Derbyshire, Tel: 03316
2834

Thurlaston Gun Club
Normanton Park, Normanton Dairy
Farm, Thurlaston, Nr. Leicester, Tel:
Thurlaston 210

LINCOLNSHIRE

**Penningtons Shooting Ground
Ltd**
Peartree Hill Road, Whaplode Drive,
Holbeach, Spalding, Tel: 040 634
362
*Facilities - Clay pigeon shooting. Gun
fitting facilities and non supervised
individual practice available. Closed
on Mondays. Wide selection of trophies
and leatherwear. Catalogues supplied*

Spinneys Shooting Ground
Willoughby Alford , Lincs, Tel: 05212
2357

NORFOLK

Mid Norfolk Shooting School
Deighton Hills Shooting Ground,
Taverham, Norwich, Tel: 0603 860436

**Barnham Broom Hotel Golf &
Country Club**
Barnham Broom, Norfolk, Tel: 060545
393

Wayland Gun Club
Summer Lane, Carbrooke, Thetford,
Norfolk, Tel: 0362 820309

NOTTINGHAMSHIRE

Cavendish Gun Club
Clipstone Drive, Forest Town, Mansfield, Tel: Mansfield 25988

Nottingham & District Gun Club
Nine Miles North of Nottingham on the A614, Nottingham, Tel: Nottingham 273492

NORTHUMBERLAND

Blagdon Shooting Ground
Dinnington, Northumberland, Tel: 0632 322776

Bywell Shooting Ground

Bywell Shooting Ground

Bywell Farm, Felton, Newcastle Upon Tyne, Tel: 0661 25885
Facilities - 4 DTL, 3 ABT. Skeet and sporting shoots held twice monthly. Clubhouse and refreshments. Cartridges available

Northumbria Clay Club
c/o 4a/b Albion Road, North Shields, Tyne & Wear, Tel: 0632 577510

OXFORDSHIRE

Heythrop Shooting Grounds
Chipping Norton, Oxford, Tel: 0608 2924

Plough Shooting Grounds
Sporting-Tucker Radclive Nurseries, Follyhill, Farringdon, Tel: 0295 65819

SHROPSHIRE

Oswestry Shooting Club
Trench Farm, Red Hall Lane, Penley, Nr. Ellesmere, Tel: 0691 653761

West Midlands Shooting Ground
Corndean, Nr. Hodnet, Market Drayton, Tel: 093 924 644

Wrekin Shooting Ground
11 Broomfield Road, Admaston, Wellington, Tel: 0952 3556

SOMERSET

Cheddar Valley Gun Club
Draycott Moor, Draycott, Nr. Cheddar, Tel: 0934 742 563

Pitts Wood Shooting Ground
Hornsmead, Bodden, Shepton Mallet, Tel: 0749 2728

STAFFORDSHIRE

Brown Edge Shooting Ground
Broad Lane, Brown Edge, Tel: 0782 534750

Garlands Shooting Ground

Raddle Farm, Edingale, Tamworth, Tel: 082 785 216
Facilities - ABT, DTL Sporting, skeet and Olympic Trap. Gun shop. Catering. Non supervised individual practice guns available. Gun fitting facilities

Rowley Shooting Club
Rowley House Farm, Shooting Ground, Croxton, Eccleshall, Tel: Newcastle Under Lyme 561768, or Market Drayton 4228, or Wetwood 248

Leek & District Gun Club
Westwood Shooting Ground, Leek, Tel: Leek 386127

Midland Counties Shooting Ground
Oakedge, Wolsey Bridge, Nr. Stafford and at 7 Market Square, Stafford. Tel:0785 44191, Tel: 021 236 7451

SUFFOLK

Kettleburgh Lodge Shooting School
Framlington, Tel: 0728 723523
Facilities - Sporting DTL, skeet flushes (20 to 132 birds) Practice guns available. Gun fitting facilities. Refreshments. Equipment for sale. Practice and tuition by appointment. Open, private or invitation shoots. Complete provision for shoots elsewhere. Mobile unit in operation for both competition and instruction. Cartridges, equipment for sale or loan. Please telephone for further information

SURREY

Mr Clay Pigeon's Club
N.R.A. Ranges, Brookwood, Tel: 04867 88282

Wishanger Clay Club
Wishanger Stud, Frensham Lane,, Churt, Tel: 025 125 4170

SUSSEX EAST

Catsfield Shooting Centre
Catsfield Place Farm, Catsfield, Nr. Battle, Tel: 042 483 511
Facilities - 4 skeet layouts, 3 DTL 1 ABT, Tower and sporting layouts

Diamond Guns
Pounsley, Nr. Blackboys, Tel: 04352 3295

The Essex Shooting School
25 Duck Lane, , Thornwood, Essex, Tel: 0378 76726

SUSSEX WEST

Weald Shooting Ground
Trowell Cottage, Pound Street, Petworth, Tel: 0798 43042

TYNE & WEAR

Northumbria Clay Club
Bomarsund, Old Pit, Stakeford, Nr. Bedlington, Tel: 0632 577510/580799

WARWICKSHIRE

Ian Butler
c/o Astwood Guns, 4 High Street, Studley, Warwickshire, Tel: 052 785 4963

Coventry Shooting School & CPC
The Bund, Stoneleigh, Tel: 0203 503709
Facilities - Sporting DTL, Ball trap. Refresments. Cartridge sales. Practice guns and non supervised individual practice available. Coaching by appointment only

Edge Hill Shooting School
16 Smith Street, Warwick

The Falcon Clay Pigeon Club
Honiley Aerodrome, Wroxall, Tel: 05645 2914

Watling Gun Club
Barby Lane, Rugby, Tel: 0788 860744

WEST MIDLANDS

Bridgenorth & District Gun Club
Great Moor Road, Pattingham, Wolverhampton, Tel: Pattingham 700313

WILTSHIRE

Barbury Guns Shooting School
44/45 High Street, Marlborough, Wilts., SN8 1HQ, Tel: 0672 52862
Expert coaching for the experienced and novice game and clay shooter by John King, qualified C.P.S.A senior sporting coach. Individual and group practice facilities available.

Roses Wood Shooting Ground
Butter Cottage, Haugh, Winsley, Bradford on Avon, Tel: 02216 2310

White Horse Clay Pigeon Club
Yatesbury Old RAF, Tel: 0793 23075

YORKSHIRE

Beamsley Estate Shooting School
Beamsley Estate, Beamsley, Nr. Ilkley, Tel: 075 671 344

Greetland Shooting Club
New Rock Tavern, Barkisland, Nr Halifax, Tel: 0422 76906

Harrogate Shooting Grounds
Penny Pot Lane, Harrogate

Heathcote-Walker R E
The Cottage, Gomersal House, Lower Lane, Gomersal, BD19 4HY, Tel: 0274 877498
Facilities - coaching for clay pigeon teams , small bore and air weapon teams. Also individual tuition on pupil's own premises. Portable equipment available.

Holmfirth Shooting School
Edge End Farm, Nr. Ford Inn, Holmfirth, Huddersfield, Tel: 048 468 2767

North Yorkshire Moors Shooting School
9/10 Queen Street, Scarborough, Tel: 0723 360904

Redmires Shooting Ground
Redmires Road, , Sheffield 10, Tel: 0742 28920
Facilities, DTL, ABT & Skeet layouts English ISU tower. Practice every Sunday. Tuition every Saturday by appointment. CPSA coaching in attendance. For more information se advert at beginning of section

Yorkshire Gun Room Shooting Ground
Bishop Thornton, Nr. Harrogate, Tel: 076586 602

Westfield Shooting Grounds
Westfield House, Cone Lane, Silkstone Common, Nr. Barnsley, Tel: 0226 790524

**West Yorkshire Shooting
Ground**
Knaresboro' Forest, 39 Cookridge
Drive, Cookridge, Leeds 16, Tel: 0532
674785

PRACTICE &
TUITION GROUNDS
SCOTLAND

HIGHLANDS &
ISLANDS

Highland Guns Ltd
53 High Street, Dingwall, Tel: 034 987
258

Kilmartin Farm
Glenurquhart, Inverness, Tel: 04564
268

LOTHIAN

**Dicksons Colzium Shooting
School**
**Colzium Farm, Nr. Kirknewton, Tel:
031 225 4218**
*Facilities - excellent natural Sporting
layouts under expert surveillance for
gun fitting, coaching tuition and
practice by appointment. Address for
bookings-John Dickson & Son, 21
Frederick Street, Edinburgh. Tel:031
225 4218*

PRACTICE &
TUITION GROUNDS
WALES

CLWYD

North Wales Shooting School
Sealand Manor, Sealand, Deeside Nr
Chester, Tel: 0244 812219
Manager - N Jones.
*Facilities - ABT, Olympic Trap, DTL,
English and ISU Skeet, Sporting. Non
supervised individual practice amd
practice guns available. Gun fitting
facilities. Gun sales.*

DYFED

County Shooting Grounds
Deep Lake, Haverfordwest, Tel: 0473
3740

POWYS

The Lake Country House Hotel
Llangammarch Wells, Tel: 05912 202

PRACTICE &
TUITION GROUNDS
IRELAND

CO.DOWN

**Hollow Farm Shooting
Grounds**
Co. Down, Tel: 0238 528381

Advertiser's Index

THE ASSOCIATIONS

ASSOCIATIONS

The Birmingham Proof House
Banbury Street, Birmingham, B5 5RH, Tel: 021 643 3860

The British Association for Shooting & Conservation (BASC)
National Headquarters/Centre, Marford Mill, Rossett, Clwyd, LL12 OHL, Tel: 0244 570881

Founded in 1908 as the Wildfowlers' Association of Great Britain and Ireland and with membership in excess of 75,000. The B.A.S.C. is the National Representative body for sporting shooting: dedicated to preserving the sport and wildlife conservation. It represents all those with shooting interests and gives advice on wildlife management and conservation. It is the voice of sporting shooting - seeking to ensure the future of the sport and lawful gun ownership. HRH The Prince Philip, Duke of Edinburgh KG, KT, OMM Patron
Key Personnel: The Viscount of Arbuthnott DSC,MA,JP, President
Mr Simon Cussons FCA Chairman
John Anderton OBE, VRD, Director
Colin Barwell, MinstAM, Director Administration
John Swift, MPhil, MBOU, Director Conservation and Research
Tom Cave, Head of membership
Pamela Brogan Public relations officer
Scottish Office Buchanan Home Farm, Drymen, Glasgow, Tel:0360 60840
Key Personnel:David Cant, Director development (Scotland)

British Deer Society
Church Farm, Lower Basildon, Reading, Berks, RG8 9NH, Tel: 073 57 4094

Patron:His Royal Highness The Prince of Wales, KG,KT,GCB,ADC,(P)
President:The Lord Dulverton,CBE,TD,MA,DL
Chairman:Sir Dudley Forwood,Bt
Vice Chairman:Major Hugh Oliver-Bellasis
Director:N J Foll, BSc.(Agric).

British Field Sports Society (BFSS)
59 Kennington Road, London, SE1 7PZ, Tel: 01 928 4742

With an individual memebership of 70,000 the BFSS is the largest National Organisation concerned with all matters relating to field sports. Through membership of its affiliated clubs it represents a further 350,000 sportsmen and women: committed to ensure that these sports continue to be a major activity in modern society and that their importance for wildlife and habitat conservation is recognised.
Key personnel:
Lord Margadale TD JP, President
Christopher Sporoborg, Hon Treasurer
John Hopkinson CB, Director
David Whiter MBE, Deputy Dirctor (Administration)

Peter Atkinson, Deputy Director (Public Affairs)
Charles Nodder, Information officer
Derek Starkie, Legislative secretary
Ian Goghill, Conservation officer
Peter Hunt, Senior field secretary
James McKay
Regional Secretaries
Scottish Branch
Donald Burns Glenmore Lodge, Moffat, Dumfries-shire. Tel (0683) 20571
North East
Nigel Porter, Millrace House, Netherwitton, Morpeth, Northumberland. Tel:967 027 673
Yorkshire
Rick Greenwood, 67 Prince Rupert Drive, Tockwith, York. Tel:090 15 8144
North West
Micheal Whittaker, Swingletrees, Grange in Borrowdale, Keswick, Cumbria Tel: 059 684 672
Eastern
Christopher Wells, Bush Cottage, Thurston, Bury St Edmunds, Suffolk IP3 3QE Tel:0359 31573
East Midlands
Frank Philip, The White House, Higson Road, Lincoln LN1 3XB Tel: 0522 30784
West Midlands
Bill Hoare, Curlew Cottage, Mardu, Clun, Craven Arms, Salop Tel:058 84 226
North Wales
Mike Greenwood, Tyn-y-Waen, Glasfryn, Corwen, Clwyd Tel:049 082 482
South Wales
John Carter, Clover Cottage , The Mardy, Abergavenny, Gwent Tel: 0873 4449
Greater London & South East
Pat Browne:Wilgate Farm House, Wilgate Green, Throwley, Faversham, Kent Tel; 079 589 244
Southern
Richard Colvile, Church Corner House, Michelmersh, Romsey, Hants, Tel:0794 68590
Wessex
Pat Stcpoole, Crossways House, Market Lavington, Divizes, Wiltshire Tel: 038 081 2380
South West
Arlin Rickard, Haye House, Callington, Cornwall Tel:0579 43573
Northern Ireland
John Beach, The Land Stewards House, Shanes Castle, Antrim, NI Tel:084946 3282

British Shooting Sports Council
Pentridge, Salisbury, Wiltshire, SP5 5QX, Tel: 07255 370

Formed and financed by the shooting sports organisations and the manufacturers of firearms and ammunition, the British Shooting Sports Council is the officially recognised central representative body for its member associations. It promotes and safeguards the lawful

use and manufacture of firearms and ammunition for sporting and recreational purposes in the UK
Key Personnel:
Sir John Farr, MP ChairmanThe Lord Swansea DL;Vice Chairman
JPG Lawrence CBE
PA Gouldbury MBE Secretary

British Sporting Rifle Club (BSRC)
National Rifle Association, Bisley Camp, Brookwood, Woking Surrey

The aims of the BSRC are:to encourage and promote the sporting rifle competitions, to seek to improve the facilities available for such competitions in Great Britain and to ensure that this country is worthily represented in the Sporting Rifle Championships and Olympic Games. It is affiliated to the NRA, NSRA and the Surrey Rifle Association. The events that it covers are;100 metre Running Deer moving target, full bore rifle; 100 metre Roe Buck, Sitting Fox static target, full bore rifle; 50 metre Running Boar (Olympic event) .22 rifle 10 metre Running Boar., .177 air rifle

Clay Pigeon Shooting Association (CPSA)
107 Epping New Road, Buckhurst Hill, Essex, IG9 5TQ, Tel: 01 505 6221

Founded in 1928 the CPSA is the national governing body of the sport of clay pigeon shoooting and the officiating body for all registered clay shooting competitions.
Key Personnel:
Roy A Greatorex, President
J F Green, Chairman
I Wright, Vice Chairman
Keith Murray, Director
B P Hammond, Development Officer
Regional Committees:
North Of England
J S Hope, Chairman
R Pearce, Secretary, 11 Beech Crescent, Darrington, Pontefract, West Yorkshire, WF8 3AD
East Midlands: J F Green, Chairman
R S Groves, Secretary, 85 Brownlow Drive, Rise Park, Nottingham NG5 5BB
West Midlands:
MP Townsend, Chairman
PS James, Secretary, 17 Ebourne Close, Clinton Vale, Farmer Ward, Kenilworth, Warks
South East of England
D Hays, Chairman
G H Read, Secretary, 4 Blackborough Close, Reigate, Surrey, RH2 7BZ
South West of England
M J Collins, Chairman
Mrs J Vetralls, Secretary, Dolphins, The Stream, Catsfield, Battle, Sussex, TN33 9BD
British International Board
N Pryce Jones, Chairman, C/O Secretary CPSA, 17 Epping New Road, Buckhursy Hill, Essex, IG9 5TQ

The Countryside Commission
John Dower House, Crescent Place, Cheltenham, Gloucestershire, GL50 3RA, Tel: 0242 521381

An independant statuary body concerned with all matters relating to the conservation of landscape beauty and the provision of improved facilities for the enjoyment of the countryside in England and Wales. Free catalogue of publications available From: Publications Despatch Dept, 12-23 Albert Road, Manchester, M19 2EQ Tel:061 224 6287
Key Personnel:
Sir Derek Barber, Chairman
M Reesd, Chairman/Committee for Wales
AAC Phillips, Director
R Clarke, Assistant Director (Policy)
M Kirby Assistant director (regions)

Country Landowners Association
16 Belgrave Square, London, SW1X 8PQ, Tel: 01 235 0511

The National representative organisation for owners of agricultural and other rural land providing assistance and advice on various matters including legal and taxation problems; also responsible for organising the annual Game Fair.
Key Personel:
PR de L Gifford, President
J H M Norris, Deputy president
James Douglas, Director General
Robin Rees Webbe, Game Fair Director

English Shooting Council, The
3 Knowle Gardens, West Byfleet, Surrey, Tel: 093 23 40243

Founded in October 1979 the English Shooting Council is the central co-ordinating body for the various English competition shooting associations; represents their common interests for shooting in England and abroad. The member associations govern the competition target shooting disciplines including clay pigeon.
Key Personnel:
Lord Cottesloe, CBE,TD,DL,President
Ben Ford Esq, Chairman
EPK.J Harrison, Secretary and Treasurer

Federation of Lurcher Clubs
Key Personnel:
Lt.Col.E.G.Walsh.,President
Mr.E.Riley,Vice President
Mr.J.Corson,Chairman
Mr.R.Austin,Vice Chairman
Secretary Treasurer:Mrs.G.Riley, 16 Alexander Road,Bedworth,Nuneaton, Warks..Tel:0203 317462.Press Officer:Mr. T.Diprose,13 Battle Close,Speen,Newbury, Berks.Tel:01 427 8469

Field Trial Council
1 Clarges Street, Piccadilly, London, WIY 8AB, Tel: 01 493 6651

Consisting of one member from each of The Field Trial Societies registered at the Kennel Club, The Field Trial Council is the link betwen the Field Trial Societies and the Kennel Club Committee; discusses all matters relating to field trials and in connection with this makes recommendations to the Field Trials ~~Committee of the Kennel Club~~

Key Personnel;
J Lukies, Chairman
D Douglas, Vice Chairman

The Game Conservancy
Fordingbridge, Hampshire, Tel: 0425 52381

The Game Conservancy is an independantly financed organisation which carries out research into the shooting man's practical problems. These include dealing with today's changed conditions and so helping game and wildlife adapt, investigating modern farming pressures that restrict game abundance assisting landowners, farmers and rough shooters to get the best out of their shooting assets and ensuring that the Government and ministries are constantly made aware of the importance of game and the necessary conservation and management that also benefits other wildlife. Fourteen research projects are now in hand covering different aspects of gamebird and wildfowl and biology and management - several of them financed by special grants or groups of sponsors.

A network of skilled game advisers is available for on-the-shoot consultations, for improving habitat, showing birds to the best advantage, or improving breeding success on the rearing field and in the wild. Reducing shoot costs is an important aspect of this work.

Yearly residential courses for gamekeepers are held at Fordingbridge as well as courses for young shots and part time gamekeepers.

Symposia are held from time to time on specialised subjects. In addition, courses are held at various centres up and down the country on all aspects of game and deer management. A three day stalker's course was again held in Scotland early this year. Staff are available to give lectures on a variety of topics to farmers clubs and the like through sponsorship at open meetings. Descriptions of research work in progress appear in the Annual Review published each Spring. In addition regular newsletters keep members fully in touch and announcements of current interest are publicised through general release to the press.

Most regions of the country have their own branch which arranged interesting outings and functions, and, in addition, an annual dinner for members and guests.

Officers:
HRH The Duke of Edinburgh KG, KT<., OM Patron
HRH The Prince of Wales, KG, KT, GCB, AK, President
Key Personnel:
Th Duke of Wellington, MVO, OBE, MC, Deputy President
C A Vandervell, Chairman
The Honourable C A Morrison, MP, Vice Chairman

The Earl Peel, Vice Chairman
RM Vann Oss, MA Director
G R Potts, BsC F.Director of Research
~~RC Bucknall, Head of Membership~~
C L McKelvie, ELS Head of Publicity and Information
T McCall BSc, Deer Consultant
H Smith-Carington, Secretary/ Treasurer

The Game Farmers Association
The Cottage, Little Chart, Ashford, Kent, Tel: 023384/610

Founded in 1907 the association exists to serve the shooting public by promoting the interests of game farming. The association insists on high standards and membership is therefore restricted to farms with an established business. It maintains contact with other organisations not only with game farming but also shooting, indicating its commitment to ensure that field sports are preserved.

Key Personnel:
E J Coles President
Major L Barrington, Chairman
J Clarke, Hon Treasurer
S H Jervis-Read CBE, MC, Secretary

Guild of Taxidermists
c/o Hampshire County Museum Service, Chilcomb House, Chilcomb Lane, Bar End, Winchester, Hants, SO23 8RD, Tel: 0962 66242

Founded in 1976 by a group of taxidermists concerned with the decline in standards of taxidermy in the British Isles.
The aims of the Guild are to:
1. raise and maintain the professional status and standard of taxidermy
2. Encourage training and demonstrations in taxidermy
3. exhibit specimens of a high standard
4. the provision of information relating to taxidermy, to the public
5. promote public interest in taxidermy
Key Personnel:
J Dickinson 1985-6
C Stoate, Hon Secretary
E Morton, Honorary Treasurer

The Gun Trade Association
Fairbourne Cottage, Bunny Lane, Timsbury, Nr Romsey, Hants, SO5 0PG, Tel: 0794 684430

The GTA comprises established members from all sections of the guntrade. It maintains a close liaison with the relevant authorities, both directly and through its membership of the British Shooting Sports Council. It regularly assists the police with its unique register of stolen firearms and has its own internal newsletter
Key Personnel:
Air Commodore The Honourable Sir K. Peter Vanneck, GBE, CB, AFC, AE, MA, DSc, DL, JP, MEP, President
NS Brown, Secretary

Historial Breechloading Smallarms Assoiation
Imperial War Museum, Lambeth Road, London, SE1 6HZ, Tel: 01 735 8922

The association takes an active role in monitoring legislation regulating the

use of small arms. It is concerned primarily with safeguarding the interests of the collector and historian of breechloading firearms. The H.B.S.A. is one of the constituent bodies of the National Pistol Association and is responsible for running the 'Classical' events at the N.P.A'S May pistol meeting at Bisley.
Key Personnel:
Lt Col The Rt Hon The Lord Cottesloe, GBE, Td.D, DL, Patron
C H Roads, MA, PHd, President
C E Owen, Vice President
F W Wilkinson, Vice President and Editor of the 'Newsletter'
J B Bell, Editor of the 'Journal'
D J Penn, MA, Secretary
E Meigh, Treasurer
D B Gregory, Range Practice Secretary

The Jack Russell Terrier Club of Great Britain
National Chairman:Greg Mousley,Aston Heath Cottage,Sudbury,Derbyshire.Tel:028378 317;National Secretary:Thelma Looms,Primrose Cottage,West Street, Dormansland,Nr. Lingfield,Surrey.Tel:0342 832965.National Show Manager:Pauline Lee,141 Abingdon Road,Didcot,Oxon.Tel:0235 814778 REGIONAL SECRETARIES:Border Counties & North Midlands- Mr.R.Petts,3 Cardington Close, Newcastle,Staffs.Tel:0782 619581.London & Home Counties- Mrs.T.Looms,Primrose Cottage,West Street,Dormansland,Nr.Lingfield,Surrey. Midlands- Mrs.C.Sibbick,Springhill Farm,Camp Road,Sutton Coldfield,West Midlands.Tel:021 308 1087.North West-Mrs.D.Robinson,20 Carna Road,Stockport,Cheshire.Tel:061 442 4109.South West-Mrs.E.Harris,Prospect House,Atherington,Nr.Umberleigh,North Devon.Tel:0769 60419.Thames Valley- Mrs.P.S.Lee,141 Abingdon Road,Didcot,Oxon.Tel:0235 814778.North Wales-Mrs.J.Johnson,16 Ffordd Almer,Acton,Wrexham,Clwyd.Tel:0978 359288.

The Kennel Club
1 Clarges Street, Piccadilly, London, W1Y 8AB

Promotes the general improvement of standards for Dogs, Dog Shows, Field Trials, Working Trials and Obedience Classes. The Kennel Club is responsible for licensing shows, farming and enforcing the rules governing Exhibition of Dogs and Conduct of Field Trials; also keeps a record of shows, Trials, and Obedience Tests.
Key Personnel:
HRH Prince Michael of Kent, President
J A Macdougal, MChri, FRCS, FRCSE Chairman of general Committee

Maj Gen M H Sinnatt CB, Senior Executive & Secretary

Muzzle Loaders Association of Great Britain
PO Box 217, Newport Pagnell, Bucks, MK16 9YD

The Governing body for Muzzle Loading Shooting in the United Kingdom. Founded in 1952 and with a membership in excess of 1,500 the Association is not only interested in collecting antique firearms but also in using them for participation in rifle, clay pigeon and pistol shooting as well as for shoting game. Membership details on application. Joining fee £1 and annual subscription of £10. Journals and newsletters are published free to members throughout the year
Key Personnel:
A Courtney, Chairman
J R Taylor, Secretary
W S Curtis, Treasurer

National Game Dealers Association
1 Belgrove, Tunbridge Wells, Kent, TN1 1YW, Tel: 0892 41412/4

Founded in 1979, membership consists of wholesale game dealers and leading exporters; aims to promote and raise the standard of the industry and to this end works in close conjunction with related organisations
Key Personnel:
Dieter Dent, Chairman
John Fuller, Secretary

National Pistol Association (NPA)
Spirella Building, Bridge Road, Letchworth, Herts , SG6 4ET, Tel: 04626 79887

Formed in 1979 by Pistol Shooters for Pistol Shooters. The object of the NPA is to promote all forms of recreational pistol shooting recognised by the Association to hold an Annual Open Meeting, to organise and promote competition at all levels to conduct coaching and training, and to defend the best interests of the sport.
Key Personnel:
Brian Kett, President
Robin Macdonald, Chairman
David Penn, Vice Chairman
Ken West, Secretary/Treasurer

National Rifle Association (NRA)
Bisley Camp, Brookwood, Woking, Surrey, Tel: 04867 2213/4

The NRA is the major association for competitive full bore rifle and pistol shooting in the United Kingdom. Formed in 1860, it is based in Bisley Camp in Surrey, where there is the largest concentration of ranges for all types of shooting in the country. It organises over two hundred competitions during the annual Bisley Meeting, including H.M. The Queen's prize as the major shooting trophy. Membership is open to individuals with affiliation open to rifle and pistol clubs and associations. International full bore matches are arranged and

hosted by the NRA, with team visits to and from the commonwealth and other countries. The NRA is a certified Firearms dealer and as such can provide the following service to its members and affiliated cleubs; sale of ammunition, hire of firearms and armourers assistance.
Key Personnel:
Field Marshal Sir Roland Gibbs GCB,CBE,DSo,MC,DL
Brigadier PGA Prescott MC, Secretary

National Small-Bore Rifle Association (N.S.R.A.)
Lord Roberts House, Bisley Camp, Brookwood, Woking
Surrey, GU24 ONP, Tel: 04867 6969
The NSRA is the governing body for small bore and air gun shooting within the UK and in turn is affiliated to the world governing body, the International Shooting Union (ISU or UIT) It is also the governing body for match crossbow shooting. As part of its aim to promote and regulate small bore and air weapon shooting it organises the annual Bisley and Scottish Small-bore-Rifle meetings, the National Pistol meeting and the National Air Weapons championship as well as numerous national competitions, leagues and coaching schemes. It raises the teams of all World Championship and Olympic events in small bore rifle, pistol and air guns
Key Personnel:
General Sir Peter Hunt GCB,DSO,OBE,FBIM,President
A J Clarke Esq, MBE, Chairman
Group Captain D J.King, MBE, Secretary

The Proof House
The Gunmaker Company, 48 Commercial Road, London, EL1 1LP, Tel: 01 481 2695
Key Personnel:
G A Brooks, Proof Master

Red Deer Commission
Knowsley, 82 Fairfield Road, Inverness, IV3 5LH, Tel: 0463 31751
The Red Deer Commission's principal functions are the conservation and control of Deer in Scotland, mainly Red and Sika; with a limited responsibility for Roe Deer. The Commission advises the Secretary of State for Scotland on matters affecting Deer including the prevention of the illegal killing of all species.
Key Personnel:
N H McCulloch, Secretary
L K Stewart, Senior Deer Officer

Scottish Clay Pigeon Association (S.C.P.A.9
2 Greengill, Gilcrux, Aspatria, Carlisle, Cumbria, CA5 2RA
Founded in 1929, represents the interests of Scottish clay shooters and acts as the officiating body for all registered competitions in Scotland.
Key Personnel:
W Norval, President
D O'Briscoll, Vice President

S Shiach, Secretary
Mrs G Shiach, Ass Secretary

The Scottish Landowners Federation
18 Abercromby Place, Edinburgh, EH3 6TY, Tel: 031 556 4466
Established 1906. The officially recognised organisation representing rural landowners in Scotland. Responsible for the Game Fair every 5th Year when held in Scotland.
Key Personnel:
R C Stewart, CBE, TD, President
P C Macdonald, Convener
D J Hughes Hallett, Director

Scottish Pistol Association
80 Gowanbrae, Blairgowrie, Perthshire
The association is the governing body for pistol shooting in Scotland, and selects teams or individuals to represent the country in matches. The aim of the association is to encourage and promote the sport of pistol shooting in Scotland.
Key Personnel:
Mrs C M Johnston, Chairman
J L Aitken, Vice Chairman
J Curran, Hon Sec, Dykelaw, 15 Branscroft, Kilbarchan, Renfrewshire, PG10 2LU

Scottish Shooting Council, The
39 Pelstream Avenue, Stirling, FK7 OBG, Tel: 0786 75769
Formed in 1970, the Council promotes shooting in Scotland and is the central co-ordinating body for all competitive shooting associations in Scotland.
Key Personnel:
Jack Anderson, Chairman
G Webb, Hon Secretary & Treasurer

The Shooting Sports Trust Ltd.
Omega House, 471 King's Road, London, SW10 OLU, Tel: 01 373 2940
Formed in 1972. Full membership consists of leading manufacturers and importers of sporting guns and ammunition. Associate Membership is available to retailers of these products. Members contribute to a fund which is used to promote and develop all aspects of the sport of shooting.
Key Personnel:
Lord Swansea, DL, President
Mr F J Winfield, Secretary, P O Box 360, 75 Harbourne Road, Birmingham, B15 3DH. Tel 054 36 4636

Standing Conference on Countryside Sports
c/o College of Estate Management, Whiteknights, Reading, Berkshire, RG6 2AW, Tel: 0734 861 101 ext. 65
The Standing Conference is a forum where representatives of national organisations concerned with countryside sports, mainly hunting, shooting and fishing come together to identify and discuss major problems, so that where necessary, attention may be drawn to any action needed. The Conference is also attended by observers from government departments and agencies,

associations of local authorities and representatives of national and international bodies and individuals having concern for the future well being of the countryside. The objective of the Standing Conference is to maintain countryside sports as an integral part of the national way of life by promoting public awareness of:
1. their contribution to the employment and the national economy while complementing the primary land uses of farming and forestry
2. the contribution made by countryside sports to amenity and wildlife conservation
3. the need for action at national level on problems or issues affecting countryside sports.
4. the European Economic Community's activity in this field
Key Personnel:
Lord Porchester KCVO, KBE, DL, Chairman
RGA Lofthouse FRICS, Convenor
Captain Jeremy Stewart RN, Secretary

The U.K. Federation of Face
C/O The British Association for Shooting and Conservation, Marford Mill, Rossett, Wrexam, Clwyd, LL12 0HL., Tel: 0244 570881
Face is the federation of Field Sports Associations of the EEC. It has a secretariat in Brussels which monitors all issues and proposals for legislation that could affect field sports in any way. The UK Federation was formed by the associations set out below and is financed by contributions from the associations themselves, as well as other donations.
Members: British Falconers Club, British Field Sports Society, B.A.S.C. Country Landowners Association, The Game Farmers Association, St Hubert Club, The Game Conservancy, Federation of Deer Management Societies, Masters of Foxhounds Association, Association of Masters of Harriers and Beagles, The Atlantic Salmon Research Trust Ltd, National Anglers Council
Key Personnel:
Duke of Abercorn, President
Simon Jervis-Read, Chairman
Maj GTEN John Hopkinson, Vice Chairman
J R Greenwood, Treasurer
J A Swift, Secretary

Vintage Arms Association
11 Gardens, Bury St. Edmunds, Tel: 0284 61832
Founded in 1973 to encourage the collection and use of firearms whose prototype was in use by 1918. This includes pistols, rifles, shotguns and airguns, vintage or replica, muzzle loading or breech loading. The V.A.A. has a number of ranges in the London area, East Anglia and Scotland
Key Personnel:
Gareth Jenkins, Editor 'The Primer'
VAA Magazin

Norman Cheesewright, Membership records Secretary, 5 Duberly Close, East Perry, Huntingdon, Tel 0480 810927

Welsh Clay Pigeon Shooting Association (CPSA)
Trefane, Roch, Haverfordwest, Dyfed, Wales, Tel: 043784 219
Founded in 1930, represents the interests of Welsh Clay shooters and acts as the officiating body for all registered competitors in Wales
Key Personnel:
AJK Aston, President
L D Davies, Chairman
Miss M John, Secretary
R Hill, Treasurer
R Locke, Public Relations Offier

Welsh Pistol Association (WPA)
RX Products, Pontygwindy Industrial Estate, Caerphilly, Mid. Glam., DF8 3HV
The Association is the governing body for centrefire pistol in Wales, and is affiliated to NRA and the Regional participent ofNPA. It is responsible for the administration and organisation of c/f shooting in Wales, the Welsh Squad and team, and arranging international and representative matches, coaching and coaches' courses etc
Key Personnel:
M Banwell- Clode Chairman and Welsh National Coach
A Chadwick, Treasurer

The Welsh Shooting Council
13a Archer Road, Penarth, South Glamorgan, CF6 2HW, Tel: 0222 702463
Formed in 1975. The Council is the central coordinating body for its member associations (Welsh Clay Target Shooting Association, Welsh Smallbore Shooting Union, Welsh Rifle Association and Welsh Pistol Association). Promotes and further the shooting sport in Wales and encourages shooting at international level
Key Personnel:
Basil George 1985-6 Chairman
T Speck, Treasurer
A L Tusler, Hon Secretary
Produces Annual Handbook and conducts annual multi stage championship

World Pheasant Association
P O Box 5, Lower Basildon, Goring, Near Reading, Berkshire, Tel: 07357 5140
An international conservation organisation researching and working towards achieving their main objectives of conserving and preserving the threatened and endangered Galliformes (Gamebirds) of the world.
Key Personnel:
Dr Jean Delacour, President
KCR Howman, Chairman
Dr David Hill & Prof John Crawford, Editors
J Brown, Treasurer
C D W Savage, Secretary

BRITISH ASSOCIATION FOR SHOOTING AND CONSERVATION

TRADE MEMBERS

The following section comprises a list of the trade members of the British Association for Shooting and Conservation whose entries do not appear in any other section of the book.

A. Allison Esq, The Lodge, East Brackley, Kinross KY13 7LU.

D Arch Esq, The Maltsters Arms, Bradby, Daventry, Northants NN11.

A R P Trading Co. 35G Parsonage Street, Dursley, Glos GL11 4BP.

G H Arrowsmith Esq, Maker Lane Farm, Hoar Cross, Burton on Trent, Staff DE13 8QR.

R H Ball Esq, Barncrosh, Castle Douglas, Scotland DG7 1TX.

B & P Barnett, Unit 4, Bilston Industrial Estate, Ettingshall Road, Bilston, Staffs WV14.

K.A. Barnett Esq, Kab's Cabin, 228 Broad Street, Crewe, Cheshire CW1.

Baxter & Blanchard Ltd, 2 Bracken Avenue, Hellesdon, Norwich, Norfolk NR6 6LS.

Belgrave Gun Co Ltd, 43 Melton Road, Leicester LE4 6PN.

A D Belkl Esq, Arton Game Services, Bamff Estate, Alyth, Perthshire, Scotland PH11 8LF.

P J Bender Esq, Chestnuts Hotel, Racecourse Road, Ayr, Scotland KA7.

John Blades & Son, G/A Oct 83, L/K/A Belvedere House, Whitley Bay, Northumberland NE25 8RT.

Bluett Smith & Co Ltd (Inc Insurance Brokers), 189/195 High Street, Beckenham, Kent BR3 1AH.

T D Bone Esq, 2 Muscott Street, Northampton, Northants NN5 5EY.

Boodle & Dunthorne Ltd, 35 Lord Street, Liverpool.

Boss & Co (Holdings) Ltd, 13 Dover Street, London W1X 3PH.

Joseph Brazier Limited, Ashes Works, Ash Street, Bilston, West Midlands WV14.

M Bregoli Esq, Old Manor House Restaurant, 21 Palmerston Street, Romsey, Hants. SO5 8GF.

D S Broadway Esq, Discount Motoring, 54 Aire Street, Goole, Humberside DN14 5QE.

D M Brown Esq, 32 Hamilton Road, Bothwell, Glasgow, Scotland G71 8NA.

P Brown Esq, Tiltech Ltd, Fromehall Mill, Lodgemoor Lane, Stroud, Glos GL5 3EH.

V Brown Esq, Highcrest Roofing Co Ltd, 55 Ormskirk Road, Knowsley, Liverpool L9 5AD.

J D Burden Esq, Brambles, Shoreham Road, Otford, Kent TN14 5RL.

G Burton Esq, 106 Hollingbury Park Avenue, Brighton, Sussex BN1 7JP.

Burton McCall, Samuel Street, Leicester LE1 1RV.

P G E Butterfield Esq, Redcoates Farmhouse Hotel, Hitchin, Herts SG4 7JR.

C Campbell Esq, Nythfa House Hotel, Brecon, Powys LD3.

C B Cheney Esq, The Meads, 3 Brookside, Pontrilas, Hertfordshire HR2 0BQ.

The City Press of Chester, 45 Watergate Row, Chester CH1 2LG.

C L A Game Fair Department, Berrington House, St Alkmunds Square, Shrewsbury, Shropshire SY1 1UH.

K H Claridge Esq, Claridge's Book Shop, Church Street, Helmsley, York YO6 5AD.

M T Clarke Esq, Countrywise & Co, Hillside, Gover Hill, Tonbridge, Kent TN11 9SP.

R M Clayton, 4A The Traverse, Bury St Edmunds, Suffolk IP33 1BJ.

J Clifton Melville Esq, Country Wear, 35 Bridge Street, Ballater, Aberdeenshire AB3 5QD.

R W Cobbleddick W.Esq, Infur(Great Britain), PO Box 20, Bude, Cornwall EX23 8PF.

M J Colline Esq, Catsfield Shooting Centre, Catsfield Place, Battle Sussex TN33.

The Colt Car Company Limited, Spitalgate Lane, Cirencester, Glos GL7 2DE.

Major N Corry, Ccaw Ltd, Gunhouse, Steeple Bumpstead, Haverhill, Suffolk CB9.

Country Gent, Majestic Buildings, Whitburn Street, Bridgnorth, Shropshire WV16.

The Country Gunshop, A P Kelly Esq, 100 Panprysg Road, Pencoed, Brigend, Mid Glamorgan CF35 6LT.

Country Style Sporting Clothes, High Street, Ruabon, Wrexham, Clwyd LL14.

Country Woollens, River Mill, Afonwen, Mold, Clwyd CH7.

Countrysport Publishing Co Ltd, Claggan Road, Fort William, Inverness-shire, Scotland PH3 6QL.

Craig Caledonian, Gartinstarry, Buchlyvie, Stirlingshire, Scotland FK8 3PD.

Craven Gilpin & Sons Ltd, The Cottage, Mansion Lane, Roundhay, Leeds LS8 2HH.

George Curwen & Sons, Central Garage, Throckley, Newcastle-Upon-Tyne NE5.

C J Davis Esq, Llugwy Hall, Country House Hotel, Pennal, Machynlleth SY20 9JX.

Decorative Arts, Stainsacre Industrial Estate, Whitby, N. Yorkshire YO22 4PU.

Denmar Supplies, Walford Lodge, Walford, Baschurch, Shropshire SY4 2HL.

M H Dibble Esq, H J Blakeney Ltd, Fatting House Farm, Mill Lane, Old Sodbury, Bristol BS17 6SH.

Dirca Design, Spring Cottage, Hooe, Battle, Sussex TN33 9EU.

Carlo Donetti, Four Seasons Hotel, St Fillans, Perthshire, Scotland PH6 2NF.

Drunken Duck Inn, P A Barton Esq, Barngates, Nr Ambleside, Cumbria LA22 0NG.

Enviroment & Wildlife Ltd, Warren Farm, Boxley, Maidstone, Kent ME14 3EB.

T Epps Esq, Port Charlotte Hotel, Isle Of Islay, Argyll, Scotland.

Exmoor Guns & Fishing, G/A July 1983, L/K/A 3 The Parade, Minehead, Somerset TA 2 5NL.

Harold Faulkener, Sealand Manor, Sealand, Deeside, Clwyd CH1.

M W Festing Esq, Hele House, Hele, Taunton, Somerset TA 4 1AJ.

Michael Ruvigny Esq, The Field, Carmelite House, London EC4.

Field Sport Supplies, Boardmans Farm, Hawshaw Lane, Hawshaw, Bury, Lancs BL8 4LD.

Fine English Guns, J Lawrence Esq, Park Farm House, Waterstock, Oxon OX9 1JT.

Fores Ltd, G/A Nov 1981, L/K/A 29 Bruton Street, London W1X 7DP.

D Gaskin Esq, Candy & Country Store, Shurloch Row, Reading, Berks RG10 0PS.

B Gibson Esq, The Salmon Leap Hotel, Sleights, Whitby, N. Yorks YO

R J Gilmore Esq, 15 York House, Canterbury, Borehamwood, Herts WD6 1PF.

J A & N J Gowling, Edenhall Hotel, Edenhhall, Penrith, Cumbria CA11 8SX.

A R Graham Esq, Shooting Developments, Valley Drive, Leslie, Fife, Scotland KY6 3BQ.

H C Graham Esq, Central Dog Food Supplies, 69 Larkfield Road, Kirkintilloch, Scotland G66 3AS.

Grainstock, 96B West Avenue, Rudheath, Northwich, Cheshire CW9 7ET.

L Grant Esq, The Westwood, 75 St Johns Street, Creetown, Newton Stewart, Wigtownshire DG8 7JB.

Guns & Tackle, 81 High STreet, Whitton, Twickenham, Middlesex TW2 7LD.

A Hancock Esq, Venom Conversations, 208 High Street, Lye, West Midlands, DY9 8JZ.

Hannants Pest Control, 4 Porters CLose, Fordham Heath, Colchester, Essex CO3 5TY.

G S Harvey Esq, 5 New Cottages, The High Street, Partridge Green, W. SUssex PO19 3AU.

H Harvie Wsq, Fernhill Hotel, Portpatrick, Wigtownshire DG9

F A Hawkins Transport Ltd, 66 Totterhoe Road, Eaton Bay, Dunstable, Beds LU6 2BD.

T M Enderson Esq, Sport-E-Quip, 37 High Street, Shaftesbury, Dorset SP7 8JE.

William Hendry & Son, Petersmuir, Haddington, Scotland EH41 4JR.

B R Hickman Esq, Greenham, 28 Aldbourne Avenue, Earley, Berks RG6 2DB.

H M Supplies, 10 High Street, Camberley, Surrey GU15 3SX.

Holland & Holland Ltd, 33 Bruton Street, London W1X 8JS

Holand Textiles Ltd, Heapey Street, Macclesfield, Cheshire SK11 7JB.

Horse & Hound Ltd,115 Holburn Street, Aberdeen, Scotland AB1 0BQ.

Horton Crossbows Ltd, Peddiston, Cromarty, Ross-shire, Scotland IV11 8XX.

Howard & King, Pond Hall Game Farm. Gainsborough Lane, Ipswich, Suffolk IP3 0EU.

David Hughes (Sculptor), 7 Ardenflats, Dorridge, Solihull, Warks B93 8HH.

P M Hughes Esq, Pontycoedcae Boarding Kennels, Tyrcoed Road, Glanamman, Ammanford, Dyfed SA18.

Inch Park Hotel, 1-2 St Leonards Bank, Perth, Scotland PH2 8EB.

K Jones Esq, Cross Keys Grange, Glebe Road, Loughor, Swansea SA4.

Andrew Kay Shooting Supplies, Pinfolds, Welham, Retford, Notts DN22 0SQ.

R I Kennedy Esq, Midland Tree Surgeons, Corner House, Draycott In The Clay, Sudbury, Derbyshire DE6 5BT.

The Keysder Gallery, Corston, Malmesbury, Wiltshire SN16 0HJ.

Kippen Smoke-House, The Garrique, Kippen, Stirling KF8 3JN.

D & D Kitson, Banks Ghyll Kennels, Lothersdale, W.Yorks BD20 8HB.

K S R International Ltd, Sandiron House, Beachief, Sheffield,Yorks S7 2RA.

Lakeland Plastics, ALexandra Buildings, Station Precinct, Windermere, Cumbria LA23 1AH.

Peter Lapper & Assoc, Estate Agents, 3 Imperial Square, Cheltenham, Glos GL50 1QB.

Leisure Sports Of Dronfield, 2 High Street, Dronfield, SHeffield, Yorks S18 6PY.

P Lisney Esq, Pest Control, 2 Morris Drive, Donnington, Telford, Salford TF2 8AY.

Lombard Tricity Finance Ltd(L H Bernard Esq), Lombard House, Blaird Road, Enfield, Middlesex EN1 1TP.

P Loughrin Esq, 41 Kirk Road, Wishaw, Lanarkshire, Scotland ML2 7BL.

Luxitours Hunting Lambert Ltd, 75 Mardol, Shrewsbury, Salop SY1 1QE.

MacGourmets Ltd, Hollybush House Hotel, Holybush, Ayr, Scotland KA6 7Ea.

R A S Maconochie Esq, Riverside Cottage, Ablington, Bibury, Cirencester, Glose GL95NY.

The Manydown Company, Worting Wood Farm, Basingstoke, Hants RG.

T Marsden & Sons Ltd, Midge Hall, Leyland, Lancs PR5 3TN.

H L McConnell Esq, Miskin Arms, Miskin, Mid Glamorgan CF7 8JQ.

Mclean Bros, R Slaughter Esq, Rosebank, Cromdale, Grantown-on-Spey, Scotland PH26 2LW.

Murray Arms Hotel, Mrs Murray Usher of Cally, Cally Estate Office, Gaterhouse-of-Fleet, Scotland DG7.

Lance Nicholson, Fishing & Guns, High Street, Dulverton, Somerset TA22 9HB.

Nigel Sweeting Galleries Ltd, Church Close, Ramsdell, Basingstoke, Hants RG26 5RF.

The Northern Armoury Ltd, 67 North Methveven Street, Perth, Scotland PH1 5PX.

Northern Dogfood Supplies, 15 Leopold Street, Nairn, Scotland IV12 4BE.

R F O'Dell Esq, Sheraton House, 37 High Street, Shefford, Beds SG17 5AX.

T D Oram Esq, Cawdor Tavern, Cawdor, Nairnshire, Scotland CIV12.

J C Palmer Esq, Craig Y Dderwen Hotel, Betws-Y-Coed, Gwynedd LL24 0AS.

David Patmore Ltd, 20 Stonegate, York, Y01 2AS.

J R Redder Esq, Windsor Guns, 9 St Leonards Road, Windsor, Berks SL4 3HU.

Camping and Caravan Dist Ltd, The Pennine Centre, 109 Mill Street, Macclesfield, Cheshire SK11 6NN.

Pet Plan Ltd, 35 Horn Lane, London W13 9TA.

D Philpott & Daughter, 30 West Road, Spondon, Derby DE2 7AB.

Piranha Fieldsports and Country Clothing, 28 Middlehill Gate, Stockport, Cheshire SK1 3AY.

Works, Farfield Road, Sheffield S30 3NN.

Purdies 112 Argyll Street, Dunnoon, Argyll, Scotland PA23 7DH.

P V Guns, 133 Brockenhurst Road, Gosport, Hants PO12 3AX.

Rathburn Leather & Leisure, 141 Stamford Street, Ashton Under Lyne, Lancs OL6 6XJ.

D H Rayner Esq, Caleb Rayner Ltd, Church Hall Farm, Paglesham, Rochford, Essex SS4 2DP.

Justin Reay Associates, 62 Sheerstock, Haddenham, Bucks HO17 8EJ.

M B Redway Esq, Moor End Game Farm, Sleights, Whitby, Yorkshire YO22.

R G S Automatics & Services, 102 Hollies Avenue, Newark, Notts NG24 2AS.

R H Sporting Services, 16 London Road, Stapeley, Nantwich, Cheshire CW5 7JJ.

S J Rhodes Esq, The Red Lion, Llanfairwaterdine, Knighton, Powys LD7 1TU.

Norman Richards Esq, Burlington Publishing Co Ltd, 12-18 Paul Street, London EC2A 4JH.

Rod & Gun Sports, Abbeylands, Navan, Co Meath, Eire.

The Rod Box, 52 St George Street, Winchester, Hants SO23 8AH.

Roseland Inn, Philleigh, Truro, Cornwall TR2 8NB.

J C Rowlands Esq, Guns And Ammo, 95 Beatrice Street, Oswestry, Shropshire. SY11 1HL.

Ruthen Tower Hotel, Abbey Road, Auchterarder, Perthshire, Scotland PH3 1DN.

J L Saint Esq, I M I(Kynoch) Ltd, PO Box 216, Kynoch Works, Witton, Birmingham B6.

Scale Hill Hotel, Loweswater, Cockermouth, Cumbria CA13 9UX.

Sevenoaks Travel Ltd, Dorset Road, 4/5 Dorset Street, Sevenoaks, Kent TN13 1LL.

J B Shears & Sons Ltd, Homesteads Road, Basingstoke, Hants RG22 5RP.

M J Shefford Esq, Housty Kennels, Pale

Mawr Farm, Velindre, Swansea SA5 7PP.

David Sheldon, 6 Willow Street, Oswestry, Salop SY11 1AA.

Shooting Field Services Ltd, Great Edstons House, Kirbymoorside,York YO6 6PB.

Shooting News, Unit 25, Plymouth Road Industrial Site, Tavistock, Devon PL19.

House Of Anton, Castleton Road, Hope, Sheffield, Yorks S30 2RD.

Stanley Skinner & Company, The Mills, Stradbroke, Diss, Norfolk, IP21 5HL.

P M Skoulding Esq, Barn End, High Street, Hadleigh, Suffolk IP7.

Alan W. Smith Racing(1077) Ltd, Manchester Street, Derby DE3 3GA.

G Smith Esq, Firearms Dealers Mains of Williamston Cottages, Insch, Aberdeen AB5 6TX.

Somerset Sheepskin And G/A Nov 83, L/K/A Leatherwear, 84 High Street, Somerset, BA16 0EN.

S O S Pest Control Specialist, 13 Essex Grove, Upper Norwood, London SE19 3SX.

South East Pest Control, 19 Beaufort Road, Kingston-upon-Thames, Surrey KT1 2TH.

Sport & Leisure Camforth, 17 Market Street, Camforth, Lancs LA5 9JX.

Sporting Gun Magazine, Bretton Court, Bretton, Peterborough PE3 8DZ.

Sporting Insurance Services Ltd, 19 Quarry Street, Guildford, Surrey GU1 3UY.

Sports And Model Shop, Tulloch Street, Dingwall, Ross-shire Scotland IV15.

Sprint AIr, 26 Belle Vue Road, Salisbury, WIlts SP1 3YG.

Storrs Jewellers/Firearms, 44 Newton Street, Millom, Cumbria LA18 4DR.

K J & P Stroude, Asterby House Farm, Asterby Louth, Lincs LN11 9UF.

Sudbrooke Garden Contracting, Church View, Church Lane, Sudbrooke, Lincoln LN2 2QH.

S T Somermerson-Wright Esq, Summerston Country Holidays, 1 Carr Row, Leamside, Durham DH4 6QH.

Sun Hotel, 9 Market Square, Buckingham, Bucks MK18 1NJ.

Tackle & Guns (B L M Macmartin Esq), 918 Pollockshans Road, Glasgow, Scotland. G41 2ET.

Tanners Wine Ltd, 26 Wyle Cop, Shrewsbury, Shropshire.SY1 1XD.

Teesdale Country Fair, Spencer House, Melsonby, Richmond, N Yorkshire DL10.

T F C A Ltd, Bridgeway, St Leonards, Sussex TN38 8AP.

The Dog House, Garth Gogo, Rhyd Y Foel, Abergele, Clwyd LL22 8JE.

Frank Thompson (Crieff) Ltd, 9 East High Street, Crieff, Perthshire, Scotland,PH7 3AF.

Towy Sports, 9 King Street, Llandeilo, Dyfed SA19 6BA.

Tweed Fishing Tackle, 13 Market Street, Coldstream, Berwickshire TD12 4BO.

Vale Meat & Game Dealers, 772 Mansfield Road, Woodthorpe, Nottingham NG 3FH.

Vecta Engineering Co Ltd, Carpenters Road, St Helens, Ryde, Isle Of Wight PO33 1YW.

E. Veniard Ltd, 138 Northwood Road, Thornton Heath, Surrey CR4 8YG.

Mr & Mrs G Wade, Mount Stewart Hotel, Portpatrick, Stranraer, Wigtownshire DG9 8LE.

B Wainwright & Co, Estate Agents, 53 King Street, Blackpool, Lancs FY1.

B Wall Esq, Crossroads Farm Kennels, Caister Road, Market Rasen, Lincs, LN8 3JE.

F J Wallace Esq, Yeomanry House, Castle Hill, Reading, Berks RG1.

Walrus Waterproofs Ltd, Studio Works, 3 Mount Street, Basford, Nottingham NG7 7HX.

A Walter Esq, The Country Gun Shop, Lilliesleaf, Melrose, Rosburghshire TD6 9JD.

Ward Childs Ercall, Market Drayton, Shropshire TF9 2DA.

A Watson T/As Castle Armoury, RFD No 51, 55 Braunstone Gate, Leicester LE3 5LG.

A W Weale Esq, Trebowen, Talgarth, Brecon, Powys LD3.

M/S R Weaver, Greywalls Hotel, Gullane, East Lothian, Scotland EH31 2EG.

Wheel & Gun Rest, Ivy House Inn, Holmfield, Halifax, Yorks HX2 9TN.

White Hart Hotel, Port Ellen Islay PA42.

R S White Esq, Chalk Pit Farm, Whiteparish, Salisbury, Wilts SP5 2SD.

Whitebridge Hotel, D F Bailey Esq, Whitebridge, Inverness, Scotland IV1 2UN.

Gordon WIlliams Esq, SSW Limited, 11 Market Place, Wobury, Bedfordshire MK17 9PZ.

M T Woods Esq, Westfield Pheasantries, Cropton, Pickering, N. Yorkshire YO18 8HQ.

Woodlea Hotel, Monaive, Dumfreisshire, Scotland DG3 4EN.

J W Wycherley & Son, Maplas, Cheshire SY14.

IT'S A SIN TO CALL IT JUST CIDER.

THE SHOOTING BUYER'S GUIDE

the most comprehensive reference source available on the vast array of shooting products and services. In five, easy-to-follow, sections you will find all the major brand names together with the names and addresses of their manufacturers and distributors.

Introduction

PART 1

Guns & Ammunition
Brand Names, Manufacturers and their Distributors. Easy-reference tabular guides.

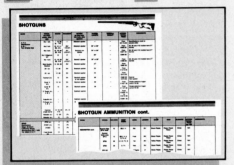

PART 2

Gunshops
Covering England, Scotland, Wales and Ireland. If you are looking for a local gunshop – this is the place to find it.

The Nissan Patrol will more than pull its weight. Comfortably.

PART 3

Game Rearing & Gun and Working Dogs

Game Farms, Game Feedstuffs and Game Rearing Equipment followed by comprehensive listings of Gun & Working Dogs accessories and breeders.

PART 4

Clothing

From Breeches to Weatherproofs, you will find all the major manufacturers and distributors listed in alphabetical sequence.

PART 5

Accessories

From Auctions & Auctioneers to 4 Wheel Drive this last section provides information on the ancillary products and services relevant to the shooting enthusiast.

READER ENQUIRY SERVICE

As a special service to readers and advertisers in the Buyer's Guide, we have incorporated a reader enquiry service. To receive further information from any advertiser in this section, please circle the appropriate reference number on the reply-paid card at the back of the guide.

CONTENTS

GUNS & AMMUNITION

CONTENTS

SHOTGUNS

ADI

A.D.I (Humberside) Ltd
Pool Bank Lane, Welton, Brough,
Humberside, Tel: 0482 667313

ALFRED J PARKER
Manufacturer: Alfred J. Parker Ltd
348 Moseley Road, Birmingham 12,
West Midlands, Tel: 021 440 1480

ANTONIO ZOLI
Distributor: Auto Alloys(Industrial
and Defence) Ltd
Berristow Lane, Hilcote, Blackwell,
Nr Alfreton, Derbys, DE55 5JB
Tel: 0733 813421
Sole distributor

ARIZAGA
Distributor: Sussex Guns Imports
203 Preston Road, Brighton, Sussex,
Tel: 0273 553222
*Barrel blacking and repairs carried
out on the premises*

ARMI TECHNICHE
Distributor: Duglan & Cooper Ltd
14-16 Church Street, Dunstable, Beds.,
Tel: 0582 64649

ARTHUR TURNER
Manufacturer: Arthur Turner
33-35 West Bar, Sheffield, SR 9PQ,
Tel: 0742 22560

AYA
Distributor: A.S.I. Alliance House
Snape Maltings, Saxmundham, Suffolk,
Tel: 072 888 555

ATKIN GRANT & LANG
Manufacturer: Atkin Grant & Lang
& Co Ltd
6 Lincolns Inn Fields, London,
WC2, 0707 42622 (Appointments
only)
*Established 1821. For rebarrelling,
restocking, repairs and new best gun
orders.*

BAIKAL
Distributor: Sports Marketing
13 Grange Way, Whitehall Road,
Colchester, Essex, Tel: 0206 65333

BAILONS
Manufacturer: Bailons Gunmakers Ltd
94-95 Bath Street, Birmingham, B4
6HG, Tel: 021 236 7593

BARHAM
Manufacturer: Barhams
95 Tilehouse Street, Hitchin, Herts,
Tel: 0462 34298

BATE
Manufacturer: G Bate (Gunmakers)
Ltd
8-10 Colmore Circus, Birmingham,
B4 6AT, Tel: 021 236 7451
Also 7 Market Square, Stafford ST16
2JN
Tel 0785 44191

BENNELLI
Distributor: Parker Hale Ltd
Golden Hillock Road, Birmingham,
B11 2PZ, Tel: 021 7738481

BENJAMIN WILD
Manufacturer: Benjamin Wild & Son
55 Price Street, Birmingham, B4 6J2,
Tel: 021 359 2303

BERETTA
Distributor: Gunmark Ltd
The Armoury, Fort Wallington,
Fareham, Hants, Tel: 0329 231531

BERNADELLI
Distributor: Surrey Guns Ltd
9 Manor Road, Wallington, Surrey,
Tel: 01 647 0017

BLOOMFIELD
Manufacturer: Bloomfield Gunmaker
Hill Farm, Radlett, Herts, Tel:
09276 4639

BOSS
Manufacturer: Boss & Co Ltd
13 Dover Street, London, W1, Tel: 01
493 1127/0711

BRETTON
Distributor: Viking Arms Ltd
Summerbridge, Harrogate, N. Yorks,
Tel: 0423 780810

BRNO
Distributor: Edgar Brothers
Catherine Street, Macclesfield,
Cheshire, Tel: 0625 613177

AA BROWN & SONS
Manufacturer: A A Brown & Sons
1 Snake Lane, Alvechurch,
Birmingham, B48 7NT, Tel: 021 445
5395
*Sole manufacturers of the Supreme de luxe
sidelock ejector sporting guns and best
Boxlock. Made to order. All British
manufacture.*

BROWNING
Distributor: Browning Sports Ltd
37d Milton Trading Estate, Milton,
Abingdon, Oxon, OX14 4RT, Tel:
0235 833939

CAPRINUS
Distributor: Holland & Holland Ltd
33 Bruton Street, London, W1X 8JS,
Tel: 01 499 4411

CENTURY
Distributor: Hilton Gun Co Ltd
60 Station Road, Hatton, Derby, DE6
5EL, Tel: 0283 814488

CHAPLIN
Manufacturer: B E Chaplin
(Gunmakers) Ltd
6 Southgate Street, Winchester,
Hampshire, Tel: 0962 52935
Leading gunmakers of the South.

CRAIG M WHITSEY
Manufacturer: Craig M Whitsey
(Gunmakers) Ltd
Unit D 10/12 Fitzalan Road,
Arundei, West Sussex, Tel: 0903
883102

I M CRUDGINGTON LTD
Manufacturer: I M Crudgington Ltd
37 Broad Street, Bath, Avon, BA1 5LT,
Tel: 0225 64928 or 66325

David Mckay Brown(Gunmaker)

DAVID McKAY BROWN
SCOTLAND's GUNMAKER

32 Hamilton Road, Bothwell,
Glasgow, G71, 0698 853727
*Specialists in the manufacture of 12
and 20 bore round action guns.*

DENTON & KENNELL
Manufacturer: Denton & Kennell
West Street, Somerton, Somerset,
Tel: 0458 73732/72065

DERBYSHIRE FIREARMS
Distributor: Auto Alloys (Industrial
and Defence)Ltd
Berristow Lane, Hilcote, Blackwell,
Nr Alfreton, Derbyshire, DE55 5JB,
Tel: 0773 813421
Sole distributor

DICKSON ROUND ACTION

John Dickson & Son
21 Frederick Street, Edinburgh, Tel:
031 225 4218

EL CHIMBO
Distributor: Direct Arms Imports
208 High Street, Lye, Nr Stourbridge,
West Midlands, Tel: 038 482 2496

ELDERKIN

**Elderkin & Son (Gunmakers)
Ltd**
Spalding 3, Lincolnshire, PE11 1TG,
Tel: 0775 2919/4621

FABARM
Distributor: Leslie Hewett Ltd
Upton Cross, Liskeard, Cornwall,
Tel: 0579 62319

FAMAR
Distributor: Leslie Hewett Ltd
Upton Cross, Liskeard, Cornwall,
Tel: 0579 62319

FERLIB
Distributor: Hilton Gun Co Ltd
60 Station Road, Hatton, Derby,
DE6 5EL, Tel: 0283 814488
C[BASC]N

F.I.A.S.
Distributor: Oliver J. Gower Ltd
Unit K1, Cherrycourt Way, Stanbridge
Road, Leighton Buzzard, Bedfordshire,
Tel: 0525 377730

FOSTER
Manufacturer: Fosters Countrysport
1 Cleveland Street, Co. Durham, Tel:
0325 51351

FRANCHI
Distributor: A.S.I. Alliance House
Snape Maltings, Saxmundham, Suffolk,
Tel: 072 888555

GAMBA
Distributor: Leslie Hewett Ltd
Upton Cross, Liskeard, Cornwall,
Tel: 0579 62319

GREENFIELDS
Manufacturer: H S Greenfield & Son
4-5 Upper Bridge Street, Cantrbury,
Kent, Tel: 0227 456959

GOROSABEL
Distributor: Denton & Kennell
West Street, Somerton, Somerset,
Tel: 0458 73732/72065

HAYGARTH
Manufacturer: C H Haygarth & Sons
The Cottage Gun Shop, Dunnet,
Caithness, Scotland, Tel: 084785
602

HARTMANN & WEISS
Manufacturer: Hartmann & Weiss
Ltd

Folly Meadow, Hammersley Lane,
Penn, Bucks, Tel: 049481 2836

HEATHWALK
Manufacturer: R E Heathcote-
Walker
The Cottage, Gomersal House,
Lower Lane, Gomersal, West
Yorkshire, BD19 4HY, Tel: 0274
877498

Hellis, Beesley & Watson
(Gunmakers)
33 South Parade, Mollison Way,
Edgware, Middlesex, HA8 5QL, Tel: 01
952 1579

HOLLAND & HOLLAND
Manufacturer: Holland & Holland
Ltd
906 Harrow Road, London, NW10
5JT, Tel: 01 960 4358

HOPKINS
Manufacturer: H G Hopkins & Sons
53-55 High Street, Sandbach, Cheshire,
CW11 0AL, Tel: 09367 2404

YOU'LL FIND OUR RANGE OF AMMUNITION WELL WITHIN RANGE OF YOUR POCKET.

Winchester GB 1oz & 1¹/₁₆oz
Chasse 1¹/₁₆oz Game loads: Trap 100/200
Winning clay laods: Ranger 16g and 20g game
loads: AA Skeet the top skeet cartridge.

WINCHESTER
THE AMMUNITION COMPANY
CUTNALL GREEN, DROITWICH,
WORCESTERSHIRE WR9 0NS. 1

IAB

Distributor: Goss Petcher Guns Ltd

The Gun Room, Wighay Bridge,
Annesley Road, Hucknall, Notts,
Tel: 0602 633430

IMPERIAL

Distributor: Hilton Gun Co Ltd

60 Station Road, Hatton, Derbys, Tel:
0283 814488

INVESTARM

Distributor: Olver J. Gower Ltd

Unit K1, Cherrycourt Way, Stanbridge
Road, Leighton Buzzard, Beds., Tel:
0525 377730

G. BATE
(GUNMAKERS) LTD
ESTABLISHED 1850

2

Retail shops:
8-10 Colmore Circus,
Birmingham B4 6AT.
Telephone: 021-236 7451
7 Market Square, Stafford
ST16 2JN
SHOOTING GROUND:
Midland Counties. S.G.
Oakedge, Wolseley Bridge,
Nr. Rugeley Staffs.
Tuition, Gunfitting, Refreshments.
Sporting practice each Sat: from 10am
Open Sporting Shoots
2nd Sunday each month.

INVESTARM

Distributor: Intergun
PO Box 1, Probus, Truro, Cornwall,
Tel: 087252 243

ITHACA

Distributor: Essex Gun
6 Eastbrook Drive, Rush Green,
Romford, Essex, Tel: 01 593 3502

IVOR ROBERTS

**Manufacturer: Roberts & Quin
(Gunmakers)**
Commercial Street, Newtown, Powys,
Tel: 0686 26579

JASON ABBOT

Jason Abbot(Gunmakers)Ltd
1-3 Bell Street, Princes Risborough,
Nr Aylsbury, Buckinghamshire,
HP17 0AD, 08444 6677
English Gun specialists.

JOHN POWELL

John Powell
45 Church Street, Reigate, Surrey, Tel:
07372 44111

JOHN RIGBY

**Manufacturer: John Rigby & Co
(Gunmakers) Ltd**
5 King Street, Covent Garden,
London, WC2E 8HN, Tel: 01 734
7611

JOHN WILKES

**Manufacturer: John Wilkes Gun &
Rifle Makers**
79 Beak Street, Regent Street, London,
W1, Tel: 01 437 6539

KESTREL

Distributor: Gunmark Ltd
The Armoury, Fort Wallington,
Fareham, Hants, Tel: 0329 231531

KRIEGHOFF

Distributor: Tony Kennedy Guns
6 Church Street, Lauceston, Cornwall,
Tel: 0566 4465

LANBER

Distributor: Gunmark Ltd
The Armoury, Fort Wellington,
Fareham, Hants, Tel: 0329 231531

LAURONA

Distributor: Frank Dyke & Co Ltd
1-7 Ernest Avenue, West Norwood,
London, SE27 ODG, Tel: 01 670 2224

LINCOLN

**Distributor: David Nickerson
(Tathwell) Ltd**
The Old Vicarage, Tathwell, Louth,
Lincs, LN11 9ST, Tel: 0472 840536

LINSLEY BROTHERS

Manufacturer: Linsley Brothers Ltd
28 Kirkgate, Leeds, LE2 7DR, Tel
0532 452790
*Manufacturers of Linsley Bros
shotguns.*

MANU ARM

Distributor: Oliver J. Gower Ltd
Unit K1, Cherrycourt Way, Stanbridge
Road, Leighton Buzzard, Beds, Tel:
0525 37730

MARLIN

Distributor: Leslie Hewett Ltd
Upton Cross, Liskeard, Cornwall,
Tel: 0579 62319, Telex: 338172
Safari Birmingham

MAROCCHI

Distributor: Gamebore Cartridge Co
Great Union Street, Hull, North
Humberside, Tel: 0482 223707

MB 80

Distributor: Duglan & Cooper Ltd
14-16 Church Street, Dunstable,
Beds., Tel: 0582 64649

MERKEL

Distributor: Parker Hale Ltd
Golden Hillock Road, Birmingham, W.
Midlands, B11 2PZ, Tel: 021 773 8481

MIDLAND
Distributor: Parker Hale Ltd
Golden Hillock Road, Birmingham, W.
Midlands, B11 2PZ, Tel: 021 773 8481

MIROKU
Distributor: Browning Sports Ltd
37d Milton Trading Estate, Milton,
Abingdon, Oxon., Tel: 0235
833939

THE MISTRAL
Distributor: John Rothery
(Wholesale) Co Ltd

MOSSBERG
Distributor: Intergun
PO Box 21, Probus, Nr. Truro,
Cornwall, TR2 4JJ, Tel: 087252 243

PARKER HALE
Distributor: Parker Hale Ltd
Golden Hillock Road, Birmingham,
West Midlands, B11 2PZ, Tel: 021 773
8481

PEDRETTI
Distributor: Hilton Gun Co Ltd
60 Station Road, Hatton, Derby, DE6
5EL, Tel: 0283 814488

PEDERSOLI
Distributor: Coach Harness
Haughley, Stowmarket, Tel: 0449
673258

PEDRO ARRIZABALAGA
Distributor: J Roberts & Son
5 King Street, Covent Garden,
London, WC2E 8HN, Tel: 01 240
3186

PERAZZI
Distributor: Leslie Hewett Ltd
Upton Cross, Liskeard, Cornwall,
Tel: 0579 62319

PIOTTI
Distributor: Hilton Gun Co Ltd
60 Statin Road, Hatton, Derbyshire,
DE6 5EL, Tel: 0283 814488

POINTER
Distributor: SSM International
Tedstone Wafre, Nr. Bromyard,
Herefordshire, Tel: 08867 646 &
284

PURDEY
Manufacturer: James Purdey & Sons
Audley House, 57-58 South Audley
Street, London, WIY 6ED, Tel: 01
499 1801

RALPH GRANT & SON
Distributor: Ralph Grant & Son Ltd
Green Lane Road and Rosebery Street
(off East Park Road), Leicester, LE5
4PD, Tel: 0533 767551
Boxlock 8 bore and Single barrel 4 bores

REMINGTON
Distributor: Hull Cartridge Co Ltd
Bontoft Avenue, National Avenue,
Hull, North Humberside, HU5 4HZ,
Tel: 0482 42756/445679

**RIZZINI SIDES BY SIDES (TOP OF
RANGE)**
Distributor: Hilton Gun Co Ltd
60 Station Road, Hatton, Derbyshire,
Tel: 0283 814488

RIZZINI (BATTISTA)
Distributor: Pardoe Importers
Wychbold, Droitwich, Worcestershire,
WR9 0BX, Tel: 052786 517

J ROBERTS & SON
Manufacturer: J Roberts & Son
5 King Street, Covent Garden,
London, WC2E 8HN, Tel: 01 240
3186

**Roding Armoury
(Gunsmiths)**
Silver Street, Market Place, Abridge,
Romford, Essex, Tel: 037 881 3570

ROTA LUCIANO
Distributor: Hilton Gun Co Ltd
60 Station Road, Hatton, Derbys., Tel:
0283 814488

ROTTWEIL
Distributor: Leslie Hewett Ltd
Upton Cross, Liskeard, Cornwall,
Tel: 0579 62319

RUGER
Distributor: Viking Arms Ltd
Summerbridge, Harrogate, N. Yorks,
HG3 4BW, Tel: 0423 780810

SARRIUGARTE
Distributor: Surrey Guns Ltd
9 Manor Road, Wallington, Surrey,
Tel: 01 647 0017

SARRIUGARTE
Distributor: Wellington Country
Sports
Fore Street, Wellington, Somerset,
Tel: 082347 2120
*Distributers of all Sarriugarte shotguns
including Multichokes and Sidelock
over and unders*

W & C SCOTT
Manufacturer: W&C Scott
Premier Works, Tame Road, Witton,
Birmingham, B6 7HS, Tel: 021 328
4107

SILMA
Distributor: A.D.I. Humberside Ltd
Pool Bank Lane, Welton, Brough,
North Humberside, Tel: 0482 667313

C SMITH & SONS
Manufacturer: C Smith & Sons
(Newark) Ltd
Clinton House, Lombard Street,
Newark, Notts., Tel: 0636 703839

SMITH & WESSON
Distributor: Parker Hale Ltd
Golden Hillock Road, Birmingham,
B11 2PZ, Tel: 021 773 8481

SPORTARMI
Distributor: Direct Arms Imports
208 High Street, Lye, Nr. Stourbridge,
West Midlands, Tel: 038 482 2496

SPRINGFIELD FIREARMS
Distributor: Auto Alloys (Industrial
and Defence)Ltd
Berristow Lane, Hilcote, Blackwell,
Nr Alfreton, Derbyshire, DE55 5JB,
Tel: 0773 813421
Sole distributor

THOMAS BLAND
Manufacturer: Thomas Bland &
Sons Ltd
21-22 New Road, St. Martin's Row,
London, WC2, Tel: 01 836 9122

THOMAS WILD
Manufacturer: Rowland Watson
32 Lower Loveday Street, Birmingham,
19, Tel: 021 359 1830

TONY KENNEDY
Manufacturer: Tony Kennedy Guns
6 Church Street, Launceston,
Cornwall, Tel: 0566 4465
Distributers of Caprinus, Sweden

UGARTECHA
Distributor: Parker-Hale Ltd
Golden Hillock Road, Birmingham,
West Midlands, B11 2PZ, Tel: 021 773
8481

UNION ARMERA
Distributor: Hilton Gun Co Ltd
60 Station Road, Hatton, Derbys., DE6
5EL, Tel: 0283 814488

Uttings Tackle & Gun Shop
54 Bethel Street, Norwich, NR2
1NR, Tel: 0603 621776
Send or ring for quotations.

VERNEY CARRON
Distributor: David Nickerson
(Tathwell) Ltd
The Old Vicarage, Tathwell, Louth,
Lincs, Tel: 0472 840536

VIKING SHOTGUNS
Distributor: Viking Arms Ltd
Summerbridge, Harrogate, N.Yorkshire,
HG3 5JA, Tel: 0423 780810
Pump action and automatic

WESTLEY RICHARDS
Manufacturer: Westley Richards &
Co
40 Grange Road, Birmingham, Tel:
021 472 1701

WILLIAM EVANS
Manufacturer: William Evans Ltd
67a St. James' Street, London, SW1,
Tel: 01 493 0415

WILLIAM POWELL
Manufacturer: William Powell &
Son (Gunmakers) Ltd
35-37 Carrs Lane, Birmingham, B4
7SX, Tel: 021 643 0689 or 021
643 8362

WINCHESTER.
Distributor: Winchester UK, Site 7
Kidderminster Road, Cutnall Green,
Droitwich, Worcester, WR9 ONS,
Tel: 029 923 461

F J WISEMAN & CO
Manufacturer: F J Wiseman & Co Ltd
3 Price Street, Birmingham, B4 6JX,
Tel: 021 359 1256

WOODS OF SWAFFHAM
Manufacturer: Woods of Swaffham
7-11 Mangate Street, Dereham Road,
Swaffham, Norfolk, Tel: 0760 22609

RIFLES

ANSCHUTZ
Distributor: Frank Dyke & Co Ltd
1/7 Ernest Avenue, West Norwood,
London, SE27 ODG, Tel: 01 670 2224

Atkin Grant & Lang & Co Ltd

6 Lincolns Inn Fields, London,
WC2, 0707 42622 (Appointments
only)
*Established 1821. For rebarrelling,
restocking, repairs and new best gun
orders.*

Baytree Arms
10 Baytree Hill, Liskeard, Cornwall,
Tel: 0579 46636

BERETTA
Distributor: Gunmark Ltd
The Armoury, Fort Wallington,
Fareham, Hants, Tel: 0329 231531

BRNO
Distributor: Edgar Bros.
Catherine Street, Macclesfield, Tel:
0625 613177

BROWNING
Distributor: Browning Sports Ltd
37d Milton Trading Estate, Milton,
Abingdon, Oxon, OX14 4RT, Tel:
0235 833939

BSA
Manufacturer: BSA Guns Ltd
Armoury Road, Birmingham, B11 2PX,
Tel: 021 773 0845

CHAPLIN
Manufacturer: B E Chaplin
(Gunmakers) Ltd
6 Southgate Street, Winchester,
Hants, Tel: 0962 52935

CHARTER ARMS
Distributor: Viking Arms Ltd
Summerbridge, Harrogate, N.
Yorkshire, Tel: 0423 780810

DAVID LLOYD STALKING RIFLES
Manufacturer: David Lloyd
Pipewell Hall, Kettering, Tel: 0536
760300

RWS DIANA
Distributor: Leslie Hewett Ltd
Upton Cross, Liskeard, Cornwall,
Tel: 0579 62319
Match rifles

ERMA(WEST GERMANY)
Distributor: Edgar Brothers
Catherine Street, Macclesfield,
Cheshire, Tel: 0625 613177

FEINWERKBAU
Distributor: A.S.I. Alliance House
Snape Maltings, Saxmundham, Suffolk,
Tel: 072 888555

**FULTON FULLBORE TARGET
RIFLES**

G E Fulton & Son
Bisley Camp, Brookwood, Woking,
Surrey, Tel: 048 673204

GEVARM
Distributor: Gamebore Cartridge Co
Great Union Street, Hull, Tel: 0482
223707

GRUNIG AND ELMIGER
Distributor: John Powell Gunmakers
45 Church Street, Reigate, Surrey, Tel:
07372 44111

HART
Manufacturer: G L & I J Hart
46 Winchester Way, Cheltenham,
Glos., Tel: 0242 519020

HARTMANN & WEISS
Manufacturer: Hartmann & Weiss
Ltd

Folly Meadow, Hammersley Lane,
Penn, Tel: 049481 2836

HECKLER & KOCH
Distributor: Parker Hale Ltd
Golden Hillock Road, Birmingham,
B11 2PZ, Tel: 021 773 8481

HEATHWALK
Manufacturer: R E Heathcote-Walker
The Cottage, Gomersal House, Lower Lane, Gomersal, West Yorkshire, BD19 4HY, Tel: 0274 877498

HEYM
Distributor: The Shooting Lodge Ltd 28-30 Victoria Street, Skipton, North Yorkshire, BD23 1JE, Tel: 0756 5825

HOLLAND & HOLLAND
Manufacturer: Holland & Holland Ltd
906 Harrow Road, London, NW10 5JT, Tel: 01 960 4358

I.M.I. (Israel Military Industries)
Distributor: Pat Walker Guns 143 Alexandra Road, Gateshead, Tyne & Wear, Tel: 0632 78636 and 091478 6736
[BBASC]N

JOHN RIGBY, Sporting rifles
Manufacturer: John Rigby & Co (Gunmakers) Ltd
131 Pall Mall, London, SW1Y 5LU, Tel: 01 734 7611

KLEINGUENTHER
Distributor: Southern Gun Co 4 Market Street, Bodmin, Cornwall, Tel: 0208 5915

KRICO
Distributor: Leslie Hewett Ltd Upton Cross, Liskeard, Cornwall, Tel: 0579 62319

MANNLICHER
Distributor: Hilton Gun Co Ltd 60 Station Road, Hatton, Derby, Tel: 0283 814488

MANURHIN
Distributor: Viking Arms Ltd Summerbridge, Harrogate, N. Yorks, Tel: 0423 780810

MARLIN
Distributor: Leslie Hewett Ltd Upton Cross, Liskeard, Cornwall, Tel: 0579 62319

MAUSER
Distributor: The Shooting Lodge Ltd 28-30 Victoria Street, Skipton, North Yorkshire, BO23 1JE, Tel: 0756 5825

MOSSBERG, .22 Sporting rifles
Distributor: Intergun PO Box 1, Probus, Nr. Truro, Cornwall, TR2 4JJ, Tel: 087 252 243

MUSGRAVE, Full bore target rifles
Distributor: G E Fulton & Son Bisley Camp, Brookwood, Woking, Surrey, Tel: 048 673204

PARKER HALE
Manufacturer: Parker Hale Ltd Golden Hillock Road, Birmingham, B11 2PZ, Tel: 021 773 8481
Sporting, Stalking and target rifles, military rifles, black powder rifles

PROCTOR
Manufacturer: T T Proctor Ltd 88A Water Lane, Wilmslow, Cheshire, Tel: 0625 526654
Sporting rifles. Restocking and overhauls of shotguns and rifles.

PURDEY
Manufacturer: James Purdey & Sons Ltd
Audley House, 57-58 South Audley Street, London, WIY 6ED, Tel: 01 499 1801

RECK
Distributor: Phoenix Arms Co Ltd Phoenix House, Churchdale Road, Eastbourne, Sussex, Tel: 0323 645131
Sporting rifle

REMINGTON
Distributor: Hull Cartridge Co Ltd Bontoft Avenue, National Avenue, Hull, HU5 4HZ, Tel: 0482 42756/445679

ROBERTS
Manufacturer: J Roberts & Son 5 King Street, Covent Garden, London, WC2, Tel: 01 240 3186
Lightweight stalking rifles and heavy calibre big game rifles

Manufacturer:
Ronald Wharton From Rigby's
100 St Martins Lane, London, WC2

RUGER
Distributor: Viking Arms Ltd Summerbridge, Harrogate, Yorks, Tel: 0423 780810

SAKO/TIKKA
Distributor: Gunmark Ltd The Armoury, Fort Wallington, Fareham, Hants, Tel: 0329 231531

SHILEN
Distributor: G L & I J Hart 46 Winchester Way, Cheltenham, Glos., Tel: 0242 519020
Target rifles

SMITH & WESSEN
Distributor: Parker Hale Ltd Golden Hillock Road, Birmingham, B11 2PZ, Tel: 021 773 8481

STEYR-MANNLICHER
Distributor: Hilton Gun Co Ltd 60 Station Road, Hatton, Derby, Tel: 0283 81488

SWING
Swing Target Rifles Ltd P O Box 17, Tonbridge, Kent, Tel: 0732 357908

TIKKA FINLAND
Distributor: JLS Arms Co Ltd Scoltock House, Perry Street, Wednesbury, WS10 0AU, Tel: 021 556 9658

UNIQUE
Distributor: Arthur E S Matthews

Epworth House, 25/35 City Road, London, EC1, Tel: 07373 50670
.22 Target rifles. Agents for Unique rifles.

VOERE (AUSTRIA) & VOERE (WEST GERMANY)
Distributor: Edgar Brothers Catherine Street, Macclesfield, Cheshire, Tel: 0625 613177

VOSTOK
Distributor: Majex (UK) 25 High Street, Egham, Surrey, Tel: 0784 31488

WALTHER
Distributor: Accuracy International (Shooting Sports) Ltd 43 Gladys Avenue, North End, Portsmouth, Hants, Tel: 0705 660371/2

WEIHRAUCH
Distributor: Edgar Brothers Catherine Street, Macclesfield, Cheshire, Tel: 0625 613177

WESTLEY RICHARDS
Manufacturer: Westley Richards Grane Road, Birmingham, Tel: 021 472 1701

WINCHESTER
Distributor: Winchester UK

Site 7, Kidderminster Road, Cutnall Green, Droitwich, Worcester, WR9 0NS, Tel: 029 923 461

CRAIG M WHITSEY
Manufacturer: Craig M Whitsey Unit D 10-12 Fitzalan Road, Arundel, West Sussex, Tel: 0903 883102

WHITWORTH
Distributor: Interarms UK Ltd 1 Worsley Street, Manchester, 15, Tel: 061 833 0701
Sporting rifles

HANDGUNS

Accuracy International Ltd

43 Gladys Avenue, North End, Portsmouth, Hants, Tel: 0705 660371/2
Distributers of Walther Pistols

Arminex UK Ltd
639 Commercial Road, London, E14, Tel: 01 790 1896

Arthur E S Matthews Ltd
Epworth House, 25/35 City Road,
London, EC1, Tel: 07373 50670
'Unique pistols'

Baytree Arms
10 Baytree Hill, Liskeard, Cornwall,
Tel: 0579 46636

Berdan (Gunmakers) Ltd
Unit 1 Rabans Close, Rabans Lane
Ind. Estate, Aylesbury, Bucks, Tel:
0296 87408

Browning Sports Ltd
37d Milton Trading Estate,
Abingdon, Oxon, OX14 4RT, Tel:
0235 833939
Browning Pistols

DAN WESSON
Matlock Inter
61-63 Smedley Street, , East Matlock
Derbyshire, Tel: 0629 3892

Duglan & Cooper Ltd
14-16 Church Street, Dunstable,
Beds, Tel; 0582 64649
LI

Edgar Brothers
Catherine Street, Macclesfield,
Cheshire, Tel: 0625 613177

**Edgcumbe Arms (Gunmakers)
Ltd**

1-11 Ramdolph Road, Parkstone,
Poole, Dorset, Tel: 0202 740743
*New Guns Super Ten Series I P.O.A.,
Super Ten Series II P.O.A., Super Ten
Series III P.O.A., New Edgcumbe
Arms Target 32. Subsidiary of Majex
(UK) Ltd.*

ERMA PISTOLS
Pennine Arms

PENNINE
SHOOTING CENTRE

Manorley Lane,, Bradford, BD6
2HF, Tel: 0274 603665
Erma Pistols

Gamebore Cartridge Co
Great Union Street, Hull, Tel: 0482
223707
*Distributors of Auto Ordnance.
Thompson 45 ACP 1911 AI Pistols*

Gunmark Ltd
The Armoury, Fort Wallington,
Fareham, Hants, Tel: 0329 231531

Intergun
PO Box 1, Probus, Truro, Cornwall,
Tel: 087252 243

John Slough of London

John Slough of London

35 Church Street, Hereford, Tel:
0432 55416

Majex (UK) Ltd
25 High Street, Egham, Surrey, Tel:
0784 31488
*Distributors of Vostok Pistols: AMT
target and combat pistols, Meister
(MP Express) target and combat
pistols; Hallocks .45 accessories,
Mihan Corp .45 ACP accessories;
Wilson .45 ACP accessories
Wilson .45 ACP combat accessories;
Carville .45 ACP accessories.*

May of London
35 Cherry Tree Rise, Buckhurst
Hill, Essex, Tel: 01 504 5946

Oliver J Gower Ltd
Unit K1, Cherrycourt Way, Stanbridge
Road, Leighton Buzzard, Beds., Tel:
0525 377730

ORIGINAL
Frank Dyke & Co Ltd
1/7 Ernest Avenue, West Norwood,
London, SE27 ODG, Tel: 01 670 2224

PANTHER
Distributor: Phoenix Arms Co Ltd
Phoenix House, Churchdale Road,
Eastbourne, Sussex, Tel: 0323 645131

PARDINI/FIOCCHI
Hull Cartridge Co
Bontoft Avenue, National Avenue,
Hull, North Humberside, HU5 4HZ,
TEL: 0482 42756/445679

Parker Hale Ltd
Golden Hillock Road, Birmingham,
B11 2PZ, Tel: 021 773 8481

Pat Walker Guns
143 Alexandra Road, Gateshead,
Tyne & Wear, Tel: 0632 786736
*Sole importers of IMI (Israeli Military
Industries) Uzi, Mini, Uzi, Desert
Eagle Pistols*

Phoenix Arms Co Ltd
Phoenix House, Churchdale Road,
Eastbourne, Sussex, Tel: 0323 645131

PRACTISPORT/ARMALON
Practisport
44 Harrowby Street, London, W1H
5HX , Tel: 01 262 1881

Precision Arms Co
Unit One, 2 Maidstone Road, Paddock
Wood, Tunbridge, Kent, Tel: 089283
6622

RELUM TORNADO
Manufacturer: Relum Ltd
5 Chalk Farm Road, London, NW1
8AD, Tel: 01 267 0171

SAKO
JLS Arms Co Ltd
Scoltock House, Perry Street,
Wednesbury, W. Midlands, Tel: 021
556 9658/1322

SLAVIA
Distributor: Edgar Brothers
Catherine Street, Macclesfield,
Cheshire, Tel: 0625 613177

Springfield Fire Arms Ltd
8 Eastbourne Road, St. Austell,
Cornwall, Tel: 0726 72733

STERLING
**Manufacturer: Sterling Armament Co
Ltd**
Rainham Road, South Dagenham,
Essex, Tel: 01 595 2226

Distributor: Surrey Guns Ltd
9 Manor Road, Wallington, Surrey,
SM6 OBZ, Tel: 01 647 0017
*Distributors of Vincenzo Bernardelli
pistols and Arminius pistols*

UNIQUE
Arthur E S Matthews Ltd

Epworth House, 25-35 City Road,
London, EC1Y 1AR, Tel: 07373
50670
Agents for Unique pistols.

Viking Arms Ltd
Summerbridge, Harrogate, N. Yorks,
HG3 4BW, Tel: 0423 780810

WALTHER
**Distributor: Accuracy International
(Shooting Sports) Ltd**

43 Gladys Avenue, North End,
Portsmouth, Hants, Tel: 0705
660371/2

WEBLEY
Manufacturer: Webley & Scott Ltd
Frankley Industrial Park, Tay Road,
Rubery, Birmingham, B45 OPA,
Tel: 021 453 1864

WEIHRAUCH
Distributor: Edgar Brothers
Catherine Street, Macclesfield,
Cheshire, Tel: 0625 613177

AIR WEAPONS

Air Logic Ltd
3 Medway Buildings, Lower Road,
Forest Row, Sussex, Tel: 034282 4433
Whisperer airgun silencer

ANSCHUTZ
Distributor: Frank Dyke & Co Ltd
1/7 Ernest Avenue, West Norwood,
London, SE27 0BG, Tel: 01 670 2224

ASI
Distributor: A.S.I. Alliance House
Snape, Saxmundham, Suffolk, Tel: 072
888555

BAIKAL
Distributor: Air Arms
Station Road Industrial Estate,
Hailsham, E.Sussex, Tel: 0323 845853

BAIKAL
Distributor: Sports Marketing
13 Grange Way, Whitehall Road,
Colchester, Essex, Tel: 0206 65333

Baytree Arms
10 Baytree Hill, Liskeard, Cornwall,
Tel: 0579 46636

BSA
Manufacturer: BSA Guns Ltd
Birmingham
PCB11 2PX
Tel: 021 773 0845

The Country Gunshop
Lissiesleaf, Melrose, Roxburghshire,
Tel: 0835 7315

CROSMAN AIR GUNS
Manufacturer: Crosman Air Guns
Unit 2, Parish Wharf Estate, Harbour
Road, Portishead, Bristol, Tel: 0272
845024

CROSMAN AIR GUNS
Distributor: Scalemead Arms Co
3 Medway Buildings, Lower Road,
Forest Row, Sussex, Tel: 034282 4433

DAYSTATE
Manufacturer: Daystate Limited
Newcastle Street, Stone, Staffs, Tel:
0785 812473

EL GAMO
Distributor: A.S.I. Alliance House
Snape Maltings, Saxmundham, Suffolk,
Tel: 072 888 555

FAS
Distributor: Oliver J Gower Ltd
Unit K1, Cherrycourt Way, Stanbridge
Road, Leighton Buzzard, Beds., Tel:
0525 377730

FEINWERKBAU
Distributor: ASI
Alliance House, Snape Maltings,
Saxmundham, Suffolk, Tel: 072 888555

GALAXY
Manufacturer: Saxby & Palmer
3 Swan Industrial Estate, Avenue Farm,
Birmingham Road, Stratford on Avon,
Tel: 0789 298830

GAT
Distributor: Oliver J Gower Ltd
Unit K1, Cherrycourt Way, Stanbridge
Road, Leighton Buzzard, Beds., Tel:
0525 377730

GOLD CUP SPORTING MATCH
Manufacturer: Phoenix Arms Co Ltd
Phoenix House, Churchdale Road,
Eastbourne, Sussex, Tel: 0323 645131
Air rifle

HAENEL
Distributor: Viking Arms Ltd
Summerbridge, Harrogate, Yorks, Tel:
0423 780810

HOT SHOT AIR PISTOL
Distributor: Scalemead Ltd
3 Medway Buildings, Lower Road,
Forest Row, Sussex, Tel: 034282 4433

Hull Cartridge Co
Bontoft Avenue, National Avenue,
Hull, Tel: 0482 42756/445679

LINCOLN
Distributor: David Nickerson
(Tathwell) Ltd
The Old Vicarage, Tathwell, Louth,
Lincs, Tel: 0472 840530

MANUARM
Distributor: Oliver J Gower Ltd
Unit K1, Cherrycourt Way, Stanbridge
Road, Leighton Buzzard, Beds., Tel:
0525 377730

MAUSER
Manufacturer: Phoenix Arms Co Ltd
Phoenix House, Churchdale Road,
Eastbourne, Sussex, Tel: 0323 645131

May of London
35 Cherry Tree Rise, Buckhurst
Hill, Essex, Tel: 01 504 5946

Optima Leisure Products Ltd
Gilnow Mill, Spa Road, Bolton,
Lancs, BL1 4LF, Tel: 0204 386899

PANTHER
Manufacturer: Phoenix Arms Co Ltd
Phoenix House, Churchdale Road,
Eastbourne, Sussex, Tel: 0323 645131

RECORD
Distributor: John Rothery
(Wholesale) Co Ltd

*John Rothery & Co.
(Wholesale) Ltd*

22 Stamshaw Road
Portsmouth, Hants
Tel: 0705 667323

RWS/DIANA
Distributor: Leslie Hewett Ltd
Upton Cross, Liskeard, Cornwall,
Tel: 0579 62319

SHARP
Hull Cartridge Co
Bontoft Avenue, National Avenue,
Hull, North Humberside, HU5 4HZ,
Tel: 0482 42756/445679

SIROCCO
Manufacturer: Theoben Engineering
Stephenson Road, St Ives,
Huntingdon, Cambs, PE17 4WJ
*Manufacturers of Sirocco air rifle
using unique Theoben power system.*

SOFT
Battle Orders
71 Eastbourne Road, Lower
Willingdon, Eastbourne, East Sussex,
Tel: 032 12 7309
*H & K SD3 Mini Custom U21 S & W
59 KG9 all these and more available
as pellet firing replicas.*

WALTHER
Distributor: Accuracy International
Ltd
43 Gladys Avenue, Northend,
Portsmouth, Hants. PO2 9AZ. Tel:
0705 660371
*Distributors of walther air rifles and
air pistols*

WEBLEY
Manufacturer: Webley & Scott
Frankley Industrial Park, Tay Road,
Rubery, Birmingham, B45 0PA,
Tel: 021 453 1864

WEIRAUCH
Distributor: Edgar Brothers
Catherine Street, Macclesfield,
Cheshire, Tel: 0625 613171

WEIHRAUCH
Distributor: Hull Cartridge Co
Bontoft Avenue, National Avenue,
Hull, North Humberside, HU5 4HZ,
Tel: 0482 42756/445679

SHOTGUN AMMUNITION

BAIKAL
Distributor: Sports Marketing
13 Grange Way, Whitehall Road,
Colchester, Essex, Tel: 0206 65333

Baytree Arms
10 Baytree Hill, Liskeard, Cornwall,
Tel: 0579 46636

BOSS
Manufacturer: Boss & Co Ltd
13 Dover Street, London, W1, Tel: 01
493 1127/0711

British Sports
107 Praed Street, Paddington,
London, W2, Tel: 01 402 7511
*Stockists of all @types of shotguns,
rifles, handguns, air guns, cartridges
and ammunition. Replica weapons
and clothing also available. Export
enquiries welcome. Open 9.00 - 6.00
Mon-Sat.*

BROWNING
Manufacturer: Browning Sports Ltd
37D Milton Trading Estate, Milton,
Abingdon, Oxon, OX14 4RT, Tel:
0235 833939

CALEDONIAN
Manufacturer: Caledonian Cartridge
Co
Arrat Works, Brechin, Angus, Tel:
067481 342
*Top quality game and trap cartridges -
the top cartridges for top shots.*

**CHEDDITE (FORMERLY
GEVELOT)**
Distributor: Gamebore Cartridge Co
great Union Street, Hull, N.
Humberside, Tel: 0482 223707,
Telex: 527185 GABOR G

COUNTY
Distributor: H S Greenfield & Son
4-5 Upper Bridge Street, Canterbury,
Kent, Tel: 0227 456959

Distributor: Dan-Arms Ltd
8a Cannock Road, Burntwood,
Staffs, Tel: 05436 76638

EATON MASCOTT
Distributor: South Shropshire Game
Farm
Eaton Mascott Hall, Cross Houses,
Shrewsbury, Tel: 074375 540

ELEY
Manufacturer: Eley
PO Box 705, Witton, Birmingham,
B6 7UT, Tel: 021 356 8899

FEDERAL
Distributor: Viking Arms Ltd
Summerbridge, Harrogate, N. Yorks,
Tel: 0423 780810

F.D.
Manufacturer: Frank Dyke & Co Ltd
1-7 Ernest Avenue, West Norwood,
London, SE27 ODG, Tel: 01 670 2224

FIOCCHI
Distributor: Hull Cartridge Co Ltd
Bontoft Avenue, National Avenue,
North Humberside, HU5 4HZ, Tel:
0482 42756/445679

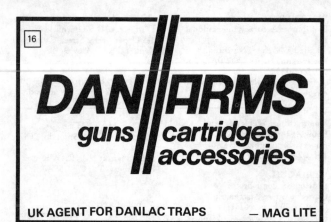

16

DAN ARMS
guns cartridges accessories

UK AGENT FOR DANLAC TRAPS — **MAG LITE**

GAMEBORE
Manufacturer: Gamebore Cartridge
Co

Gamebore

Established 1973

Great Union Street, Hull, North
Humberside, Tel: 0482 223707,
Telex: 527185 GABOR G

HULL
Manufacturer: Hull Cartridge Co Ltd
Bontoft Avenue, National Avenue,
Hull N.Humberside, HU5 4HZ,
0482 42756/445679

INTERSTATE
Manufacturer: Interstate Cartridges
Great Western Road, Martock
Industrial Estate, Martock, Somerset,
Tel: 0935 823201
*A complete range of shotgun cartridges
manufactured in Somerset from the
best components. Available
nationwide. Telephone above for
details and nearest stockist.*

KENT
Manufacturer: Kent Cartridge
Manufacturing Co Ltd
Branbridges Industrial Estate, East
Peckham, Tonbridge, Kent, TN12 5HF,
Tel: 0622 872255

KENTISH FIRE
Distributor: H S Greenfield & Son
4-5 Upper Bridge Streett, Canterbury,
Kent, Tel: 0227 456959

MAIONCHI
Distributor: Mediterranean Shooting
Supplies Ltd
P O Box 7, Evesham, Worcs.,
WR11 6YT, Tel: 0386 3654
*Sole distributor of Maionchi shotgun
cartridges.*

MARCH
Distributor: A.W. Wright & Sons,
Fenland Gunsmith Ltd
98 Creek Road, March, PE15 8RD,
Tel: 0354 53290

MSS
Distributor: Mediterranean Shooting
Supplies Ltd
Four Pools Industrial Estate,
Evesham, Worcs., WR11 6XJ, Tel:
0386 3654, Telex: 335286 MEDSS
G
*Sole distributor of MSS Special Game
cartridges.*

Distributor: David Nickerson
(Tathwell) Ltd
Tathwell, Louth, Lincs, LN11 9ST,
Tel: 0472 840536

NIKE
Distributor: Viking Arms Ltd
Summerbridge, Harrogate, N.Yorks,
Tel: 0423 780810

PHILLIPS
Manufacturer: Phillips Game
Technology Ltd
Unit 16, Branbridges Ind Est, Peckham,
Tonbridge, Kent, Tel: 0622 872255

RAKER
Raker Cartridges
2 Jocelyn Court, Burntmills Ind Est,
Basildon, Essex, Tel: 0268 727689

ROTTWEIL
Distributor: Leslie Hewett Ltd
Upton Cross, Liskeard, Cornwall,
Tel: 0579 62319

RW
Distributor: Ray Ward (Gunsmith)
41 Holland Close, Redhill, Surrey, Tel:
0737 66715

SELLIER AND BELLOT
Distributor: Edgar Brothers
Catherine Street, Macclesfield,
Cheshire, Tel: 0625 613177

SMI
Distributor: SSM International
Tedstone Wafre, Nr. Bromyard,
Herefordshire, Tel: 08867 646 &
284

SUN
Distributor: Mediterranean Shooting
Supplies Ltd
Four Pools Industrial Estate,
Evesham, Worcs, WR11 6XJ, Tel:
0386 3654, Telex: 335286 MEDSS
G
*Sole distributors of Sun shotgun
cartridge.*

THREE CROWNS
Manufacturer: Hull Cartridge Co Ltd
Bontoft Avenue, National Avenue,
Hull, N.Humberside, Tel: 0482 42756/
445679

TOPMARK & KENT
Manufacturer: Kent Cartridge
Manufacturing Co Ltd
Branbridges Industrial Estate, East
Peckham, Tonbridge, Kent, TN12 5HF

TOPMARK & KENT
Distributor: David Nickerson
(Tathwell) Ltd
North Ormsby, Louth, Lincs, LN11
9ST, Tel: 0472 840536

WILLIAM POWELL
Manufacturer: William Powell &
Son (Gunmakers) Ltd
35/37 Carrs Lane, Birmingham, B4
7SX, Tel: 021 643 0689/8362

WINCHESTER
Manufacturer: Winchester UK

WINCHESTER.

Site 7, Kidderminster Road, Cutnall
Green, Droitwich, Worcs., WR9
ONS, Tel: 0299 23461

RIFLE & PISTOL AMMUNITION

British Sports
107 Praed Street, Paddington,
London, W2, 01 402 7511

*Stockists of all types of shotguns, rifles,
handguns, air guns, cartridges and
ammunition. Replica weapons and
clothing also available. Export
enquires welcome. Open 9.00 - 6.00
Mon-Sat.*

Edgar Brothers
Catherine Street, Macclesfield,
Cheshire, SK11 6SG, Tel: 0625 613177

ELEY
Eley
PO Box 705, Witton, Birmingham,
B6 7UT, Tel: 021 356 8899

Empire Arms Co
14 Empire Parade, Great Cambridge
Road, Edmonton, London, N18
1AA, Tel: 01 807 3802
*Vintage and modernn ammunition.
Lee, R.C.B.S. loading equipment.
Lyman, CCI primers, hard cast heads.
Manufacturers of ammunition
including 455; (Discounts on 1000).
D.P.M. and waterproofs. Repairs/
gunservicing by qualified gunsmith.*

FEDERAL
Distributor: Viking Arms Ltd
Summerbridge, Harrogate, Yorks, Tel:
0423 780810

FIOCCHI
Distributor: Hull Cartridge Co Ltd
Bontoft Avenue, National Avenue,
Hull, North Humberside, HU5 4HZ,
Tel: 0482 42756/445679

GECO
Distributor: Leslie Hewett Ltd
Upton Cross, Liskeard, Cornwall,
Tel: 0579 62319

LAPUA
Distributor: Accuracy International

43 Gladys Avenue, North End,
Portsmouth, Hants, Tel: 0705
660371/2

LAWSON LEAD CAST BULLETS
R S Lawson Firearms &
Ammunition
Great Western Road, Martock Ind Est,
Martock, Tel: 0935 823201

MOUNTAIN & SOWDEN LTD
Mountain & Sowden Ltd
PO Box 5, Horsforth, Leeds, LS18
5TH, Tel: 0532 58266

NORMA
Distributor: Parker-Hale Ltd
Golden Hillock Road, Birmingham,
B11 2PZ, Tel: 021 773 8481

NOSLER
Modern & Antique Firearms
147 Tuckton Road, Southbourne,
Bournemouth, Dorset, BH6 3JZ,
Tel: 0202 429369

REMINGTON
Distributor: Hull Cartridge Co Ltd
Bontoft Avenue, National Avenue,
Hull, Tel: 0482 42756/445679

RWS
Distributor: Leslie Hewett Ltd
Upton Cross, Liskeard, Cornwall,
Tel: 0579 62319

SAKO
Distributor: JLS Arms Co Ltd
Scoltock House, Perry Street,
Wednesbury, W.Midlands, Tel: 021
556 9658/1322

SAMSON
Distributor: Conjay Arms
118 Craven Park Road, London,
NW10, Tel: 01 965 7116

SELLIER & BELLOT
Distributor: Edgar Brothers
Catherine Street, Macclesfield, Tel:
0625 613177

VOSTOCK
Distributor: Majex (UK) Ltd
25 High Street, Egham, Surrey, Tel:
0784 31488

WINCHESTER
Distributor: Winchester UK, Site 7

WINCHESTER.

Kidderminster Road, Cutnall Green,
Droitwich, Worcester, WR9 ONS,
Tel: 029 923 461

AIRGUN PELLETS

Baytree Arms
10 Baytree Hill, Liskeard, Cornwall,
Tel: 0579 46636

BSA
BSA Guns Ltd
Birmingham, B11 2PX, Tel: 021 773
0845

CALEDONIAN

milbro

Manufacturer: Milbro Caledonian
Pellet Co
Carfin Industrial Estate, Black 4
Unit 4,G., Motherwell, Lanarkshire,
Tel: 0698 732411
*Manufacturers of Caledonian pellets,
air gun darts and targets*

CHAMPION
Manufacturer: L J Cammell
(Merseyside) Ltd
53 Borrowdale Road, Moreton, Wirral,
Merseyside, L46 ORE, Tel: 051 677
6689

CHAMPION
Distributor: Cobra Arms International
Ltd
53 Borrowdale Road, Moveton, Wirral,
Merseyside, Tel: 051 677 6689

CROSMAN
Manufacturer: Crosman Air Guns
Unit 2, Parish Wharf Estate, Harbour
Road, Portishead, Bristol, Tel: 0272
845024

CROSMAN
Distributor: Scalemead Arms Co
3 Medway Buildings, Lower Road,
Forest Row, Sussex, Tel: 034282 4433

DIABLO
Distributor: Abbey Supply Co
197 Great Knollys Street, Reading,
RG1 7HA, Tel: 0734 584767

ELEY
Distributor: Eley
PO Box 705, Witton, Birmingham,
B6 7UT, Tel: 021 356 8899

EL GAMO
Distributor: A.S.I. Alliance House
Snape Maltings, Saxmundham, Suffolk,
Tel: 072 888 555

HAENDLER & NATERMAN
Distributor: Frank Dyke & Co Ltd
1/7 Ernest Avenue, West Norwood,
London, SE27 ODG, Tel: 01 670 2224

HUSTLER
Distributor: Scalemead Arms Co
3 Medway Buildings, Lower Road,
Forest Row, Sussex, Tel: 034 282 4433

JACKAL JETS
Distributor: Phoenix Arms Company
Limited
Phoenix House, Churchdale Road,
Eastbourne, Sussex, Tel: 0323 645131

MARKSMAN
Manufacturer: Lincoln Jeffries
54/56 Summer Lane, Birmingham, B19
3TH, Tel: 021 359 3343

NICKERSON
Distributor: David Nickerson
(Tathwell) Ltd
The Old Vicarage, Tathwell, Louth,
Lincs, Tel: 0472 840536

PROMETHEUS
Manufacturer: Pax Guns Ltd
166 Archway Road, London, N6,
Tel: 01 340 3039

PROMETHEUS
Distributor: John Knibbs
Gillia Blackfirs Lane, Bickenhill,
W.Midlands, Tel: 021 779 3391

RWS
Distributor: Leslie Hewett Ltd
Upton Cross, Liskeard, Cornwall,
Tel: 0579 62319

SABO
Distributor: Westhaven Marketing
Ltd
Unit 3, Manor Industrial Park,
Manor House Avenue, Millbrook,
Southampton, Tel: 0703 780505

SAXBY & PALMER
Manufacturer: Saxby &
Palmer(Manufacturers)
3 Swan Industrial Estate, Avenue Farm
Birmingham Road, Stratford on
Avon, Tel: 0789 298830

TITAN BLACK
Titan Airgun Products
98 Bath Street, Birmingham, B4 6HG,
Tel: 021 779 3391
Manufacturer and Distributor

WEBLEY
Manufacturer: Webley & Scott Ltd
Frankley Industrial Park, Tay Road,
Rubery, Birmingham, B45 OPA,
Tel: 021 453 1864

RELOADING

Accuracy International
(Shooting Sports) Ltd

43 Gladys Avenue, North End,
Portsmouth, Hants, Tel: 0705
660371/2
*Distributers of Bonanza reloading
equipment, SIERRA bullets, Lapua
ammunition and reloading
components*
Manufacturer: Ballistic Precision Ltd
PO Box 172, Birmingham, Tel: 021 233
1640

Manufacturers of bullets and ammunition components

Ballistic Products UK
6 Whitewell, Catterall , Garstang, Lancs, Tel: 09952 4251
UK agents for Ithaca 'Mag Ten'

Caer Urfa Guns and Ammo
399 Stanhope Road, South Shields, Tyne and Wear, Tel: 0632 551045

Caisson Supplies Ltd
91-95 Nottinghill Gate, London, W11 3JZ, Tel: 01-727-0530, Telex: 24301 G
Distributors of Dillon Precision Products Inc (Factory Appointed

European Warrenty Centre) and RDP Progressive (Sole European Distributor)

Davies of Bolton
128 Deane Road, Bolton, Gtr.Manchester, Tel: 0204 24893
Good selection of reloading equipment available

Dillon Precision Products Inc
Practisport, 44 Harronby Street, London, WIH 5HX, Tel: 01 262 1881

Edgar Brothers
Catherine Street, Macclesfield, Cheshire, Tel: 0625 613177

Edgcumbe Arms (Gunmakers) Ltd
1/11 Randolph Road, Parkstone, Poole, Dorset, Tel: 0202 740743
General Gunsmithing and reloading services available. Subsidiary of Majex (UK) Ltd.

Empire Arms Co
14 Empire Parade, Great Cambridge Road, Edmonton, London, N18 1AA, Tel: 01 807 3802
Vintage and modern ammunition. Lee, R.C.B.S. loading equipment. Lyman, CCI primers, hard cast heads. Manufacturers of ammunition including 455; (Discounts on 1000). D.P.M. and waterproofs. Repairs/gunservicing by qualified gunsmith.

Francis Bros.
49 Roberts Street, Rushden, Northants, Tel: 09334 311760

Frank Dyke & Co Ltd
1/7 Ernest Avenue, West Norwood, London, SW27 ODG, Tel: 01 670 2224

Gamebore Cartridge Co

Gamebore

Established 1973

Industrial Estate, Great Union Street, Hull, Tel: 0482 223707
Sole distributors of:SNPE Vectan AO, A1 and as shotgun powders BA5, BA9 and BA10 pistol powders 12G original brenneke slug heads and 8 bore plastic wads

F Hall (Gunmakers) Ltd
Beetwell Street, Chesterfield, Derbyshire, Tel: 0246 73133
Makers of special purpose reloading tools. Suppliers of all types of components

C H Haygarth & Sons
The Cottage Gun Shop, Dunnet, Caithness, Tel: 084785 602

Hull Cartridge Co Ltd
Bontoft Avenue, National Avenue, Hull, N.Humberside, HU5 4HZ, Tel: 0482 42756/445679

Intergun
PO Box 1, Probus, Nr. Truro, Cornwall, TR2 4JJ, Tel: 087 252 243

Jack Laurance Bowes Ltd
4 Third Avenue, Luton, Chatham, Kent, Tel: 0634 407805

Leslie Hewett Ltd
Upton Cross, Liskeard, Cornwall, Tel: 0579 62319
Lyman reloading equipment and case preparation equipment. RWS components

Marper R D
Cleatham, Kirton Lindsey, Gainsborough, Lincs, Tel: 0652 648466
Muzzle loading and large bore reloading equipment a speciality. Suppliers of Turner Richards gundog equipment

Mediterranean Shooting Supplies
PO Box 7, Evesham, Worcestershire., WR11 6YT, Tel: 0386 3654, Telex: 335286 MEDSS G
Sole distributors of Martignoni empty cases.

Modern & Antique Firearms
147 Tuckton Road, Southbourne, Bournemouth, BH6 3JZ
Suppliers of all reloading equipment and accessories

Mountain & Sowden Ltd
PO Box 5, Horsforth, Leeds, LS18 5TH, Tel: 0532 582666

North Devon Firearms Services
3 North Street, Braunton, Devon, Tel: 0271 813624

Oliver J Gower Ltd
Unit K1, Cherry Court Way, Stanbridge Road, Leighton Buzzard, Beds, Tel: 0525 377730

Parker-Hale Ltd
Golden Hillock Road,, Birmingham, B11 2PZ, Tel: 021 773 8481

Peter Dyson Ltd
29-31 Church Street, Honley, Huddersfield, Tel: 0484 661062

Plaswads Ltd
155 Atteborough Lane, Attenborough, Beeston, Nottingham, Tel: 0602 221233

Prime Reloading Co
30 Chiswick End, Meldreth, Royston, Herts, Tel: 0763 60636

Propellant Powders Ltd
48 Crown Street, Reading, Berkshire, Tel: 0491 680487

Sheldon Bush & Patent Shot Co Ltd
Cheese Lane, Bristol, B52 OJL, Tel: 0272 20636

SSM International
Tedstone Wafre, Nr Bromyard, Herefordshire, Tel: 08867 646 & 284
Distributors of SNIA powders and wads

Thomas Bland & Sons (Gunmakers) Ltd
22-22 New Row, St Martins Lane, London, WC2, Tel: 01 836 9122

Tim Hannam
The Granary, Wakefield Road, Swillington, Leeds, LS26 8UA, Tel: 0532 862175

Viking Arms Ltd
Summerbridge, Harrogate, Yorks, Tel: 0423 780810

Wamadet
Silver Springs, Goodleigh, Barnstaple, Devon, Tel: 0271 71194

Winchester UK

WINCHESTER.

Cutnall Green, Droitwich, Worcester, Tel: 0299 23461

RIFLE & PISTOL RANGES

Aylestone Gun Co, Pistol Range
Shearsby Spa, Leicestershire, Tel: 0533 832828
For specialist sales and service

Exelair Shooting Club
346 Sheffield Road, Birdwell, Barnsley, S Yorks, Tel: 0226 747107

Norfolk Gun Trading Co Range
Thornham Range, Thornham, Norfolk, Tel: 04853 33600

Pennine Indoor Pistol Range
Manorley Lane, Bradford, Tel: 0274 603665

Wednesbury Marksmen
Scoltock House, Perry Street, Wednesbury, W. Midlands, Tel: 021 556 9658/1322
Handgun training courses a speciality from beginner to expert

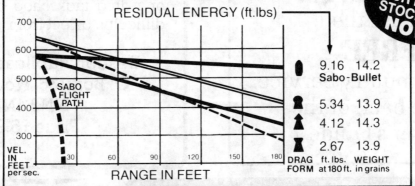

SHOTGUNS

MAKE	MODEL inc over/ under, side/ side	GAUGE	CHAMBER	ACTION eg side lock, box lock, plus ejectors	BARREL LENGTH	OVERALL WEIGHT	APPROX RETAIL PRICE	COMMENTS
A.Y.A. Distributors **A.S.I.** Tel: 072888 555	No. 1 s/s	12, 16, 20 28, .410	—	Sidelock ejector	—	—	From £2115.00	Specifications made to special order
	No. 2 s/s	12, 16, 20 28, .410	2¾" (.410 3")	Sidelock ejector	26" or 28"	—	From £929.00	20, 28 and .410 models have 27" barrels
	No. 3 s/s	12, 16, 20 28, .410	2¾" (.410 3")	Boxlock non ejector	26" or 28"	—	From £357.50	20, 28 and .410 models have 27" barrels
	No. 3 Magnum s/s	12	3"	—	29"	—	£390.60	—
	No. 4 s/s	12, 16, 20 28, .410	2¾" (.410 3")	Boxlock ejector	26" or 28"	—	From £460.00	20, 28 and .410 models have 27" barrels
	Best Quality Boxlock	12, 20, 28	2¾"	Boxlock ejector	27"	—	From £895.00	
	25" s/s	12, 20	2¾"	Sidelock ejector	25"	—	From £1315.00	
	25" s/s	12, 20	2¾"	Boxlock ejector	25"	—	From £815.00	
	Yeoman s/s	12	2¾"	Boxlock ejector or non ejector	28"	—	£335.00 £279.00	Ejector Non ejector
	Coral 'A' o/u	12, 16	2¾"	Boxlock ejector	28"	—	From £1021.30	Single selective trigger extra £76.00
	Coral 'B' o/u	12	2¾"	Boxlock ejector	28"	—	From £1137.50	Single selective trigger extra £76.00
	37 Super o/u A, B, C	—	—	Sidelock ejector			From £3320.10 to £4316.50	
	Augusta o/u	—	—	Sidelock ejector			£4281.35	
	79 Super o/u A, B, C	—	—	Boxlock ejector			From £787.10 to £1374.15	
	Cosmos single barrel	12, 16, 20 .410	2¾"/3"	—	28" or 30"	—	£137.65	
	Matador o/u	12, 20	2¾"	Boxlock ejector	26" or 28"	—	£541.50	
	Matador o/u	10	3½"	Boxlock ejector	32"	—	£512.50	
BRNO Distributors **Edgar Brothers** Catherine Street, Macclesfield SK11 6SG Tel: 0625 613177	ZP49 s/s	12	2¾"	Sidelock ejector	28"	app 6½lbs	N/A	Solid rib
	ZH301 o/u	12	2¾"	Boxlock n/e	28"	app 7¼lbs	N/A	Vent rib
	ZH302	12	2¾"	Boxlock n/s	26" Skeet with Muzzle Brakes	app 7lbs	N/A	Solid rib
	Field Grade s/s	12	2¾"	Boxlock n/e	26"	app 6½lbs	N/A	Solid rib
BROWNING Manufacturers **Browning Sports Ltd,** 37d Milton Trading Estate, Milton, Abingdon, Oxford Tel: 0235 833939	205	12	2¾"	Boxlock	27½"	7lbs 3oz	£2070+	All Browning B25s are available in different grades of finish
	206	12	2¾"	Boxlock	30"	7lb 10oz	£2070+	
	Trap 2 & 6	12	2¾"	Boxlock	30"	7lb 10oz/7lb 11oz	£2070+	Trap 2 has 16mm rib. Trap 6 has 12mm
	Skeet 105	12	2¾"	Boxlock	27½"	7lb 3oz	£2070+	
	Game 13	12, (20)	2¾"	Boxlock	27½" (26")	6lb 10oz (6lb 1oz)	£2500+	Swan neck stock. Narrow tapered rib
	B125 Sport	12	2¾"	Boxlock	28"	3.4kg	£1625	Pistol grip stock.'Invector Choke System'
	B125 Game	12	2¾"	Boxlock	27½"	3.0kg	£1625	Swan neck stock. 'Invector Choke System'
	B80	12	2¾"	Gas-auto	28"	3.5kg	£435	Available with or without invector choke system
	BPS	12	3"	Pump	28"	3.5kg	£490	3" mag. bottom ejection, shotgun safety
CITORI RANGE	Trap High Rib	12	2¾"	Boxlock	30"	7lb	£895	Top barrel has normal full choke. Bottom barrel has Browning 'Invector choke'.
	Trap Low Rib	12	2¾"	Boxlock	30"	8lb	£1065	New Browning style trap stocks.
	Sporting 1	12	2¾"	Boxlock	28"	7lb 8oz	£895	)
	Grade 3	12	2¾"	Boxlock	28"	7lb 8oz	£1195	) All with 'Invector choke system'
	5	12	2¾"	Boxlock	28"	7lb 8oz	£1500	) 13mm RVR.

SHOTGUNS cont.

MAKE	MODEL inc over/ under, side/ side	GAUGE	CHAMBER	ACTION eg side lock, box lock, plus ejectors	BARREL LENGTH	OVERALL WEIGHT	APPROX RETAIL PRICE	COMMENTS
BROWNING cont.	Game Grade 1	12	2¾″	Boxlock	28″	6lb 12oz	£895	6.2mm RVR)
	3	12	2¾″	Boxlock	28″	6lb 12oz	£1195	6.2mm RVR) All with 'Invector
	3	20	2¾″	Boxlock	28″	6lb	£1195	5.5mm RVR) chokes'. Auto safe.
	5	12	2¾″	Boxlock	28″	6lb 12oz	£1500	6.2mm RVR)
A A BROWN & SONS Manufacturer A A Brown & Sons 1 Snake Lane, Alvechurch, Birmingham B48 7NT Tel: 021 445 5395	Supreme De Luxe s/s	12, 16, 20 28, .410	2½″ or 2¾″	Self opening Sidelock ejector	25″ to 30″	12 bore 6lb 2oz to 6lb 8oz	From £7500	Self, easy or standard opening Choice of barrel lengths, chokes, ribs, bore, stocks, engraving etc.
	"Best" s/s	12	2½″ or 2¾″	Self opening Boxlock ejector	25″ to 30″	12 bore 6lb 2oz to 6lb 8oz	From £4000	Self, easy or standard opening Choice of barrel lengths, chokes, ribs, bore, stocks, engraving etc.
DAN ARMS	Game o/u	12	3″ Mag	Boxlock ST ejector	26″ or 28″		£300	Non ejector and double trigger available
	Sporter o/u	12	3″ Mag	Boxlock ST ejector	30″		£300	Non ejector available
	Trap o/u	12	2¾″	Boxlock ST ejector	30″		£450	—
	Skeet o/u	12	2¾″	Boxlock ST ejector	26″		£450	—
	Multichoke o/u	12	3″ Mag	Boxlock ST ejector	28″		£410	—
	Game o/u	20	3″ Mag	Boxlock ST ejector	28″		£300	—
	Imperial Game s/s	12	3″ Mag	Boxlock DT NE	28″		£250	—
	Imperial Game s/s	20	3″ Mag	Boxlock DT NE	28″		£250	—
DENTON & KENNELL Manufacturers Denton & Kennell, West Street, Somerton, Somerset Tel:0458 73732	Folding Hammer	.410	3″	Folding	28″		From £69	Single barrel & double barrel available
	De-Luxe s/s	12, 16, 20 28, .410	2¾″ (.410 3″)	Boxlock non ejector	26″ 27″ 28″		From £169	
	De-Luxe s/s	12, 16, 20 28, .410	2¾″ (.410 3″)	Boxlock ejector	26″ 27″ 28″		From £215	
	Best Grade s/s	12, 20	2¾″	Boxlock non ejector	25″ 28″		From £198	25″ has Churchill rib
	Best Grade s/s	12, 20	2¾″	Boxlock ejector	25″ 28″		From £239	25″ has Churchill rib
	No. 3 Magnum s/s	12	3″	Boxlock ejector or non ejector	30″		From £198	Pistol grip Beavertail forend
	Silverpoint o/u	12, 20	2¾″	Boxlock non ejector	26″ 28″		From £201	Available D/T S/T or SST
	Silverpoint o/u	12, 20	2¾″	Boxlock ejector	26″ 28″		From £249	D/T, S/T or SST 20g available with 3″ chambers
	Silverpoint Grade 2 s/s	12	2¾″	Sidelock ejector	28″		£269	
	Silverpoint Best Grade s/s	12, 20	2¾″	Sidelock non ejector	27″		£239	
	Silverpoint Best Grade s/s	12, 20,16	2¾″	Sidelock ejector	25″ 27″ 28″		From £315	Single trigger £75 extra
	Braemar s/s	12, 16, 20	2¾″	Sidelock ejector	28″		£375	Single trigger £75 extra
	Silverpoint s/s (2 B) (2 sets barrels)	12	2¾″	Sidelock ejector	25″/28″		£465	Price includes 2 sets barrels
	Blackpoint s/s	12, 20	2¾″	Sidelock ejector	27″ 28″ 25″		From £425	
	Black Classic s/s	12, 20	2¾″	Sidelock ejector	27″ 28″		From £485	Totally hand engraved
	Richmond s/s	12, 20	2¾″	Sidelock ejector	28″		£465	
	Black Game s/s	12, 20	2¾″	Sidelock ejector	27″ 28″		£690	Lightweight All hand engraved
	Windsor s/s	12, 20, 16	2¾″	Sidelock ejector	27″ 28″		£690	Rounded action
	No. 1 Best Grade	12, 20	2¾″	Sidelock ejector	25″ 27″ 28″		£1250	Hand built Assisted opener available

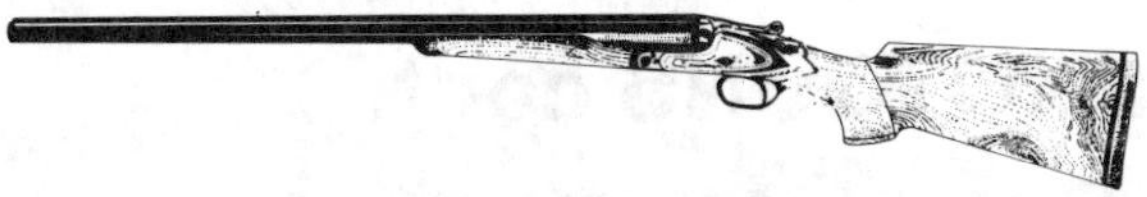

SHOTGUNS cont.

MAKE	MODEL Inc over/ under, side/ side	GAUGE	CHAMBER	ACTION eg side lock, box lock, plus ejectors	BARREL LENGTH	OVERALL WEIGHT	APPROX RETAIL PRICE	COMMENTS
FABARM Distributor Leslie Hewett Ltd, Tel: 0579 62319	Gamma o/u	12	2¾"	Boxlock ejector	27" to 29"	6.2 kg to 7.8 kg	£479.22 to £567.73	Trap, and Sporting versions
	Ellegi Multichoke	12	2¾"	Gas op. auto	24"	6.9 kg	£371.29	Multichoke
	Ellegi Mag.	12	3"	Auto	30"/32"	7.4 kg	£357.67	
	Ellegi Slug	12	2¾"	Auto	24½"	6.9 kg	£363.34	
	Pump Martial	12	3" Mag.	Pump	20"	6. kg	£244.12	
	Pump SDASS	12	3" Mag.	Pump	20"	6.6kg	£274.77	
	Pump Multichoke	12	3" Mag.	Pump	24½"	6.6kg	£269.09	Multichoke
	Other barrels available for Elligi							
	Goosegun	12	3" Mag.		41.5"	7.6 kg	£146.45	Multichoke
	Standard	12	2¾"		28"	6.9 kg	£119.22	Multichoke
	Spare barrels for Pump	—	—	—	—	—	£90.83	
F.I.A.S. Distributor Oliver J. Gower Ltd. Tel: Leighton Buzzard 0525 377730	Jaguar o/u	12	2¾"	Boxlock n/e	28"	6¾lbs	£257	Double or selective single trigger
	Olimpo o/u	12	2¾"	Boxlock ejector	28"	6¾lbs	£302	D.T. or S.S.ST. ¼ or ¾ chokes
	Skeet o/u	12	2¾"	Boxlock ejector	26"	7lbs	£325	S.S.T. Skeet choked
	Trap o/u	12	2¾"	Boxlock ejector	30"	7¾lbs	£360	S.S.T. Vent side ribs. Raised top rib
	Fulgar o/u	12	2¾"	Boxlock ejector	30"	8lbs	£417	S.T. Trapgun custom grade
	Artimedes o/u	12	2¾"	Boxlock ejector	28"	7lbs	£475	5 Multichokes, Sideplates Custom grade
	Saba d/b	12	2¾"	Boxlock non ejector	28"	6½lbs	£248	¼-¾ choked
	Sirio d/b	12	2¾"	Boxlock ejector	28"	6¾lbs	£338	¼-¾ choked
FRANCHI Distributors A.S.I. Tel: 072888 555	Barrage o/u	12	2¾"	Ejector	28", 29" 30"	—	£1176	Skeet and Trap models Single trigger
	Dragon o/u	12	2¾"	Ejector	28" or 30"	—	£835	Skeet, Trap and Sporting models Single trigger
	Alchione o/u	12	2¾"	Ejector	27" or 28"	—	From £523.50 to£878.75	Single or double triggers Auto safety
	Falconet o/u	12	2¾"	Ejector	27" or 28"	—	From £550 to £878.75 Standard £429.93	Single or double triggers Auto safety
	Admiral SL o/u	12	2¾"	Auto	71cm	—	£1500	
	Prestige o/u	12	2¾"	Auto	24"	—	£455	Variomix barrel and chokes
	Elite o/u	12	2¾"	Auto	24"	—	£497.50	Variomix barrel and chokes
	Hunter o/u	12	2¾"	Auto	28"	—	£311.20	Ventilated rib
	Standard o/u	12	2¾"	Auto	28"	—	£295	Ventilated rib
	Magnum o/u	12	2¾"	Auto	32"	—	£497.50	Ventilated rib
	Pump PA7						£259	
GUNMARK Distributor Gunmark Ltd, The Armoury, Fort Wallington, Farehame, Hants PO16 8TT Tel: 0329 231531	Viscount s/s	12, 20	2¾"	Sidelock ejector	Various	6¾lbs (6lbs 20 gauge)	£699	Choice of scroll or game engraving
	Crown Sabel s/s	12, 20	2¾"	Sidelock ejector	Various	6½-6¾lbs	£998 £1225	Single trigger version available
	Royale s/s	12, 20	2¾"	Sidelock ejector	Various	6½lbs	£1050	Engraved game scenes. 25" versions available with Churchill rib
	Gold s/s	12	2¾"	Sidelock ejector	Various	6½lbs	£2050	Easy opener. Can be made to individual requirements
	Regale s/s	12	2¾"	Sidelock ejector	Various	6½lbs	£2740 £3760	Easy opener. Can be made to individual requirements
	Sovereign s/s	12	2¾"	Sidelock ejector	28"	6½lbs	£2460	Easy opener
KESTREL Distributors Gunmark Ltd, Tel: 0329 231531	s/s	12, 16, 20	2¾"	Boxlock non ejector	28"	6¾lbs (6lbs 20 gauge)	£207-£225	
	s/s	10	2¾"	Boxlock non ejector	32"	11lbs	£265	Pistol grip
	s/s	28, .410	2¾"	Boxlock non ejector	26"	6lbs	£225	

SHOTGUNS cont.

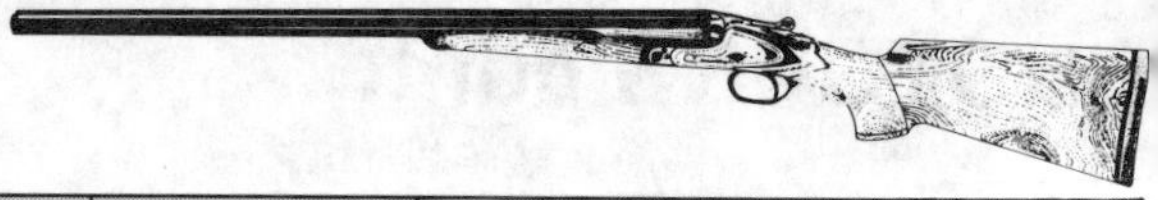

MAKE	MODEL inc over/ under, side/ side	GAUGE	CHAMBER	ACTION eg side lock, box lock, plus ejectors	BARREL LENGTH	OVERALL WEIGHT	APPROX RETAIL PRICE	COMMENTS
KESTREL cont.	s/s	12 Mag.	3"	Boxlock non ejector	30"	7¾lbs	£230	Magnum. Pistol Grip
	s/s	12, 16, 20	2¾"	Boxlock ejector	28"	6¾lbs (6lbs 20 guage)	£270-£287	
	s/s	12 Mag.	3"	Boxlock ejector	30"	7¾lbs	£299	Magnum. Pistol Grip
	Churchill Rib s/s	12	2¾"	Boxlock ejector	27"	6¾lbs	£287	
	Polychoke s/s	12	2¾"	Boxlock ejector	28"	6¾lbs	£365	Multichoke
	s/s	12	2¾"	Sidelock ejector	28"	6¾lbs	£399	
KRIEGHOFF Distributors Tony Kennedy Guns Tel:0566 4465	K80 o/u	12	2¾"	—	26" or 28"	—	From £2350	Skeet or Trap Sporting
LANBER Distributors Gunmark Ltd. Tel: 0329 231531	Field o/u	12	2¾"	Non ejector	28"	7¼lbs	£260	Single selective trigger
	Field o/u	12	2¾"	Ejector	28"	7½lbs	£282	Single selective trigger
	Magnum	12	3"	Non ejector	30"	7½lbs	£282	Single selective trigger
	Magnum	12	3"	Ejector	30"	7½lbs	£425	Single selective trigger Multichoke
	Multichoke	12	2¾"	Ejector	28", 30"	7¼-7½lbs	£399 to £480	Sporting, Trap and Field versions
MARLIN (Goose guns)	55	12	3" Mag.	Bolt Action 2 shot	56¾"	8lb	£213.72	
	5510	10	3½" Mag.	Bolt Action 2 shot	55½"	10½lb	£350.73	
MAROCCHI Distributors Gamebore Cartridge Co., Spyvee Street, Hull Tel: 0482 223707	America Trap o/u	12	2¾"	Boxlock	29"	3.6kg	£1283	High ventilated rib Coloured trap stock Red foresight bead
	Cup Trap o/u	12	2¾"	Boxlock	29"	3.6kg	£1190	Red foresight bead High ventilated rib Coloured trap stock
	Trapper LM Range o/u	12	2¾"	Boxlock	28"	3.1kg	From £302 to £388	
	Marocchi SM 57 LM o/u	12	2¾"	Boxlock	26", 28",30"	3.1kg	From £217 to £250	
	Marocchi Standard o/u	12	2¾"	Boxlock	28"	—	From £195 to £220	
MIROKU Distributors Browning Sports Ltd. Tel: 0235 833939	3800 o/u Trap	12	2¾"	Boxlock	30" or 32"	3.4kg	£795+	Conventional trap gun design Grades 1 & 3
	3800 o/u Skeet	12	2¾"	Boxlock	28"	3.4kg	£760+	Conventional skeet gun Grades 1, 3 & 4
	7000 Trap	12	2¾"	Boxlock	29½"	3.6kg	£1030+	High rib trap gun with invector chokes
	6000 Trap	12	2¾"	Boxlock	29½"	3.6kg	£860+	High rib trap gun Grades 1, 3 & 5
	6000 Skeet	12	2¾"	Boxlock	27"	3.4kg	£860	
	6000 Game	12	2¾"	Boxlock	26" or 28"	2.9/3.0kg	£780+	Lightweight game. Auto safe Grades 1 & 3, 6mm rib
	6000 Sport	12	2¾"	Boxlock	28" or 29"	3.4/3.5kg	£795+	Grades 1 & 3, 13mm rib
	7000 Sport	12	2¾"	Boxlock	28" or 29"	3.4/3.5kg	£895+	Invector chokes
	7000 Game	12	2¾"	Boxlock	28"	3.05kg	£895+	Grades 1 & 3, auto safe
	3000	12	2¾"	Boxlock	28"	—	£599	Invector choke
MISTRAL Distributors John Rothery (Wholesale) Co Ltd. Tel: 0705 667323	DTNE o/u	12	2¾"	Boxlock non ejector	28"	7lbs	N/A	Raised + lateral ventilated rib
	STEJ o/u	12	2¾"	Boxlock ejector	28"	7lbs	N/A	Raised + lateral ventilated
	DTES o/u	12	2¾"	Boxlock ejector	28"	7lbs	N/A	Raised + lateral ventilated rib

SHOTGUNS cont.

MAKE	MODEL inc over/under, side/side	GAUGE	CHAMBER	ACTION eg side lock, box lock, plus ejectors	BARREL LENGTH	OVERALL WEIGHT	APPROX RETAIL PRICE	COMMENTS
PARDOE Distributors Pardoe Importers Wychbold, Droitwich, Worcs WR9 0BX Tel: (052 786) 517	P12NE s/s	12	3″	Anson & Deely Boxlock Double trigger Non ejector Straight hand stock	28″	7lbs	£199	English style flat cut rib XXXX/XXX
	P20NE s/s	20	3″	Anson & Deeley Boxlock Double trigger Non ejector Straight hand stock	27½″	6½lbs	£199	English style flat cut rib XXXX/XXX
PERAZZI Distributors Leslie Hewett Limited Upton Cross, Liskeard, Cornwall Tel: 0579 62319	MX3 STD Trap o/u	12	2¾″	Detachable box lock ejector	29½″/31½″	—	£1912.47	
	MX3 B STD Trap o/u	12	2¾″	Detachable box lock ejector	29½″/31½″	—	N/A	
	MX3 STD SK o/u	12	2¾″	Detachable box lock ejector	29½″	—	£1912.47	
	MX3 C STD Skeet o/u	12	2¾″	Detachable box lock ejector	27½″	—	£1980.10	
	MX3 C STD Game o/u	12	2¾″	Detachable box lock ejector	27½″	—	£1980.10	
	MX3 Game o/u	20/12	2¾″/3″	Detachable box lock ejector	⅝″/27½″	—	£1912.47	
	MX3 C Sporting	12	2¾″	Detachable box lock ejector	29½″	—	£1980.10	
	MX3 BL Trap o/u	12	2¾″	Detachable box lock ejector	29½″/31½″	—	£2347.14	Engraved
	MX3 L Sk o/u	12	2¾″	Detachable box lock ejector	27½″	—	£2347.14	Engraved
	MX3 C L SK o/u	12	2¾″	Detachable box lock ejector	27½″	—	£2414.74	Engraved
	MX3 CL Game	12	2¾″	Detachable box lock ejector	27½″	—	£2414.74	Engraved
	MX3 L Game	20/12	2¾″	Detachable box lock ejector	26⅝″/27½″	—	£2347.14	Engraved
	MX3 C L Sporting	12	2¾″	Detachable box lock ejector	29½″	—	£2414.74	Engraved
	MX3 B SCO Trap o/u	12	2¾″	Detachable box lock ejector	29½″/31½″	—	£5249.78	Engraved
	MX3 SCO Sk	12	2¾″	Detachable box lock ejector	27½″	—	£5249.78	Engraved
	MX3 C SCO Skeet o/u	12	2¾″	Detachable box lock ejector	27½″	—	£5317.57	Engraved
	MX3 C SCO Game o/u	12	2¾″	Detachable box lock ejector	27½″	—	£5317.57	Engraved
	MX3 SCO G	20/12	2¾″ (12) 3″ (20)	Detachable box lock ejector	27½″ (12) 26″ (20)	—	£5249.78	Engraved
	MX3 C SCO Sport o/u	12	2¾″	Detachable box lock ejector	29½″	—	£5317.57	Engraved
	MX3 B SCO/O Trap o/u	12	2¾″	Detachable box lock ejector	29½″/31½″	—	£6237.75	Engraved (Gold)
	MX3 SCO/O Skeet o/u	12	2¾″	Detachable box lock ejector	27½″	—	£6237.75	Engraved (Gold)
	MX3 C SCO/O Skeet o/u	12	2¾″	Detachable box lock ejector	27½″	—	£6305.55	Engraved (Gold)
	MX3 C SCO/O Game o/u	12	2¾″	Detachable box lock ejector	27½″	—	£6305.55	Engraved (Gold)
	MX3 SCO /O Game o/u	20/12	2¾″ (12) 3″ (20)	Detachable box lock ejector	27⅝″ (12) 26″ (20)	—	£6237.75	Engraved (Gold)
	MX3 C SCO/O Sporting	12	2¾″	Detachable box lock ejector	29½″	—	£6305.55	Engraved (Gold)
	MX8 Trap o/u	12	2¾″	Detachable box lock ejector	29½″/31½″	—	£2366.45	
	MX8 Skeet o/u	12	2¾″	Detachable box lock ejector	27½″	—	£2366.45	
	MX8 H.G. Sporting	12	2¾″	Detachable box lock ejector	27½″	—	£2366.45	
	MX2 Trap High Rib	12	2¾″	Detachable box lock ejector	29½″	—	£2578.84	

SHOTGUNS cont.

MAKE	MODEL inc over/ under, side/ side	GAUGE	CHAMBER	ACTION eg side lock, box lock, plus ejectors	BARREL LENGTH	OVERALL WEIGHT	APPROX RETAIL PRICE	COMMENTS
PERRAZI cont.	MX8 Trap adj b choke	12	2¾"	Detachable box lock ejector	29½"/31½"	—	£2511.34	
	MX2 Trap adj b choke	12	2¾"	Detachable box lock ejector	29½"	—	£2723.83	
	MX2 Light-weight o/u	12	2¾"	Detachable box lock ejector	29½"	—	£2578.94	
	MX2 l/weight adj b choke	12	2¾"	Detachable box lock ejector	29½"	—	£2723.83	
	MX8 SC3 Trap	12	2¾"	Detachable box lock ejector	29½"/31½"	—	£3825.96	Engraved
	MX8 SC3 Sk o/u	12	2¾"	Detachable box lock ejector	27½"	—	£3825.96	Engraved
	MX8 SC3 Sp. o/u	12	2¾"	Detachable box lock ejector	29½"	—	£3825.96	Engraved
	SC3 Trap adj b choke o/u	12	2¾"	Detachable box lock ejector	29½"/31½"	—	£3971.24	Engraved
	MX2 SC3 o/u	12	2¾"	Detachable box lock ejector	29½"	—	£4087.47	Engraved
	MX2 SC3 adj. b choke o/u	12	2¾"	Detachable box lock ejector	29½"	—	£4232.76	Engraved
	MX2 L/weight SC3 o/u	12	2¾"	Detachable box lock ejector	29½"	—	£4087.47	Engraved
	MX2 L/weight SC3 Ad b c	12	2¾"	Detachable box lock ejector	29½"	—	£4232.76	Engraved
	MX8 SCO Trap	12	2¾"	Detachable box lock ejector	29½"/31½"	—	£6005.29	Engraved
	MX8 SCO/SK.	12	2¾"	Detachable box lock ejector	27½"	—	£6005.29	Engraved
	MX8 SCO Sporting	12	2¾"	Detachable box lock ejector	27½"	—	£6005.29	Engraved
	SCO Trap ad bot. choke	12	2¾"	Detachable box lock ejector	29½"	—	£6150.56	Engraved
	SCO Game 20g	20	2¾"/3"	Detachable box lock ejector	26"/27½"	—	£6276.49	Engraved
	MX8 SCO/O Trap o/u	12	2¾"	Detachable box lock ejector	29½"/31½"	—	£7022.31	Engraved (Gold)
	MX8 SCO/O Skeet o/u	12	2¾"	Detachable box lock ejector	27½"	—	£7022.31	Engraved (Gold)
	MX8 SCO/O Sport o/u	12	2¾"	Detachable box lock ejector	27½"	—	£7022.31	Engraved (Gold)
	MX 4 B Std. Trap	12	2¾"	Detachable box lock ejector	29½"/31½"	—	£2076.67	Adjustable trigger
	MX4 Std. Skeet	12	2¾"	Detachable box lock ejector	27½"	—	£2076.67	Adjustable trigger
	MX4 C Std. Skeet	12	2¾"	Detachable box lock ejector	27½"	—	£2144.	Adjustable trigger
	MX4 Std. Sporting	12	2¾"	Detachable box lock ejector	27½"	—	£2076.67	Adjustable trigger
	MX4 C Spl. Sporting	12	2¾"	Detachable box lock ejector	28"	—	£2144.30	Adjustable trigger
	MX4B SC3 Trap	12	2¾"	Detachable box lock ejector	29½"/31½"	—	£3525.53	Engraved
	MX4 SC3	12	2¾"	27½"	—		£3525.53	
	MX4 B SC3 Trap	12	2¾"	Detachable box lock ejector	29½"/31½"	—	£5325.53	Adjustable trigger Engraved
	MX4 SC3 Skeet	12	2¾"	Detachable box lock ejector	27½"	—	£3525.53	Adjustable trigger Engraved
	MX4C SC3 Skeet	12	2¾"	Detachable box lock ejector	27½"	—	£3593.14	Adjustable trigger Engraved
	MX4 SC3 Sporting	12	2¾"	Detachable box lock ejector	27½"	—	£3525.53	Adjustable trigger Engraved
	MX4 SC3 Sporting	12	2¾"	Detachable box lock ejector	27½"	—	£3593.14	Adjustable trigger Engraved
	MX4 SCO Trap	12	2¾"	Detachable box lock ejector	29½"/31½"	—	£5553.92	Adjustable trigger De-Luxe Engraved
	MX4 SCO/O Trap	12	2¾"	Detachable box lock ejector	29½"/31½"	—	£5795.40	Adjustable trigger Engraved (Gold)

SHOTGUNS cont.

MAKE	MODEL inc over/under, side/side	GAUGE	CHAMBER	ACTION eg side lock, box lock, plus ejectors	BARREL LENGTH	OVERALL WEIGHT	APPROX RETAIL PRICE	COMMENTS
PERAZZI cont.	MX5 Game	12	2¾"	Non Detachable	26⅝"/27½"	—	£1228.00	Selective trigger
	MX5 C Game	12	2¾"	Non Detachable	27½"	—	£1270.74	Selective trigger
	MX5 20 Game	20	2¾" - 3"	Non Detachable	26"	—	£1778.00	Selective trigger
REMINGTON Distributors Hull Cartridge Co. Ltd. Bontoft Ave,. National Ave,. Hull	M1100 Field	12/20	2¾"	Semi Auto	30" 28" 26"	7¾ lbs	—	Left hand available
	M1100 Mag.	12/20	3"	Semi Auto	30" 28"	7¾ lbs	—	Left hand available
	M1100 Skeet T Skeet	12/20	2¾"	Semi Auto	26"	7¾ lbs	—	Left hand available
	M1100 Trap Trap M/Carlo T Trap T Trap M/Carlo	12	2¾"	. Semi Auto	30"	8¼ lbs	—	Left hand available
	M1100	28/.410	2¾"	Semi Auto	25"	6½ & 7 lbs	—	
	M1100	.410	3"	Semi Auto	25"	7¼ lbs ·	—	
	M870	12/20	3"	Pump Action	30"/28"/26"	7 & 6 lbs	—	Left hand available
	M870	12/20	3"	Pump Action	18"/20"	7 & 6 lbs	—	Left hand available rifle sight option. Plain barrel option
	M870 Comp Trap Trap Monte Carlo Trap	12	2¾"	Pump Action	30"	8½ lbs	—	
	M870	28/.410	2¾"	Pump Action	25"	7¾ lbs	—	
RIZZINI Distributors Pardoe Importers Wychbold, Droitwich, Worcs WR9 0BX Tel: (052 786) 517	Multichoke o/u	12	2¾"	Boxlock SST ejector	28"	6¾ lbs	£399	5 screw chokes key ¼/½/¾ full
	Game o/u	12	2¾"	Boxlock SST ejector	28"	6¾ lbs	£408	Ventilated rib choke ¼/¾
	Game Deluxe	12	2¾"	Boxlock with dummy sideplates SST ejector	28"	7 lbs	£565	Ventilated rib choke ¼/¾
	Skeet o/u	12	2¾"	Boxlock SST ejector	26"	7 lbs	£429	Ventilated rib choke sk/sk
	Trap o/u	12	2¾"	Boxlock SST ejector	30"	8 lbs	£447	Ventilated rib choke ¾/full
	Trap 2000 extra o/u	12	2¾"	Boxlock with dummy sideplates SST ejector	30"	8¼ lbs	£703	Ventilated rib choke ¾/full
	Special o/u Sporting	12	2¾"	Boxlock SST ejector	28" or 30"	6¾ lbs	£450	Ventilated rib choke IC/½
	Special o/u Sporting MkII	12	2¾"	Boxlock SST ejector	28" or 30"	6¾ lbs	£475	Ventilated rib choke IC/½
W & C SCOTT Manufacturers W & C Scott (Gunmakers) Ltd. Tel: 021 328 4107	Chatsworth	12, 16 20, 28	2¾"	Boxlock ejector	25" to 30"	To specification	From £3542	All guns built to customers specifications and measurements Choice of stock wood. All extras and refinements are available
	Bowood	12, 16 20, 28	2¾"	Boxlock ejector	25" to 30"	To specification	From £2379	
	Kinmount	12, 16 20, 28	2¾"	Boxlock ejector	25" to 30"	To specification	From £1747	
	Blenheim	12, 20	2¾"	Sidelock ejector	26" to 30"	To specification	From £5335	A 'best' sidelock gun built to customers requirements
F. J. WISEMAN Manufacturers F. J. Wiseman & Co Ltd, 3 Price Street, Birmingham B4 6JX Tel: 021-359 1256	County Range S/S	20, 16 or 12	2½" or 2¾"	Sidelock ejectors and boxlock ejectors	As req.	As req	From £3000	Guns made to individual requirements

RIFLES

MAKE	MODEL	CALIBRE	TYPE eg sporting, target, stutzen varmint etc	ACTION eg bolt arm, under lever etc	BARREL LENGTH	OVERALL WEIGHT	MAGAZINE CAPACITY	APPROX RETAIL PRICE	COMMENTS
ACCURACY INTERNATIONAL Distributor Accuracy International Ltd Tel: 0705 660371/2	S/S	.243 .308 Win .708 Rem	Target	Bolt action	630mm	5kg 5.5kg	Singleshot		For NRA or UIT comps
	CISM	.243 Win .308 Win .708 Rem	Target	Bolt action	630mm	5kg	10 shot		For UIT CISM competition
ANSCHUTZ Distributors Frank Dyke & Co 01 670 2224	1813	.22	Target	Bolt action	69cm	7.0kg	—	N/A	
	1811	.22	Match	Bolt action	69cm	5.4kg	—	N/A	
	1810	.22	Match	Bolt action	69cm	7.0kg	—	N/A	
	1807	.22	Match	Bolt action	66cm	4.9kg	—.	N/A	
	1403	.22	Match	Bolt action	64cm	3.5kg	—	N/A	
	1808 ED Super	.22	Moving target	Bolt action	83cm rifling 49cm	4.2kg	—	N/A	
	54, 18 MS	.22	Target	Bolt action	57cm	3.7kg	—	N/A	
	64 MS	.22	Target	Bolt action	55cm	3.6kg	—	N/A	
	Mark 2000	.22	Target	Bolt action	64cm	3.3kg	—	N/A	
	1403 Rep	.22	Target	Bolt action	64cm	3.7kg	10	N/A	
	1807 Rep	.22	Target	Bolt action	66cm	5.4kg	10	N/A	
	1365	.9mm	Vermin	Auto loader	61cm	2.3kg	Single shot	N/A	
	1388	.22 l.r.	Vermin	Bolt action	50cm	2.2kg	Single shot	N/A	
	520	.22 l.r.	Vermin	Auto loader	61cm	2.9kg	—	N/A	
	1450	.22 lr.	Sporting	Bolt action	50cm	2.2kg	5	N/A	
	1415	.22 l.r.	Sporting	Bolt action	58cm	2.8kg	5	N/A	
	1515	.22 Magnum	Sporting	Bolt action	58cm	2.8kg	4	N/A	
	1430	.22 Hornet	Sporting	Bolt action	61cm	3.0kg	5	N/A	
	1530	.222 Rem	Sporting	Bolt action	61cm	3.0kg	3	N/A	
BRNO Distributors Edgar Brothers Catherine Street, Macclesfield SK11 6SG Tel: 0625 613177	ZKK	.308W .223 R .243 W .270 W .375 H&H .458 W.Mag. .22 Hornet .222 Rem.	Sporting	Bolt action	Various	According to calibre	5/6	N/A	
	ZKM452	.22	Sporting	Bolt action	24¾"	6½lbs	5	N/A	10 shot mag. optional
	CZ511	.22	Sporting	Semi-auto	22"	6lbs	8	N/A	
BROWNING Manufacturers Browning Sports Ltd, 37d Milton Trading Estate, Milton, Abingdon, Oxon Tel: 0235 833939	BBR	.22-250 Rem. .243 Win. .308 Win. .270 Win.	Sporting/ Varmint	Bolt (9 lugs)	22"	8lbs	4, detachable	£480	
	BBR 'A Bolt'	.22-250 Rem. .243 Win. .308 Win. 6.5 × 55 .270 Win.	Sporting/ Varmint	B/A (3 lugs)	22½"	6lb 10oz+	4, detachable	£425	
	BAR	.243 Win. .270 Win. .308 Win. .30 - 065pr	Sporting	Auto loading	22"	7lb 8oz	4, detachable	£550	
	BAR	.22	Sporting	Auto loading	20¼"	6lb 4oz	15 LR	£295	
	BLR	.22	Sporting	Lever	20"	5lb	22 shot 15 LR	£295	
	Auto	.22	Sporting	Auto loading	19¼"	4lb 12oz	11LR	£320	
	BPR	.22	Sporting	Pump	20¼"	6lb 4oz	11 LR	£295	
	O/U "Express"	9.3 × 74R 7 × 65R .30-065pr .270 Win.		B/L	650mm 650mm 610mm 610mm	3.45kg 3.45kg 3.15kg 3.15kg		))) £2500+)	

RIFLES cont.

MAKE	MODEL	CALIBRE	TYPE eg sporting, target, stutzen varmint etc	ACTION eg bolt arm, under lever etc	BARREL LENGTH	OVERALL WEIGHT	MAGAZINE CAPACITY	APPROX RETAIL PRICE	COMMENTS
B.S.A. Manufacturers B.S.A. Guns Ltd, Armoury Road, Birmingham B11 Tel: 021 772 8543	CF2	222R .22/250 .243W	Sporting	Bolt action	23.6"	3.4 kg to 3.64 kg	3 to 5 depending on calibre	£278.75	Single trigger All calibres also available with set trigger £303.95 All calibres also available with heavy barrel £311.20 Heavy barrel and set trigger £336.60 CF2 fitted with full length Stutzen stock £295.50 CF2 Carbine £278.75
		6.5 × 55							
		7 × 57 7mm R. Mag 7mm R. Mag .270W .308W 30/60 .300W Mag							
	B.S.A. Classic	Calibres as above						£295.50 £326.00 £336.60	Single trigger Set trigger Heavy barrel
ERMA Distributors Edgar Brothers Tel: 0625 613177	EG 712	.22	Sporting	Under lever	18"	6lbs	15	N/A	
	Em-1	.22	Sporting	Semi-Auto	17½"	6lbs	10	N/A	Military style
	EGm-1	.22	Sporting	Semi-auto	17½"	7lbs	5	N/A	Sporter version EM-1
FEINWERKBAU Distributors A.S.I. Tel: 072888 555	2000 UIT	.22	—	—	—	—	—	From £433	Universal, Standard and running target models
	KK Super Match Free rifle	.22	—	—	—	—	—	£764.85	Mechanical trigger
KRICO Distributors Leslie Hewett Ltd. Lower Lake, Upton Cross, Liskeard, Cornwall Tel: 0579 62319	260 EA/LA	.22 LR	Sporting	Semi automatic	600mm	3.1kg	5/10	£188.94	Beech Tangent rear sight
	300 E	.22 LR/.22 or Mag.	Sporting	Bolt action repeater	600mm	3.0kg	5/10	£197.66	Tangent Beech
	300 D	.22 LR/or Mag.	Sporting	Bolt action repeater	600mm	3.0kg	5/10	£220.90	Walnut Fixed
	300 D ST	.22 LR/or .22 Mag	Sporting	Bolt action repeater	600mm	3.0kg	5/10	£220.90	Walnut Fixed
	320 L		.22 LR/WMR	Sporting					
	320 L	.22 LR/WMR	Sporting	Bolt action repeater	500mm	2.8kg	5/10	£284.88	Walnut/carbine Fixed
	320 L ST	.22 LR/WMR	Sporting	Bolt action repeater	500mm	2.8kg	5/10	£284.88	Walnut/carbine Fixed
	340 S	.22 LR/WMR	Sporting	Bolt action repeater	500mm	2.8kg	5/10	£284.88	Walnut/carbine Fixed
	340 S	.22	Match	Bolt action single shot	—	—	N/A	£337.20	Walnut Grooved for scope
	400 E	.22 Hornet	Sporting	Bolt action repeater	600mm	3.1kg	5/10	£383.13	Beech Fixed
	400 EST	.22 Hornet	Sporting	Bolt action repeater	600mm	3.1kg	5/10	£283.13	Beech Fixed
	400 D	.22 Hornet	Sporting	Bolt action repeater	600mm	3.1kg	5/10	£336.02	Walnut Fixed
	400 DST	.22 Hornet	Sporting	Bolt action repeater	600mm	3.1kg	5/10	£336.02	Walnut Fixed
	420 L	.22 Hornet	Sporting	Bolt action repeater	500mm	2.8kg	5/10	£386.63	Walnut Fixed
	420 LST	.22 Hornet	Sporting	Bolt action repeater	500mm	2.8kg	5/10	£386.63	Walnut Fixed
	430 S	.22 Hornet	Match	Bolt action/Single shot	600mm	3.9kg	N/A	£316.86	Walnut
	600 A	See note	Sporting	Bolt action/Repeater	600mm	3.2kg	3/5	£362.78	Walnut Grooved for scope
	600 D	See note	Sporting	Bolt action/Repeater	600mm	3.2kg	3/5	£470.92	Walnut Fixed
	600 DL	See note	Sporting	Bolt action/Repeater	600mm	3.2kg	3/5	£581.95	Walnut/Luxury Fixed
	620 L	See note	Sporting	Bolt action/Repeater	550mm	3.1kg	3/5	£531.39	Walnut/Carbine Fixed
	620 DL	See note	Sporting	Bolt action/Repeater	550mm	3.1kg	3/5	£651.15	Walnut/Luxury carbine Fixed
	630 S	See note	Competition	Bolt action/Single shot	600mm	4.0kg	3/5	£517.44	Walnut Grooved for scope
	640 L	See note	Sporting	Bolt action/Repeater	600mm	3.7kg	3/5	£505.23	Walnut Grooved for scope
	640 S	See note	Match Bench Rest	Bolt action/Repeater	600mm	4.1kg	3/5	£666.26	Walnut Grooved for scope

RIFLES cont.

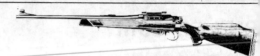

MAKE	MODEL	CALIBRE	TYPE eg sporting, target, stutzen varmint etc	ACTION eg bolt arm, under lever etc	BARREL LENGTH	OVERALL WEIGHT	MAGAZINE CAPACITY	APPROX RETAIL PRICE	COMMENTS
KRIKO cont.	640 S Sniper	See note	—	Bolt action/Repeater	—	—	—	£656.97	Walnut Grooved for scope
	700 A	See note	Sporting	Bolt action/Repeater	600mm	—	3/5	£362.78	Walnut
									Grooved for scope
	700 D	See note	Sporting	Bolt action/Repeater	600mm	—	3/5	£494.76	Walnut Grooved for scope
	700 DL	See note		Bolt action/Repeater	600mm	—	3/5	£612.78	Walnut/Luxury Grooved for scope
	720 D	See note		Bolt action/Repeater	550mm	3/5		£571.48	
	720 D	See note		Bolt action/Repeater	550mm	—	3/5	£571.48	Walnut/carbine Grooved for scope
	720 DL	See note		Bolt action/Repeater	550mm	—	3/5	£694.19	Walnut Luxury carbine Grooved for scope

Note re calibres
SHORT ACTION (600 Series)
Model 600 A only available in :- .222 Rem, 243 Win, .308 Win, 22-250 Rem
Other calibres, .17 Rem, .222 Rem Mag 5.6 × 50 Mag 5.6 × 51 RWS
Medium Ation (700 series)
Model 700 A only available in :- 7 × 64 .30-06
Other calibres, 6.5 × 55 .270 Win 9.3 × 68
Magnum Action (700 series)
Model 700 series available in 700mm Rem Mag .300 Win Mag 6.5 × 68 7.5 Swiss
Left hand stocks available in all 600, 700 series models
Left hand action & stock available in De Luxe version only

MAKE	MODEL	CALIBRE	TYPE	ACTION	BARREL LENGTH	OVERALL WEIGHT	MAGAZINE CAPACITY	APPROX RETAIL PRICE	COMMENTS
MARLIN Distributors Leslie Hewett Ltd. Upton Cross, Liskeard, Cornwall Tel: (0579) 62319	15Y	.22	Sporting	Bolt action	33¼"	4½lbs	Single	£115.15	
	780	.22	Sporting	Bolt Action	41"	5½lbs	7 shot	£166.39	
	70	.22 LR	Sporting	Semi auto	36½"	5lbs	7 shot	£123.97	
	995	.22 LR	Sporting	Semi auto	36¾"	5lbs	7 shot	£163.45	
	60	.22 LR	Sporting	Semi auto	40½"	5½lbs	18 shot	£123.97	
	990	.22 LR	Sporting	Semi auto	40¾"	5½lbs	18 shot	£174.91	
	1894S	.44 WMR	Sporting	Lever action	37½"	6lbs	10 shot	£374.20	
	1894CS	357 Mag. .38 Special	Sporting	Lever action	36"	6lbs	9 shot		
	39A	.22	Sporting	Lever action	40"	6½lbs	26 short 21 long 19 Long R.	£336.66	

MAKE	MODEL	CALIBRE	TYPE	ACTION	BARREL LENGTH	OVERALL WEIGHT	MAGAZINE CAPACITY	APPROX RETAIL PRICE	COMMENTS
T.T. PROCTOR Manufacturer T. T. Proctor 88a Water Lane, Wilmslow, Cheshire Tel: 0625 526654		all calibres	Stalking	Mauser/Sako	18"-26"	8-9lb	4-5rds	From £1700 + VAT	Spec scope mounts French walnut
	African	.375-458	Big game	BRNO Mauser mag.	18"-24"	10-12lb	5rds	£900 + VAT	English express rifle

MAKE	MODEL	CALIBRE	TYPE	ACTION	BARREL LENGTH	OVERALL WEIGHT	MAGAZINE CAPACITY	APPROX RETAIL PRICE	COMMENTS
RWS Distributors Leslie Hewett Ltd Tel: 0579 62319	820S/82	.22 LR	—	Bolt Action	660mm	4.7kg	—	£496.32	
	820S/75	.22 LR	—	Bolt Action	660mm	4.7kg	—	£452.52	
	820SF/82	.22 LR	—	Bolt Action	690mm	5.0kg	—	£504.60	
	820/K Match rifles	.22 LR	—	Bolt Action	660mm	3 pieces each 50gms	—	£436.40	

MAKE	MODEL	CALIBRE	TYPE	ACTION	BARREL LENGTH	OVERALL WEIGHT	MAGAZINE CAPACITY	APPROX RETAIL PRICE	COMMENTS
REMINGTON Distributors Hull Cartridge Co. Ltd. Bontoft Ave., National Ave., Hull	700 ADL	Various Calibres	Sporting	Bolt Action	22" & 24"	7¼ to 7¾lbs	3 & 4 Varies with calibre	—	Adjustable blade rear sight long action models only
	700 Classic	Various Calibres	Sporting	Bolt Action	22" & 24"	7¼ to 7¾lbs	3 & 4 Varies Calibres		
	700 BDL	Popular Calibres	Sporting	Bolt Action	22" & 24"	7¼ to 7¾lbs	3, 4 & 5 Varies with calibre		Adjustable blade rear sight long action models only
	700 BDL Left Hand	.270 Win .30-06 7mm Rem Mag	Sporting	Bolt Action	22" & 24"	7¼ to 7¾lbs	3 & 4 Varies with calibre		Adjustable blade rear sight
	700 BDL Heavy Barrel Varmint	Various Calibres	Varmint	Bolt Action	22" & 24"	9 lbs	4 & 5 Varies with calibre		

RIFLES cont.

MAKE	MODEL	CALIBRE	TYPE eg sporting, target, stutzen varmint etc	ACTION eg bolt arm, under lever etc	BARREL LENGTH	OVERALL WEIGHT	MAGAZINE CAPACITY	APPROX RETAIL PRICE	COMMENTS
REMINGTON cont.	700 Safari	.375 H & H Mag .45 Win Mag	Big game	Bolt Action	24″	9 lbs	3		
	Model 7	Various Calibres	Light weight Sporting	Bolt Action	18½″	6½ lbs	4 & 5 Varies Calibres		Adjustable blade rear sight
	Model 4 and 7400	Various Calibres	Sporting	Semi auto	22″	7½ lbs	4		Adjustable blade rear sight
	Model 6 and 7600	Various Calibres	Sporting	Pump Action	22″	7½ lbs	4		Adjustable blade rear sight
	Sportsman 74	30-06	Sporting	Semi auto	22″	7½ lbs	4		Adjustable rear sight
	Sportsman	30-06	Sporting	Pump Action	22″	7½ lbs	4		Adjustable rear sight
	Sportsman 78	.243 Win .270 Win .30-06 .308 Win	Sporting	Bolt Action	22″	7 lbs	4		Adjustable rear sight
	572 A & BDL	.22 LR	Sporting	Pump Action	21″	5¾ lbs	15		
	552 A & BDL	.22 LR	Sporting	Semi auto	21″	5¼ lbs	15		
	Nylon 66	.22 LR	Sporting	Semi auto	19⅝″	4 lbs	14		
SAKO Distributors Gunmark Ltd. The Armoury, Fort Wallington, Fareham, Hants PO16 8TT Tel: 0329 231531	Finnscout	.22LR .22 Hornet	Sporting	Bolt action	57cm	2.7kg	5	£355 to £380	Heavy barrel and sporter versions
	Vixen	.17 Rem .222 Rem .223 Rem	Sporting	Bolt action	61cm	3.0 to 3.8kg	5	£460 to £1140	Standard, heavy barrel, full stock, de luxe and super de luxe models
	Forester	.22-250 Rem .243 Win .308 Win	Sporting	Bolt action	58cm or 61cm	3.3 to 3.8kg	5	£460 to £1140	Standard to super de luxe models
	Finnbear	.270 Win .30-06 .375 H&H Magnum	Big game	Bolt action	61cm	3.7kg	4-5	£470 to £1180	Standard to super de luxe models
STEYR-MANNLICHER Distributors Hilton Gun Co Ltd. Tel: 0283 814488	SL	.222 Rem .223 Rem 5.6-50 Mag	Sporting	Bolt action	50.8cm 60cm 65cm	2.7 to 3.6kg	5	N/A	Full stock, half stock or varmint versions
	L	5.6 × 57 .243 Win .308 Win	Sporting	Bolt action	50.8cm 60cm 65cm	2.8 to 3.6kg	5	N/A	Full stock, half stock or varmint versions
	M	6.5 × 57 .270 Win 7 × 64 .30-06 6.5 × 55 7.5 Swiss 8 × 57JS 9.3 × 62	Sporting	Bolt action	50.8cm 60cm	3.1 to 3.15kg	5	N/A	Full or half stock
	S	6.5 × 68 7mm R Mag .300 Win Mag 8 × 68S .375 H&H mag	Sporting	Bolt action	65cm	3.8kg	4	N/A	
	S/T	9.3 × 64 .375 H&H Mag .458 Win Mag	Sporting	Bolt action	65mm	4.10kg	4	N/A	
	Luxus	6.5 × 57 .270 Win 5.6 × 57 7 × 64 .243 30-06 .308 8 × 68S 5 × 68 .300 Win Mag 7mm Rem	Sporting	Bolt action	50.8 or 60cm	3.3 to 3.5kg	6	N/A	
	Sport Match	.308 Win .243 Win		Bolt action	65cm	3.90kg	5	N/A	
	Match	.308 Win .243 Win		Bolt action	65cm	4.4kg	5	N/A	

RIFLES cont.

MAKE	MODEL	CALIBRE	TYPE eg sporting, target, stutzen varmint etc	ACTION eg bolt arm, under lever etc	BARREL LENGTH	OVERALL WEIGHT	MAGAZINE CAPACITY	APPROX RETAIL PRICE	COMMENTS
SWING Manufacturers & Distriburors Swing Target Rifles Ltd. PO Box 17 Tonbridge Kent Tel: 0732 357908	Sin 71M4 Sin 71M4H Sin 71M4 (Longrange Pistol)	.308 Win .708 Rem 6.5 × 55 6.5 ×284 Win .22-250 Rem 7mm Rem Mag 8mm Rem Mag Other calibres to order	Target & Sporting	Bolt action	26" 28" 30" Barrels supplied. Different profiles and weight to order.	Varying from NRA target rules, ISU rules and free rifle weights	Single	N/A	A variety of target rifle, Free rifle, ISU rifle, Match rifle, longrange pistols and combination of barrels and calibres available
TIKKA Distributors Gunmark Ltd, The Armoury, Fort Wallington, Fareham, Hants PO16 8TT	M55 Standard	.17 Rem .222 Rem .223 Rem .22-250 6mm Rem .243 Rem .308 Rem	Sporting		52cm	3.3Kilo		£420	
	M 55 Trapper	.17 Rem .222 Rem .223 Rem .22-250 6mm Rem .243 Rem .308 Win	Sporting		52cm	2.8Kilo		£435	
	M55 Continental	.222 Rem .223 Rem .22-250 .243 Win .308 Win	Sporting		62cm	4 Kilo		£450	
	M55 DeLuxe	.17 Rem .222 Rem .223 Rem .22-250 6mm Rem .243 Win .308 Win	Sporting		58cm	3.3 Kilo		£450	
	M65 Standard	6.5 × 55 .25-06 .270 Win 7mm Rem Mag 7 × 64 .300 Win Mag .30-06 .308 Win	Sporting		56cm	3.4Kilo		£442	
	M65 Trapper	6.5 × 55 .25-06 .270 Win 7mm Rem Mag 7 × 64 .300 Mag .30-06 .308 Mag	Sporting		52cm	3 Kilo		£458	
	M65 Continental	6.5 × 55 .25-06 .270 Win 7mm Rem Mag 7 × 64 .300 Win Mag .30-06 .308 Win	Sporting		62cm	4.3 Kilo		£480	
	M65 DeLuxe	6.5 × 55 .25-06 .270 Win 7mm Rem Mag 7 × 64 .300 Mag .30-06 .308 Mag	Sporting		56cm	3.4 Kilo		£480	
	Mounts Standard							£26.40	Standard Mounts are available 25.4 and 26mm, Low/High
	Mounts DeLuxe							£38.80	Quick detachable lightweight mounts available as above

RIFLES cont.

MAKE	MODEL	CALIBRE	TYPE eg sporting, target, stutzen varmint etc	ACTION eg bolt arm, under lever etc	BARREL LENGTH	OVERALL WEIGHT	MAGAZINE CAPACITY	APPROX RETAIL PRICE	COMMENTS
TIKKA Distributors JLS Arms Co Ltd Tel: 021 556 1322/9658	M55 Standard Trapper DeLuxe	.17, .222 .223 .22 .250 .243 6mm .308 Win	Sporting Hunting	Bolt action	580mm 23"	3.3kg	3 to 10	£444 to £479	Sporting rifles with target rifle accuracy
	M55 Heavy barrelled Continental	.222, .22 .250 .223, .243 .308 Win	Sniping Varmint	Bolt action	620mm 24¼"	4kg	5 to 10	£479	
	M65 Standard Trapper DeLuxe Magnum Wildboar Continental	25.06, 6.5 × 55 7 × 64, .270 .308, .30-06 7mm Mag 300 Win Mag	Hunting	Bolt action	560mm 22" 520mm 620mm	3.4kg 3.4kg 4kg	3 to 7 3-7 3-7	£471 to £546 £535 £510	Seven variations available. Continental has heavy barrel
	M55 Heavy barrelled Sporter & Super Sporter	.222, .22 .250 .223, .243 .308 Win	Target Sniping Bench Rest	Bolt action	620mm 24½"	4.1kg	5 to 10	£456 to £563	Also used Running Boar and Deer
	M65 Sporter & Super Sporter	6.5 × 55 .270, .308 .30-06	Target Sniping Bench Rest	Bolt action	620mm 24½"	4.5kg	3 to 7	£499 to £610	
	M65 Super Sporter Master	.308	Match	Bolt action	620mm	4.5kg	3 to 7	£747	Thicker diameter barrel, fluted to reduce weight. Highly selected for accuracy
	Shotgun Rifle Combi MO7 Standard DeLuxe	12g/.222 12g/5.6 × 50 R Mag 12g/5.6 × 52R	Hunting	Top lever	580mm 635mm	3.2kg	N/A	£594 £622	Stecher double set trigger available as extra
VOERE Distributors Edgar Brothers Tel: 0625 613177	Titan II	All popular calibres	Sporting	Bolt action	Various	According to calibre	5/6	N/A	
	Titan Menor	.222 Rem .223 Rem .222 Rem Mag	Sporting	Bolt action	Various	According to calibre	5/6	N/A	
	2115	.22	Sporting	Semi-auto	22"	6lbs	8	N/A	optional 15 shot mag.
	1014	.22	Sporting	Semi-auto	17"	6lbs	8	N/A	Military style stock
	1007	.22	Sporting	Bolt action	18"	6lbs	5	N/A	
WALTHER Distributors Accuracy International (Shooting Sports) Ltd, 43 Gladys Ave, Northend, Portsmouth, Hants. Tel: 0705 660371/2	KKM	.22lr	Target	Bolt action	650mm	7.4kg	Singleshot		Designed for Free Rifle or English Match comp.
	UIT Match	.22lr	Target	Bolt action	650mm	5.0kg	Singleshot		For 3 Position or prone, conforms to standard rifle regulations
	UIT MT	22lr	Moving target	Bolt action	600mm	3.9kg	Singleshot		For UIT Moving Target competition
	KJS	.22lr .22 Hornet	Sporting	Bolt action	650mm	3.5kg	Singleshot		
WEIHRAUCH Disributors Edgar Brothers Tel: 0625 613177	HW60J	.22 .22 Magnum	Hornet Sporting	Bolt action	22½"	7lbs	5	N/A	
CRAIG M. WHITSEY Manufacturers Craig M. Whitsey (Gunmakers) Ltd, Unit D., 10/12 Fitzalan Road, Arundel, West Sussex Tel: 0903 883102	Rook Rifle Sporting	.222 or .223 Any calibre	Boxlock	24" Bolt action	7lbs 20" to26"	9lbs	Singleshot 4-5Rds	Walnut Walnut	Scope Sight Scope Sight

AIR WEAPONS

MAKE	PISTOL/ RIFLE	MODEL	CALIBRE	POWER	ACTION	BARREL LENGTH	WEIGHT	APPROX RETAIL PRICE	COMMENTS
ANSCHUTZ Distributors Frank Dyke & Co Tel: 01-670 2224	Rifle	380LK	.177	—	Cocking lever	51.5cm	4.4kg	N/A	Moving target air rifle
	Rifle	LG380	.177	—	Cocking lever	51.5cm	4.9kg	N/A	Match air rifle
	Rifle	333	.177	—	Break barrel	51.5cm	3.1kg	N/A	Sporting
	Rifle	335	.177, .22	—	Break barrel	51.5cm	3.3kg	N/A	Sporting
A.S.I. Alliance House, Snape Maltings, Snape, Saxmundham, Suffolk IP17 1SW Tel: 072888 555	Rifle	MC Super Match	.177	—	—	—	—	£245	
	Rifle	Magnum	.22	—	—	—	—	£69	
	Rifle	Statical	.22	—	—	—	—	£59	
	Rifle	Paratrooper single	.177 & .22	—	—	—	—	£49	
	Rifle	Paratrooper repeater	.177	—	—	—	—	£59	
	Rifle	Sniper	.177 & .22	—	—	—	—	£45	
	Rifle	Sniper repeater	.177	—	—	—	—	£55	
	Rifle	Apache	.177	—	—	—	—	£39.50	
	Pistol	Center	.177	—	—	—	—	£39.50	
	Pistol	Falcon	.177	—	—	—	—	£29.50	
B.S.A. Manufacturers B.S.A. Guns Ltd, Armoury Road, Birmingham B1 Tel: 021-772 8543	Rifle	Meteor	.177	650 fps min	Break barrel	18.5″	6lb	£49.95	
	Rifle	Meteor	.22	500 fps min	Break barrel	18.5″	6lb	£49.95	
	Rifle	Meteor S	.177	650 fps min	Break barrel	18.5″	6lb	£59.50	
	Rifle	Meteor S	.22	500 fps min	Break barrel	18.5″	6lb	£59.50	
	Rifle	Mercury	.177	700 fps min	Break barrel	18.5″	7lb	£79.95	
	Rifle	Mercury	.22	600 fps min	Break barrel	18.5″	7lb	£79.95	
	Rifle	Mercury S	.177	825 fps min	Break barrel	19.4″	7¼lb	£99.50	
	Rifle	Mercury S	.22	600 fps min	Break barrel	19.4″	7¼lb	£99.50	
	Rifle	Airsporter	.177	700 fps min	Under-lever	18.5″	8lb	£108.40	
	Rifle	Airsporter	.22	550 fps min	Under-lever	18.5″	8lb	£108.40	
	Rifle	Airsporter S	.177	825 fps min	Under-lever	19.5″	8lb	£135	
	Rifle	Airsporter S	.22	600 fps min	Under-lever	19.5″	8lb	£135	
	Pistol	Scorpion	.177	510 fps min	Break barrel	7⅞″	3.6lb	£49.95	
	Pistol	Scorpion	.22	380 fps min	Break barrel	7⅞″	3.6lb	£49.95	
	Rifle	Challenger	.177	850 fps min	Break barrel		7¼lb	£99.50	
	Rifle	Challenger	.22	625 fps min	Break barrel		7¼lb	£99.50	
	Rifle	Airsporter Stutzen	.177	850 fps min	Under-lever		7¾lb	£139.70	
	Rifle	Airsporter Stutzen	.22	625 fps min	Under lever		7¾lb	£139.70	
	Rifle	VS 2000	.177	850 fps min	Side-lever		9lb	£158.70	
	Rifle	VS 2000	.22	625 fps min	Side-lever		9lb	£158.70	
	Rifle	VS 2000 Custom	—	—	—	—	9lb	£210	As VS2000 + Custom walnut stock
CROSMAN Distributors Scalemead Arms Co Tel: 034282 4433	Rifle	Model 1	.22	535 fps	—	—	5.1lbs	£66	Sporting rifle
	Rifle	760 Pumpmaster	.177/BB	530 fps	—	—	4.2lbs	£32	Repeating rifle
	Rifle	766	.177/BB	575 fps	—	—	4.2lbs	£55	Repeating rifle
	Pistol	1322/1377 Medalist	.177/.22	—	—	—	5.6lbs	£49.95	
	Rifle	1766 Classic	.177/BB	600 fps	—	—	4.9lbs	£55.50	Repeating rifle
	Rifle	2200 Magnum	.22	535 lbs	—	—	11 lbs	£55	Sporting rifle
DAN ARMS	Rifle	Junior	.177 or .22	6 ft lbs	Break barrel	—	5lbs 1oz	£30	
	Rifle	Standard	.177 or .22	6½ ft lbs	Break barrel	—	6lbs 6oz	£39	—
	Rifle	De Luxe	.177 or .22	6½ ft lbs	Break barrel	—	6.13ozs 3.1kg	£49	—
	Pistol	Standard	.177 or .22	—	Break barrel	—	—	£35	

AIR WEAPONS cont.

MAKE	PISTOL/ RIFLE	MODEL	CALIBRE	POWER	ACTION	BARREL LENGTH	WEIGHT	APPROX RETAIL PRICE	COMMENTS
DAYSTATE Manufacturers Daystate Ltd Newcastle St., Stone, Staffs. ST15 8JU Tel: 0785 812473	Rifle	Huntsman	.22	Up to 30 ft lbs	Pneumatic	—	3.75kg	£250	Air reservoir giving 100 shots at 12 ft lb
	Rifle	Spotsman	.22	Up to 25 ft lbs	Pneumatic	—	3.55kg	£275	Pump up
	Pistol	Competa	.177 or .22	Up to 30 ft lbs	Pneumatic	—	1.30kg	£225+	Air reservoir model. Basic pistol without sights etc, from £225
DIANA/RWS Distributors Leslie Hewett Ltd Tel: 0579 62319	Rifle	24	.177, .22	574/492 fps	Break barrel	17¼"	6.0lbs	£41.86	
	Rifle	26	.177, .22	656/541 fps	Break barrel	17¼"	6.2lbs	£55.75	
	Rifle	27	.177, .22	656/509 fps	Break barrel	17¼"	6.lbs	£75.23	
	Rifle	34	.177, .22	850/625 fps	Break barrel	19½"	7.4lbs	£70.09	
	Rifle	45	.177, .22	853/665 fps	Break barrel	20½"	7.7lbs	£78.53	
	Rifle	50	.177, .22	771/623 fps	Underlever	19¼"	8.2lbs	£106.36	
	Rifle	75 Match 75 HV 75UTOI 75 KTOI	.177	N/A	Side lever	18⅞"	11.0lbs	£290.32	4 Models available
	Pistol	5g	.177	126 m/s	—	180mm	1.2kg	£62.04	
	Pistol	5gs	.177	126 m/s	—	180mm	1.2kg	£79.34	With scope
	Pistol	6g	.177	125 m/s	—	180mm	1.4kg	£98.15	
	Pistol	6gs	.177	125 m/s	—	180mm	1.4kg	£116.32	With scope
	Pistol	6m	.177	125 m/s	—	180mm	1.4kg	£118.89	
	Pistol	10RT	.177	140 m/s	—	180mm	1.5kg	£213.16	
	Pistol	10LT	.177	140 m/s	—	180mm	1.5kg	£225.71	
FAS Distributors Oliver J. Gower Ltd, Leighton Buzzard, Bedfordshire Tel: 0525 377730	Pistol	604	.177	385 fps	Top lever	190gm	£229		Recoiless
	Pistol	604	.177	385 fps	Top lever	190gm			
	Pistol	604	.177	385 fps	Top lever	190mm	990gm	£229	Recoiless pneumatic match pistol
FEINWERKBAU Distributors A.S.I. Tel: 072888 555	Rifle	300SU	.177	—	—	—	—	From £363.25	
	Rifle	300S	.177	—	—	—	—	From £315.10	
	Rifle	300 S Junior	.177	—	—	—	4.0 kg	From £284.65	
	Rifle	300S Running Target	.177	—	—	—	—	From £297.40	
	Rifle	Sport Mk 2	.177 & .22	—	—	—	—	From £135	
	Pistol	65	.177	—	—	—	—	From £268.05	Walnut and anatomical grips
	Pistol	80	.177	—	—	—	—	From £283.30	Anotomical grip 3 barrel weights
	Pistol	CO₂ Gas	.177	—	—	—	—	From £293.60	
	Pistol	90 Electronic	.177	—	—	—	—	From £332.90	Electronic trigger, adjustablle sighting
PANTHER Distributor Phoenix Arms Co Ltd Tel: 0323 645131	Pistol	Standard	.177 & .22	220 fps	Break action	7"	—	N/A	Contoured chequered grip. Target sights
	Pistol	De-Luxe	.177 &	250 fps	Break action	7¼"	—	N/A	Match grip Fore and rear sights
	Pistol	Artillery Carbine	.177	300 fps	Break action	13"	—	N/A	Micro sights Shoulder stock
RECORD Distributors John Rothery (Wholesale) Co Ltd Tel: 0705 667323	Pistol	1	.177	260 FS	Break barrel	—	610gm	£14.80	Smooth barrel
	Pistol	2	.177	283 FS	Break barrel	—	780gm	£20.52	Rifled barrel
	Pistol	68	.177	335 FS	Break barrel	—	1.45kg	£38.80	Rifled barrel
	Pistol	77	.177	389 FS	Break barrel	—	1.0kg	£28.65	Rifled barrel
	Pistol	Jumbo	.177	302 FS	Top lever	—	950 gm	£44.65	Rifled barrel
	Pistol	Jumbo DLX	.177	302 FS	Top lever	—	980 gm	£51.55	Rifled barrel

AIR WEAPONS cont.

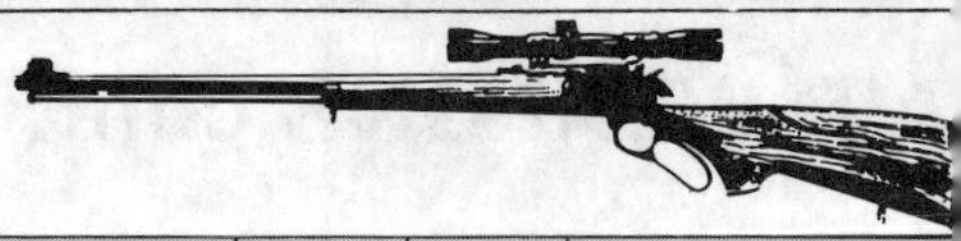

MAKE	PISTOL/ RIFLE	MODEL	CALIBRE	POWER	ACTION	BARREL LENGTH	WEIGHT	APPROX RETAIL PRICE	COMMENTS
SHARP Distributors Hull Cartridge Co. Ltd., Bontoft Avenue, National Ave., Hull	Rifle	ACE	.177/.22	—	Multi-stroke Pneumatic	608mm	2.85kg	N/A	
	Rifle	INNOVA	.177/.22	—	Multi-stroke Pneumatic	508mm	2kgs	N/A	
WALTHER Distributors Accuracy International (Shooting Sports) Ltd, 43 Gladys Ave, Northend, Portsmouth, Hants Tel: 0705 660371/2	Rifle	LGR Match	.177	Less than 12 ft lb	Single stroke Pneumatic	500mm	4.7kg	N/A	Recoilless precision target air rifle
	Rifle	LU Universal	.177	Less than 12 ft lb	Single stroke Pneumatic	500mm	4.6kg	N/A	Recoilless precision target air rifle with adjustable cheekpiece
	Rifle	LGR Moving Target	.177	Less than 12 ft lb	Single stroke Pneumatic	500mm	4.7kg	N/A	Recoilless precision target air rifle designed for UIT Running Boar
	Pistol	CP2	.177	Less than 6ft lb from regulated liquid CO_2 cylinder	CO_2	220mm	1180g with full cylinder	N/A	Recoilless precision target pistol
WEBLEY Manufacturers Webley and Scott Ltd, Frankley Industrial Park, Tay Road, Rubery, Birmingham B45 0PA Tel: 021 453 1864	Rifle	Air Wolf	.177 or .22	10 ft lbs	Break barrel	17⅜"	6lbs 2.7kg	£49.50	Rifled barrel, scope grooves, auto safe, adjustable sights
	Rifle	Victor	.177 or .22	10.7 ft lbs	Break barrel	17⅛"	7.0lbs 3.18kg	£66.50	Rifled barrel, scope grooves, adjustable sights
	Rifle	Beeman C1	.177 or .22	12 ft lbs	Break barrel	14"	6.8lbs 3.1kg	£79.50	Rifled barrel, scope grooves, safety catch, adjustable sights
	Rifle	Vulcan	.177 or .22	12 ft lbs	Break barrel	19¼"	7.75kg 3.52kg	£87.50	Rifled barrel, scope grooves, safety catch, adjustable sights
	Rifle	Vulcan DeLuxe	.177 or .22	12 ft lbs	Break barrel	19¼"	7.85kg 3.56kg	£112	Rifled barrel, scope grooves, safety catch, adjustable sights, walnut stock
	Rifle	Viscount	.177 or .22	12 ft lbs	Side lever	18½"	7.6lbs 3.45kg	£105	Rifled barrel, scope grooves, safety catch, adjustable sights
	Rifle	Viscount DeLuxe	.177 or .22	12 ft lbs	Side lever	18½"	7.7lbs 3.5kg	£129.78	Rifled barrel, scope grooves, safety catch, adjustable sights, walnut stock
	Rifle	Tracker	.177 or .22	12 ft lbs	Side lever	11⅜"	7.0lbs 3.18kg	£108.73	Rifled barrel, scope grooves, safety catch, adjustable sights, barrel weight
	Rifle	Tracker and scope	.177 or .22	12 ft lbs	Side lever	11⅜"	8.3lbs 3.76kg	£160.98	Rifled barrel, 4×32 scope, safety catch, arrester block, barrel weight
	Rifle	Tracker DeLuxe	.177 or .22	12 ft lbs	Side lever	11⅜"	7.1lbs 3.22kg	£135	Rifled barrel, scope grooves, safety catch, adjustable sights, barrel weight, walnut stock
	Rifle	Tracker Deluxe + Scope	.177 or .22	12 ft lbs	Side lever	11⅜"	8.4lbs 3.8kg	£185.54	Rifled barrel, 4×32 scope, safety catch, arrester block, barrel weight, walnut stock
	Rifle	Ranger	.177	4.0 ft lbs	Under lever	17¾"	6.4lbs 2.9kg	£174	Rifled barrel, recoilless action, scope grooves, safety catch, cleaning rod
	Rifle	Omega	.177 or .22	12 ft lbs	Break barrel	19¼"	7"9lbs 3.6kg	£125	Rifled barrel, barrel lock, two stage trigger, scope grooves safety catch, adjustable sights
	Pistol	Tempest	.177 or .22	3.6 ft lbs	Break barrel over cylinder	6⅞"	2.09lbs 0.9kg	£54.95	Rifled barrel, adjustable sights, safety catch, adjustable trigger
	Pistol	Hurricane	.177 or .22	3.6 ft lbs	Break barrel over cylinder	8"	2.4lbs 1.1kg	£64.95	Rifled barrel, click adjustable sights, safety catch, adjustable trigger.

AIR WEAPONS cont.

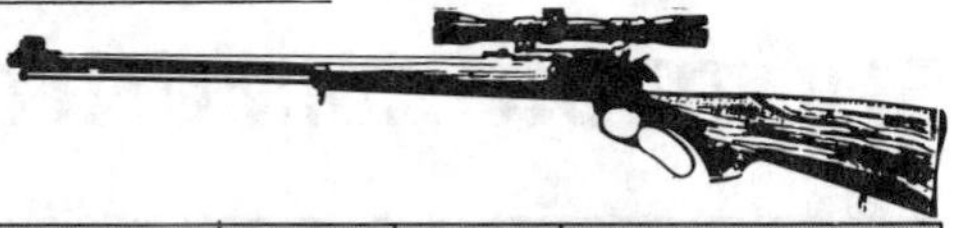

MAKE	PISTOL/RIFLE	MODEL	CALIBRE	POWER	ACTION	BARREL LENGTH	WEIGHT	APPROX RETAIL PRICE	COMMENTS
WEIHRAUCH Distributors Hull Cartridge Co. Ltd., Bontoft Avenue, National Ave., Hull	Rifle	HW30	.177/.22	—	Break barrel	430mm	2.5kg	N/A	
	Rifle	HW35	.177/.22	12ft lbs	Break barrel	500mm	3.8kg	N/A	
	Rifle	HW35E	.177/.22	12ft lbs	Break barrel	560mm	3.9kg	N/A	
	Pistol	HW45	.177/.22	6ft lbs	Break barrel Over cylinder	170mm	1.15kgs	N/A	
	Rifle	HW50	.177/.22	—	Break barrel	470mm	3.1kgs	N/A	
	Rifle	HW55	.177/.22	—	Break barrel	470mm	3.7kg - 4.1	N/A	Precision Match 4 Models
	Pistol	HW70	.177	—	Break barrel	160mm	1.10kg	N/A	
	Rifle	HW77/77K	.177/.22	12ft lbs	Underlever	470mm/370mm	4.1kg	N/A	Long Range
	Rifle	HW80	.177/.22	12ft lbs	Break barrel	500mm	4.0kgs	N/A	Long Range

SHOTGUN AMMUNITION

MAKE	MODEL	CALIBRE	SHOT SIZES	LOAD	LENGTH	CASE	WAD	CLOSURE	APPROX RETAIL PRICE	COMMENTS
CALEDONIAN Manufacturers Caledonian Cartridge Co. Ltd. Tel: 067481 342/361	C.C. Classic	12, 16, 20	4, 5, 6, 7	1oz, 1 1/16oz	67.5mm	Plastic	Fibre or plastic	Crimp	N/A	Game Cartridge
	C.C. Champion	12	7, 7½, 9	1⅛oz	67.5mm	Plastic	Plastic	Crimp	N/A	Trap and Skeet
	C.C. Supamax	12	BB, 1, 3, 4, 5	1¼oz	70mm	Plastic	Plastic	Crimp	N/A	Wildfowling
DAN ARMS	Trap	12	7½/8	1⅛oz	70mm	Red Plastic	Plastic	Crimp		
	Skeet	12	9	1⅛oz	70mm	White Plastic	Plastic	Crimp		
	Max Trap	12	7½/8	1⅛oz	70mm	Yellow Plastic	Plastic	Crimp		
	Fibre Trap	12	7½	1⅛oz	70mm	Red Plastic	Fibre	Crimp		
	Fibre Skeet	12	9	1⅛oz	70mm	White Plastic	Fibre	Crimp		
	Game 28.5	12	6/7	1oz	67mm	Green Paper	Fibre Fibre	Crimp Crimp		
	Game 30	12	6/7	1 1/16 oz	67mm	Orange Plastic	Fibre	Crimp		
	Game 32	12	5/6/7	1⅛oz	70mm	Green Plastic	Plastic	Crimp		
	Game 36	12	3/5	1¼oz	70mm	Blue Plastic	Plastic	Crimp		
	Super Max	12	/35	1½oz Copper plated	70mm	Red Plastic	Plastic	Crimp		
	Super Magnum	12	3/5	2oz Copper plated	75mm	Red Plastic	Plastic	Crimp		
	Twenty	20	6/7½/9	1oz	70mm	Yellow Plastic	Plastic	Crimp		
ELEY Manufacturers Eley Limited PO Box 705, Witton, Birmingham B6 7UT Tel: 021 356 8899	Grand Prix	12	BB, 1, 3, 4 5, 6, 7,	1 1/16	2½″/65mm	Orange Plastic	Kleena	Crimp	N/A	
	Grand Prix	12	LG SG	1 1/16	2½″/65mm	Orange Plastic	Kleena	Rolled	N/A	
	Grand Prix	12	SpecSG AAA	1 1/16	2½″/65mm	Orange Plastic	Kleena	Rolled	N/A	
	Grand Prix HV	12	BB, 1, 4, 5, 6 & 7	1⅛	2½″/65mm	Orange Plastic	Kleena	Crimp	N/A	
	Impax	12	6 & 7	1oz	2½″/65mm	Orange Plastic	Kleena	Crimp	N/A	
	Impax	12	6 & 7	1oz	2½″/65mm	Orange Paper	Kleena	Crimp	N/A	

SHOTGUN AMMUNITION cont.

MAKE	MODEL	CALIBRE	SHOT SIZES	LOAD	LENGTH	CASE	WAD	CLOSURE	APPROX RETAIL PRICE per 100	COMMENTS
ELEY cont.	Super Game	12	6	1⅛	2½"/65mm	Orange Plastic	Monowad	Crimp	N/A	
	Two Inch	12	6 & 7	⅞oz	2"/65mm	Oran/Crim Paper	Kleena	Rolled	N/A	
	International Game	12	5, 6, 7	1¹⁄₁₆	2½"/65mm	Crimson Plastic	Monowad	Crimp	N/A	
	Grand Prix	16	1, 3, 4, 5, 6, 7, BB	¹⁵⁄₁₆oz	2½"/65mm	Blue Plastic	Kleena	Crimp	N/A	
	Grand Prix	20	4, 5, 6, 7	¹³⁄₁₆oz	2½"/65mm	Yellow Plastic	Kleena	Crimp	N/A	
	Grand Prix	28	6	⁹⁄₁₆oz	2½"/65mm	Crimson Plastic	Kleena	Rolled	N/A	
	Fourten	.410	6	⁵⁄₁₆oz	2"/65mm	Crimson Plastic	Kleena	Rolled	N/A	
	Fourlong	.410	4, 5, 6	⁷⁄₁₆oz	2½"/65mm	Crimson Plastic	Kleena	Rolled	N/A	
	Extra-long	.410	6	⅝oz	3"	Crimson Plastic	Kleena	Rolled	N/A	
	Magnum	12	BB, 1, 3, 4	1⅝oz	3"/75mm	Crimson Plastic	Monowad	Crimp	N/A	
	Magnum	12	BB & 3	1½oz	2¾"/70mm	Crimson Plastic	Monowad	Crimp	N/A	
	Alphamax	12	BB, 1, 3, 4, 5, 6, 7	1¼oz	2¾"/70mm	Crimson Plastic	Monowad	Crimp	N/A	
	Alphamax	12	LG SG SPSG, AAA	1¼oz	2¾"/70mm	Crimson Plastic	Kleena	Rolled	N/A	
	Hymax	12	1, 3, 4, 5, 6	1¼oz	2¾"/70mm	Green Plastic	Monowad	Crimp	N/A	
	Maximum	12	4, 5, 6	1³⁄₁₆oz	2½"/65mm	Orange Plastic	Monowad	Crimp	N/A	
	Maximum	12	BB	1³⁄₁₆oz	2½"/65mm	Orange Plastic	Kleena	Crimp	N/A	
	Alphamax	16	4, 5, 6	1⅛oz	2¾"/70mm	Blue Plastic	Kleena	Crimp	N/A	
	Alphamax	20	4, 5, 6	1⅛oz	2¾"/70mm	Yellow Plastic	Kleena	Crimp	N/A	
	Olympic Trap	12	7½ (lead) 8	1⅛oz	2¾"/70mm	Blue Plastic	Monowad	Crimp	N/A	
	Olympic Trap	12	7½ (Nickel)	1⅛oz	2¾"/70mm	Blue Plastic	Monowad	Crimp	N/A	
	Olimpic Skeet	12	9	1⅛oz	28"/70mm	Blue Plastic	Monowad	Crimp	N/A	
	Trap Extra	12	7	1⅛oz	2½"/65mm	Green Plastic	Kleena	Crimp	N/A	
	Skeet Extra	12	9	1⅛oz	2½"/65mm	Red Plastic	Kleena	Crimp	N/A	
	Olimpic Gold	12	7½/Ni/b	1⅛oz	2¾"/70mm	Burgundy Paper	Monowad	Crimp	N/A	
	International Trap	12	7½	1⅛oz	2½"/65mm	Crimson Plastic	Monowad	Crimp	N/A	
	International Skeet	12	9	1⅛oz	2½"/65mm	Crimson Plastic	Monowad	Crimp	N/A	
FIOCCHI Distributors Hull Cartridge Co. Ltd., Bontoft Avenue, National Ave., Hull	VIP1	12	7½, 8	1⅛oz	70mm	Maroon Plastic	Plastic	Crimp	N/A	
	International Skeet	12	9½	1⅛oz	70mm	Maroon Plastic	Plastic	Crimp	N/A	
	VIP2	12	7½, 8	1⅛oz	70mm	Maroon Plastic	Plastic	Crimp	N/A	
	VIP3	12	7½, 8	1⅛oz	70mm	Maroon Plastic	Plastic	Crimp	N/A	
	Game & Target	12	7½, 8	1⅛oz	70mm	Orange Plastic	Plastic	Crimp	N/A	
	Semi Mag.	12	0, 3, 4	1⅜oz	70mm	Black Plastic	Plastic	Crimp	N/A	
	Magnum	12	0, 3, 4	1¾oz	76mm	Black Plastic	Plastic	Crimp	N/A	
	PL1	24	6, 7	20.075gms	65mm	Red Plastic	Plastic	Rolled	N/A	
	PL1	28	5, 6, 7	16.425gms	65mm	Red Plastic	Plastic	Rolled	N/A	

SHOTGUN AMMUNITION cont.

MAKE	MODEL	CALIBRE	SHOT SIZES	LOAD	LENGTH	CASE	WAD	CLOSURE	APPROX RETAIL PRICE per 100	COMMENTS
FIOCCHI cont.	PL1	.410	6	9.125gms	51mm	Red Plastic	Plastic	Rolled	N/A	
	PL1	32	6, 7	½oz	65mm	Red Plastic	Plastic	Rolled	N/A	
	PL1	.410	4, 5, 6, 7	⅜oz	65mm	Red Plastic	Plastic	Rolled	N/A	
	Flobert	9mm	7½							
GAMEBORE **Manufacturers** **Gamebore Cartridge Co.** **0482 223707**	Game	12	4, 5, 6, 7	28, 30, 32g.	67mm	Blue Plastic	Plastic cup or fibre	6 star Crimp	N/A	
	Special Game	12	BB to 7	36	69mm	Red Plastic	Plastic cup or fibre	6 star Crimp	N/A N/A	
	Special Game	12	BB to 5	42	69mm	Green Plastic	Plastic cup or fibre	Rolturn	N/A	
	20 Gauge	20	4 to 7	24, 28	67mm	Orange Plastic	Plastic cup or fibre	6 star Crimp	N/A	
	Trap Xclant	12	7	32	67mm	Black Plastic	Plastic	6 star Crimp	N/A	
	Trap Xclant Super Competition	12	7, 7½	32	69mm	Black Plastic	Plastic	6 star Crimp	N/A	
	Skeet Xclant	12	9	32	67mm	Red Plastic	Fibre wad	6 star Crimp	N/A	
	Skeet Xclant Super Competition	12	9	32	69mm	Red Plastic	Fibre wad	6 star Crimp	N/A	
	Fitasc 36	12	7, 8, 9	36	69mm	Plastic	Plastic cup	6 star Crimp	N/A	
	Special load	12	LG, SG, AA, BB	32, 36, 42	67mm	Plastic	Fibre wad	Roll turn	N/A	
	Supreme Slug	12	Brenneke	—	67mm	Plastic	Fibre wad	Roll turn	N/A	
	Super Game	12	6	32	67	Plastic	Plastic	6 star Crimp	N/A	
	Super Trap	12	7/7½	32	67mm	Plastic	Plastic	6 star Crimp	N/A	
	Super Skeet	12	9	32	67mm	Plastic	Plastic	6 star Crimp	N/A	
	.410"	.410	6/7	11.00	65mm	Plastic	Plastic	Roll burn	N/A	
HULL **Manufacturers** **Hull Cartridge Co. Ltd.,** **Bontoft Avenue,** **National Ave.,** **Hull**	Three Crowns	12	All sizes	1oz	65mm	Red-Paper/ Plastic	Fibre	Crimp	N/A	
	Three Crowns	12	All Sizes	29½gms	70mm	Red-Plastic/ Plastic	Fibre or Plastic	Crimp	N/A	
	Three Crowns	12	All Sizes	27g	65mm	Red-Paper/ Plastic	Fibre	Crimp	N/A	
	Three Crowns	16, 20	All Sizes	27g	65mm	Blue/Yellow Plastic	Fibre	Crimp	N/A	
	Competition Trap	12	7, 7½, 8	1⅛oz	70mm	Silver Plastic	Fibre or Plastic	Crimp	N/A	
	Competition	12	9	1⅛oz	70mm	Silver Plastic	Fibre or Plastic	Crimp	N/A	
	Hulmax	12	BB, 4, 5, 6		70mm	Red Plastic	Plastic	Crimp	N/A	
	Ultramax	12	BB, 4, 5, 6	1¼oz	70mm	Red Plastic	Plastic	Crimp	N/A	
KENT **Manufacturers** **Kent Cartridge** **Manufacturing Co. Ltd.** **Tel: 0622 872255**	Trap	12	7½	1⅛oz	67mm	Plastic	Plastic monowad	Crimp	N/A	
REMINGTON **Distributors** **Hull Cartridge Co. Ltd.,** **Bontoft Avenue,** **National Avenue,** **Hull**	Nitro Mag. Buffered Loads SP12 NM/HNM	12	BB, 2, 4, 6	1⅝, 1⅞oz	3"	Green Plastic	Plastic Power Piston	Crimp	N/A	

SHOTGUN AMMUNITION cont.

MAKE	MODEL	CALIBRE	SHOT SIZES	LOAD	LENGTH	CASE	WAD	CLOSURE	APPROX RETAIL PRICE per 100	COMMENTS
REMINGTON cont.	Express Mag. SP10 MAG.	10	BB, 2, 4	2oz	3½"	Green Plastic	Plastic Power Piston	Crimp	N/A	
	Express Extra Long SP12	12	BB, 2, 4, 5, 6, 7½, 9	1¼oz	2¾"	Green Plastic	Plastic Power Piston	Crimp	N/A	
	SP20	20	4, 5, 6, 7½, 9	1oz	2¾"	Yellow Plastic	Plastic Power Piston	Crimp	N/A	
	SP28	28	6, 7½	¾oz	2¾"	Green Plastic	Plastic Power Piston	Crimp	N/A	
	SP4103	.410	4, 5, 6, 7½, 9	20.075gms	3"	Green Plastic	Plastic Power Piston	Crimp	N/A	
	SHUR SHOT									
	R12H	12	4, 5, 6, 7½, 8, 9	1⅛oz	2¾"	Green Plastic	Plastic Power Piston	Crimp	N/A	
	R20M	20	4, 5, 6, 7½, 8, 9	1oz	2¾"	Yellow Plastic	Plastic Power Piston	Crimp	N/A	
	Express Power Pakt SP12RS	12	HP Rifled Slug	1oz	2¾"	Green Plastic	Fibre	Rolled	N/A	
	SP12BK	12	00 Buckshot Pellets - 9	—	2¾"	Green Plastic	Plastic Power Piston	Crimp	N/A	
	PR12 H Mag	12	BB, 2, 4	1⅞oz	3"	Green Plastic	Plastic Power Piston	Crimp	N/A	
	PR20S Mag	20	4, 6	1⅛oz	2¾"	Yellow Plastic	Plastic Power Piston	Crimp	N/A	
	PR20H Mag	20	2, 4, 6	1¼oz	3"	Yellow Plastic	Plastic Power Piston	Crimp	N/A	
ROTTWEIL Distributors Leslie Hewett Ltd. Upton Cross, Liskeard, Cornwall Tel: 0579 62319	Special MkII	12	5, 6½, 7, 8 & 9	29½g	67½mm	Plastic	Plastic	Star Crimp	£111.89	200 pack
	Club 32	12	7 & 9	32g/1⅛oz	67½mm	Plastic	7-plastic 9-Felt	Star Crimp	£115.58	200 pack
	Club 32	16	7	27g	67½mm	Plastic	Plastic	Star Crimp	£118.99	200 pack
	Club 32	20	6½	25½g/⅞	67½mm	Plastic	Plastic	Star Crimp	£120.33	200 pack
	CX Trap	12	7	32g/1⅛oz	67½mm	Plastic	Plastic	Star Crimp	£120.33	200 pack
	CX	12	8	32g/1⅛oz	67½mm	Plastic	Plastic	Star Crimp	£120.33	200 pack
	CX Skeet	12	9	32g/1⅛oz	67½mm	Plastic	Felt	Star Crimp	£120.33	200 pack
	Nickel Trap	12	7	32g/1⅛oz	67½mm	Plastic	Plastic	Star Crimp	£140.50	200 pack
	Supertrap	12	7	32g/1⅛oz	70mm	Plastic	Plastic	Star Crimp	£201.48	200 pack
	Stern	12	9	32g/1⅛oz	67½mm	Plastic	Greased Felt	Star Crimp	£174.01	200 pack
	Game 32	12	4, 5 & 6½	32g/1⅛oz	67½mm	Plastic	Plastic	Star Crimp	£121.76	200 pack
	Game 20	20	6½	25½g	67½mm	Plastic	Plastic	Star Crimp	£115.56	200 pack
	Tiger	12	4, 5 & 6½	32g/1oz	67½mm	Plastic	Plastic	Star Crimp	£156.72	200 pack
	Tiger Game	16	6½	27g	67½mm	Plastic	Plastic	Star Crimp	£156.72	200 pack
	Tiger Game	20	5 & 6½	25½g	67½mm	Plastic	Plastic	Star Crimp	£156.72	200 pack
	Waidmann- sheil	12	BB, 1, 2, 3, 4 & 5	36g/1¼oz	70mm	Plastic	Plastic	Star Crimp	£208.84	200 pack
	Waidmann- sheil	20	BB, 4 & 5	27g	70mm	Plastic	Plastic	Star Crimp	£208.84	200 pack
	Waidmann- sheil	16	BBB, BB, 4 & 6½	31g	70mm	Plastic	Plastic	Star Crimp	£208.84	200 pack
	Express	12	SSG	32g	67½mm	Plastic	Greased Felt	Star Crimp	£208.84	200 pack
	Express	12	SP-SG	32g	67½mm	Plastic	Greased Felt	Star Crimp	£208.84	200 pack
	Brenneke	12	Slug	31g	70mm	Plastic	Greased Felt Plastic comb.	Star Crimp	£362.60	200 pack
	Express	12	SG/LG	32g	67½mm	Plastic	Greased Felt	Star Crimp	£208.84	200 pack
	Rottweil	.410	6½	—	12mm	Plastic	Plastic	Star Crimp	£139.65	200 pack

SHOTGUN AMMUNITION cont.

MAKE	MODEL	CALIBRE	SHOT SIZES	LOAD	LENGTH	CASE	WAD	CLOSURE	APPROX RETAIL PRICE per 100	COMMENTS
SELLIER & BELLOT Distributors Edgar Brothers Catherine Street, Macclesfield SK11 6SG Tel: 0625 613177	Trap	12	6½	1⅛oz	67mm	Red Plastic	Felt	Crimp	N/A	
	Skeet	12	9	1⅛oz	67mm	Red Plastic	Felt	Crimp	N/A	
	Mk III	12	4, 5, 6, 7	1⅛oz	67mm	Red Plastic	Felt	Crimp	N/A	
	Mk II	12	4, 5, 6, 7	1⅛oz	67mm	Orange Paper	Felt	Crimp	N/A	
	Trap Super	12	6½	1⅛oz	67mm	Red Plastic	Plastic	Crimp	N/A	
	Skeet Super	12	9	1⅛oz	67mm	Red Plastic	Plastic	Crimp	N/A	
	Practice	12	6½ & 9	⅞oz	60mm	Red Paper	Felt	Crimp	N/A	
	Black Star	12	BB, 2, 4 & 5	1¼oz	70mm	Black Paper	Felt	Crimp	N/A	
	Orange Tiger	12	SG, LG, AAA	1⅛oz	67mm	Orange Paper	Felt	Rolled	N/A	
	Special Trap	12	6½	1⅛oz	67mm	Red Paper	Plastic	Crimp	N/A	
TOPMARK UNIVERSAL Manufacturers Kent Cartridge Manufacturing Co. Ltd. Tel: 0622 872255	Skeet	12	9	32g	67mm	Plastic	Plastic or Fibre	—	—	
	Trap	12	7½	32g	67mm	Plastic	Plastic or Fibre	—	—	
	Game	12	4, 5, 6	32g	67mm	Plastic	Plastic	—	—	
	Game	12	5, 6, 7	30g	67mm	Plastic	Plastic	—	—	
	Game	12	6	30g	67mm	Plastic	Fibre	—	—	
TOPMARK PIGEON	Economy	12	5, 6, 7½ 9	32g	67mm	Plastic	Plastic	—	—	
	1oz	12	6, 7½	28g	67mm	Plastic	Plastic	—	—	
	G.P. Turbo's General purpose	12	5, 6, 7½, 9	32g	67mm	Plastic	Plastic	—	—	
	Topmark Duck & Goose Wildfowling	12	3, 4, 6	36g	70mm	Plastic	Plastic	—	—	
		12	1, 3	42g	70mm	Plastic	Plastic	—	—	

AIRGUN PELLETS

MAKE	MODEL	CALIBRE	PELLET TYPE	PELLET WEIGHT	APPROX RETAIL PRICE per 100	COMMENTS
A.S.I. Tel: 072888 555 Alliance House, Snape Maltings, Snape, Saxmundham, Suffolk IP17 1SW		.177 or .22	Waisted & Pointed		0.98 to £1.10 tin of 500	
BEEMAN Distributors Webley and Scott Ltd. Tel: 021 453 1864	Silver Jet	.177	Tri-ring pointed	8.48 grains	£3.75 per tin of 500	Precision hunting pellet with three sealing rings
	Silver Jet	.20	Tri-ring pointed	11.21 grains	£3.60 per tin of 300	Precision hunting pellet with three sealing rings
	Silver Jet	.22	Tri-ring pointed	15.00 grains	£3.50 per tin of 250	Precision hunting pellet with three sealing rings
BULLDOG Manufacturers Lanes Pellets Ltd. 01 - 511 - 1312		.177	Diablo	7.3 grains	£1.20 per 500	An accurate all purpose pellet
		.22	Diablo	14. grains	£1.65 per 500	An accurate all purpose pellet
ELEY Manufacturer Eley Limited PO Box 705, Witton, Birmingham B6 7UT Tel: 021 356 8899	Wasp Match	.177 .177	Sporting & Target Target Match	7.5 grains 7.5 grains	N/A N/A	
	Wasp	.22	Sporting & Target	14 grains	N/A	

AIRGUN PELLETS cont.

MAKE	MODEL	CALIBRE	PELLET TYPE	PELLET WEIGHT	APPROX RETAIL PRICE per 100	COMMENTS
HUSTLER Distributors Scalemead Arms Co. Tel: 034282 4433		.177	Needlepoint twin ring	9 grains	£1.73 (500)	
		.22	Needlepoint twin ring	14 grains	£2.30 (500)	
	Harrier	.22	Twin ring	14 grains	£1.90 (500)	
	Tri-jet	.177	Triple ring needlepoint	—	£2.0 (500)	
	Strike	.177	Needlepoint	9 grains	£1.45 (500)	Free stick-on target in each tin
MARKSMAN Please note that we are sole manufacturers of Marksman Airgun Pellets. Distributors Lincoln Jeffries Tel: 021 359 3343		.177	General purpose/nunting	.53 grams	N/A	
		.22	General purpose/hunting	.9 grams	N/A	
		.22	Pointed	1.0 gram	N/A	
PROMETHEUS Distributors John Knibbs Gillia, Blackfirs Lane, Birmingham B37 7JE Tel: 021 779 3391		.22	Hunting	9.12 grains	£2.50 (100)	Lead free
		.177	Hunting	6 grains	£2.50 (125)	Lead free
		.22	Truncated	8.75 grains	£2.50 (100)	Lead free — Field target pellet
		.177	Truncated	6.00 grains	£2.50 (125)	Lead free — Field target pellet
RWS Distributors Leslie Hewett Ltd, Upton Cross, Liskeard, Cornwall Tel: 0579 62319	Hobby	.177	Practice	0.45g	£2.17	Packed in round boxes
	Hobby	.22	Practice	0.76g	£3.86	Packed in round tins
	Diablo	.22	Competition	0.5g	£3.22	Packed in round tins
	Diablo	.22	Competition	0.8g	£4.50	Packed in round tins
	Superpoint	.177	Hunting	0.5g	£3.22	Packed in round tins
	Superpoint	.22	Hunting	0.94g	£4.50	Packed in round tins
	Super H Point	.22	Hunting		£4.50	Packed in round tins
	Superdome	.177	Practice & Hunting		£3.22	Packed in round tins
	Superdome	.22	Practice & Hunting		£4.50	Packed in round tins
	Meisterkugein	.177 Airgun	Competition	0.54g	£3.24	Packed in round tins 500
	Meisterkugein	.177 Airgun	Competition	0.54g	£9.45	Match packs of 100
	Meisterkugein	.177 Airgun	Competition	0.54g	£7.84	Match refill packs
	Meisterkugein	.177 Airpistol	Competition	0.50g	£13.45	Match pack of 100
	Meisterkugein	.177 Airpistol	Competition	0.50g	£11.57	Match refill packs
	Meisterkugein	.177 Air rifle	Competition	0.54g	£13.45	Match pack of 100
	Meisterkugein	.177 Air rifle	Competition	0.54g	£11.57	Match refill packs
SABO Distributors Westhaven Marketing Ltd		.22	Hunting	14.0 grains	£1.85 (100)	Copper plated lead
		.177	Hunting	9.3 grains	£2.85 (200)	Copper plated lead. No dispenser required
TITAN BLACK manufacturer & Distributor Titan Airgun Products 98 Bath Street, Birmingham B4 6HG Tel: 021 779 3391	Titan Black	.177	Hunting	9.0 grains	£3.50(100)	Precision hunting pellet made specifically for F.A.C. rated and customised air rifles.
	Titan Black	.22	Hunting	13.4 grains	£3.50(100)	Precision hunting pellet made specifically for F.A.C. rated and customised air rifles
WEBLEY Manufacturers Webley and Scott Ltd, Frankley Industrial Park, Tay Road, Rubery, Birmingham, B45 0PA	Special	.177	Round nose diablo	8.3 grains	£1.24 per tin of 500	Ideal all round pellet
	Special	.22	Round nose diablo	13.7 grains	£1.70 per tin of 500	Ideal all round pellet
	GP	.177	Round nose diablo	7.3 grains	£1.76 per tin of 500	Perfect hunting pellet with high energy retention and accuracy
	GP	.22	Round nose diablo	14.3 grains	£2.48 per tin of 500	Perfect hunting pellet with high energy retention and accuracy
	Flying Scot	.177	Twin ring round nose diablo	7.3 grains	£2.02 per tin of 500	High velocity round nose hunting pellet
	Flying Scot	.22	Twin ring round nose diablo	14.2 grains	£2.40 per tin of 500	High velocity round nose hunting pellet

GUNSHOPS
CONTENTS

GUNSHOPS

The following list of gunshops does not purport to be a comprehensive list of all the retail trade outlets. The shops have been selected to provide suitable lists of outlets in each area. Some of the shops listed are BASC and GTA members where customers may be assured of receiving good service.

AVON

Avon Shooting Ltd
2 Market Place, Radstock, Avon, BA3 3AE, Tel: 0761 33167
Specialist in sporting guns, fishing tackle and accessories. Coaching, gun fitting and practice available at our own clay shooting range.

G J Bissex (Avon Shooting) Ltd
Hollowdene, 2 Market Place, Radstock, Tel: 0761 33167

County Firearms
'Woodlands' Warminster Road, Nr. Claverton, Bath, Tel: 022122 2224

I M Crudgington Ltd

37 Broad Street, Bath, BA1 5LT, Tel: 0225 64928/66325

Fish 'n Shoot
5 Cleveland Place East, Bath, Tel: 0225 336620

George Gibbs Ltd
3-4 Perry Road, Park Row, Bristol, BS1 5BQ, Tel: 0272 24824
Gunmakers, retailers and repairs. We are also game fishing specialists. Open 6 days a week 9.15 am to 5.00 pm.

Rowland's Limited
15 Green Street, Bath, BA1 2JZ, Tel: 0225 62911

Scott Tackle (R Crocker & P Kent)
42 Soundwell Road, Staple Hill, Bristol, BS16 4QP

Sheppard's Rod, Gun & Sports Centre
46 Bond Street, Bristol, BS1 3LZ, Tel: 0272 273351

JOHN EASTAFF

Elstow Storage Depot · Kempston Hardwick Bedford MK45 3NU
Telephone: Bedford 740834 (8 lines)
Telex: 826318
REGISTERED FIREARMS DEALER

A comprehensive range of shotguns, rifles, pistols & air weapons from Winchester, AYA, Beretta, Laurona, Kestral, Lanber, Perazzi, Baikal, etc.
Many types of stalking rifles.
Full overhauling & repair service.
A large selection of shooting accessories for the clay & game shooter; including clothing, clays, traps, cartridges, etc.

215

J B Sports

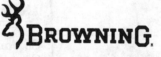

3 Repton Road, Sandy Park, Brislington, Bristol, 4, Tel: 0272 772633

BEDFORDSHIRE

Airmasters
2 Hibbert Street, Luton, Tel: 0582 26217

Bedford Target Supplies
Duck Mill Lane, Bedford, Tel: 0234 217838/9
The Shooting Specialist. A large selection of equipment for both the beginner and the beginner and the experienced shooter. Shotguns, sporting air rifles and pistols, match air rifles and pistols. Complete range of accessories. Comprehensive gunsmithing service. Open Monday to Saturday 9-6.

Bleak Hall Bird Farm (Kempston) Ltd
1 High Street, Kempston, Bedford

W Darlow
46 Ashburnham Road, Bedford, MK40 1EE, Tel: 0234 52056

Duglan & Cooper Ltd
14-16 Church Street, Dunstable, Tel: 0582 64649

John Eastaff

Elstow Storage Depot, Kempston, Hardwick, Bedford, Tel: 0234 740834
Full overhauling and repair service. A large selection of shooting accessories for the clay and game shooter, including clothing, clays, traps, cartridges etc.

Tom Lindars
82 North Street, Leighton Buzzard, Tel: 0525 372416

BERKSHIRE

Astral Sports
86 Northbrook Street, Newbury, Tel: 0635 35166
35166

Roxton Sporting Ltd
10 Bridge Street, Hungerford, Tel: 0488 82885

Thomas Turner Gunmaker
208 Gosbrook Road, Caversham, Reading RG4 88L, Tel: 0734 481699

Windsor Guns & Field Sports
9 St Leonards Road, Windsor, Tel: 07535 54023

BUCKINGHAMSHIRE

Benskins County Sports
15 Market Square, Winslow, Tel: 029671 2580

Berdan (Gunmakers) Ltd
Unit 1, Rabans Close, Rabans Lane Ind. Estate, Aylesbury, HP10 3RT, Tel: 0296 87408

W Cox
23 High Street, Chesham, HP5 1BG, Tel: 0494 771340

Fish & Field
62 Nelson Street, Buckingham, Tel: Buckingham 814495

Hartmann & Weiss Ltd (Gunmaker)
Folly Meadow, Hammersley Lane, Penn, Tel: 049481 2836

Jason Abbot Gunmakers Ltd

1-3 Bell Street, Princes Risborough, HP17 OAD, Tel: 08444 6677/6672

Rods 'n Guns
Rickmansworth Lane, Chalfont St. Peter, SL9 OJR, Tel: 024 027 5326

Wooburn Green Guns

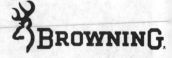

6 The Green, Wooburn Green, Tel: 062 85 28718

Wycombe Armoury
Westbourne Street, High Wycombe, HP11 2PZ

CAMBRIDGESHIRE

J A Cochrane & Son
24-25 Old Market, Wisbech, PE13 1NB

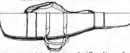
Gallyons
5 Cowgate, Peterborough, Tel: 0733 43152

John Bradshaw
Perio Mill, Fortheringhay,
Peterborough, PE8 5HU

Sheltons Gun and Tackle
67 South street, Stanground,
Peterborough, Tel: 0733 65287

The Cambridge Gun Centre
243-245 Newmarket Rd,
Cambridge, Tel: 0223 322161

Theoben Engineering
Stephenson Road, St Ives,
Huntingdon, Cambs, PE17 4WJ
High quality accessories for air rifle enthusiasts.

Thornton & Son
46-47 Burleigh Street, Cambridge, CB1
1DJ, Tel: 0223 358709

P G Woodward
Daintree Road, Ramsey St. Mary,
Huntingdon, PE17 1T, Tel: 073129 354

**A W Wright & Sons, Fenland
Gunsmith Ltd**

FENLAND GUNSMITH LTD.

98 Creek Road, March, PE15 8RO,
Tel: 0354 53290

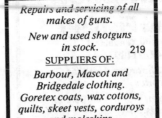
CHANNEL ISLANDS

M F Gotel Guns

14 Brighton Road, St. Helier, Jersey,
Tel: 0534 76588

The Gun Shop
7 Hauterville, St. Peter Port, Guernsey,
Tel: 0481 22409

Newton & Newton Ltd
3 Colomberie Parade, St Helier, Jersey,
Tel: 0534 33697

CHESHIRE

A Branthwaite
6-8 Ravenoak Road, Cheadle Hulme,
Tel: 061 485 1199

**Chester Gun Company (M + A
Foxton)**
23 Charles Street, Hoole, Chester.,
Tel: 0244 314694

The Countryman
Holly Bank, Manchester Road, Rixton,
Warrington, Tel: 061 775 2842

Foxton Gunsmiths

23 Charles Street, Hoole, Chester,
CH2 3AY, Tel: 0244 314694

Henry Monk (Gunmaker) Ltd

8 Queen Street, Chester, CH1 3LG,
Tel: 0244 20988
Game guns, rifles, clothing, Knives, game fishing tackle. A huge selection of books on shooting, fishing bags and their training and so much more.

**H G Hopkins & Sons
(Gunmakers)**

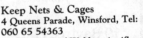

53-55 High Street, Sandbach, Tel:
09367 2404

E Jackson Gunsmith
37 Chester Road, Whitby, South
Wirral

Keep Nets & Cages
4 Queens Parade, Winsford, Tel:
060 65 54363
Wide selction of Webley air rifles and pellets, witby knives and shooting accessories. Also Shakespeare and Mitchell tackle. Open 6 days per week 9.00-5.30

Lymm Sports Centre
8 The Cross, Lymm, Tel: 092 575
3021
Specialist in all target disciplines. Gun repair

North Wales Shooting School

Sealand Manor, Sealand, Chester, Tel:
0244 812219

T T Proctor Ltd
88a Water Lane, Wilmslow, Tel:
0625 526654
Restocking and overhauls of shotguns and rifles

Sporting & Militaria Arms Ltd
Kerfield House, Knutsford, Tel: 0565
3344/4861

John W Simpson [22]
Shooting and Fishing

6 Bridge Road, Stokesley, Cleveland
Telephone: (0642) 711892

Large selection of Rifles, Shotguns, Air Rifles
and Accessories

Main dealer for Browning, Miroku, Winchester, Beretta,
Parker-Hale and B.S.A.

Extensive range of Barbour, Belstaff and other country clothing.

Also main stockists for Hardy, Shakespeare, Bruce Walker
and East Anglian Rod Co.

CLEVELAND

John F Gent Ltd
Firearms & Fishing Tackle Ltd, 161
York Road, Hartlepool, TS26 9EQ,
Tel: 0429 72585

ARMS

10 Baytree Hill, Liskeard, Cornwall, TEL: LISKEARD 46636
Registered Firearms Dealer

[23]

J W Simpson
6 Bridge Road, Stokesley, Tel: 0642
711892

A.Ward Thompson
5-6 Albert Road, Stockton-on-Tees,
Tel: 0642 607060

CORNWALL

Baytree Arms
10 Baytree Hill, Liskeard

Country Sports
Crantock Street, Newquay

R Drew Whurr (Specialist Gunsmith)
The Old Mill House, Helland Bridge,
Bodmin, PL30 4QR, Tel: St. Mabyn
(020884) 206

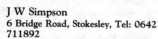

Forsyth Firearms

St Mary's Street, Truro, Tel: 0872
71744

A B Harvey & Son Ltd
1-2 Market Strand, Falmouth, TR11
3DA, Tel: 0326 312796

Helston Gunsmiths
The Clies, Meneage St, Helston, Tel:
03265 3385, Telex: 45117G

John Langdon
20 St. Mary Street, Truro, TR1 2AF

Kernow Feeds & Guns Ltd
4 St. Nicholas Street, Bodmin, Tel:
0208 6024

Lower Lake Shooting Grounds
Upton Cross, Liskeard, Tel: 0579
62319

Roy Dutch Firearms
21 High Cross Street, St Austell, Tel:
0726 72960

Southern Gun Co
4 Market Street, Bodmin, Tel: 0208
5915

Tackle Box
4 Market Square, Mevagissey, Tel:
072684 3513

Tony Kennedy Guns

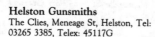
6 Church Street, Launceston, Tel: 0566
4465

CUMBRIA

J Albright (Ulverston) Limited
Ulverston, Tel: 0229 55641

Thomas Atkinson & Son
14 Stricklandgate, Kendal, Cumbria,
Tel: 0539 20300

Border Guns
10 Botchergate, Carlisle

Cumbria Countryman
Market Place, Ambleside, Tel: 096 63
3145

N John Ferguson
1/3 Fisher Street, Workington, Tel:
0900 61559
Over 100 weapons by leading makers,
English and foreign in stock. Clothing,
cartridges, clays, traps and accessories
for the game and clay shooter. Repairs,
overhauls and re-stocking.

Gun Shop, Ian Nicholson
Jubilee Bridge, Cockermouth, Tel: 0900
822058

W N Holmes & Son
45 Main Street, Egremont

Mr J W McHardy
South Henry Street, Carlisle, Tel:
022823988

John Norris of Penrith
21/22 Victoria Road, Penrith, Tel:
0768 64211

R Raine & Co
21 Warwick Road, Carlisle, Tel: 0228
23009

R A Sanders(Firearms)
Rocklands, Hard Cragg,Cartmel,Grange
Over Sands , Tel: 044854 476

Charles R Sykes
4 Great Dockray, Penrith, Tel: 0768
62418

Wells (Barrow) Ltd
56 Crellin Street, Barrow In Furness,
Tel: 0229 22681

Geoff Wilson Practical Gunsmiths
36 Portland Place, Carlisle, CA1 1RL,
Tel: 0228 31542

DERBYSHIRE

K Bancroft
82 Spire Hollin, Glossop, Tel:
04574 2599
All types of new and second hand
shotguns including Winchester/
Parker Hale. Also rifles and pistols,
ammo etc. Resident working
gunsmith.

F. Hall (Gunmakers) Ltd. [24]
Est. 1880
Beetwell Street,
CHESTERFIELD
Derbyshire
Tel: (0246) 73133

REGISTERED GUNSMITHS

MANUFACTURERS OF "HALLRITE"
SPORTING, TARGET & INDUSTRIAL
FIREARMS.
Appointed Distributors for:
COLT & BROWNING, SMITH &
WESSON SPECIALIST FOR OVER 35
YEARS. LARGE STOCK OF RIFLES,
PISTOLS & SHOTGUNS.
AIR WEAPONS BY LEADING MAKERS.
ALL TYPES OF ACCESSORIES &
RELOADING EQUIPMENT IN STOCK.
RFD 15 Derbys

J V Burrows Guns & Antiques
Sheeplea, Baslow Road, Eastmoor,
Chesterfield

Derby Shooting Supplies Ltd
1 and 3 Peel Street, , Derby, Tel: 0332
369500

Fosters Sporting Services Ltd
32 St John Street, Ashbourne, Tel:
0335 43135

F Hall Gunmakers Ltd
Beetwell Street, Chesterfield, S40
1SH, Tel: 0246 73133

Hilton Gun Co

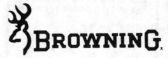
BROWNING

62 Station Road, Hatton, Tel: 0283
814141/814463

Matlock Gun Co
61/63 Smedley Street, East Matlock,
Tel: 0629 3892

J F Neville

6 King Street, Alfreton, Tel: 0773
834451
All leading makes of shotguns at
competitive prices. Part/exchange
welcome. Repairs and alterations by
our own gunsmith. Guns, ammunition
and clothing. Open 9.30
- 5.30 Mon-Sat, Thurs - 7pm.

W Parr (Firearms) International
32 Market Place, Belper, EE5 1F2,
Tel: 077382 6955
*Largest gunshop in the Midlands.
Over 500 guns in stock, including
sporting and military rifles. Extensive
shooting accessory dept closed
Wednesday, late night Friday 9.00
am - 8.00 pm*

Yeaveley Shooting Ground

Yeaveley, Ashbourne, Tel: 033 523 247

DEVON

**Atwell & Phipps, The
Gunsmiths**
16 Litchdon Street, Barnstaple, Tel:
0271 7807

Country Sports
9 William Street, Tiverton, Tel: 0884
254770

Drum Sports Ltd
47 Courtnay Street, Newton Abbot,
Tel: 0626 65333
*Pop in for our guns and accessories
range which includes air rifles and
pistols, cartridge belts and bags, rifle
slings and an excellent selection of
Barbour clothing.*

E Gale & Son Ltd
2-3 Mill Street, Bideford, Tel:
02372 72508

Gun & Sport Shop, The
76 Fore Street, Heavitree, Exeter,
EX1 2RR, Tel: 0392 71701
*Specialist gun, pistol and rifle
stockists. Air rifles ammunition,
knives, fishing tackle and militaria
weapons. We buy guns, rifles
and accessories.*

Gun Room, The
2 Church Street, Modbury, Ivybridge,
Tel: Modbury 830203

Gun Room & Sports Centre

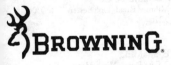

139 High Street, Ilfracombe, Tel:
0271 64546
*Stockists of Browning, Miroku,
Beretta etc. Large range of guns can be
tried before purchase.*

Keep, The
30 Brook Street, Tavistock, Tel: 0822
2509

Ladd's Guns & Sports

86/87 High Street, Crediton, Tel:
03632 2666

Mayson Firearms
170 Grenville Road, St Judes,
Plymouth, Tel: 0752 266436

M J W Sports Ltd

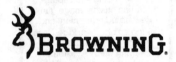

7/7a Dartmouth, Paignton

Neroche Armoury
High Street, Honiton, Tel: 0404 2100

Frank Richard (Gunsmiths)
25 Silver Street, Taunton, Tel: 0823
81487

Sportsman, The
7 Dartmouth Road, Paignton,
TQ5AB, Tel: 0803 558142/
551275

Staffords Gunsmiths
279 Union Street, Plymouth, Tel: 0752
664865

Stanley's Tackle Centre
12 Middle Street, Brixham, Tel:
Brixham 3080

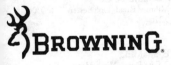

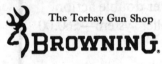

The Torbay Gun Shop

36 South Street, Torbay

John Webber (Sports)
79 Queen Street, Exeter, Tel: 0392
74975

DORSET

Arthur Conyers Ltd
3 West Street, Blandford, Tel: 0258
52307

**Edgcumbe Arms (Gunmakers)
Ltd**
1/11 Randolph Road, Parkstone,
Poole, Tel: 0202 740743
Subsidiary of Majex (UK) Ltd

Gunsports
871 Christchurch Road, Pokesdown,
Bournemouth, Tel: 0202 425735

Gunstock
23 Church Road, Parkstone, Poole,
Tel: 02027 35296

Messrs Hayman
13 Trinity Road, Weymouth

C Jeffrey & Sons
25 High East Street, Dorchester
GTA

John March (Firearms) Ltd

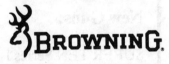

19 Westborough, Wimborne, Tel: 0202
888504

Modern & Antique Firearms
147 Tuckton Road, Bournemouth,
Tel: 0202 429369

Sport Equip
37 High Street,, Shaftsbury, Tel:
Shaftsbury 2511

Wessex Gun Sales
Clay Pigeon Cafe, Wardon Hill, Nr
Dorchester, Tel: 093 58 3368

DURHAM

Messrs W P Adams
42 Duke Street, Darlington, Tel: 0325
468069

**A & J Corbett Guns, Cartridges,
Clothing Etc**
Greenfoot, Stanhope, Tel: 0388 528306

Elvet Game Centre
8 New Elvet, Durham City, Tel:
0388 819500
*We sell best quality English guns.
Large selection of shooting accessories,
air weapons and firearms. Clothing
for all outdoor tastes. Open 9.00-5.00
Mon-Sat. 1/2 day Weds.*

Fosters Country Sport
1 Cleveland Street, Darlington, Tel:
0325 51351

A Ward Thompson
5/6 Albert Road, Stockton On Tees,
Cleveland

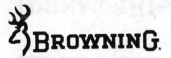
ESSEX

GLOUCESTERSHIRE

Allsports
126/128 Eastgate Street, Gloucester,
Tel: 0452 27324/22756

Chambers & Co Gunmakers

**Ideal Gunworks, Northleach, Tel:
04516 372**
Gloucestershire's leading gunsmiths. High class gun and rifle repairs of all descriptions carried out on the premises. Established 1870.

Corinium Gunshop

The **Corinium**
Gunshop

22 Castle Street, Cirencester, Tel:
0285 67527
Comprehensive range of weapons, clothing and auxilliary equipment. Repairs undertaken on the premises.

F J Cole (Cirencester) Ltd
26 Castle Street, Cirencester, Tel: 025
3832

Ian Coley

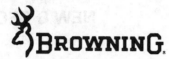

442/444 High Street, Cheltenham, Tel:
0242 582270/522443

Forest of Dean Armoury
Canberra New Road, Coalway,
Coleford, Tel: 0594 33908
Suppliers of rifles, pistols, shotguns and all shooting equipment.

Gloucester Rod & Gun Room
67 Alvin Street, Gloucester, Tel: 0452
410444

Shipston Gun Co Ltd
Blenheim Farm, Moreton in Marsh,
Tel: 0608 50349

GREATER LONDON

Bapty & Co Ltd
703 Harrow Road, London, Tel: 01
969 6671

J Blanch & Son
37B New Cavendish Street, London ,
W1 M8JR

**Thomas Bland & Sons
(Gunmakers) Ltd**

21/22 New Row, St Martins Lane,
London, Tel: 01 836 9122

Boss & Co Ltd

13 Dover Street, London, Tel: 01 493
1127

British Sports
107 Praed Street, 15 Norfolk Place,
Paddington, W2 1NT, Tel: 01 402
7511/3 Lines
Stockists of all types of shotguns, rifles, handguns, air guns, cartridges and ammunition. Replica weapons and clothing also available. Export enquiries welcome. Open 9.00 - 6.00 Mon-Sat.

Catford Gun Co
9 Eros House, Catford, Tel: 01 697
0830

**Chubbs of Edgware
(Gunmakers) Ltd.,**

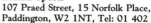

33 South Parade, Mollison Way,,
Edgware
TL}Tel: 01 952 1579

**Cogswell & Harrison (Gun
Agency)**
5 King Street, Covent Garden,
London, WC2E 8HN, Tel: 01 240
3186

Collins Brothers (Southern Armoury) Ltd
171 New Kent Road, Nr Elephant & Castle, Tel: 01 407 2278

D & P Guns
134 Blenheim Road, Harrow, Middlesex, Tel: 01 863 5873

Empire Arms Co
14 Empire Parade, Great Cambridge Road, Edmonton, London, N18 1AA, Tel: 01 807 3802
Vintage and modern ammunition. Lee, R.C.B.S. loading equipment. Lyman, CCI primers, hard cast heads. Manufacturers of ammunition including 455; (Discounts on 1000). D.P.M. and waterproofs. Repairs/gunservicing by qualified gunsmith.

William Evans Ltd
67a St James Street, London, Tel: 01 493 0415

C Farlow & Co Ltd
5 Pall Mall, London, Tel: 01 839 2423

Field Arms Ltd
10 Tilney Street, Audley Square, London

Fulham Armoury Ltd
185 Fulham Palace Road, London, W8 8QX, Tel:01 385 9902

Guncraft
11 Woodcock Hill, Kenton, Harrow, HA3 0XP, Tel: 01 907 3651

The Gun Makers Co
The Proof House, 48 Commercial Road,, London, Tel: 01 481 2695

Guns & Tackle

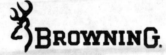

81 High Street, Whitton, Twickenham, Tel: 01 898 3129

Hellis Beesley and Watson Gunmakers
33 South Parade, Mollison Way, Edgware, Tel: 01 952 1579

Holland & Holland Ltd
33 Bruton Street, London, Tel: 01 499 4411

Messrs Judds of Hillingdon
3 Westbourne Parade, Uxbridge Road, Hillingdon, Middlesex, Tel: 01 573 0196

London Armoury
639 Commercial Road, London, Tel: 01 790 6094

London Gun Co

The London Gun Company

622 Greenford Road, Greenford, Middlesex, Tel: 01 575 2934

Manor Firearms

421 High Street, Manor Park, London, E12 6TL, Tel: 01 552 9036

Parabellum Sports
475 Upper Richmond Road West, London, Tel: 01 878 7003

Pax Guns Ltd
166 Archway Road, London, Tel: 01 340 3039

James Purdey & Sons Ltd
Audley House, 57/58 South Audley Street, London, Tel: 01 499 1801

John Rigby & Co (Gunmakers) Ltd
5 King Street, Covent Gardens, London, WC2E 8HN, Tel: 01 734 7611

J Roberts & Son
5 King Street, Covent Garden, London, Tel: 01 240 3186
Gun agency for Logswell & Harrison

Shooters Supply Co Ltd
149 Cleveland Street, London, Tel: 01 387 8330

Solis Gunshop
487b Green Lanes, Haringey, London, Tel: 01 340 9593

Stratford Gun Room
30 Vicarage Lane, London, E15, Tel: 01 519 7411

Streatham Armoury
90 Mitcham Lane, London SW16, Tel: 01 769 0671

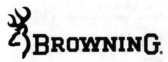
Thames Water Sports (Brian Fedder Investments) Ltd
179/181 Fulham Palace Road, London,
Tel: 01 381 0558

John Wilkes, The Gun & Rifle Makers
79 Beak Street, Regent Street, London,
W1R 3LF, Tel: 01 437 6539

Woodys of Wembley

BROWNING.

565 High Road, Wembley, Tel: 01 902
7217

GREATER MANCHESTER

Davies of Bolton
128 Deane Road, Bolton, Tel: 0204
24893
A wide range of accessories, firearms and clothing

John Dickson
128 Mauldeth Road, Burnage,
Manchester, Tel: 061 445 2976

Hurley's Sports
93 Piccadilly, Manchester, Tel: 061 228
2888

Manchester Air Guns
470 Oldham Road, Failsworth,
Manchester, Tel: 061 681 1671

Pearsons Tackle & Guns (M/CR) Ltd
292 Manchester Street, Oldham,
061 633 6199

Penine Shooting Centre
Gorrels Way, Rochdale, OL11 2NR,
Tel: 0706 30502

Oliver Somers
6/10 Mesnes Street, Wigan,
Manchester, Tel: 0942 42384

T Stensby & Co Ltd
33 Shudehill, Manchester, Tel: 061 834
6589

Weston Supplies
398/400 Ashton Road, Hathershaw,
Oldham

HAMPSHIRE

Accuracy International (Shooting Sports) Ltd

43 Gladys Avenue, North End,
Portsmouth, Tel: 0705 660371/2

Astral Sports
18 New Market Square, Basingstoke,
Tel: 0256 22255

Bassetts
4-6 Swan Street, Petersfield, Tel: 0730
64238

B E Chaplin (Gunmakers) Ltd

6 Southgate Street, Winchester, Tel:
0962 52935
Shotguns and stalking rifles built to order. Large selection of new and second hand English and Imported guns. Over 150 held in stock.

Cole & Son (Devizes) Ltd
67 High Street, Andover, Tel: 0264
51773

Custom Rifles
100a St Mary Street, Southampton,
Tel: 0703 30253

Greenfield of Salisbury Ltd
16 Market Place, Ringwood, Tel: 04254
3223

Gunmark Ltd
The Armoury, Fort Wallington,
Fareham, Tel: 0329 231531

Herriard Sporting Guns

Alton Road, Herriard, Basingstoke,
Tel: 025 683 277
An excellent range of guns and equipment for the clay and game shooter. Accessories include cartridges, clays, knives etc.

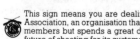

Jennings & Paterson
High Street, Fareham, Tel: 0329
234343

Lockerley Game Services
2 Barley Hill Cottages, Dumbridge,
Romsey, Tel: 0794 40851

Marlborough Gun Shop
138a Weyhill Road, Andover, Tel:
Andover 53957

Maskells Guns
18 Camp Road, Farnborough, Tel:
0252 518062
*Stockists for Webley, ASI, Weihrauch,
B.S.F., Original, Feinwerkau, Ensign
and Sharp. Scopes by Tasco, Rhino,
Kassnar, ASI. Large selection of
pellets, gun covers and accessories.*

McCrabtree,
Portsmouth Gun Centre, 295 London
Road, Portsmouth

Modern & Antique Firearms
147 Tuckton Road, Southbourne,
Bournemouth, BH6 3JZ

Multi Sports (High Sarin Ltd)
225 Old Christchurch Road,
Bournemouth, Tel: 0202 26319

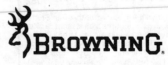
Parvin Brothers
79 High Street, West End,
Southampton, Tel: 0703 465656

Portsmouth Gun Centre

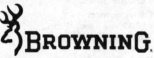

295 London Road, North End,
Portsmouth, Tel: 0705 660574

Rawson & Sons
2 Park Road, Farnborough

John Rothery Co Ltd

*John Rothery & Co.
(Wholesale) Ltd*

22 Stamshaw Road, Stamshaw,
Portsmouth, Hants, Tel: 0705
667323

Southampton Firearms
100a St Mary Street, Southampton,
Tel: 0703 30253

Sporting & Firearms Centre
41 Brookley Road, Brockenhurst, SO4
7RB

Test Valley Sporting Guns
35 High Street, Overton, Nr
Basingstoke, Tel: 0256 770872

Town & Country Sports
19 The Square, Botley, Tel: 04892
87962

W C & P J Turner
133 Brockhurst Road, Gosport
GTA

HEREFORD & WORCESTER

E C Ashthorpe
Severn Stoke, Worcester

Carey (Gunmakers) Ltd
88 The Homend, Ledbury, Tel: 0531
2838

Davies Baker Gun Co
The Village, Clifton on Teme

F Durrant & Son

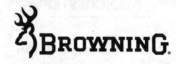

3 Mealcheapen Street, Worcester,
Tel: 0905 25247
*We are a long established business and
specialise in good quality English guns.
A shooting ground is available for
either tuition or trial of a gun.*

G B Sports
10 Broad Street, Ross on Wye, Tel:
0989 63723

Grange Gun Company
Hewell Park, Nr Redditch, Tel: 0527
46096

M A Grinnal
10 York Street, Stourport on Severn,
Tel: 029 932212

D Monk Ltd
Unit 32K Heming Road, Washford Ind
Estate, Redditch, Tel: 0527 20829

Phillip Morris & Sons

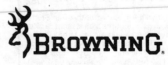

21/23 Widemarsh Street, Hereford,
Tel: 0432 269501

W J Pierce & Son
The Country Gun Shop, Monderfield,
Nr Bromyard, Hereford, HRT 4JY,
Tel: 08853 201

Powells
28 Mount Pleasant, Redditch, Tel: 0527
62669

R B Shooting Supplies
Inside Amber Joinery Centre,
Stourport Road, Foley Park,
Kidderminster, Tel: 0562 751159

John Slough of London
35 Church Street, Hereford, Tel:
0432 55416

**Upton Marina Chandlery
(Marina Arms)**
East Waterside, Upton Upon Severn,
Worcestershire, Tel: 06846 3404

**Worcestershire Black Powder
Supplies Ltd**
Units 15/17 Craft Centre,
Wribbenhall, Bewdley, Tel: 0299
402154

Worcestershire Gunsmiths
17/20 New Road, Kidderminster, Tel:
0562 3776

HERTFORDSHIRE

Barhams
95 Tilehouse Street, Hitchin, Tel: 0462
34298

Bloomfield (Gunmaker)

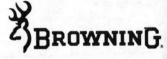

Hill Farm, Radlett, Tel: 09276
4639

P R Godfrey (Gunsmith)
14 Laxton Gardens, Baldock, Tel: 0462
892963

The Gun Room (NF Cooper)
50 Hockerhill Street, Bishops
Stortford, Tel: 0279 52166

Gunner One & Co
1/2 Parkstreet Lane, Parkstreet, St
Albans, Tel: 0727 72646

Hertford Guns
31 St Andrews Street, Hertford, Tel:
0992 553582

Marks Sports Shop
50 Market Street, Watford, Tel: 0923
39824/50070

T Takats
73 High Street, Ware, Tel: 0920 2057

HUMBERSIDE NORTH

H H E Akrill (Gunmaker)
18 Market Place, Beverley

The Cartridge (Beverley)

EYGC Bygot Wood, Cherry Burton, Beverley

Duncans (Gunmakers) Ltd
8 Paragon Square, Hull, HU1 3QT, Tel: 0482 28150

Shotguns, firearms, air rifles and pistols, shooting accessories, new and second hand guns. Part exchange on all weapons. Prompt gunservicing and repairs. Open Mon-Sat 9.00 - 6.00.

G W Hutchinson Gunmaker
31 Anlaby Road, Hull
All leading makes of rifles, pistols and shotguns. Cartridges and ammunition. Fishing tackle also stocked.

HUMBERSIDE SOUTH

Lightwoods of Grimsby
172 Cleethorpe Road, Grimsby, Tel: 0472 43536

ISLE OF MAN

G Corlett
6 Castle Street, Douglas, Tel: 0624 76762

The Country Gun Shop, J A Quillam

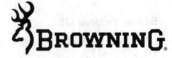

Santon Shooting Centre, Ballagick, Santon, Tel: 0624 74392

Raynors Gun Shop
1 Murray's Road, Douglas, Tel: 0624 75706

ISLE OF WIGHT

Arnold Heal Ltd
86B Upper St James Street, Newport

Island Gun Centre

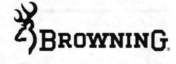

26 Birmingham Road, Cowes, Tel: 0983 299154

KENT

F A Anderson
73a High Street, Ashford, Kent, Tel: 0233 37717

T M Dunnell Gunsmith
Rumstead Lane, Stocbury Valley, Sittingbourne, Tel: 0795 842200

Don Gray Guns
7 Railway Street, Chatham, Tel: 0634 43032

Gentrys

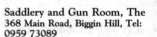

32/34 Park View Road, Welling, Tel: 01 304 9922

H S Greenfield & Son
4/5 Upper Bridge Street, Canterbury, Tel: 0227 456959

Jack Laurence Bowes Ltd
4 Third Avenue, Luton, Chatham, Tel: 0634 407805

Kent Small Arms
134 High Street, Herne Bay, Tel: 022 73 64833

Medway Gunrooms Ltd
115 Canterbury Street, Gillingham, Tel: 0634 576332

Chris Potter Guns

43 Camden Road, Tunbridge Wells, Tel: 0892 22208

Saddlery and Gun Room, The
368 Main Road, Biggin Hill, Tel: 0959 73089

A Sanders (Maidstone) Ltd
85 Bank Street, Maidstone, Tel: 0622 52707

Colin P Smith
61 The Street, Ash, Canterbury, Tel: 0304 812224

Herriard Sporting Guns
Working Dogs & Country Shop
ALTON ROAD, HERRIARD, HAMPSHIRE
Telephone : 025 683 277

We offer a wide range of guns and equipment for the clay and game shooter.
We stock:

SHOTGUNS	Browning, Miroku, Rossini, Beretta, etc.
CLOTHING	Barbour, Mascott, Belstaff, etc.
FOOTWEAR	Regent

41

All shooting accessories including cartridges, clays, knives etc., also gun-servicing and repairs available. Open 6 days a week. We also have our own shooting ground, where members or visitors are welcome. Practice and tuition by appointment only. Regular shoots held.

LANCASHIRE

Ballistic Products UK

6 Whitewell, Catterall, Garstang, Tel: 09952 4251

UK agent for Itaqcha 'Mag Ten'. All reloading requirements, rebarrelling, sleeving, 4,8, and 10 bore. 'MAG MAX' cartridges 8, 10 and 12 bore magnum. Grouse shooting trips to Scotland.

44

Town & Country Sports Ltd

- We offer a large selection of new and secondhand shotguns for the Game and Clay shooter.

- Full range of clothing and footwear.

- Cartridges & Accessories

Buy With Confidence

Members of Gun Trade Association, B.A.S.C., B.F.S.S. and Game Conservancy.

19 THE SQUARE, BOTLEY, HAMPSHIRE SO3 2EA TELEPHONE (04892) 87962

R Bamford

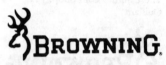

207 The Green, Eccleston, Nr Chorley, PR7 5PX, Tel: 0257 451274

John Slough of London

47

35 Church St., Hereford.
Tel: Hereford (0432) 55416

Sole importer and factory distributor of
THE AT 84 9mm PISTOL—made in Switzerland, .410 Shotgun Walking Sticks, and Sword Canes made in France,
THE KINETIC BULLET PULLER—made in Texas.
We are a large retail shop with a full range of rifles, shotguns, pistols, revolvers and airguns.
We do repairs and modifications in our workshops here in Church St., Hereford.
We have an extensive clothing department stocking all types of shooting and country clothing.
We also stock every sort of shooting accessory. We are open six days a week —Monday-Saturday 9.00-5.30.

Bond & Bywater

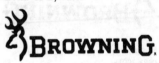

42 Fylde Street, Preston, Tel: 0772 58980

S Entwhistle

161 Church Street, Blackpool, Tel: 0253 20192

Ferrand Custom Arms
Riverside Works, Todmorden Road, Littleborough, Tel: 0706 78545

GUNS
OVER 300 SHOT GUNS AND AIR GUNS IN STOCK

CASH DISCOUNTS
PART EXCHANGES

R. BAMFORD
207 The Green, Eccleston, Nr. Chorley, Lancs.
PHONE 0257 451274

42

Hiller Airguns & Publications
92 Chorley Old Road, Whittle le Woods, Chorley, Lancs, Tel: 02572 65489

We have :—
Our own cartridges in 12, 16 & 20 bore
Our own Shooting School
Our own workshop for every kind of repair and renovation
Our own Shooting Suits specially made for us.
We stock all kinds of guns and every kind of shooting accessory.
We are shooters ourselves with shotgun, rifle and pistol and our expert advice is free.

THE GUN ROOM
(Norman F. Cooper)
50 Hockerill Stret,
Bishop's Stortford, Herts.
CM23 2DW
Telephone B.S. (0279) 52166

45

James S Kirkman (Firearms Dealer)
12D Blackpool Old Road, Poulton le Flyde, Tel: 0253 882262/885799

CHRIS POTTER GUNS OF TUNBRIDGE WELLS
Specialists in Game & Clay Shooting

* Guns
* Cartridges (low priced)
* Accessories
  Whatever your requirements we are sure we can save you money! Why not give us a call!

Chris Potter Guns
43 Camden Road,
Tunbridge Wells
Kent. Tel: 0892 22208

46

Lancashire Guns

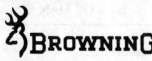

88 Bank Street, Rawtenstall, Tel: 0706 220559

THE STAMFORD GUN ROOM LTD
THE place in South Lincs for all your Shooting requirements.

We are interested in buying Antique and Collectors' Guns and Old Fishing Tackle

8 ST MARY's HILL, STAMFORD, LINCOLNSHIRE
Telephone (0780) 62796

Approved Browning/Miroku Dealer Registered Game Dealer Member of G.T.A.

43

T & J J McAvoy (Guns)
3 High Street, Standish, Wigan, Tel: Standish 426129

LARGE SELECTION
Guns—Rifles— Airweapons
FULL REPAIR & ALTERATION SERVICE
(specialist in Choke alterations)
New & Sleeved barrels—Blacking & Browning.
All carried out in our own Workshop by Skilled & Experienced Staff

Clothing—Accessories —Cartridges

FREE: Insurance Estimates & Gun Condition Check

BLOOMFIELD Gunmaker
HILL FARM, RADLETT, HERTS. Tel-(09276) 4639

48

'Macks' Jim Grooby
33a Parliament Street, Burnley, Tel: 0282 27386

Meggison
8a Main Street, Bolton by Bowland, Clitheroe, Tel: 02007 602

Pennine Shooting Centre
Gorrels Way, Rochdale, OL11 2NR, Tel: 0706 30502

Ray Fox Guns
48 Bolton Street, Chorley, Tel: 0257 262938

Mike Roberts
Park Hill, Garstang, Nr Preston, Tel: 09952 3925

Shooters Gunroom

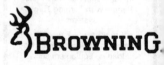

56 Darwen Street, Blackburn, Tel: 0254 663547

Stephen J Fawcett
7 Gt John Street, Lancaster, LA1 1NQ,
Tel: 0524 32033

Towers of Rochdale
52 Whitworth Road, Rochdale, Tel:
Rochdale 46171

K Varey
4 New Market Street, Clitheroe, Tel:
0200 23267

West End Gun Co
18 Alexandra Road, Morecambe, Tel:
0524 412049

LEICESTERSHIRE

Aylestone Gun Co

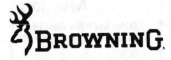

1/3 Paigle Road, Aylestone, Tel:
0533 832828
For specialist sales and service.

Belgrave Gun Co. Ltd.,

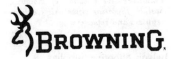

43 Melton Road, Leicester, Tel: 0533
663505

**Roger Bolstridge, Sports Guns
& Fishing Tackle**
32 High Street, Coalville, Tel: 0530
32515

Alan Bray (Guns & Tackle)
5 Waterloo Road, Hinckley, LE10
OQJ, Tel: 0455 634317
*Call in for an excellent selection of
shotguns, rifles, pistols, air weapons,
scopes, knives, clothing and many
more accessories*

Charnwood Gun & Tackle
(Prop Mr L Jones)
48 Chapel Street, Ibstock, Tel: 0530
60901

Clay Shooters' Supplies

32 St Mary's Road, Market
Harborough, Tel: 0858 66616

Galway Silencer & Gun Co
2 Old Green, Medbourne Green, Tel:
085883 706

Ralph Grant & Son Ltd
Grants Gunroom, Green Lane Road &
Roseberry Street, (Off East Park Road)
Leicester, Tel: 0533 767551
BASC:Y

D J Jones
30 Sherrard Street, Melton Mowbray

**Loughborough Gun & Angling
Centre**
34 Nottingham Road, Loughborough,
Tel: 0509 230627

LINCOLNSHIRE

**J Blanch & Son (Gunmakers)
Ltd**

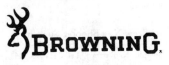

29 Station Road, Corby Glen,
Grantham, Tel: 047684 628
Repairs

Leslie Bowler Ltd
The Post Office, High Street, Little
Bytham, Grantham, NG33 4QJ, Tel:
078081 200
*Gun specialist for all pistol shooting
requirements.*

P E Charity, The Gun Shop
34 Westgate, Grantham, Tel: 0476
63074

Coppin, Peter

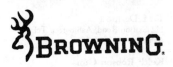

Spinneys Shooting Ground,
Willoughby, Alford, Lincs, Tel: 0521
22357

**Elderkin & Son (Gunmakers)
Ltd**
17 Broad Street, Spalding, Tel: 0775
2919/4621

Gun & Tackle Shop
Churchgate, Whaplode, Spalding

**R N & G M Hargrave
Gunmakers**
9 Market Place, Horncastle, Tel: 06582
3366

G Harrison & Son
55 Croft Street, Lincoln, Tel: 0522
23834

**Humberside Armoury &
Angling Co**
73 Ladysmith Road, Grimsby, Tel:
0472 52029

**Lincolnshire Gun Co and Air
Gun Centre**
6 Eastgate, Louth, Tel: 0507 603861

R D Marper

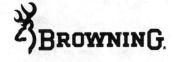

Cleatham, Kirton Lindsey,
Gainsborough, Tel: 0652 648466

Slingsbys
19 Westgate, Sleaford

Stamford Gun Room Ltd

8 St Mary's Hill, Stamford, Tel:
0780 62796

J Wheater (Gunmakers) Ltd

3-9 Tentercroft Street, Lincoln, Tel:
0522 21219

Ian Wilson (Gunmaker)

53 Wide Bargate, Boston, Tel: 0205
65668

MERSEYSIDE

Merseyside Armoury
83 Lark Lane, Liverpool 17, Tel: 051
728 8390

Rainford Field Sports
21 Church Street, Rainford, St
Helens, Merseyside, Tel: Rainford
5580
LIShotguns and air rifles bought, sold
or part exchanged. Gun repairs and
a good selection of shooting
accessories. Valumix and Skinners
dogfood.

Henry Whitty & Son
37/39 School Lane, Liverpool, L1 3DA

NORFOLK

Darlow & Co (Gunsmiths) Ltd

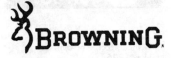

8 Orford Hill, Norwich, Tel: 0603
623414

Dereham Gun & Tackle Shop
26 Norwich Street, Dereham, Tel: 0362
66926

Gallyon & Sons Ltd
9/11 Bedford Street, Norwich, Tel:
0603 623414

Gun Room The
234 Wroxham Road, Sprowston,
Norwich, Tel: 0603 49227

J H Ling
Eye Road, Hoxne, Eye, Tel: 037975
315

Norfolk Gun Trading Co
14 Greevegate, Hunstanton, Tel:
04853 33600
For specialist sales and service.

J W Powell (Fakenham) Ltd
5/14 Oak Street, Fakenham, Tel: 0328
2232

Sporting Guns
The Street, Helhoughton, Fakenham,
Norfolk, Tel: 048522 789

Uttings Tackle & Gun Shop

54 Bethel Street, Norwich, Tel:
0603 621776

Woods of Swaffham

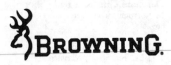

7/11 Mangate Street, Swaffham, Tel:
0760 22609

NORTHAMPTONSHIRE

Brackley Gunsmiths Ltd

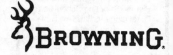

95 High Street, Brackley, Tel: 0280
702519
*Specialists in all quality guns (English
and Continental). Guns repaired/
refurbished in our own workshop,
gunfitting our speciality. Cash paid for
'best' guns.*

Peter Crisp Ltd
7 High Street, Rushden, Tel: 0933
56424

T J Grimley Gunsmith
65 Occupation Road, Corby, Tel: 0536
60719

Northampton Gun Co
136 St James Road, Northampton,
Tel: 0604 51206
*Northamptons only specialist gunshop,
stocking a wide range of clay and
game shooting guns and accessories,
firearms and air rifles. Full repair
service available.*

Sparfield Sporting Guns
19 High Street, Irthlingborough, Tel:
0933 650296

Sportsman's Lodge

44 Kingsthorpe Road, Northampton,
Tel: 0604 713399

T H Thursby & Son
Sheep Street, Northampton, Tel: 0604
38225

NORTHUMBERLAND

Game Fair
12 Marygate, Berwick Upon Tweed,
Tel: 0289 305119

T McDermott
112 Station Road, Ashington, Tel:
Ashington 812214

Keith Robson Guns
17 St Mary's Chare, Hexham, Tel:
Hexham 605569

NOTTINGHAMSHIRE

Armstrong's Gunsmiths
360 Carlton Hill, Carlton,
Nottingham, Tel: 0602 873313
*Comprehensive selection of shotguns,
Stalking/Sporting rifles, Air weapons
retailers and repairers*

Belvoir Shooting Supplies

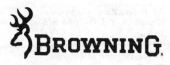

Orston, Nottinghamshire, Tel: 0949
50556
*Main stockists for Beretta, Browning,
Miroku. Traps, clays and cartridges.
All shooting accessories*

Goss Petcher Guns Ltd
The Gun Room, Wighay Bridge,
Annesley Road, Hucknall, Tel: 0602
633430

Andrew Kay Shooter Supplies
Mount Pleasant Farm, Sturton Le
Steeple, Nr Retford, Tel: 0427 880914

**The Nottingham Gun Centre
Ltd**
155 Attenborough Lane, Beeston

C Smith & Sons (Newark) Ltd
Clinton House, Lombard Street,
Newark on Trent, Tel: 0636 703839

OXFORDSHIRE

Banbury Gunsmiths

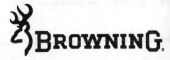

47a Broad Street, Banbury, Tel:
0295 65819
*Fine quality English guns and main
dealer for A.Y.A., Browning, Beretta,
Miroku.; Firearms, air weapons, all
accessories and clothing. Tuition and
repairs, part exchange welcome.*

Bicester Rod & Gun
9 Kingsley Road, Bicester, Tel: 0869
241002

R F Bridgman
76 High Street, Witney, Tel: 0993 2587

Burton & Morgan (Gunsmiths)
The Old Bakery, Lower Icknield
Way, Chinnor, Oxford, Tel: 0844
53655

Casecraft (G H Hawarth)
The Old Telephone Exchange,
Kingston Blount, Nr Oxford
Anschutz target rifles and equipment

Cotswold Guns
Church Street, Charlbury, Tel: 0608
810891

The Gun Counter

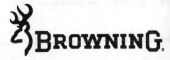

67 High Street, Wallingford, Tel:
0491 34343

Hammants
26/28 Bell Street, Henley on
Thames, Tel: 0491 574545
*Good selection of shotguns, rifles, air
weapons, cartridges, clothing, knives
and shooting accessories always in
stock. Repairs carried out on our own
premises.*

Mark Henshall Country Sports
5/7 Mill Street, Wantage, Tel: 023
57 2610

John Kent
5/7 Mill Street, Wantage,

Jonathan Lawrence
Park Farm House, Waterstock, Tel: 08447 469
Best English Guns and Rifles

Thame Shooting Supplies

 THAME SHOOTING SUPPLIES

1st Floor, 15 Cornmarket, Thame, Oxon, Tel: 084421 4122
Shotguns : Cartridges - Dan Arm - Rottweil - SMI - Fiocchi - Baikal : Clays : Air Weapons : Pellets : Britton Belstaff Wax clothing : Ganton shooting vests : plus shooting accessories for the clay, game and rough shooting enthusiast.

H J Wadley & Son Ltd
30 Market Square, Bicester

Windrush Guns Ltd
19 Corn Street, Witney, OX8 7DE, Tel: 0993 3035

SHROPSHIRE

Ebrall Brothers
Smithfield Road, Shrewsbury, Tel: 0743 3048

Gordon Forrest
 BROWNING
2 Wyle Cop, Shrewsbury, Tel: 0743 56878

Guns & Ammo
95 Beatrice Street, Oswestry, Tel: 0691 653761

Paint & Tool Stores (Wellington) Ltd
29 New Street, Telford

A & B Smith
London House, Market Street, Craven Arms, Tel: 05882 2368

Sporting & General Supply Co Ltd
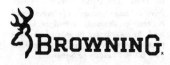 BROWNING
1a Swan Hill, Shrewsbury, Tel: 0743 50991

Herbert Tucker
The Square, Newport, Salop

Vickers Owen Ltd
Wharf Gun Shop, Mill Street, Whitchurch, SY13 1SE, Tel: 0948 2609

W R Wood
Holly Dale, Buildwas Road, Iron Bridge

SOMERSET

Bridgewater Guns Ltd
22 St Mary Street, Bridgewater, Tel: 0278 423441

Victor Coates Gunsmith
2 Saturday Market Place, Kings Lynn, Tel: 0553 63673
Agents for all leading makes of shotguns and air rifles. Repairs carried out on the premises. Wide range of accessories

Denton & Kennell
West Street, Somerton, Tel: 0458 73732/72065

The Flintlock
17A High Street, Glastonbury, Tel: 0458 31525
Air gun specialists. Also antique firearms. All accessories, ammunition. Part exchange.

Lance Nicholson Fishing & Guns
High Street, Dulverston, Tel: 0398 23409

Neroche Armoury
Rose Mill, Hort Bridge, Ilminster., Tel: 0460 53722

Frank Richards
25 Silver Street, Taunton, Tel: 0823 81487

Sherwood Guns & Cartridges
Littlemore Road, Mark, Nr Highbridge, Tel: 027864 419

Shotgun Supplies
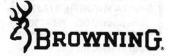 BROWNING
Lower Odcombe, Yeovil, Tel: 093 586 2712

That Tackle Shop
29 Princes Street, Yeovil, Tel: 0935 74600

Wesley Hamm
Winchester Farm, Wells Road, Cheddar, Tel: 0934 742563
LI

STAFFORDSHIRE

G Bate (Gunmakers) Ltd
7 Market Square, Stafford, Tel: 0785 44191

John Birks (Sports)
293 Uttoxeter Road, Normacott, Stoke on Trent, ST3 5LQ

Thomas Blakemore
Excelsior Works, Bath Street, Walsall

G R Bourne (Guns & Tackle)

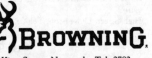

40 King Street, Newcastle, Tel: 0782 625385

Catton Gunsmiths
Catton Hall, Burton on Trent, DE12 5LN

Tom Cooper
Hanley Gunshop Ltd, 28-30 Pall Mall, Hanley, Stoke on Trent, Tel: 0782 281589

R E Garland
Edingale, Nr Tamworth, Tel: 0827 85216

J M Green Guns & Tackle
42 Crewe Road, Alsager, Stoke on Trent, Tel: 09363 2983

Lakefield Armoury
1/3 Church Street, Audley, Stoke on Trent

Lichfield Gun Co
13 Lyn Avenue, Lichfield, Tel: 054 32 22416

M B Guns

MB
TEL. 32479

Rear 187 Waterloo Street, Burton on Trent, Tel: 0283 32479
For a huge range of guns and accessories, discount cartridges, knives and sheaths, game bags and carriers plus many more. Pop in between 9.30 and 5.00 Tuesday to Saturday.

Morlands Shotgun Supplies (Prop R M Blythe)
3 Lightoaks Level, Oakamoor

Practical Weaponry
162 Bucknall New Road, Hanley, Stoke on Trent, Tel: 0782 29712

Wm Riley & Sons Ltd
High Street, Halmer End, Stoke on Trent, Tel: 0782 720212

Rugeley Guns & Tackle
5 Market Square, Rugeley, Tel: 08894 79002

Specialist Military Sales (Prop Mr P Bark)
109 Hednesford Road, Heath Hayes
All types of shotguns, air rifles, section 1 rifles, pistols and section 5

R A York & R D Wallin
3 Pendeford Mill Lane, Bilbrook, Wolverhampton

SUFFOLK

Alfred Clark
69 St Matthews Street, Ipswich, Tel: 0473 52498

Anglia Arms

96 Risbygate Street, Bury St Edmunds, Tel: 0284 61470

R M & D Clayton
Town Hall Gun Works, 4a The Traverse, Bury St Edmunds, Tel: 0284 4559

Coach Harness
Haughley, Stowmarket

East Coast Gunroom
29 Beach Station Road, Felixtowe, IP11 8DR, Tel: 0394 282100
Cartridge mail order list :- £1.00 for inert pistol and rifle ammunition for collectors. 1860-1985 (No licence required) Guns, antiques and vintage firearms. Closed all day Monday

Morgan Guns Ltd
Eurosports Village, Shotley Gate, Nr Ipswich, Tel: Shotley 717/740

A Richardson & Sons (Gunsmiths)

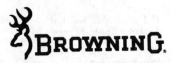

32 Quay Street, Halesworth, Tel: 09867 2520

Rod & Gun Shop
18 Church Street, Woodbridge, Tel: 039 43 2377

Suffolk Gun Club
42/44 Upper Orwell Street, Ipswich, Tel: 0473 210914

R Tilney (Gunsmith)
17 Small Gate, Beccles, Tel: 0502 712105

SURREY

A E Clarke & Son (Yateley) Ltd

55 London Road, Blackwater, Camberley, Tel: 0276 35615

Cranleigh Field Sports, (Gunsmiths)
Ewhurst Road, Cranleigh, Tel: 0483 272071

Dees Sports

7 Manor Road, Wallington, SM6 0BZ, Tel: 01 647 7742

Dorking Gun Company (Gunmakers)
243A High Street, Dorking, RH4 1RT, Tel: 0306 883451

Egham Gun Centre
83 High Street, Egham, Tel: 0784 33424
Founded some 15 years. The shop carries a wide range of shotguns being agents for Winchester, Beretta, Remington, Mossbert etc. Also airweapons and handguns. All normal shooting accessories stocked. One of the largest range of knives in the area is available plus a comprehensive range of dog training equipment. Personally run by the owners.

Farnham Saddlers
7 West Street, Farnham, Tel: 0252 713004

Jeffreys of Guildford

BROWNING.

34 High Street, Guildford, Tel: 0483
05055

Masters Gunmakers Ltd
Cannon Works, Ockley Road, Beare
Green, Dorking, RH5 4PU, Tel:
0306 711435

John Powell Gunmakers
5 Church Street, Reigate, Tel: 073 72
4111

Surrey Guns Ltd
Manor Road, Wallington, Tel: 01
647 00177

Andrew Tucker Ltd
68 Portsmouth Road, Cobham,
KT11 1HY, Tel: 0932 62921

Walton Tackle Shop
66 Station Road, Addlestone, Tel:
0932 42528

Ray Ward

BROWNING.

41 Holland Close, Redhill, RH1 1RT,
Tel: 0737 66715

Richard Wells (Sporting Guns)
The Gun Shop, Lionmead, Shottermill,
Haslemere, GU27 3NH, Tel: 0428
51913

Weybridge Guns & Tackle Ltd
180 Oatlands Drive, Weybridge, KT13
9ET, Tel: 0932 42675

SUSSEX EAST

F A Anderson

BROWNING.

12 East Street, Brighton, Tel: Brighton
23066

The Armoury Nappers
High Street, Mayfield, TN20 6AB, Tel:
0435 873288

Diamond Guns
67 High Street, Heathfield, Tel: 042 52
3295

Hestons
37 Coombe Terrace, Brighton, Tel:
0273 693248

S A Lambert (Gunsmith)
5 Friarshill Terrace, Guestling,
Hastings, Tel: 0424 813299

Lewes Gun Room
127 High Street, Lewes, Tel: Lewes
474669

Sussex Guns
203 Preston Road, Brighton, Tel:
0273 553222

D Townsend (Gunsmiths)
63 Preston Street, Brighton, Tel: 0273
25245

Wisdens (G.Hastings) Ltd
1 Trinity Street, Hastings, Tel: 0424
421240

SUSSEX WEST

Anscombe & Hall
2 Caudle Street, Henfield, Tel:
Henfield 494340

Chichester Armoury, The

BROWNING.

43 West Street, Chichester, Tel:
0243 774687/786173

Churchley Brothers Ltd
282 Goring Road, Worthing, Tel: 0903
46301

Craig M Whitsey (Gunmakers)
Ltd

Craig M. Whitsey

Unit D, 10/12 Fitzalan Road,
Arundel, West Sussex, Tel: 0903
883102
*Shotgun and rifles made and repaired
in our own workshop. English firearms
bought and sold.*

Horsham Gun Shop
42 East Street, Horsham, Tel: 0403
52684
*Fine selection of all types of shotguns
and airguns. Purdey trained gunsmith
on premises. Comprehensive range of
country clothing for the shooter .*

Kirkman (Crawley) Ltd
Starway Nurseries, Copthorne
Common, Crawley, RH10 3JU, Tel:
0293 26670

Michael Miller
The Lamb, 8 Cuckfield Road,
Hurstpierpoint, Tel: 0273 834567

Sports & Radio
25/29 Aldwick Road, Bognor Regis

Sussex Gun Room
The Covert, East Street, Petworth,
Tel: 0798 43118

Worthing Gun Shop
80 Broadwater Street West, Worthing,
Tel: 0903 37378

TYNE & WEAR

Bagnall & Kirkwood Ltd
52 Grey Street, Newcastle, Tel: 0632
325875

G P Bradford (Firearms)
Dene Croft, Front Street, Burnopfield,
Newcastle Upon Tyne, Tel: 0207 70295

Caer Urfa Guns and Ammo
399 Stanhope Road, South Shields,
Tel: 0632 551045
*Lowest prices in the North for rifles,
pistols, shotguns and air weapons.*

Coast & Country Sports
3 Derwent Street, Sunderland, Tel:
0783 659666

The County House
123/125 Clayton Street West,
Newcastle Upon Tyne, Tel: 0632
616669

J R Murdy
Unit 15, Swan Road, Swan Ind Est,
District 9, Washington

Pat Walker Guns
143 Alexandra Road, Gateshead,
Tel: 0632 786736

Steve Smith Gunmaker

BROWNING.

37 Nelson Street, Newcastle, Tel: 0632
322776

WARWICKSHIRE

Astwood Guns
4 High Street, Studley, Tel: 052 785
4963

Cartridge, The
16 Smith Street, Warwick, Tel:
0926 491087

Highfield Gun Co Ltd
158 Highfield Road, Hall Green,
Birmingham, B28 0HT, Tel: 021 778
5465

William Howell
63 Price Street, Birmingham, Tel: 021
359 3452

J L S Arms Co Ltd
Scoltock House, Perry Street,
Wednesbury
*Rifle specialists. Used shotguns pistol
and firearms a speciality.*

Guns & Sports

26 Henley Street, Stratford Upon
Avon, Tel: 0789 67100

Gun Shop, The

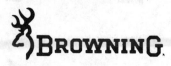

62a Lawford Road, Rugby, Tel: 0788
751198

**Hogan & Colbourne
Gunmakers**
Phoenix Works, Alscot Park, Stratford
on Avon, Tel: 078987 764

Sidelock Guns

1a Coleshill Road, Atherstone, Tel:
08277 2903

WEST MIDLANDS

Accles & Shelvoke Ltd
Palford Street, Aston, Birmingham 6,
Tel: 021 3593277

Alfred J Parker
348 Moseley Road, Birmingham 12,
Tel: 021 440 1480

Bailons Gunmakers Ltd
94/95 Bath Street, Birmingham, Tel:
021 236 7593

G Bate (Gunmakers) Ltd
8/10 Colmore Circus, Birmingham,
Tel: 021 236 7451

A A Brown & Sons
1 Snake Lane, Alvechurch,
Birmingham, Tel: 021 445 5395

City Air Weapons & Firearms
260 Lyndon Road, Olton, Solihull, Tel:
021 742 1329

William Ford Ltd
352 Moseley Road, Birmingham

Godiva Guns (Coventry)
191 Canley Road, Coventry, CV5 6AS,
Tel: 0203 76077

Peter Gordon
84 High Street, Dudley, Tel: 0384
52413

W W Greener Ltd
Belmont Row, Birmingham , Tel:
021 3595757

Clive C Lemon Gunmaker
Malt Mill Lane, Halesowen, West
Midlands, Tel: 021 559 5717

G E Lewis & Sons
32/33 Lower Loveday Street,
Birmingham, Tel: 021 359 2750

J Manton & Co Ltd
140 Bromsgrove Street, Birmingham,
B6 6RQ

**William Powell & Son
(Gunmaker) Ltd**
35/37 Carrs Lane, Birmingham,
Tel: 021 643 0689/8362

The Elephant

TRADE MARK

is back!

W. W. GREENER

Makers of fine guns since 1829

Best quality shotguns manufactured in 12, 16 and 20 bores.
Rifles made to order. Full range of shooting accessories
and repairs to W. W. Greener guns.

W. W. GREENER LTD., BIRMINGHAM B4 7SA.
Telephone: 021-359 5757 or 066-641 351.

65

WILLIAM POWELL & SON (GUNMAKERS) LTD.

Gunmakers since 1802

One of the largest selections
of shotguns, accessories and
clothing in the country.
Retail shop adjoins their
factory in Birmingham
City Centre.

**35-37 Carrs Lane,
Birmingham B4 7SX
Tel: 021-643 0689**

66

MALT MILL LANE HALESOWEN

WEST MIDLANDS B62 8JF · ENGLAND
TELEPHONE 021-559 5717

67

Our range of oils, waxes and
polishes for gunstock finishing are
exactly the same as those used by
Clive C. Lemon, Maker of Fine
English Shotguns of Halesowen,
West Midlands.
They are used to produce the
traditional 'English' stock finish
which is well known throughout
the world and they are actually
mixed and blended by the
Gunmakers themselves to the old
trade recipes together with one or
two new ones specially developed
by CCL.

We also supply materials for
gunstock preparation before
finishing. These include lacquer
stock finish remover, gunstock
stain and grain sealer to
complement our range of finishes.

*Send S.A.E. for description
leaflet on our whole range.*

*Available through
Gunmark Stockists
Everywhere.*

Westley Richards & Co Ltd
Birmingham, Tel: 021 4721701

Salisburys Gunsmiths
2a Lower Loveday Street,
Birmingham, Tel: 021 359 7362

Victor Simmons
2 Manor Road, Streetley, Sutton
Coldfield, Tel: 021 353 9795

**H Smith & Sons (Gunmakers)
Ltd**
Price Street, Birmingham 4, Tel: 021
359 1680

**Frank Spittle (Guns) & (Martial
Arts)**
16 Bushbury Road, Fallings Park,
Wolverhampton, Tel: 0902 731383

Trapshot
8 High Street, Lye, Nr Stourbridge,
Tel: 038 482 4644/2496

Turner Richards
Cardigan Street, Birmingham, B4 7SA

Venom Arms Co
Unit 1, Gun Barrel Ind Centre,
Hayseech Road, Cradley Heath,
Warley, Tel: 021 501 3794

Rowland Watson
32 Lower Loveday Street, Birmingham,
Tel: 021 359 1830

Benjamin Wild & Son
624 Bristol Road South, Northfield,
Birmingham, Tel: 021 477 4350

Wiseman of Birmingham
3 Price Street, Birmingham, Tel: 021
359 1256

WILTSHIRE

Barbury Guns Ltd
44/45 High Street, Marlborough,
SN8 1HQ, Tel: 0672 52862
*Full range of Shotguns, Air Weapons,
Sporting Firearms, Ammunition and
accessories for the field sportsman and
clay shooter. Credit facilities available
on all guns over £100.*

The Fieldsman
10 Rodbourne Road, Swindon

Greenfield of Salisbury Ltd

BROWNING.

21 Milford Street, Salisbury, Tel:
0722 333795/6
*Our skilled craftsmen are here to help
you for all your gun repair
requirements, plus all leading makes
of country clothing in stock.*

Chris Harding Guns
Cresswell Lane, Lea, Malmesbury, Tel:
06662 2447
*New and second hand guns, guaranteed.
Prompt gun repairs and sevicing carried
out on premises.*

WESTLEY RICHARDS & CO., LTD.

68

Established in the Reign of King George III

**Gun and Rifle makers by warrants of appointment to
the Royal Family for over 100 years.**

Currently in production we have Best Quality sidelocks,
Connaught Model boxlocks, Double Rifles and Magazines
Rifles. Full repair service available in our own workshops.

*Full brochure available including full list of second hand
Shotguns and Rifles. Further details contact:-*

WESTLEY RICHARDS & CO LTD
Grange Road, Bournbrook, Birmingham B29 6AR.
Telephone: 021 472 2953. Retail sales 021 472 1701

Limmex Field Sports
High Street and Wood Street, Old
Town, Swindon, Tel: 0793 22056

Kenlis R Ponting

Kenlis R. Ponting

Tadpole Farm, Blunsdon, Swindon,
Tel: 0793 770305
*For fine quality English guns. Kenlis R
Ponting, bring you, the customer, the
best of both worlds. Clothing and
footwear by all leading
manufacturers.*

Westbury Guns

BROWNING.
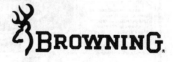

12 Edwards Street, Westbury Wilts,
BA13 BD, Tel: 0373 826081
*High class stockists of all leading
brands of shotguns, shooting
accessories and coaching facilities.
Excellent selection of Browning,
Beretta etc. Repair and alteration
service available.*

BARBURY GUNS

183

We carry a full range of shotguns including the latest models.
Browning, Miroku, Winchester, Beretta A.Y.A., Lanber, Rizzini, Kestrel, etc.
Air Weapons, Sporting Firearms, Clothing, Ammunition and accessories for the Field Sportsman and Clay Shooter.

Credit facilities available on all guns over £100

Cartridges: **Rottweil, Eley, Winchester, Viri, Gamebore and our own Gamebore custom loads**

Expert coaching given for the experienced or novice game and clay shooter

Full Gun Repair Facilities

We will be pleased to make arrangements for you to try your new gun at our own shooting school, and offer a free lesson including cartridges when you purchase a gun over £400.

For further details contact:
44/45 HIGH STREET, MARLBOROUGH
Tel: Marlborough (0672) 52862

Wiltshire Rod & Gun

23 High Street, Old Town, Swindon, Tel: 0793 47455
Main dealers of Browning, Beretta, Miroku, Aya and all leading gunmakers. A wide range of accessories and outdoor clothing. Gunfitting services available.

Wiltshire Shooting Centre
Station Road, Devizes, Tel: 0380 77282

Wiltshire Small Arms Company
P O Box 36, Devizes, Wiltshire, SN10 1UZ, Tel: 0380 6610

YORKSHIRE NORTH

Messrs J Anderson & Son
4 Saville Street, Malton, Tel: 0653 2367

Barrington C Davies
4/6 Cheltenham Parade, Harrogate, Tel: 0423 55677

Bulmers Gunsmiths

BROWNING

1/7 Lord Mayors Walk, York, Tel: 0904 20788

Cawood Gun Co
Sherburn Street, Cawood, Nr Selby, Tel: 075 786 223

John Gretton Shooting & Fishing

BROWNING

28 Northway, Scarborough, Tel: 0723 368771
Comprehensive range of shotguns, air rifles, full and small bore rifles and pistols. New and second hand. Part exchange welcome. Full repair service - restocking a speciality.

Gun Shop, The (Otley) Ltd
36 Cross Green, Pool Road, Otley, Tel: 0943 462770

Hargers for Guns
Cheapside, Settle, Tel: 07292 3751

R G Hodgson
7 Queen Street, Rippon, Tel: 0765 3029

Hookes of York Ltd
28/30 Coppergate, York, Tel: 0904 55073

John A Jackson
9/10 Queen Street, Scarborough, Tel: 0723 360904
Gun fitting facilities, cartridges and gun hire available.

W Metcalf & Son
5 Market Place, Richmond, Tel: 0748 2108

R J & B Morley
7 Bishopsthorpe Road, York, Tel: 090◄ 23007

Shooting Lodge, The

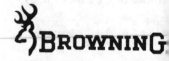

28/30 Victoria Street, Skipton, Tel: 0756 5825

H & J R Smith
8 High Street, Knaresborough, Tel:
423 863322

Thirsk Gunrooms
Finkle Street, Thirsk, Tel: 0845
4355

York Guns
King Street, York, Tel: 0904 31913

Yorkshire Gun Room

35/37 Swan Road, Harrogate, Tel:
0423 61182
*Specialising in English ejector guns.
Also quality repairs and alterations*

Yorkshire Gun Room

4 Finkle Street, Thirsk, Tel: 0845
24355

YORKSHIRE SOUTH

A1 Sporting Guns & Ammo
50 Wicker Street, Sheffield, S3 8JB,
Tel: 0742 24602

Doncaster Shooters Supply Ltd

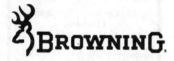

12 Copley Road, Doncaster, Tel: 0302
67615

Exelair Shooting Club
346 Sheffield Road, Birdwell,
Barnsley, Tel: 0226 748629
*The facilities of this fine indoor
shooting range include an armoury
and work area with a well stocked gun
shop supplying guns and accessories of
all types*

Field Sports Supplies,
YMCA Buildings, 10 Pitt Street,
Barnsley, Tel: 0226 206326

**Guns & Ammo, The Gunsmiths
& Shooting Centre**
50 Wicker, Sheffield 3, Tel: 0742
24602

Guns International

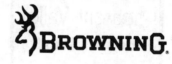

502 Doncaster Road, Stairfoot,
Barnsley, Tel: 0226 289155

GUNSPORT

125 Wellgate, Rotherham, Tel:
0709 377406

Hardy's Gunshop
367 Eccleshall Road, Sheffield, Tel:
0742 663403

Northern Arms Co

62b Copley Road, Doncaster, Tel: 0302
60265

George Wood & Co Ltd
113/115 Pinstone Street, Sheffield, Tel:
0742 23334

YORKSHIRE WEST

B & I Bancer
18 Pontefract Road, Castleford, Tel:
0977 554339
£I

Carters of Bradford Ltd
15 Bridge Street, Bradford, Tel: 0274
726215

The Castle Air Gun Centre
6 Castle Way, Castleford, Tel: 0977
511452

Dobson & Robinson
46 The Grove, Ilkey, West
Yorkshire, LS29 9EE, Tel: 0943
608549

Peter Dyson Ltd
31 Church Street, Honley,
Huddersfield, Tel: 0484 661062

R E Heathcote Walker
The Cottage, Gomersal House,
Lower Lane, Gomersal, BD19 4HY,
Tel: 0274 877498

A J Jewson
1 Westgate, Halifax, Tel: 0422 541146

Richard Jones
7 Horsefair, Wetherby, LS22 4JG, Tel:
0937 65919

J P S Guns
22 Lower Warrengate, Wakefield, Tel:
0924 379215

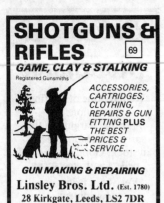
Kirklees Gun Shop

17 Lord Street, Huddersfield, Tel:
0484 44600

Henry Krank & Co Ltd
108 Lowtown, Pudsey, Tel: 0532
569163/0532 565167

Linsley Brothers Ltd

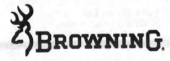

28 Kirkgate, Leeds, LE2 7DR, Tel:
0532 452790

Park Lane Service Station
Park Lane,, Keighley, Tel: 0535 605445

Pennine Shooting Centre
Manorley Lane, Bradford, Tel: 0274
603665

B G Pollard, Thornhill Armourers Shop
88 Thornhill Street, Calverley, Leeds,
Tel: 0532 568356

David J Rimington
Rathwell, Leeds, Tel: 0532 822540

Sambrook Shooting Sports
180 Leeds Road, Newton Hill,
Wakefield, Tel: 0924 365384

Silsden Sporting Guns
31 Skipton Road, Silsden, Nr Keighley
PC
Tel: 0535 56058

Swillington Shooting & Stable Supplies

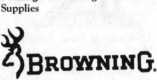

Home Farm, Wakefield Road, Leeds,
Tel: 0532 864097

Pennington's Sporting Arms and Ammunition
67 Bridge Street, Castleford

Pheasant Valley Shooting Ground
Unit 6, Tower Works, Globe Road,
Leeds, Tel: 0532 460003

Swillington Shooting & Stable Supplies
Home Farm, Wakefield Road,
Swillington, Tel: 0532 864097

Yorkshire Air Weapons
209 Stanningley Road, Armley, Leeds

SCOTLAND

BORDERS

Country Gun Shop, The
Lilliesleaf, Melrose, Roxburghshire,
TD6 9JD, Tel: 083 57315
*Established 1966. Closed all d.
Monday. Suppliers of Sporting gur
rifles and pistols. Also accessori
including our own custom loade
Eildon cartridges. A wide range
clothing. Gun repairs by skill
craftsmen.*

Game and Country Enterprises
6-8 Cannon Gate, Jedburgh,
Roxburghshire

Ian Fraser Sports
1 Bridgegate, Peebles, Tel: 0721 2097

John Dickson & Son
35 The Square, Kelso, Tel: 0573
24687

R Welsh & Son

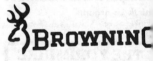

28 Castle Street, Duns, TD11 3D, T
0361 83466

CENTRAL

D Crockhart & Son

15 King Street, Stirling, FK8 1DN
Tel: 0786 73443
The friendly shop with the reputation. Shotguns-Rifles-Weapons-Ammunition-Clothing Accessories including Small k second hand weapons bought and se

Glasgow Range Supplies Ltd
6 Main Street, Menstrie, Tel: 0259
61301

K Angling & Guns

BROWNING.

101 Mary Square, Laurieston,
Falkirk, FK2 9PR, Tel: 0324 23156

Alex Martin
0 Royal Exchange Square , Glasgow

McLaren's of Bridge Allen
Allanvale Road, Bridge of Allen,
K9 4NU
All goods and equipment for the
sporting man and woman. Clothing
and accessories available.

DUMFRIES & GALLOWAY

Castle Douglas Guns & Tackle

BROWNING.

St Andrews Street, Castle Douglas,
el: 0556 2977

Gordon Sports
7 High Street, Lockerbie, Tel: 05762
400

M McCowan & Son
1/43 High Street, Dalbeattie, DG5
AN

M McCowan & Son
0-52 King Street, Castle Douglas,
G7 1AE, Tel: 0556 2009

Pattie's of Dumfries
09 Queensberry Street, Dumfries,
G1 1BH, Tel: 0387 52891

Solway Shooting Supplies
The Green, Eastriggs, Annan,
el:TN

The Gun Shop
0 Queen Street, Newton Stewart,
Wigtownshire, Tel: 0671 2570

The Post Office
he Green, Eastriggs, Tel: 04614 201

FIFE

John A Stewart
Ladywynd, Cupar, KY15 4DE

Were Game

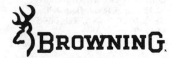

126 St Clair Street, Kirkcaldy, 0592
54301

GRAMPIAN

Anderson Guns

BROWNING.

201 Hardgate, Aberdeen, AB1 2YP,
Tel: 0224 201179

Countrywear
35 Bridge Street, Ballater,
Aberdeenshire, Tel: 0338 55453

George D Manson
45 Gordon Street, Huntly, Tel: 0466
2482

George Smith & Co
15 Bridge Street, Ballater, Tel: 0338
55432

Grampian Guns
Ravensmead, Newmachar, Aberdeen,
AB5 0PU, 06517 2273

R M Jeffries
39 New Street, Rothes, Tel: 034 03 407

Macsport Ltd
4 Bridge Street, Banchory, Tel: 03302
2855

Robertson Sports
1/3 Kirk Street, Peterhead,
Aberdeenshire

HIGHLANDS & ISLANDS

C H Haygarth & Sons
The Cottage Gun Shop, The Dunnet,
Caithness, KW14 8XQ, Tel: 084785
602

J Graham & Co Ltd
71 Castle Street, Inverness, Tel: 0463
233178

Gray & Co Gunmakers
30 Union Street, Inverness, Tel: 0463
233225

Knox House
Shore Road, Brodick, Isle of Arran,
Tel: 0770 2416

Leisuropa Ltd
6/8 Inglis Street, Inverness, Tel: 04632
39427

MacLean Sports

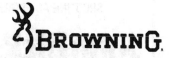

33 high Street, Dingwall, Ross-shire,
Tel: 0349 63147

R Macleod & Son

14 Lamington Street, Tain, Ross Shire,
Tel: 0862 2171

G G Mortimer & Son
61 High Street, Grantown on Spey,
Tel: 0479 2684

Ormiston & Co
Market Brae Steps, Inverness, Tel:
0463 222757

Rod & Gun Shop
68 High Street, Fort William, Tel: 0397
2656

Robert H Hall (Guns)
Willowburn Road, Kirkwall, Orkney,
Tel: 0856 2880

Rob Wilson Rod & Guns

Brora, Tel: 0408 21373

Wilson & Nolf
1 Francis Street, Wick, KW1 5PZ, Tel:
0955 4284

Wilson & Nolf
28/29 Breadlbane Terrace, Wick

ISLE OF SKYE

A Hodgson
4 Luib, Broadford

ORKNEY ISLANDS

Mr R M Hall
Willowburn Road, Kirkwall, KW15
1NE

LOTHIAN

Country Life
229 Balgreen Road, Edinburgh, Tel:
031 337 6230

David Taylor
Tel: 031 332 4873

John Dickson & Son
21 Frederick Street, Edinburgh, EH2
2NE, Tel: 031 225 4218

Edinburgh Gun Makers
73 Rose Street, Edinburgh, Tel: 031
2252641

Field & Stream Ltd
61 Montrose Terrace, Edinburgh, EH7
5DP, Tel: 031 661 4282

Shooting Lines Ltd
23 Roseburn Terrace, Edinburgh,
EH12 5NG, Tel: 031337 8616

F & D Simpson
28 West Preston Street, Edinburgh,
EH8 9PZ

M B Thompson & Son
19 East London Street, Edinburgh, Tel:
031 556 5682

Shooting Lines Ltd
23 Roseburn Terrace, Edinburgh, Tel:
031 337 8616
Tackle and shooting retailers

STRATHCLYDE

Alexander Dalgleish
11 Montgomery Street, Eaglesham,
Glasgow, G76 0AS

Crocket, The Ironmonger Ltd

BROWNING.

136 West Hill Street, Glasgow, Tel:
041 332 1041

Gamesport
60 Sandgate, Ayr, KA7 1BX, Tel: 0292
263822

Glasgow Range Supplies Ltd
6 Main Street, Menenstrie, Nr Stirling,
Tel: 0259 61301

Guns & Tackle
25 Portland Place, Hamilton, Tel: 0698
422904

James Kirk Tackle & Guns

BROWNING.

Union Arcade, Ayr, Tel: 0292
263390

John Dickson & Son
20 Royal Exchange Square, Glasgow,
Tel: 041 221 6794

D McKay-Brown Gunmaker
32 Hamilton Road, Bothwell,
Glasgow, G71 8NA, Tel: 0698
853727

McCririck & Sons
38 John Finnie Street, Kilmarnock, Tel:
0563 25577

Pitchers Sports
23 Moss Street, Paisley, Tel: 041
8896969

918 Pollokshaws Road
Glasgow, G41 2ET, Tel: 041 632
2733

Ian Tyrell Guns
165 High Street, Dumbarton, Tel:
0389 34438
*Scotlands leading supplier of shotguns
including Winchester, Browning,
AYA. Trade terms for Uniroyal
products. Barbour clothing*

TAYSIDE

**Angus Gun Room & Fishing
Tackle Centre**
98 Ferry Road, Dundee, Tel: 0382
453668

Highlands Guns & Tackle
Blair Atholl, Tel: 079681 303

Highland Gathering
Pitlochry, Tel: 0796 3047

James Crockart & Son
26 Allan Street, Blairgowrie, PH10
6AD, Tel: 0250 2056

John R Gow & Sons
12 Union Street, Dundee, DD1
4BM, Tel: 0382 25427
*Guns, rifles, air weapon
ammunition, clothing, knive
binocluars etc. Gun repairs and fishi
tackle.*

W R Hardy Gunsmith
153 East High Street, Forfar, Tel: 030
66635

A J.Kerr
213 High Street, Auchterarder

MG Guns & Tackle
51 York Place, Perth, Tel: 0738
25769
*We stock a complete range of shooti
and fishing accessories at excelle
rates. Also firearms, shotguns, de
stalking and our own shooting scho
Open 8.30 - 6.00 Mon-Sat.*

W Phillips
180 High Street, Montrose, Tel: 0674
72692

Shotcast Ltd
8 Whitehall Crescent, Dundee, DD
4AU, Tel: 0382 25621

Sporting Guns & Ammo
55 North Methven Street, Perth, Tel: 0738 23679

Tayside Tackle & Guns

259 Old High Street, Perth, Tel: 0738 32316

WALES

CLWYD

Fieldsports Equipe,
20a Elwy Street, Rhyl, Flintshire, LL18

Harry's Tackle
Unit 20, Queens Supermarket, High Street, Rhyl, Tel: 0745 54765

North Wales Shooting School

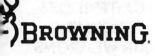

Sealand Manor, Sealand, Chester, Tel: 0244 812219

R D Pickering & Son
Abergele Road, Colwyn Bay, Tel: 492 2551

Rucksack 'N' Rifle
Abbot Street, Wrexham, LL11 1TA, Tel: 0978 350553

Shooting Sports Co
Lambpit Street, Wrexham, Tel: 978 359009

Strathyre Armoury
Harland Lane, Rossett, Wrexham, Tel: 7883 2550

DYFED

Aber Guns & Tackle
13 Terrace Road, Aberystwyth, SY23 1NY, Tel: 0970 3340

Anglers Corner
65 Robinson Street, Llanelli, SA15 1TT

Consumer Technical Supplies
'Efailfach'
Llanfair, Clydogau, , Lampeter, SA48 8LG
Mail order service available

County Sports

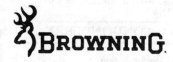

3 Old Bridge, Haverfordwest, Tel: 0437 3740

G T Griffiths
Teifi Valley Shooting Supplies, , Llechryd, Cardigan, Tel: 023987 204

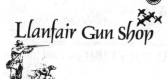

Llanfair Gun Shop

Llanfair Clydogau, Lampeter, Tel: 057045 356

L J Williams & Son, Gun Dealers
Garth, Llanrhystyd, SY23 5DQ

GLAMORGAN MID

Coed Y Brain
4 Bartlett Street, Caerphilly, Tel: 0222 882802

Country Gunshop, The
100 Penprysg Road, Pencoed, Nr Bridgend, CF35 6LT, Tel: 0656 860252

Keen's Tackle & Guns
97 Bridgend Road, Aberkenfig, Nr Bridgend, Mid Glamorgan, CF32 9AP, Tel: 0656 722448

Lloyds
40 Canon Street, Aberdare, CF44 7A, Tel: 0685 873717

GLAMORGAN SOUTH

A Bale & Sons Ltd
3 Frederick Street, Cardiff, Tel: 0222 29929

Countryside Promotions, Neath Gun Shop
44 Briton Ferry Road, Neath

Crown House Armoury Ltd
Cogan Hill, Windsor Road, Penarth, Tel: 0222 706181

Lakeside Guns (Prop RS Schulz)
4 Dynevor Road, Cyncoed, Cardiff, CF37 HZ

GLAMORGAN WEST

Lewis Sports

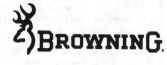

64 Commercial Road, Port Talbot, Tel: 0639 882312

West Wales Gun Co

6 James Street, Pontardawe, Tel: 0792 863181

GWENT

H H Keeling & Sons
48 Monnow Street, Monmouth, NP5 3EN

D J Litt (Firearms) Ltd

Unit 3, Maesglas Ind Estate, Newport, Tel: 0633 50025

Herbert Tucker
The Square, Newport, Salop

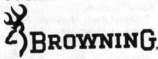
GWYNNED

Angling & Gun Centre
11/13 High Street, Porthmadog, Tel: 0766 2464

Angling & Gun Centre
11/13 High Street, Porthmadog, Tel: 0766 2464

Gwynned Firearms
99 High Street, Bangor, Tel: 0248 351641
Shotguns, Rifles, Pistols, Airguns, Large range of rifle and pistol ammunition. Military weapons a speciality. Government surplus equipment and clothing. Janes Book stockist specialising in military vehicle and shooting publications. Part exchange welcome.

W E Pugh Sports Dealer
74 High Street, Bala, Tel: 0678 520248

POWYS

N J Guns (Prop Mr N Jones)
2A High Street, Builth Wells, Tel: 0982 552174

Roberts & Quin
Commercial Street, Newtown, Tel: 0686 26579

A W Weale (Gunsmith)
Trebowen, Talgarth, LD3 OBB, Tel: 0874 711 443
Restoration and repair of antique and modern sporting guns and appliances. Also a good selection of cartridges and shooting accessories.

NORTHERN IRELAND

ANTRIM

C F Beattie

66 Main Street, Ballycarry, BT38 9HH, Tel: 09603 72462

Hugh Craig & Sons
16 The Square, Ballyclare, B39 9BD, Tel: 09603 22329

Lisburn Sports Centre
9 Smithfield Square, Lisburn, BT28 1TH, Tel: 08462 77975

James Matthews
72 Ballymoney Street, Ballymena, BT43 6A

Kenneth Rankin Ltd
131 Royal Avenue, Belfast, BT1 1FG

Spence Bros
32 New Street, Randalstown, BT41 3AF, Tel: 08494 72248

ARMAGH

T H Lavery
56 Clonmakate Road, Birches, Portadown, BT62, Tel: 0762 851215

Victor Mateer
7 Main Street, Donaghcloney, Craigavon, Co Armagh, Tel: 0762 881235

CO DOWN

Joseph Bradell & Son
9 North Street, Belfast, BT1 1AN

John M Clegg & Co Ltd
48 Regent Street, Newtownards, BT23 4LP, Tel: 0247 812585

Comber Sports Centre Ltd
18 Castle Street, Comber , BT23 5DZ, Tel: 0247 872846

Hollow Farm Shooting Grounds
35 Drumkirk Road, Comber, Co Down, Tel: 0238 528381

John C Smyth
5/7 Kildare Street, Newry, BT34 1D, Tel: 0693 5303

B A Thompson Firearms Unlimited
463 Gransha Road, Bangor, BT19 2PX

Traps & Tackle
6 Seacliff Road, , Bangor, Co Down, Tel: 0247 458515

FERMANAGH

Lakeland Tackle
Sligo Road, Enniskillen, Tel: 0365 23774

LONDONDERRY

H Burke & Son

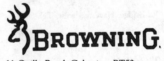

11 Quilly Road, Coleraine, BT52

H Burke & Son
70-76 Long Commons, Tel: Coleraine 2804/3496 after 6p.m.

J A McGuigan
95 Main Street, Maghera, BT46 5AB

Smyth Bros
15 Church Street, Coleraine, BT52 1A, Tel: 0265 52957

J C Stewart
1/2 Union Road, Magherafelt, BT45 5DA, Tel: 0648 32392

TYRONE

R J Farmer
23 Killyman Street, Moye, Duncannon, Co Tyrone, Tel: 08687 84556

S Kyles & Sons
Fivemiletown, Co Tyrone, Tel: 03655 21207

MC.Vey Bros
49/51 Molesworth Street, Cookstown, BT80 8NX, Tel: 0 24 92026

REPUBLIC OF IRELAND

Cal Flavin Ltd
100/101 North Main Street, Youghal, Co Cork, Tel: 024 92026

Francis Nelson & Sons Ltd
42 Castle Street & Market Street, Sligo, Tel: 071 2651

Barton Smith Est (1788)
Hyde Bridge, Sligo, Tel: 071 2356

Michael O' Connell Gunshop
24 Liberty Square, Thurles, Co Tipperary, Tel: 0504 21672

GAME REARING & GUNDOGS

CONTENTS

GAME FARMS/ ENGLAND

AVON

Patrick Pinker Game Farm Ltd
Latteridge, Iron Acton, Nr Bristol, Tel: 045422 416

BEDFORDSHIRE

Marlborough Game Farm
Miletree Road, Heath & Reach, Leighton Buzzard, Beds, LU7 9LA, Tel: 052 523563
Breeders and suppliers of pheasant and partridge eggs, chick, poults and adult stock

BERKSHIRE

Holme Park Game Hatcheries
Wokingham, Berkshire, Tel: 0734 782911

BUCKINGHAMSHIRE

Arthur Davis Game Farm
Denner Hill, Great Missenden, Tel: 024 028 200

Lodge Hill Game Farm
Butlers Cross, Wendover, Tel: 0296 625114

CAMBRIDGESHIRE

Cambridgeshire Pheasantries
Orchard Farm, Short Drove, Cottenham, CB4 4RW, Tel: 0954 50593

G L Poulter
Manor Farm, Wennington, Huntingdon, Tel: 04873 274

CHESHIRE

Cheshire Game Services

The Alpines, Twemlows Avenue, Higher Heath, Whitchurch, Shrops, Tel: 0948 840994 or 08298 306

CORNWALL

Cathacombe Game Farm
Cathacombe Street, Germans Saltash, Cornwall, Tel: 0503 30282
Pheasants, day old and poults. Mallard day old and six week old. Equipment and feed on request

CUMBRIA

Cumberland & Solway Game Farm
Castletown, Rocliffe, Carlisle, Tel: 022 874 268
Pheasant eggs, day olds, poults and partridges

Underlay Game Farm
Kirby Lonsdale, Tel: 0468 36 218

DERBYSHIRE

R Bestwick
Dale House, Tupton, Chesterfield, Tel: 0246 863826
Quality venison carcases constantly wanted. Top prices.

Derbyshire Pheasantries
Matlock Road, Walton, Chesterfield

DEVON

G R P Game Farm
Brno Lodge, Hillcroft, Staverton, Nr Totnes, TQ9 6AL, Tel: 080426 646, or 0364 43691

North Devon Game Farm
Venton, Monkleigh, Bideford, Tel: 08052 3200

Southern Partridges
Court Barton, Yarnscombe, Barnstaple, Tel: 0769 60505

DORSET

Chase Farm
Stanbridge Mill, Nr Wimborne, Dorset, Tel: 0258 840356

Cranborne Game Farm
Wedge Hill, Woodlands, Wimborne, Tel: 0202 824561
Pheasant eggs, chicks and poults

Dorset Game Services Ltd
15 Caster Bridge Estate, London Road, Dorchester, Dorset, Tel: 0305 67630

Derbyshire Pheasantries
Matlock Road, Walton, Chesterfield

Ridout Manor Farm
East Chelborough, Dorchester, Tel: 0935 83225/83615
Specialist in pheasant and partridge eggs, day old chicks and poults

DURHAM

Lambton Game Farm
Lambton Park, Chester Le Street, Co Durham, Tel: 0385 852435
Quality pheasants. Day olds and poults from six weeks

ESSEX

Field Game
Rogers Field, Hadleigh Road, Holton St Mary, Colchester, Tel: 0473 310319

Eastern Counties Game Farm
17 Butlers Drive, Stewardstone, Chingford, E4, Tel: 01 524 0518

GLOUCESTERSHIRE

Colnbrook Game Farm
Withington, Nr Cheltenham, GL54 4BW

Conigre Game Farm

LUCKY 7

Staple Farm, Withington, Nr Cheltenham, Tel: 0242 89 412

Cotswold Game Farm Ltd
Stroud, Tel: 028 582 208

Cotswold Game Hatcheries
Honeysuckle Cottage, The Camp, Stroud, Tel: 028582 458

Homestead Game Farm
Little London, Longhope, Gloucester, Tel: 0452 830263

GREATER MANCHESTER

Hamer Incubators
Bradshaw, Bolton, BL2 4JP, Tel: 0204 852555

HAMPSHIRE & ISLE OF WIGHT

Bramshot Game Birds
Rainbow End, Hoakley Farm, Tumbridge Lane, Ramshot, Liphook, Hants, Tel: 0428 723013

Hampshire Game Ltd
Clanville, Andover, Tel: 026470 294

Hi Bird Game Farm
Foley Estate, Liphook, Hampshire, Tel: 0428 722131
Pheasant eggs, chicks and eight week old poults

Lockerley Game Services
2 Barley Hill Cottages, Dunbridge, Romsey, Tel: 0794 40851

J R T Staley
Old Somerley House, Somerley, Hants, Tel: Ringwood 5628

HEREFORD & WORCESTERSHIRE

Newbridge Farm Products
Aylton, Ledbury, Herefordshire, Tel: 053183 386

G W Parker & Son
Astley Burf, Stourport on Severn, Hereford & Worcester, Tel: 02993 4593

M G Walker & Son
The Lodge, Four Ashes, Enville, Nr Stourbridge, Tel: 0384 88295

KENT

County Game Farms
Hothfield, Ashford, Tel: 0233 25580

Knuston Game Farms
Pilgroves Farm, Four Elms, Kent, Tel: 073 270 425

Mr Martin Wise
12 Wealden Close, Hildenborough, Nr Tonbridge, Tel: 0732 838402

Mid Kent Game Farm
Langley, Maidstone, Tel: 0622 861901

LANCASHIRE

Bickerstaffe Hall Game Farm
Ormskirk, Tel: 0695 22023

Hy Fly Game Hatcheries
Pilling Lane, Preesall, Nr Blackpool, FY6 0HH, Tel: 0253 810307
Specialists in the production of day old mallard and pheasants

Jim Clark
New Hall Farm, Lea, Preston, Tel: 0772 726486

LINCOLNSHIRE

Limes Pheasantries
The Limes, Boston Road, Sibsey, Boston, Tel: 0205 750409

Lincolnshire Pheasantries
Tumby, Boston, Tel: 06583 218
Pheasants, English and French partridges, Mallard, Bobwhite and Japanese quail.

Marshcroft Pheasantries
Gayton Top, Alford, Tel: 0521 50498

Meer Booth Game Farm
Antons Gowt, Nr Boston, Tel: 0205 73 250/0205 750306

Ormsby Game Services
North Ormsby, Louth, Tel: 0472 840536

Sporting Game Services
Roughton Moor, Woodhall Spa, Tel: 0526 52638/42468

West Lodge Game Farm

Whisby Moor, Lincoln, Tel: 0522 681720
Pheasant eggs, chicks and poults. Also partridges. Licensed game dealers

NORTHAMPTONSHIRE

Warwickshire Pheasantries
The Hemploe, Welford, NN6 7HF, Tel: 085 881 534

NORTHUMBERLAND

Ray Game Hatcheries
Herpath Lodge, Kirkwhelpington, Tel: 8030 403480

NOTTINGHAMSHIRE

Averham Park Pheasantries
Averham Park, Newark, Tel: 0636 702856

Shelford Pheasantries
Norwell, Woodhouse, Newark, Tel: 063686 447
Pheasant, Red and Grey partridge. Eggs, day olds, 6/8 week poults. Custom hatching

OXFORDSHIRE

Best Nest Hatcheries
Kingston House, Kingston Blount, Tel: 0844 51216
Pheasant and partridge available

Rockhill Farm & Game Hatchery
London Road, Chipping Norton, Tel: 0608 2929

Shipton Slade Game Farm
Woodstock, Oxford, OX7 1QQ, Tel: 0993 811280
For pheasant chicks and poults. Also custom hatching

SHROPSHIRE

Graham Davies Farms, Hatchery Department
Pontesford House, Pontesford, Salop, Tel: 0743 790821

Llansilin Game Farm
Oswestry, Tel: 069 170 349

North Shropshire Game Farm
Broughall, Whitchurch, Tel: 0948 3849

Peter Howe Ltd,
Sutton Camp Game Farm, Stoke Heath, Market Drayton, Tel: 063 083 236
All hardy stock caught up from one of our estate shoots. Pheasants - day olds and poults. French partridge - day olds and poults. Mallard ducklings.

Shropshire & North Wales Game Farm
Ryefields, Whixall, Whitchurch, Tel: 0948 3849

South Shropshire Game Farm
Eaton Mascott Hall, Cross Houses, Shrewsbury, Tel: 074375 540

SOMERSET

Brympton Mallard
Keepers Cottage, Camp Road, West Coker, Nr Yeovil, Tel: 093586 2044
For eggs, day olds, 5 and 6 week old ducklings by rearing only ducks and using wild drakes for breeding we produce hardy, high flying mallard

Empire Game Farm (A J Bennet & Sons)
Templecombe, Tel: 0963 70502
Pheasant and partridge eggs. Chicks and strong hardy 7 week old poults. All at very competitive prices

Empire Game Ltd
Lower Vagg, Nr Yeovil, Tel: 0935 840052

Kingstonwell Game Farm and Sporting Services
Coultings Farm, D.Fiddington, Nr Bridgewater, Tel: 0278 652272

Sedgemoor Game Farm
Fivehead, Taunton, Tel: 046 08 624

Somerset Game
Tel: 0935 840052

STAFFORDSHIRE

Sandon Pheasants
The Moathouse, Sandon, Tel: 08897 417

Brook Farm
Kirby Cane, Bungay, Suffolk, Tel: 0986 2703

Clopton Green Game Farm
Rattlesden, Bury St Edmunds, Tel: 044 93 319

Clover Lea Game Farm
Baddingham, Woodbridge, Tel:072875 633

Forest Game Farm
Brandon, Suffolk, Tel: 0842 810370

Hardwick Farms
Horsecroft Road, Bury St Edmunds, Tel: 0284 4611
Pheasant and partridge chicks and poults. Custom hatching. Extensive range of new and used equipment.

Julie Litton Waterfowl
Meadow Cottage, Linstead Parva, Halesworth, Tel: 098 685 249
Over 50 species of ornamental ducks and geese. Selection of Sawbill, Dabbling, S.Diving, Perching, Treeducks, Sea Ducks and Shelducks. Also Dutch Call Ducks (Various colours) SAE for price list.

Kettleburgh Lodge Shooting School
Woodbridge, Framlingham, Tel: 0728 723523

F W May & Son, St Bartholomews Game Farm
Sudbury, Suffolk, CO10 6XP, Tel: 078 73 72152

Pond Hall Game Farm
Gainsborough Lane, Ipswich, Tel: 0473 77117
Pheasant and partridge eggs, chicks, poults and equipment

Stow of Norton
Norton, Bury St Edmunds, Tel: 0359 30268

Winston Game Farm
Gillingham, Beccles, NR34 0HH, Tel: 0502 712260 or 717477
We specialise in pheasants, partridges and mallard. Cartridges and all rearing equipment

SURREY

Birtley Pheasantries
Birtley House, Bramley, Tel: 0483 892082

Lower Lodge Game Farm
Lower Lodge, Fernhurst, Haslemere, Tel: 0428 54351/53097

SUSSEX

Coneybury Game Farm
West Hoathly, East Grinstead, West Sussex, Tel: 0342 810200

Oakwood Game Farm
Chichester, West Sussex, PO18 9AL, Tel: 0243 786701/775089
Partridge specialists - Tony Sherlock for all your partridge requirements

Sussex Game Farm
Kirford, Billingshurst, Tel: 040377 456/417

WARWICKSHIRE

Gamekeepa Feeds Ltd
Southerley Park, Binton, Stratford Upon Avon, Tel: 0789 772429

Heart of England Partridges
Finham, Nr Coventry, Tel: 0203 418899

WILTSHIRE

Avon & Airlie Game Farms
Avon, Chippenham, Tel: 024974 225
Scottish Address: Grange of Airlie, by Kirriemuir, Angus,Tayside Tel:057 56 235

Bowood Estate
Caine, Tel: 0249 812102

David Hitchings
Knapp Farm, Broadchalke, Salisbury, Tel: 0722 780322

Rupert Cady (Game Services) Ltd
Cloverdale, East Gomeldon, Salisbury, Tel: 0980 610090

YORKSHIRE

Abbey Quail Products
Raw Lane, Stainton, Nr Rotherham, South Yorkshire, Tel: 0709 815160/ 812461
Windyridge, Huby, Leeds

Marcon Game Stock
Flaxton, York, Tel: 090486 588 (Day)

Moor End Game Farm
Sleights, Whitby, North Yorkshire, Tel: 0947 810609
Pheasant, partridge and duck. All rearing accessories

Perdix Gamen Stocc
Flinton Sproatley, Nr Hull, Tel: 04017 7171

Westfield Pheasantries
Cropton, Pickering, North Yorkshire, Tel: 07515 264/0751 73383

SCOTLAND

BORDERS

G F Burn
Bewliehill, Melrose, Tel: 08357 246

Lammermuir Game Services
Swallow Eaves, Westruther, Gordon, Berwickshire, Te 05784 258
Pheasants, grey and red leg partridges, eggs, chicks ,poults and adults

Tweed Valley Poultry Company
Tel: Peebles 22746 (day) Innerleithen 830740 (Night)

FIFE

Fife Pheasants
The Kiers, Upper Largo, Fife, Tel: 033 36 250
Day old pheasant and partridge chicks, pheasant and partridge poults,ex laying stock

Dumfries and Galloway
Glenhapple Farm, Newton Stewart, Tel: 0671 2854

GRAMPIAN

Spey Pheasantries
Tulchan Estate, Grantown on Spey, Morayshire, Scotland, Tel: 08075 200/257
Top quality pheasants and poults, day olds also French and English partridge and ducks available.

LOTHIAN

D C Watson & Sons (Fenton Barns) Ltd
Fenton Barns, North Berwick, East Lothian, Tel: 062085 201
Grey partridge specialists

A J Weare Game Services
Carberry Gardens, Musselburgh, E Lothian, Tel: 031665 4486

PERTHSHIRE

Ballechin Pheasantries Ltd
The Home Farm, Ballechin, Strathtay, Tel: 08874 380

TAYSIDE

Avon & Airlie Game Farms
Little Kenny, Lintrathen, By Kirriemuir, Angus, Tel: 05756 235

Fife Pheasantries
The Kiers, Upper Largo, Fife, KY8 6ED, Tel: 033336/250

Flawcraig Game Farm (PA Leslie)
Rait By Perth, Tayside, Tel: 08217 306

WALES

ANGLESEY

Anglesey Game Farm
Tyncae, Bachav, Llanerchymedd, Tel: 024 876 644

DYFED

Carmarthenshire & Wales Game Farm
Llanfyndd
Carmarthen, Dyfed[TWN]
Tel: 05584 491

Dyfed Game Farm
Banc Farm, Cross Inn, Llanon, Dyfed, Tel: 09746 634
Dyfed Game Farm - For the highest quality pheasants, ducks and partridges at most competitive prices. Full range of food and equipment also for sale.
Charles Grisedale.
Banc Farm, Croff Inn, Llanon, Wales - 09746 634

POWYS

Mid-Wales Game Farm
Dullas, Biew, Nantmel, Rhyader, Tel: 0597 810745

NORTHERN IRELAND

TYRONE

Dennett Game Services
Lower Rouskey, Dunnamanagh, Strabane, BT82 0SG, Tel: 050 489 235

AUTOMATIC FEEDERS

E Parsons & Sons Ltd
Blackfriars Road, Nailsea, Bristol, Avon, BS19 2BU, Tel: 0272 854911

GAME FEEDSTUFFS

Arum Feeds (Southern) Ltd
The Mill, Sincox Lane, Shipley, Horsham, Sussex, Tel: 040387 473

Barker Hickman Ltd
Upton Mill, Shifnal, Shropshire, Tel: 0952 461111
Manufacturers of starter crumbs, mini pellets, growers pellets and poult pellets

Centrepoint Dog Foods
P O Box 22, Huntingdon, Cambridgeshire, Tel: 0487 842351

Gamekeepa Feeds Ltd
Southerly Park, Binton, Stratford Upon Avon, Warks, Tel: 0789 772429
Suppliers of 'Gamekeepa feedstuffs'. Also grits

George H Elt
Eltex Works, Bromyard Road, Worcester, Tel: 0905 422377

Heygate & Sons Ltd
Bugbrooke Mills, Northampton, Tel: 0604 830381

F C Lowe & Son Ltd
Thames Street, Louth, Lincolnshire, LN11 7AE, Tel: 0507 601141
We've been around for a long time, quietly helping shooting folk enjoy their sport. Our contribution? The best dog foods, game food, cartridges and accessories.

Meer Booth Game Farm
Antons Gowt, Nr Boston, Lincs, Tel: 0205 73 250/0205 750306

Minsups Ltd
Winsford, Cheshire, CW7 3RG, Tel: 06065 56161

Micro Biologicals Ltd
Fordingbridge, Hants, Tel: 0425 52205

Pagefeeds,
The Mill, Tadcaster, North Yorks, Tel: 0937 833853

Pilwood Feeds Ltd (part of Pauls Agriculture))
Woodington Mill, East Wellow, Romsey, Hants, Tel: 0794 22693
Manufacturers of silverwood game feeds

Sportsman Game Feeds
3a West Market Place, Cirencester, Glos, Tel: 0285 68884
The Nitrovit range of Sportsman Game Feeds

Spratts Game Foods, Feed

Spratt's Game Foods

Services Centres
Old Dock, Avonmouth, Bristol, Tel: 0272 821316

Stow of Norton
Norton, Bury St Edmunds, Suffolk, Tel: 0359 30268

GAME COVER CROPS

W A Church (Bures) Ltd
Bures, Suffolk, CO8 5JQ, Tel: 0787 227654

Farmacre Game Cover
Tilston Close, Tilston, Malplas, Cheshire, Tel: 08 298 228

Gamekeepa Feeds
Southerly Park, Binton, Stratford Upon Avon, Warwicks, Tel: 0789 772429

Nicholson Nurseries
Kralingen, Steeple Aston, Oxford, Tel: 0869 40342

Rosewood Farm
Bickerstaffe, Ormskirk, Lancashire, Tel: 0695 423413

GAME HABITAT IMPROVEMENT

W A Church (Bures) Ltd
Bures, Suffolk, CO8 5JQ, Tel: 0787 227654

Oliver & Lang Brown
Brewham, Bruton, Somerset, BA10 0JP, Tel: 074 985 378

J F & F R Southgate
Creake Farm, New Common Marsh, Terrington Street, Clement, Kings Lynn, Norfolk, PE34 4JW, Tel: 0533 829571

GAME MEDICANTS

Coopers Animal Health Ltd
Crewe Hall, Crewe, Cheshire, CW1 1UB, Tel: 0270 580131

Crown Chemical Co Ltd
Lamberhurst, Kent, Tel: 0892 890491
Mebenvet wormers

David Nickerson (Tathwell) Ltd
The Old Vicarage, Tathwell, Louth, Lincolnshire, Tel: 0472 840536
Distributors of 'Gapex' water soluble treatment for gapes. Distributors of wormex.

Dorset Game Services Ltd
15 Caster Bridge Estate, London Road, Dorchester, Dorset, Tel: 0305 67630

Gilbertson & Page Ltd, Corry's
Roestock Lane, Colney Heath, Herts, Tel: 0727 22614

May & Baker Ltd, Customer Services, Animal Health Dept
Dagenham, Essex, RM10 7XS, Tel: 01 592 3060

Moor End Game Farm
Sleights, Whitby, Tel: 0947 810609
Specialist suppliers of veterinary products to the game industry

Vet Health
Colne Road, Coggeshall, Essex, Tel: 0376 61548
Manufacturers and distributors of specialist game rearing hygiene products, nutrients and medicaments

GAME REARING ALARMS & SECURITY EQUIPMENT

4 Shot Ltd

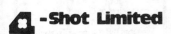

Greenacre, Station Road, Beaconsfield, Bucks, Tel: 04946 2349

Berswall Ltd
High Street, Redbourn, Herts, Tel: 058285 3707
Manufacturer of Intruder Alarm Guns to the trade. Precision Production Engineers

Carmarthenshire & Wales Game Farm
LLanfyndd, Carmarthen, Dyfed, Tel: 05584 491

Deepee Electronics Ltd
Wilderhope, Lime Walk, Dibden Purlieu, Southampton, Tel: 0703 843451

E.M.S. (Communications Division)
Grove Street, Wantage, Oxfordshire, Tel: 02357 4291
Anti poacher device

East Anglian Shooting Products

East Anglian Shooting Products

The Street, Helhoughton, Fakenham, Tel: 048 522 789

Gamekeepa Feeds Ltd
Southerly Park, Binton, Stratford Upon Avon, Warwickshire, CV37 9TU, Tel: 0789 772429
Suppliers of the 'Gamekeepa' poacher alarm system

Gilbertson & Page Ltd
Corry's, Roestock Lane, Colney Heath, Herts, Tel: 0727 22614

Helston Gunsmiths
The Clies, Meneage Street, Helston, Cornwall, Tel: 03265 3385

Kettleburgh Lodge Shooting School
Framlington, Woodbridge, Suffolk, Tel: 0728 723523
Effective range of burglar alarms. All rearing equipment accessories, medicants, disinfectants and game cover seeds. Maunfacturers of breeder houses and shelter pens

Lincolnshire Pheasantries Farm Equipment & Supply Co
Tumby, Boston, Lincs, Tel: 06583 218

Quadtag Ltd
Lordship Lane, Tottenham, London N17 6XF, Tel: 01 808 8604
Agents for E.M.S. radio poacher alarm

Stacey Electric (Wattpower) Ltd
11/15 The Grove, Reading, Berks, Tel: 0734 582758

GAME REARING EQUIPMENT

Arthur Davis Game Farm
Denner Hill, , Great Missenden, Bucks, Tel: 024 028 200

Autonest Ltd
Brampton Wood Lane, Desborough, Northants, Tel: 0536 760332
Plastic pheasant crates, drinkers, bins, plastic feeders etc.

Avon & Airlie Game Farms
Avon, Chippenham, Wiltshire, Tel: 024 974 225

Avon & Airlie Game Farms
Little Kenny, Lintrathen, Kirriemuir, Angus, Tayside, Tel: 05756 235

Axe Vale Engineering Ltd
Western Road, Axminster, Devon, EX13 5PB, Tel: 0297 32038

Brinsea Products Ltd

Broiler Equipment Co
Winnall Industrial Estate, Nr Winchester, Hants, Tel: 0962 61701

Carmarthenshire & Wales Game Farm
Llanfynydd, Dyfed, Wales, Tel: 05584 491
Pan sections made to order

Clopton Green Game Farm
Rattlesden, Bury St Edmunds, Suffolk, Tel: 04493 319

Colin F Tombs Hatchery Services
4 Mill Vue Road, Chelmsford, Essex, Tel: 0245 261207
Maintenance and spares for incubators. Suppliers of new and second hand incubation equipment

---

Conigre Game Farm

LUCKY 7

Staple Farm, Withington, Nr Cheltenham, Gloucs, Tel: 0242 89 412

Cope & Cope Ltd
57 Vastern Road, Reading, Berkshire, RG1 8BX, Tel: 0734 54491
Suppliers of Incubators, brooders, de-beakers, dry plucking machines and egg cleaners.

J B Corrie Fences
1-3 Princes Avenue, Watford, Hertfordshire, Tel: 0923 2882/29737

Cotswold Game Farm Ltd
Stroud, Gloucestershire, Tel: 028582 208

County Game Farms
Home Farm, Hothfield, Ashford, Kent, Tel: 0233 25580

Dorset Game Services Ltd
15 Caster Bridge Estate, London Road, Dorchester, Dorset, Tel: 0305 67630

East Anglian Shooting Products

East Anglian Shooting Products

The Street, Helhoughton, Fakenham, Norfolk, Tel: 048522 789
Manufacturers of automatic game feeders

Electrical Thermometers Co Ltd
Napier Place, Thetford, Norfolk, Tel: 0842 5831

Electrogame Hatchers
7 Fenview, Thorndon, Nr Eye, Suffolk, Tel: 037 971 403

Eyles Hatchers
5 West End, Avening, Tetbury, Gloucestershire, Tel: 0453 83 2947

Fife Pheasants
The Kiers, Upper Large, Fife, Tel: 03336 250

Gamekeepa Feeds
Southerly Park, Binton, Stratford Upon Avon, Warks, Tel: 0789 772429
All rearing equipment, accessories, medicines, disinfectants and game cover seeds. Manufacturers of breeder houses and shelter pens,

Game Protection Ltd
Charlswoods Road, East Grinstead, Sussex, Tel: 0342 28646
Pen netting. Steel pens.

George H Elt Ltd
Eltex Works, Bromyard Road, Worcester, Tel: 0905 422377

Gilbertson & Page Ltd
Corry's, Roestock Lane, Colney Heath, St Albans, Herts, AL4 0QW, Tel: 0727 22614

Robin Haigh Incubators
Abbey Bridge Farm House, Colonel's Lane, Chertsey, Surrey, Tel: 093 28 60236
Main agents for all 'Marsh' incubators

Hamer Incubators
Bradshaw, Bolton, Greater Manchester, BL2 4JP, Tel: 0204 852555
Manufacturers of Hamer incubators - Setter - Hatchers, separate hatchers or setters only. 25 to 10,000 egg capacities. Hamer electric hen brooders, 125-250 chick capacities. Electric hen brooder blankets

Hardwick Farms
Horsecroft Road, Bury St Edmunds, Suffolk, Tel: 0284 4611
Plastic setting inserts for pheasant and partridge eggs. The Hardwick brooder - 250 + 150 chick size gas brooder, thermostatically controlled. The Cleanmatic MK1, 180 egg capacity, thermostatically controlled washing machine.

Holme Park Game Hatcheries
Wokingham, Berkshire, Tel: 0734 782911

Incubators Unlimited
Easton Mascott Hall, Cross Houses, Shrewsbury, Tel: 074 375 540

Ivan & Cooper Ltd
Moorside Works, Cauldon Lowe, Stoke on Trent, ST0 3ET, Tel: 0538 702282

Jacksons Fencing
Stowting Common, Nr Ashford, Kent, Tel: 023375 393

Jacksons Fencing
New Rock, Chilcompton, Nr Bath, Somerset, Tel: 0761 232666

Jacksons Fencing
Wrexham Road, Belgrave, Chester, Cheshire, Tel: 0244 674804

Jacksons Fencing
Ramshawfield, Bardon Mill,, Hexham, Northumberland, Tel: 04984 555

W M James & Co (Bridport) Ltd
The Court, Bridport, Dorset, Tel: 0308 56666

A E Jennings
Iron Cross, Salford Priors, Evesham, Hereford & Worcester, WR11 5SH, Tel: 0386 870321

John Male Ltd

Church Norton, Selsey, Chichester, PO20 9DS, Tel: 0243 603040

Keene Game Products (UK) Ltd
Rockwell End Farm, Rockwell End, Hambleden, Henley on Thames, Oxon, RG9 6NG, Tel: 0491 571302

Knowle Nets
(Dept SH), 20 East Road, Bridport, Dorset, DT6 4NX, Tel: 0308 24342
Nets for covering release pens and breeding pens

Lambournes (B'Ham) Ltd
Colman House, Station Road, Knowle, Solihull, West Midlands, B93 0HL, Tel: 05645 70122

Lammermuir Game Services
Swallow Eaves, Westruther, Gordon, Berwickshire, Tel: 05784 258

The Limes Pheasantries
Boston Road, Sibsey, Boston, Lincs, PE22 0TD

Lincolnshire Pheasantries & Farm Equipment Supply Co
Tumby, Boston, Lincolnshire, Tel: 06583 218

Lockerley Game Services
2 Barley Hill Cottages, Dunbridge, Nr Romsey, Hants, Tel: 0794 40851
Suppliers of a complete range of game rearing equipment; heaters, feeders, rearing accessories, drinkers, vermin control medicants and hygiene, security

Malborough Game Farm
Miletree Road, Heath & Reach, Leighton Buzzard, Beds, LU7 9LA, Tel: 052 523 563
Manufacturers of huts, sections, shelter pens and construction equipment

Maywick (Hanningfield) Ltd
Rettendon Common, Chelmsford, Essex, Tel: 0245 400637
Manufacturers of gas-fired heaters/ brooders

Moor End Game Farm
Sleights, Whitby, North Yorkshire, Tel: 0947 810609
Suppliers of the Moor End game ring brails

A Neaverson & Sons Ltd, Portable Building Manufacturers
Peakirk, Nr Peterborough, Cambridgeshire, Tel: 0733 252225

Newbridge Farm Products
Aylton, Ledbury, Herefordshire, Tel; 053183 386

North Shropshire Game Farm
Broughall, Whitchurch, Shropshire, Tel: 0948 3849

Oakwood Equipment Supplies, Oakwood Game Farm
Chichester, Sussex, PO18 9AL, Tel: 0243 786701/775089

Oakwood game Farm
Chichester, West Sussex, Tel: 0243 786701

Ormsby Game Services Ltd
North Ormsby, Louth, Lincolnshire, Tel: 0472 840536

E Parsons & Sons Ltd
Blackfriars Road, Nailsea, Bristol, Avon, BS19 2BU, Tel: 0272 854911
Manufacturers of the Parsons automatic feeder for pheasants, partridges, cattle, fish, for export. Also automatic pop-hole door for poultry, ducks, chickens, cats and dogs

G A Patch
Whitehouse Farm, Rotherwick, Basingstoke, Hampshire, Tel: 025672 3700
Lamping package. New unique approach. Head fitting 55 watt 12 volt. Complete outfit ready to use. Write or phone for brochure.

Sandon Pheasants
The Moat House, Sandon, Staffordshire, Tel: 0889 7417 (Mr K Butler)
Penning, netting, sheeting, eggs. Day olds and poults

South Shropshire Game Farm
Eaton Mascott Hall, Cross Houses, Shrewsbury, Tel: 074375 277
Manufacturers of rearing pens and 'Eaton Mascott' gas brooders

Spey Pheasantries
Tulchan Lodge, Grantown on Spey, Morayshire, Scotland, Tel: 08075 200/257

Sporting Game Services
Roughton Moor, Woodhall Spa, Lincs, Tel: 0526 52638

Springfield Country Services
Dairy Cottage, Vigo Road, Fairseat, Kent, Tel: 0732 52638

West Dorset Nets 1985
80 North Allington, Bridport, Dorset, Tel: 0308 23576

Western Incubators
Springfield Road, Burnham on Crouch, Essex, CM0 8TA, Tel: 0621 782999

Westfield Pheasantries
Cropton, Pickering, North Yorkshire, Tel: 0751 73383

William Davies & Sons
Lynwood, Lugwardine, Hereford & Worcester, Tel: 0432 850729

S Young & Sons (Misterton) Ltd
Misterton, Crewkerne, Somerset, Tel: 0460 73461

Chertsey & District Pest Control
62 Fairway, Chertsey, Surrey, Tel: 09328 60422
All types of vermin traps supplied. Plus a complete pest control service (discounts to BASC members)

County Game Farms
Home Farm, Hothfield, Kent, Tel: 0233 25580

Deepee Electronics Ltd
Wilderhope, Lime Walk, Dibden Purlieu, Southampton, Tel: 0703 843451

Dick Brothers, Field Sports Equipment
23 St Thomas Road, Edinburgh, EH9 2LY, Tel: 031 667 3874
Specialist manufacturers and suppliers of snares, nets and traps for the trade.

East Anglian Shooting Products

East Anglian Shooting Products

The Street, Helhoughton, Fakenham, Norfolk, Tel: 048522 789

A Fenn & Co
Hoopers Lane, Astwood Bank, Redditch, Worcestershire, Tel: 052789 2881
Officially approved traps for all purposes. Also live catch cages.

Galway Silencer & Gun Co
2 Old Green, Medbourne, Market Harborough, LE16 8DX, Tel: 085883 706/733

Gilbertson & Page
Corry's, Roestock Lane, Colney Heath, Hertfordshire, AL4 0QW

Imperial Chemical Industries PLC, Plant Protection Division
Fernhurst, Haslemere, Surrey, GU27 3JE, Tel: 0428 4061

ICI PLC United Kingdom Department
Woolmead House, Bear Lane, Farnham, Surrey, GU9 7UB, Tel: 0252 724525

Infur (GB)
Dept SH, PO Box, Bude, Cornwall, EX23 8PF, Tel: 0288 3187

Jamie Wood Ltd
Cross Street, Polegate, East Sussex, Tel: 03212 3813

Kestrel Pest Control Ltd
PO Box 5, Desborough, Kettering. Northampton., Tel: 0536 523205

Patrick Pinker (Game Farm) Ltd
Latteridge, Iron Acton, Bristol, Avon, BS17 1TY, Tel: 045422 416
Manufacturers of Bristol Incubators and Still Air Hatchers. Distributors of Western Game Setters. Suppliers of pheasant eggs, chicks and poults. All necessary game rearing equipment

Perimeter Security & Protection Ltd
30 Castle Gate, Newark, Notts, Tel: Newark 77404

P & G Keeper Supplies
Heathwood Road, Higher Heath, Whitchurch, Shropshire, Tel: 0948 840994
Suppliers of everything for the gamekeeper - rearing equipment, game medicants etc

Pintafen Ltd
93 Hospital Road, Bury St Edmunds, Suffolk, Tel: 0284 2828
Incubators, feeders etc

Quadtag Ltd
197 Lordship Lane, Tottenham, London, N17 6XF, Tel: 01 808 8604/6414
Suppliers of wing tags and applicators

Redport Nets Co Ltd
94 East Street, Bridport, Dorset, Tel: 0308 22592
Game rearing nets

R.G.S. Automatics & Services
102 Hollies Avenue, Winthorpe Road, Newark, Notts, Tel: 0636 73062

Reliable Thermostst Co
95 Main Street, Bramley, Rotherham, South Yorkshire, Tel: 0709 542393

Roy Wrenn
Broomfield, 12 Wellesley Park, Wellington, Somerset, TA21 8PY, Tel: 082 347 7586

VERMIN CONTROL

C.T.F. Ltd
11 Langley Park Road, Sutton, Surrey, Tel: 01 642 5871

K P & S Nets

Castle Street, Axminster, Devon, Tel: 0297 33920
Snares and traps. Largest stockists of D.I.Y. kits etc.

Lincolnshire Pheasantries, Farm Equipment & Supply Co
Tumby, Boston, Lincolnshire, Tel: 06583 218
Manufacturers of cage traps and suppliers of all vermin control equipment

Nets & Sporting Supplies
P O Box 21, Dorchester, Dorset, Tel: 0305 67630

Ormsby Game Services Ltd
North Ormsby, Louth, Lincolnshire, Tel: 0472 840536
Manufacturers of 'Ratef' rat poison

E Parsons & Sons Ltd
Blackfriars Road, Nailsea, Bristol, Tel: 0272 854911
Manufacturers of Decoy Lofting poles for poking out pigeon nets and squirrel dreys

Patrick Pinker Game Farm Ltd
Latteridge, Iron Acton, Nr Bristol, Tel: 045422 416

R Sellars Pest Control Services Ltd
The Old Vicarage, Himbleton, Droitwich, Hereford & Worcester, Tel: 090 569 669
Suppliers of rat and mouse poisons and all traps and nets. Also pest control services, mole skin trousers and sporting books

Warwickshire Pheasantries
The Hemploe, Welford, Northampton, NN6 7HF, Tel: 085881 534

West Dorset Nets 1985
80 North Allington, Bridport, Dorset, Tel: 0308 23576

S Young & Sons (Misterton) Ltd
Misterton, Crewkerne, Somerset, Tel 0460 73461

GUN & WORKING DOG ACCESSORIES

Antidrift

Tanyard House, South Witham, Grantham, Lincs, Tel: 057283 676
Dog cushions filled with polystyrene beads with attractive fabric zip covers

Arnolds

1, Old Winch Hill Cottages, Winch Hill, Wandon End, Luton, Beds, Tel: 0582 34955

Athag Ltd UK, Guardsman
Carylon Road, Atherstone Ind Est, Atherstone, Warks, Tel: 08277 3040

Bala Pet Beds
Riverside, Stars Lane, Cold Hatton Heath, Wellington, Telford, Shropshire, Tel: 095283 380

Brettonbank Fieldsports
460 Cherryhinton Road, Cambridge, Tel: 0223 240368

Canac Pet Products, DRI Dog Bags
Beck Mill, Westbury Leigh, Westbury, Wilts, Tel: 0373 864 775

Dog Nests
Grimston, Melton Mowbray, Leics, Tel: 0664 812751

Ferry, Valerie, 'Burns Gill'
Vicarage Lane, Capel, Dorking, Surrey, Tel: 0306 711248
Supersnug beanbag pet beds and Supersnug towelling dry bags

R E Heathcote Walker Marketing,
The Cottage, Gomersal House, Lower Lane, Gomersal, West Yorkshire, BD19 4HY, Tel: 0274 877498

John Male Ltd

Church Norton, Selsey, Chichester, PO20 9DS, Tel: 0243 603040

Mill Accessory Group Ltd
Two Counties Mill, Easton Bray, Beds, Tel: 0525 220671

SSM International
Tedstone Wafre, Nr Bromyard, Herefordshire, Tel: 08867 646 & 284
Pointer gundog training accessories

Three Shires Pet Supplies Ltd
111 High Street, Marshfield, Nr Chippenham, Wilts, Tel: 0225891 232

GUNDOG BREEDERS

Chas Morris
Whitlocks End Farm, Bills Lane, Shirley, Solihull, West Midlands, Tel: 021 745 4891

Clod Hall Boarding Kennels and Cattery
Almington, Market Drayton, Shropshire, TF9 2PQ.W, Tel: 0630 2623

Clulee Peter 'Larford Gundogs' Greig Pitt
Chorley, Brignorth, Shropshire, Tel: 074632 620

Dapper Jack Russels
Five Acres, Calcott Hill, Sturry,
Canterbury, Kent, Tel: Canterbury
710537
*Jack Russels and working cocker
spaniels*

Mr Derry Argue
Millers Place, Fendom, Tain, Ross
Shire, Tel: 0862 2337

Ditchingham Gundogs
Buckenham Hall Farm, Strumpshaw,
Norwich, Tel: 0603 713873

Dog Breeders Associates
1 Abbey Road, Bourne End, Bucks,
Tel: 06285 29000
*Holders of a comprehensive list of
breeders relating to retrievers,
spaniels, labradors and jack russel
terriers*

**Dog Details, The Canine
Contact Agency**
7c High Street, Princes Risborough,
Bucks, Tel: 08444 7738

Drakeshead Gun Dogs
The Lodge, Lodge Bank, Brinscall,
Chorley, Lancs, Tel: 0254 831363
*Labradors. Black and yellow labrad r
stud dogs allfield trials champions.*

K A Erlandson
Ty Newydd, Froncysylite, Llangollen,
Clwyd, Tel: 0691 773327 or 0978
822068

Flightline Gundogs (P Sinclair)
Willowdene, Causeway End, Felsted,
Essex, Tel: 0371 820547
*Labrador and Golden Retriever field trial
winners at stud. Trained dogs and puppies
for sale*

Gaudin Gundogs
Clover Cottage, Mardy, Abergavenny,
Gwent, NP7 6HT, Tel: 0873 4449

**German Shorthaired Pointer
Association**
The Old Rectory, Rectory Lane,
Nailstone, Nuneaton, Tel: 0530 60581

Gunstock Kennels
Whitford, Holywell, Clwyd, North
Wales, Tel: 0745 560306

**Halstead J Mr & Mrs
(Drakehead Gun Dogs)**
The Lodge Bank, Brinscall, Chorley,
Lancs, Tel: 0254 831363
*Labrador puppies for sale, black and
yellow labradors at stud. Springer
spaniels at stud*

Mrs Hamnett
3 Redbrick Cottages, Ravensden
Road, Wilden, Bedford, Tel: 913
771000
*Pet and working dogs at very
competitive rates*

Hendon & Aldenham Kennels
Tylers Way, Watford by Pass, Watford,
Herts, WD2 8HQ, Tel: 01 950 1320

Holloway
Little Garth, Thorp Thewles, Stockton,
Cleveland, Tel: 0740 30801

Housty Kennels
Pal Mawr Farm
[TW]Felindre, South Wales
Tel: 0792 883687
*Gundogs trained to owners
requirements in ideal surroundings.
Puppies and adult dogs for sale.*

John Keith, Mr & Mrs
Denholm Farm, Peterhead,
Aberdeenshire, Tel: 0779 4403

Mirstan Gundogs (Stan Harvey)
Charlton House, Donkey Lane,
Stanningfield, Nr Bury St Edmunds,
Tel: 0284 828374

Navara Gundogs
Quarry Road, Witney, Oxon, Tel:
0993 72412

Paul D J & M
Ivory Farmhouse, Burghclere,
Newbury, Berks, Tel: 063527 362
*Dual purpose black labradors bred,
also Jack Russell Terriers*

Scales, Mr & Mrs
Culverdown, Great Henny, Sudbury,
Suffolk, Tel: 078729 252

**Shamdale Gundogs (Brian
Gough)**
Littlebury, Endale, Kimbolton, Nr
Leominster, Herefordshire, Tel: 0568
3580

Spatchcock Gundogs
Riverside Cottage, Ablington,
Bibury, Cirencester, Glos, Tel:
028574 431
*English Springers, Labradors, working
Cockers and working Golden
Retrievers*

**Sunstar Enterprises W O & A
Harrison**
Beacon Hill Cottage, West Morden,
Wareham, Dorset, Tel: 092 945 364

Tefhow Labradors
4 Wolverhampton Road, Hatton, Nr
Shifnall, Salop, Tel: 0952 461532
*Labradors, will work, bred for grace,
beauty and as good companions.
Tested for P.R.A.*

Trioaks Gundogs (Sam Seal)
The Bungalow, Worlds End,
Hambledon Hants, PO7 6QX, Tel:
0705 264370

**Wallace, Guy (Cross Llyde
Kennels)**
Fawley, Hereford, HR1 4SP, Tel:
043270 398

**York House Boarding Kennels
and Cattery**
Station Road, Laxfield, Suffolk, IP13
8HG, Tel: 098683 664
*Breeder of Dajumari Labradors,
sound in limb and temperament, for
work and show. Jack Russell terriers
by working parents, puppies usually
available*

GUNDOG & WORKING
DOG FEEDSTUFFS

B P Nutrition (UK) Ltd, Speciality Division
Stepfield, Witham, Essex, CM8 3AB, Tel: 0376 513651

Canine Foods Ltd
College Road, Aston Clinton, Aylesbury, Bucks, Tel: 0296 630291

Centrepoint Dog Foods
P O Box 22, Huntingdon, Cambs, PE17 3RF, Tel: 0487 842351

Championship Foods Ltd
Orwell, Royston, Herts, Tel: 0223 208081

Delta Pet Supplies
Hartley House, Mariners Street,, Goole, N Humberside, Tel: 0405 768301

Dogano Pets Shop
224 Stockport Road, Cheadle Heath, Stockport, Cheshire, SK3 0LX, Tel: 061 428 8836
Comprehensive range of complete feeds including frozen meats. Deliveries in North West

B Dugdale & Son (Petfoods) Ltd
Bellman Mill, Salthill, Clitheroe, Lancashire , BB7 1QW, Tel: 0200 27211
Manufacturers of Dugdales high performance dog foods

Evenlode Products Ltd
Station Mill, Chipping Norton, Oxfordshire, Tel: 0608 2321

Gamekeepa Feeds Ltd
Southerly Park, Binton, Stratford upon Avon, Warks, CV3 9TU, Tel: 0789 772429
Stockists: I Dominey, 19 Mallory Close, Kings Acre Road, Hereford Tel:0432 56176, D Martin, 3 Croft Road, Hungerford Tel:0488 82495. Wollerton Mill, Wollerton, Market Drayton, Salop Tel:063 084 635 Stockists in Guildford, Ipswich, Boston, Taunton, Bristol, Bridgnorth, Leicester, Ayr, Inverness and Aberdeen

Gilbertson & Page Ltd
Corrys, Roestock Lane, Colney Heath, St Albans, Hertfordshire, AL4 0QW, Tel: 0727 22614

Heygate & Sons Ltd
Bugbrooke Mills, Northampton, TEL: 0604 830381
Manufacturer of a complete coarse-mix for gundogs and working dogs

Kennel Nutrition Ltd
Dalmires Lane, Ripon, North Yorkshire, Tel: 0765 5156

K Feeds
Mount Pleasant Farm, Sturton le Steeple, Lincs, Tel: 0427 880914

Knockley Dog Foods
1 Hill Street, Lydney, Gloucestershire, Tel: 0594 41352

Linton Petfoods, Simon Thornton
Linton Mill, Wintringham, Malton, North Yorks, Tel: 09442 8181/2/3/4

Lowfield Game Farm
North Scarle, Lincoln

Luda Meaties Ltd
Thames Street, Louth, Lincolnshire, LN11 7BR, Tel: 0507 601141

Andrew Kay Shooting Supplies
Mount Pleasant Farm, Sturton Le Steeple, Nr Retford, Notts, DN22 9HS, Tel: 0427 880916
Manufacturers and suppliers of Alpha complete dog meals. Agents required. Contact Andrew Kay on 0427 880914

Nestles Ltd (Pet Foods Division)
Danesfield House, Medmenham, Marlow, Bucks, SL7 2ES, Tel: 06284 6021
Manufacturers of 'Go Dog' range of complete dog food and 'Marrow Meal' mixer biscuits

Omega Pet Products (Edward Baker) Ltd
Cornard Mills, Sudbury, Suffolk, Tel: 0787 72353

Paul D J & M
Ivory Farmhouse, Burchlere, Newbury, Berks, Tel: 063 527 362

Pedigree Pet Foods, National Office
Waltham on the Wolds, Melton Mowbray, Leics, Tel: 0664 64171

Roberts & Co, (Dunarch) Ltd
Dunchurch, Rugby, Warks, Tel: 0788 810283

Stanley Skinner & Co
The Mills, Stradbroke, Eye, Suffolk, IP21 5HL, Tel: 037984 247/434

Spratts Sporting Dog Foods,

Spratt's Game Foods

Feed Services Centre
The Old Dock, Avonmouth, Bristol, Tel: 0272 821316

Vet Health
17 Butler Road, Halstead, Essex, Tel: 0787 472450
Producers of the unique Vethealth range of feed additives and tonics for breeeding and working dogs - includes B-Sorb (iron and vitamin B tonic) and Hypernutrient (complete nutritional supplement)

Warwickshire Pheasantries
The Hemploe, Welford, Northampton, NN6 7HF, Tel: 085 881 534
Wholesale agent to Gilbertson & Page Limited for the supply of Valu-Mix Complet dog food

The vital difference you can see

It's the 100% natural goodness of Wilson's that helps to keep dogs on top form, bright-eyed and full of life.

Wilson's is a unique blend of high quality meat proteins and energy-giving cereal which provides a complete, balanced and satisfying meal for working dogs, show dogs and family pets. And dogs love it.

Wilson's cereal is cooked and rolled, so it's very digestible even for young dogs. It is rich in high-fibre bran and fortified with all the minerals and vitamins a healthy, lively dog needs, including selenium to boost the effectiveness of vitamin E.

Wilson's is formulated for top dogs, with only the best ingredients and with linseed oil to keep even the most challenging coats in peak condition.

Feed your dog on Wilson's and see the difference. It's called vitality.

NOW also with GRAVY

WILSON'S
TRADE MARK
DOG MEAL
with linseed oil

Nose to tail vitality

Distributed by
Beecham Animal Health, Broadmead Lane, Keynsham, Bristol BS18 1ST.

124

Wilson & Sons (Dundee) Ltd,
Part of Beecham Animal Health

Broadmead Road, Kynsham, Nr Bristol, Avon, BS18 1ST, Tel: 02756 67101

Manufacturers of Wilsons dog Meal and Wilsons Health care products

---

GUNDOG & WORKING DOG KENNELLING SUPPLIES

Athag Ltd, Guardsman
Carlyon Road, Atherstone Ind Estate, Atherstone, Warks, Tel: 08277 3040

Avon & Airlie Game Farms
Avon, Chippenham, Wilts, Tel: 024974 225

County Game Farms
Home Farm, Hothfield, Ashford, Kent, Tel: 0233 25580

Lindee Lu Products
Unit 4, Taverners, Southfield Road, Nailsea, Avon, Tel: 0272 853800

A Neaverson & Sons Ltd
Peakirk, Nr Peterborough, Cambs, Tel: 0733 252225

Kennel manufacturers

Scotts of Thrapston
Bridge Street, Thrapston, Northants, Tel: 08012 2366

Wylie J
Pinehawk Kennels, Carlton, Nr Newmarket, Suffolk, Tel: 022029 249 or 778

GUNDOG TRAINERS

Abbotsleigh Black Labradors
Sarah Coomber, Little Abbotsleigh, Loughton, Lewes, East Sussex., BN8 6AJ, Tel: 032183 541
We have three field trial champions and a young dog with hip pass, S.T. and championship show awards. all big, strong, good looking with superb temperament. Eyes clear.

Brackenbank Kennels
Brackenbank Lodge, Penrith, Cumbria, Tel: 076883 241

Chas Morris
Whitlocks End Farm, Bills Lane, Shirley, Solihull, West Midlands, Tel: 021 745 4891

Chudley J & K Harpersbrook Kennels
Brigstock, Kettering, Northants, Tel: 053 673 243

Clulee, Peter 'Larford Gundogs',
Greig Pitt, Chorley, Bridgnorth, Shropshire, Tel: 074632 620

D & F Roskell Sporting Services
Trasha Hill Kennels, Pilling, Lancashire, PR3 6BD, Tel: 099 52 2761

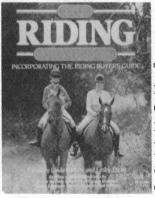
Mr Derry Argue
Millers Place, Fendom, Tain, Ross shire, Tel: 0862 2337

Ditchingham Gun Dogs
Buckenham Hall Farm, Strumpshaw, Norwich, Tel: 0603 713873

Drakeshead Gun Dogs
The Lodge, Lodge Bank, Brinscall, Chorley, Lancs, Tel: 0254 831363
Specialising in training Labradors and Springers Spaniels

Dukes R
Isle of Rhea, Bodenham, Nr Hereford, Hereford & Worcester, Tel: 056 884 367

Erlandson K A
Ty Newfydd, Froncyslte, Llangollen, Clwyd, Wales, Tel 0691 773327 or 0978 822068

Gavosie Gundogs
Newholdings, Eyton, Baschurch, Shrewsbury, SY4 2JH, Tel: 0939 260339
Gavosie Gundogs have training vacancies for labradors and spaniels of suitable age and breeding. Puppies and older dogs sometimes for sale.

Gunstock Kennels
Whitford, Holywell, Clwyd, Wales, Tel: 0745 560306

Halstead J
Drakeshead Gun Dogs, The Lodge Bank, Brnscall, Chorley, Lancs, Tel: 0254 831363

Specialising in training and boarding Labradors and Springer Spaniels

Howlett, Holkham Gun Dog Kennels

Holkham Park, Wells, Norfolk, Tel: 0328 710367

Jack Mayall (Saddleworth)

Clod Hill, Markey Drayton, Shropshire, Tel: 0630 2623

James Douglas, Conalter Kennels
Conalter, Ochtertyre, Creiff, Perthshire, Tel: 0764 2608

CONSISTENT SHOW WINNING
WORKING DOG AT STUD TO
APPROVED BITCHES
HOME REARED PUPPIES
SOMETIMES AVAILABLE

**TUTMUR
BORDER
TERRIERS**

JACK RUSSELL
TERRIERS ALSO
AVAILABLE

Mrs Ann Tuttle
20 Great Common   TELEPHONE
Inkpen, Newbury, Berks   04884 272

John Male Ltd

JOHN MALE LIMITED

Church Norton, Selsey, Chichester, PO20 9DS, Tel: 0243 603040

Kelvinhead Kennels
Auchenheath, Lanark, Tel: 0555 894198
Spaniels and retrievers trained by full time professional gundog trainer. Every facility. Consult Ron Montgomery.

Longville, R
Bell's Mill, Bell's Lane, Wordsley, Stourbridge, West Midlands, Tel: 0384 298169

Mirstan Gun Dogs (Stan Harvey)
Charlton House, Donkey Lane, Stanningford, Nr Bury St Edmunds, Suffolk, IP29 4RA, Tel: 0284 828374

Norleigh Kennels
Ardersier, Inverness, Tel: 06676 2386

Rivertrees Gundog Training Kennels
Griggs Farm, , Coggeshall, Colchester, Essex, Tel: 0376 61186
Field Trial Champion Keswich Hamish and other dogs at stud. Young dogs and puppies for sale. Apply to Bob Walker

Rutherford, John
Martins Hill, Stow on the Wold, Gloucestershire, Tel: 0451 30206

Saddleworth Gundogs
Clod Hall Kennels, Market Drayton, Shropshire, Tel: 0630 2623
Have your gundogs trained under ideal conditions. Please telephone Jack Mayall on above number. Obedience training for all other breeds

Salston Hotel
Ottery St Mary, Nr Exeter, Devon, Tel: 040 481 2310
Well established gun dog seminars. June and September

Shamdale Gundogs
Littlebury, Endale, Kimbolton, Nr Leominster, Herefordshire, Tel: 0568 3580
Puppies - trained and part trained usually available. Trained dogs for export a speciality

Sinclair, P (Fighting Gundogs)
Willowdene, Causeway End, Felstead, Essex, Tel: 0371 820547

Spatchcock Gundogs
Riverside Cottage, Ablington, Bibury, Cirencester, Glos, Tel: 028574 431
Trained and part trained dogs for sale

Sunstar Enterprises W O & A Harrison
Beacon Hill Cottage, West Morden, Wareham, Dorset, Tel: 092945 364

Trioaks Gundog Kennels (Sam Seal)
The Bungalow, Worlds End, Hambledon, Hants, PO7 6QX, Tel: 0705 264637
All gundog breeds prosfessionally trained to owners' requirements. Training and Boarding for Gundog breeds only

Wallace Guy (Cross Llyde Kennels)
Fawley, Hereford, HR1 4SP, Tel: 043270 398

Wylie, J, Pinehawk Kennels & Livestock Shipping
Carlton, Nr Newmarket, Suffolk, Tel: 022029 249 or 778

GUNDOG TRAINING EQUIPMENT

Antidrift

Tanyard House, South Witham,
Grantham, Lincs, Tel: 057283 676
*Manufacturers of Spliced nylon rope
leads. Folding dog spike*

Arnolds
1 Old Winch Hill Cottages, Winch
Hill, Wandon End, Luton, Beds, Tel:
0582 34955

Athag Ltd UK Guardsman
Carlyon Road, Atherstone Ind Estate,
Atherstone, Warks, Tel: 08277 3040

Brettonbank Fieldsports
460 Cherry Hinton Road, Cambridge,
Tel: 0223 240368

**Dick Brothers, Field Sports
Equipment**
23 ST Thomas Road, Edinburgh,
EH9 2LY, Tel: 031 667 3874
Suppliers of dog and slip leads

Dogano Pets Shops
224 Stockport Road, Cheadle Heath,
Stockport, Cheshire, SK3 0LX, Tel:
061 428 8836

Herbie Jacon Ltd
Gillingham, Dorset, Tel: 07476 4101

HJR Productions
81 Stoughton Road, Oadby,
Leicester, LE2 4FQ, Tel: 0533
714691

J Hudson & Co (Whistles) Ltd
Barr Street, Birmingham, West
Midlands, B19 3AH, Tel: 021 554 2124
Full range of 'Acme' dog whistles

Intervideo Publications Ltd
Bonnyton House, , Inverarity,
Tayside, Tel: 0307 82327

John Male Ltd

Church Norton, Selsey, Chichester,
PO20 9DS, Tel: 0243 603040

Ralph Grant & Son Ltd
Green Lane Road, Leicester, Tel: 0533
767551/2

Turner Richards
Cardigan Street, Birmingham, B4
7SA, Tel: 021 359 5577

Winners of Halstead
17 Butler Road, Halstead Essex, Tel:
0787 472450

GUNDOGS/WORKING TERRIERS

Mrs Ann Tuttle
20 Great Common, Inkpen,
Newbury, Berks, Tel: 04884 272

D.J. & M. Paul
Ivory Farmhouse, Burghclere,
Newbury, Berkshire., Tel: 063527
362

GUNDOGS/LURCHER EQUIPMENT

Turner Richards
Cardigan Street, Birmingham, B4
7SA, Tel: 021 3595577

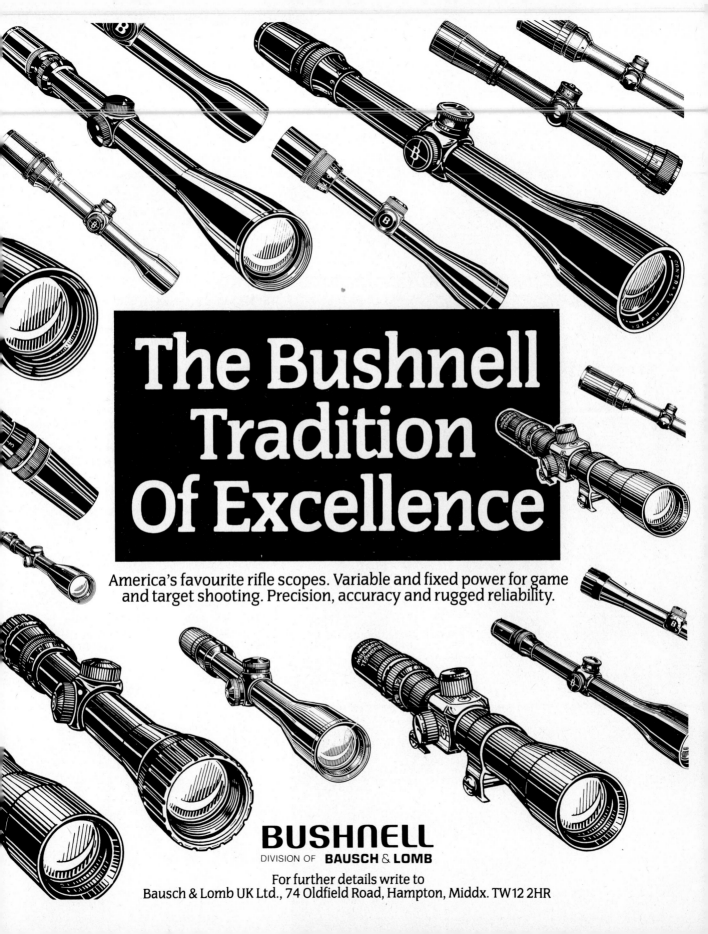

The Bushnell Tradition Of Excellence

America's favourite rifle scopes. Variable and fixed power for game and target shooting. Precision, accuracy and rugged reliability.

BUSHNELL
DIVISION OF **BAUSCH & LOMB**

For further details write to
Bausch & Lomb UK Ltd., 74 Oldfield Road, Hampton, Middx. TW12 2HR

Watch for the fox!

CLOTHING

CLOTHING

M - MANUFACTURER

W - WHOLESALER

R - RETAILER

Academy Leisure
112a Broadway, Bexleyheath, Kent, Tel: 01 304 4547
Wholesalers of Field boots

**Accuracy International
(Shooting Sports) Ltd**

43 Gladys Avenue, North End, Portsmouth, Tel: 0705 660371/2
Distributors of SAUER Shooting Clothing. Target shooting jackets, trousers and gloves

M — Afonwen Woolen Mill
Afonwen, Nr Mold, Clwyd, Wales, Tel: 0352 720427

M — Allen & Caswell Ltd
'Regent Works', Cornwall Road, Kettering, Northants, Tel: 0536 512804
'Regent' shooting boots. Leather and Veldtscheon

R — Andrew Tucker Ltd
58 Portsmouth Road, Cobham, Surrey
Retailers of shooting clothing

M — Antidrift

ANTIDRIFT

Tanyard House, South Witham, Grantham, Lincs, Tel: 057283 676
Hand knitted shooting stockings, mittens, garters, jerseys

M — Aquabeta (Specialist Products) Ltd

Aquabeta

Unit 23, Cibyn Industrial Estate, , Caernarfon, Gwynedd, LL55 2BD
Manufacturer of Gore-Tex fabric countrywear, waterproof breathable clothing.

Aran Wear
Old Lodge Farm, Westwood Heath Road, Coventry, Tel: 0203 463265
Hand knitted Aran sweaters. Stockings

R — Armstrong of Aberfoyle
Aberfoyle, Stirling, Central Scotland, Tel: 08772 221
Retailers of a range of shooting and country clothing, including knitwear, hats, shooting mitts and all clothing accessories. Tweeds by the yard

R — Armstrong's Gunsmiths
360 Carlton Hill, Carlton, Nottingham, Tel: 0602 873313
'Elch' loden clothing. Regent and Hawkins leather boots. Classic Rubber boots

M W — Ashdown Field Sports
Oast Farmhouse, Felcourt, East Grinstead, Sussex, Tel: 0342 833356

M — J Barbour & Sons Ltd
Simonside, South Shields, Tyne & Wear, NE34 3PD, Tel: 0632 552251

R — Barbury Guns Ltd
44/45 High Street, Marlborough, Wilts, SN8 1HQ, Tel: 0672 52862
Comprehensive range of clothing for the field sportsman and clay shooter. Including: Barbour, Keeperwear, Ganton, J.C.P., Gunmark, Puffa etc.

Battle Orders
71 Eastbourne Road, Lower Willingdon, Eastbourne, East Sussex, Tel: 032 12 7309
Suppliers of martial arts, karate suits and ninja black suits, also protective martial arts equipment.

M — Beaver of Bolton Ltd
Gilnow Mill, Spa Road, Bolton, Tel: 0204 386824

M — Belstaff International Ltd
Caroline Street, Longton, Stoke on Trent, Staffordshire, ST3 1DD, Tel: 0782 317261

M — Bertram Dudley & Son Ltd
Commercial House, 1 Foundry Terrace, Bradford Road, Cleckheaton, Yorks, Tel: 0274 873015

W — Bob Church & Co Ltd
16 Lorne Road, Northampton, Tel: 0604 713674

M — Born & Bred
78 Fulham Road,, London, SW3 6HH, Tel: 01 584 2451

M — 'Brafferton'
Marsh Lane, Leeds, Tel: 0532 446391/453716
Top quality heavyweight moleskin, cord, tweed, cavalry twill trousers and breeks

M — Bridgedale
Samuel Street, Leicester, Tel: 0533 538781

M — British Bata Shoe Co Ltd
East Tilbury, Essex, Tel: 03752 3400/9
Manufacturers of 'Derri Boots'

R — British Sports
107 Praed Street, Paddington, London, W2, Tel: 01 402 7511
Stockists of all types of shotguns, rifles, handguns, air guns, cartridges and ammunition. Replica weapons and clothing also available. Export enquiries welcome. Open 9.00 - 6.00 Mon-Sat.

M — Burton McCall Ltd
Samuel Street, Leicester, LE1 1RU, Tel: 0533 538781
The original Bridgedale military sweater. Dry boots and waterproof footwear. Also rubber walking boots and thermal underwear

M — Buttshop Specialist Sportswear
Newcastle House (Business Centre), High Spen, Tyne & Wear, NE39 2BL, Tel: 0207 542484
Manufacturers of jackets for target rifle shooting and air weapon shooting

R — Caer Urfa Guns & Ammo
399 Stanhope Road, South Shields, Tyne and Wear, Tel: 0632 551045
Large range of country clothing [D]

Caisson Supplies
91-95 Nottinghill Gate, London, W11 3JZ, Tel: 01-727-0530, Telex: 24301 G
Distributors of Eluminator Boots and associated products, also body armour and bomb suits, protective helmets etc.

M — Cambrian Factory
Llanwrtyd Wells, Powys, Tel: 05913 211

R — Cambrian Fly Fishers
The Old Vicarage, Trevor, Llangollen, Clwyd, Wales, Tel: 0978 821789,820880

M — Chevin Coats
47 West Busk Lane, Otley, West Yorks, LS21 3LY, Tel: 0943 463295

M — Clay Shooters Supplies
32 St Mary's Road, Market Harborough, Leics, Tel: 0858 66616
Manufacturers of Welland Royal clothing and shooting vest coats

M — Commando Knitwear
Unit 42 Faircharm Trading Estate, Leicester, LE3 2BU, Tel: 0533 891414

M — H Cooper Ltd
57 Kirkgate, Silsden, W Yorks, Tel: 0535 53338

M — Copnor Services Ltd
Gurnard House, Westlands, Birdharm, Chichester, West Sussex, Tel: 0243 512797

R — Cordings of Piccadilly
19 Piccadilly, London, W1V 0PE, Tel: 01 734 0830
Retailers of a wide range of shooting and country clothing

R — Country Corner

COUNTRY CORNER
35/37 Swan Road, Harrogate, N Yorks, Tel: 0423 61182
Ladies and Gents quality country clothing including full range of Barbour, Husky, Puffa. Country prints. Teviotdale ornaments, sporting accessories.

The Country Gun Shop
Lilliesleaf, Melrose, Roxburghshire, TD6 9JD, Tel: 083 57315
Suppliers of Quittey waistcoats and waxed jackets etc

R — Country Ways
115 Holburn Street, Aberdeen, AB1 6BQ, Tel: 0224 585150

M — Courtaulds Ltd, Viscose Division
13/14 Margaret Street, London , W1A 3DA, Tel: 01 580 8501

M — Countrystyle Sporting Clothes

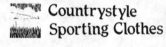 **Countrystyle Sporting Clothes**

High Street, Ruabon, Wrexham, Clwyd, LL14 6BL, Tel: 0978 821237

R — Country Wear
35 Bridge Street, Ballater, Aberdeenshire, Tel: 0338 55453
Retailer of country and shooting clothing and accessories. Large range of ladies and gents cashmere.

M — Countrywear
9 Bridge Close,, Romford, Essex, Tel: 0708 755 992

M — Countrywide
P O Box 1, , Liphook, Hampshire, Tel: 042 876 329

M — Crocket & Jones
Perry Street, Northampton, Tel: 0604 31515

R Cudworth (Norden) Ltd
Baitings Mill, Norden, Rochdale, Lancs, Tel: 0706 41771

M — Custom Caps
10 Marshalsea Road, London, SE1 1HL, Tel: 01 403 1717

David Ripper & Son

WHOLESALE DISTRIBUTORS
TO THE GUN TRADE

139

For Quality in
SHOOTING SUITS,
KNITWEAR,
GLOVES, SOCKS,
& TIES

*Silt Street, Mill, Macclesfield, Cheshire
Telephone Macclesfield (0625) 25899*

R — **E W Forbes & Son**
126/130 Eastgate, Louth, Lincolnshire

PERFECTOS
WATERPROOF CLOTHING

140

PERFECTOS Waterproof Clothing is manufactured in Scotland by **Douglas Fraser & Sons (Mfg) Ltd.**

It is designed to give complete protection whatever the weather—combining good looks with **outstanding performance** and **complete comfort.**

PERFECTOS Waterproof Clothing is **GUARANTEED** for Waterproofness, Quality and Performance.

For more details, contact:

Perfectos
Douglas Fraser & Sons (Mfg) Ltd.
PERFECTOS Tackle & Gun Division
Frockheim, Angus, Scotland, DD11 4TU
Telephone (024 12) 341

R — **Fowler Bros (Brigg)**
Main Street, Howsham, Lincolnshire,
LN7 6LD, Tel: 06527 565

W — **Frank Dyke & Co Ltd**
1/7 Ernest Avenue, West Norwood,
London, SE27, Tel: 01 670 2224

R — **Frasers Farmwear**
47 Burns Statue Square, Ayr,
Strathclyde, Scotland, Tel: 0292 281530

M — **Gamekeepa Feeds Ltd**
Southerley Park, Binton, Stratford-
on-Avon, Warwickshire, Tel: 0789
772429

M — **Ganton Manufacturing Ltd**
Ridings House, Depot Lane,
Scarborough, N Yorks, Tel: 0723
371910

M — **Arthur Garstang & Co Ltd**
213 Preston New Road, Blackburn,
Lancs, Tel: 0254 59357
Manufacturers of shirts to measure

M — **George Jeffries Gloves**
Fairfield Road, Warminster, Wilts,
Tel: 0988 212716

M — **Giddons Gloves & Leatherwear Ltd**
39 Princess Street, Yeovil, Somerset,
Tel: 0935 23468

R — **Gordon Lowes Ltd**
179/180 Sloane Street, London, SW1
X9QG, Tel: 01 235 8484/5

R — **Gordon Lowes Ltd**
16 Kings Parade, Cambridge, Tel: 0223
60274

M — **G T Hawkins Ltd**
Overstone Road, Northampton, Tel:
0604 32293
Leather shooting boots

M — **Haythornthwaite & Sons Ltd**
Grenfell House, Rylands St, Burnley,
Lancs, Tel: 0282 216211
Manufacturers of Grenfell outdoor clothing and rainwear

M — **Hebden Cord Co Ltd**
Hebden Bridge, West Yorkshire, HX7
6EW, Tel: 042284 3152

M — **Herbert Johnson Ltd**
13 Old Burlington Street, London,
W1X 1LA, Tel: 01 439 7397

M — **J Herbert Smith (Leicester)**
Saddington Hall, Leicester,
Leicestershire, LE8 0QH, Tel: 0533
402374
Shooting socks/stockings

M — **Hides & Deecs**
Pesterford Bridge, Stansted, Essex,
Tel: 0279 812638
Clothing manufacturer and supplier

R — **Highland Countrywear**
James Square, Creiff, Perthshire, KY8
4HE, Tel: 0592 713285

R — **Highland Countrywear**
17 College Street, Buckhaven, Fife,
Tel: 0764 4322

M — **A T Hogg Ltd**
5 Strathmiglo, Fife, Scotland, Tel: 033
76/202

R — **Holland & Holland Ltd**
33 Bruton Street, London, W1X
8JS, Tel: 01 499 4411
Suppliers of a complete range of shooting accessories and clothing

M — **House of Hardy**
Willowburn, Alnwick,
Northumberland, Tel: 0665 602771

M — **H Huntsman & Sons Ltd**
11 Saville Row, London, W1X 2PS,
Tel: 01 734 7441

M — **Husky of Tostock Ltd**
115 Bury Street, Stowmarkey, Suffolk,
Tel: 0499 674474

W — **Jack Carter Agencies**
61 Main Street, Burton Joyce,
Nottingham, NG14 9ED

R — **James Lock & Co Ltd**
6 St James Street, London, SW1A 1EF,
Tel: 01 930 5849

James Purdey & Sons (Accessories) Ltd
84 Mount Street, London, W.1.,
Tel: 01 499 5292
Designers and stockists of a comprehensive range of waterproof waxed fabric clothing and loden wear

R — **Jamie Wood Ltd**
Cross Street, Polegate, E Sussex, Tel:
03212 3813

JCP Ivor Sound Ltd
Unit 1004, 80 Como Street, Romford,
Essex, RM7 7DT, Tel: 0708 755992
(Factory)

J K Angling & Guns
Mary Square, Laurieston, Falkirk,
Scotland, Tel: 0324 23156
Wide selection of country clothing and rubber footwear.

R — **John Brocklehurst**
Bridge Street, Bakewell, Derbyshire,
DE4 1EE, Tel: 062 981 2089
Retailers of a wide range of country clothing

John Eastaff
Elstow Storage Depot, Kempston,
Hardwick, Bedford, Tel: 0234
740834

R — **John R Gow & Sons**
12 Union St6reet, Dundee, DD1
4BH, Tel: 0382 25427
Retailers of waterproof and quilted clothing, deerstalkers, gloves, mittens, rubbers boots and waders

John Male Ltd

JOHN MALE LIMITED

Church Norton, Selsey, Chichester,
PO20 9DS, Tel: 0243 603040

R — **John Norris**
21 Victoria Road, Penrith, Cumbria,
Tel: 0768 64211

M — **John Partridge**
New Power Station Road , Trent
Meadows, Rugeley, Staffs, Tel: 08894
4438

W — **John Rothery (Wholesale) Co Ltd**

John Rothery & Co. (Wholesale) Ltd

22 Stamshaw Road, Stamshaw,
Portsmouth, Hants, Tel: 0705
667323
The largest distributor of Uniroyal Boots and Waders in the country. Whether it's one or one-hundred pairs, despatch is same day of ordering. Delivery is possible 48 hours. Derri boots also sold.

M — **Katie Kwilt**
Carpenters Cottage, Torton Lane,
Torton, Kidderminster, Hereford &
Worcester, DY10 4HX, Tel: 0299
250727

M — **Kebcote Country Wear**
P O Box 5, Dept 14, W Yorks,
HX7 6EY, Tel: 0422 842248
Suppliers of a complete range of clothing

M R — **C & D King**
Unit 1. Church Street Workshops,
Church Street, Dorking, Surrey, Tel:
0306 883780

M — **King of Maidstone**
3 Gabriels Hill, Maidstone, Kent, Tel:
0622 55677

W — **L Le Personne & Co Ltd**
Century House. Eley Estate, Angel
Road, Edmonton, N.1.,
Tel: 01 803 4266
Distributors of 'Rockville shooters' clothing

M — **Le Tricoteur & Co Ltd**
Pitronnerie Road, St Peter Port,
Guernsey, Channel Islands, Tel:
0481 26214
Manufacturers of traditional Guernsey sweaters

MAXPROOF
STANDARD AND LIGHTWEIGHT

- ● Thornproof
- ● Waterproof
- ● Windproof
- ● Timeproof

Since the 1920's, sportsmen who take their sport seriously have taken to Maxproof thornproof garments from Macbean. That's because Maxproof has the quality to last for many years. In fact when you buy Maxproof you are really making an investment in your future comfort and protection.

Maxproof is made from extra duty tightly woven long staple cotton which is thoroughly waxproofed. Maxproof is available in two weights. Standard—the traditional garment—and Lightweight—for lightweight luxury and comfort. Our attention to details is legendary—even the seam thread is proofed.

Macbean

Edward Macbean & Co. Limited,
**Woodilee Industrial Estate, Kirkintilloch, Glasgow G66 3UZ, Scotland.
Tel: 041-776 2511 Telex: No. 777967 Code 192**

141

"elch" Shooting Garments

142

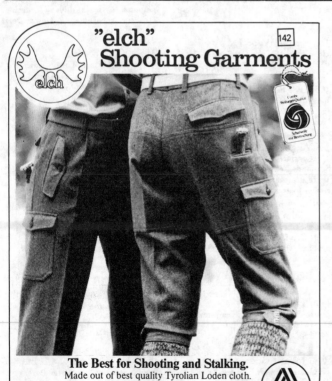

The Best for Shooting and Stalking.
Made out of best quality Tyrolian Loden cloth.
Wholesale agent: JACK CARTER, 110, Church Road, Burton Joyce, Nottingham NG14 5DQ, Tel. 0602/31 23 71
"elch" Ltd., A-5021 Salzburg/Austria, POB. 205

AUSTRIA

Leslie Hewett Ltd
Upton Cross, Liskeard, Cornwall,
Tel: 0579 62319
Sole distributors of Duchy Shooting jacket and Weathabeata clothing

143 **Farlow's**

"DID YOU KNOW THAT FARLOW'S NEW SHOP SELLS NOTHING BUT COUNTRY CLOTHING?"

By Appointment to H.R.H. The Prince of Wales
Suppliers of Fishing Tackle
and Waterproof Clothing
C. Farlow & Co Ltd London

Farlow's OF PALL MALL
5 Pall Mall, London SW1 Tel: 01-839 2423
Now open till 4p.m. on Saturdays and 6p.m. Thursdays

M — Lynton Clothes
Lynton House, Shannon Street, Leeds,
LS9 8SS, Tel: 0532 482111

R Macleod & Son
14 Lamington Street, Tain, Ross-shire,
Tel: 0862 2171

R — Malcberry Ltd
366 Croydon Road, Beckenham, Kent,
Tel: 01 650 2255

W — Mark Saddler Ltd
Gayton House, Well Lane, Gayton,
Wirral, Merseyside, Tel: 051 342 7722

R — J S Main & Sons
87 High Street, Haddington, East
Lothian, Tel: 062 082 2148

R — Map Shooting Supplies
Unit 35, Gloucester Cattle Market, St
Oswalds Road, Gloucester

M — Mars Oil Co

MARS OIL
TRADE MARK ®
Est. 1901
ORIGINAL LEATHER DRESSING

Withycombe Farm House, Drayton,
Nr Banbury, Oxfordshire, Tel: 0295
62844
Manufacturers of Mars oil original leather dressing. Use mars oil for longer lasting leather

M — Mascot Clothing
401 Old Road, Clacton on Sea,
Essex, Tel: 0255 432773
Manufacturers of waterproof clothing

M — Mediterranean Shooting Supplies
P O Box 7, Evesham, Worcs, WR11
6YT, Tel: 0386 3654
The 'Elegant' range of shooting clothing

M — Michael Clothing Co
232 Waterloo Street, Bolton, Lancs,
Tel: 0204 24846/27069

M — Mileta Sports Ltd
Heckmondwicke, W Yorks, Tel: 0924 409311
Manufacturer: Millar Gloves
Bingham Industrial Estate, Bingham, Notts, NG13 8GG, Tel: 0949 38517

M — Mister Antony (Inverness Cape Specialist)
15 Chevoit Drive, Newton Mearns, Glasgow, Tel: 041 639 7309

M — Mukluks
The Old Dairy, 98 Grove Road, Hitchin, Herts, Tel: 0462 35385

R — Nurse the Furrier Ltd
19 Magdalen Street, Cheltenham, Glos, Tel: 0242 52294

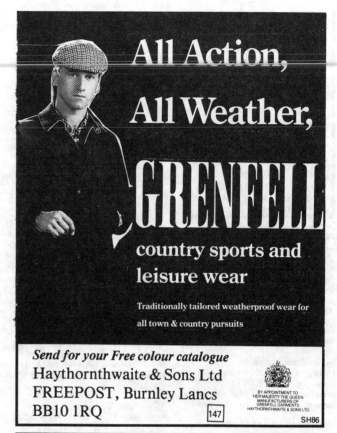

Optima Leisure Products Ltd
Gilnow Mill, Spa Road, Bolton,
Lancs, BL1 4LE, Tel: 0204 386899

R — **Orvis UK Ltd**
Nether Wallop Mill, Stockbridge,
Hants, Tel: 0264 781212

Parker Hale Ltd
Golden Hillock Road, Birmingham,
West Midlands, B11 2PZ, Tel: 021 773
8481

M — **Peter Storm**
14 High Pavement, Nottingham,
Notts, Tel: 0602 506911/3
*Waterproof clothing plus chlorofibre
thermal underwear, sweaters, socks*

**Protectorplast Ltd (Nora
Organisation)**
Nora House, Forest Road, Hainault,,
Ilford, Essex, IG6 3HT, Tel: 01
5009091

W — **Puffa, Rumward Ltd**
Crawley Mill, Witney, Oxon, OX8
5TJ, Tel: 0993 71717, 74492

W — **Ralph Grant & Son Ltd**
Green Lane Road, Leicester, Tel: 0533
7675551

M — **Redmaynes Ltd**
The Old Mill, Warwick Bridge,
Carlisle, Cumbria, CA4 8RR, Tel:
0228 61661
Manufacturers of tailored suits

M — **Richmond Field Boots**
102 Chaldon Road, Caterham, Surrey,
Tel: 0883 48666

M — **The Royal British Legion,
Cambrian Factory**
Llanwrtyd Wels, Powys, Wales, Tel:
05913 211

M — **SSM International**
Tedstone Wafre, Nr Bromyard,
Herefordshire, Tel: 08867 646 &
284
*Manufacturers of waterproof leggings,
trousers and gloves*

M — **Saville Menswear Ltd**
Marsh Lane, Leeds, Tel: 0532
453716
*Manufacturers of sporting trousers,
breeks and jackets*

M — **The Shirtmakers Guild**
78 Fulham Road, London, SW3
6HH, Tel: 01 584 2451
Suppliers of classic cut shirts to order

Shooting Developments
Valley Drive, Leslie, Fife, Tel: 0592
745029
*Repair kits for waxed cotton coats and
wellington boots*

R — **Simpson (Piccadilly), Ltd**
Piccadilly, London, W1A 2AS, Tel: 01
734 2002

M — **Skee Tex Ltd**
Battlebridge, Essex, Tel: 03744 68282

M — **Skye Crotal Knitwear**

Camus Chros, Isle of Skye, Scotland,
IV43 8QR, Tel: 04713 271
*Take this opportunity to receive direct
from the makers a hand framed, high
quality sweater. We make sweaters in
oiled Harris and Shetland Wools.
They are warm, comfortable and ideal
for any outdoor pursuit. Send now for
your free catalogue to above address.*

R — **Sporting 'n' Country Wear**
Bridge Street, Kineton, Warwick,
SCV35 0HP, Tel: 0926 640273

M — **Sporting Developments
Intl Ltd**
210 Hermitage Road, Whitwick,
Leicester, Tel: 0530 37236
*Manufacturers of 'Keeper Wear'
waterproofs. 'Kammo' brand shooting
jackets*

W — **Sterling Armament Co,**
Sterling Works, Rainham Road South,
Dagenham, Essex, Tel: 01 595 2226

M — **Stylo Matchmakers
International Ltd**
Clayton Wood Bank, Leeds, LS16 6JR,
Tel: 0532 784211

R — **Sussex Countryman**
68 High Street, Steyning, West Sussex,
Tel: 0903 812261

M — **P & L Suswin Ltd**
401 Old Road, Clacton on Sea, Essex,
Tel: 0255 432773

M — **Sutcliffe, Farrar & Co Ltd**
Hebden Bridge, W Yorks, Tel: 0422
883363

R — **Swaledale Woolens**
Murker in Swaledale, North Yorkshire,
Tel: 0748 86215/4768

M — **Thorndale Carr & Day
Matin Ltd**
Great Dunmow, Essex, Tel: 0371 2287

M — **Thwaites Country
Clothing**
The Mill, Queen Street, Barnard
Castle, Co Durham, Tel: 0833 37544/
0833 31524

M — **Toye, Kenning &Spencer
(Bedworth) Ltd**
Regalia House, Newtown Road,
Bedworth, Warks, CV12 8QR, Tel:
0203 315634
*Embroidered badges and pullovers,
club ties and headsquares*

M — **R E Trickers**
56/60 St Michaels Road, Northampton,
Tel: 0604 30595

C & D KING LTD

Buy it with Access

27 MEADOWBROOK ROAD, DORKING, SURREY · Telephone: (0306) 883780/885069
Telephone Orders for Immediate despatch, COD, Barclaycard or Access.
Callers welcome Mon.-Fri. 9-5.00 (Sun. 9.30-11 am)

VISA

155

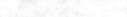

WISEWEAR WAXPROOFS
THE "BROCKHAM" JACKET

S, M, L	£34.99
XL	£37.99
XXL	£42.99

FEATURES INCLUDE:
- Large front pockets, pleated for extra fullness
- Lined hand warmer pockets
- Document breast pocket
- Large proofed interior game pocket (illustrated)
- Traditional tartan lining
- Corduroy collar
- Stud over front storm flap
- All exposed seams waxed before despatch
- Waterproof wading strip
- Elasticated storm cuffs (waterproof between cuff and end of sleeve)
- Heavy duty, double ended, non-metallic zip
- Collar studded to take hood, available as an optional extra

'CHILDREN'S' WAXPROOFS

Made in heavyweight (12oz) olive green waxed cotton.

22"	£18.49
24"	£19.49
26"	£20.49
28"	£21.99
30"	£23.49

NITE OWL
HIGH INTENSITY SPOTLIGHTS

200,000 CANDLEPOWER
(7 amp battery drain)
a)	NOVA 2 (straight cord)	**£25.99**
b)	ULTRA BEAM (smoked glare free)	**£37.99**
c)	ULTRA BLUE (blue glare free)	**£37.99**

160,000 CANDLEPOWER
3½ amp battery drain Quartz **£34.99**

300,000 CANDLEPOWER
(11 amp battery drain)
TEK **£34.99**

PRICE INCLUDES POSTAGE & PACKING

KINGS GEL POWERPACKS
(Gel batteries (non-spill) in black leather carrying case. With plug-in charger).

1.	6½ AMP/HR	£37.00
2.	8 AMP/HR (illustrated)	£48.50
3.	13 AMP/HR	£61.50

Price includes postage and packing

KINGS COMPLETE LAMPING OUTFIT

£36.00 inc P&P

a) 12 volt rechargeable lead acid battery (need your own charger)
b) 55 watt quartz halogen lamp. 250,000 candlepower.
c) red filter cover for lamp
d) When fully charged gives 1-1½ hrs continuous lamping.

KINGS DELUXE LAMPING OUTFIT

The lamp and carrying case with this outfit is identical to those with the STANDARD KINGS LAMPING OUTFIT. The battery however is a 6.5 amp/hr GEL BATTERY (non-spill).

with charger	£46.50 inc postage & packing
without charger	£40.50 inc postage & packing

NOW AVAILABLE

TATTENHAM — ladies waxproof jacket (rear centre pleat) in mid-weight blue or green waxed cotton

XS and SW £31.99	W and WX ..... £33.99 all inc. of p&p

Also available hoods for adult coats shown £4.75.

OVER TROUSERS
Boys, unlined (S.M.L.)	£9.49
Adults, unlined (S.M.L.)	£14.99
Adults, lined (S.M.L.)	£18.49

LEGGINGS
Short-stud on	£13.49
Short-pull on	£11.49
Long-stud on	£14.99
Long-Pull on	£13.49

ALL POST FREE

TRADE SUPPLIED

Send S.A.E. for full range of waxproofs, books, ferreting, trapping & dog equipment.

THE ALLWEATHER PROTECTION

RANGER

A top quality waxed jacket in olive green, ideal for all outdoor activities. Designed to be strong, long lasting and, above all comfortable, giving complete protection from the worst of elements. Heavy duty two way zipper, storm flap with press stud fastening, detachable hood, belt, collar strap, storm cuffs, extra length, zipped inside security pocket, poachers pocket, handwarmer pockets, warm acrylic lining. Sizes: S, M, L, XL, XXL

LADY

A truly fashionable jacket available in either green, burgundy or blue. Tailored for the female figure with deep side vents. A comfortable medium weight waxed coat, with a warm acrylic lining. Lined handwarmer pockets, strong two way zipper, storm flap with press stud fastening. Sizes 10, 12, 14, 16, 18 & 20

FORRESTER

The ideal boot for a day in the field, shooting or fishing. The calf top lacing ensures a snug fit; they are fully waterproof, slip resistant, light and comfortable. The Forrester is easily cleaned and can be washed inside and dried in minutes. Available in Olive Green, with a contrasting sole. Full sizes: 6-11

Ⓜ — **Tsavo Fashions**
Farfield Mill, Sedbergh, Cumbria, Tel: 0587 20169

Ⓜ — **Uniroyal Ltd, Footwear Division**
62 Horseferry Road, London, SW1, Tel: 01 222 5611
Manufacturers of the famous Hunter range of waterproof footwear

Ⓡ — **Vango (Scotland) Ltd**
Industrial Estate, Port Glasgow, Scotland, PA14 5BE, Tel: 0475 44122
bags, camping accessories

Ⓜ — **Walsden Weatherwear Ltd**
Top Floor, Hollins Mill, Rochdale Road, Walsden, Tormorden, West Yorks, Tel: 070681 2079

Ⓜ — **Waugh of Hamilton Ltd**
43 Union Street, Hamilton, Strathclyde, Tel: 0698 283188

Ⓡ — **William Powell & Son (Gunmakers) Ltd**
35/37 Carrs Lane, Birmingham, West Midlands, B4 7SX, Tel: 021 643 0689
Retailers of specialist shooting clothing. Pirsch and Damokles shooting gloves. Catalogue available

John peel
Country Clothes

REDMAYNE

S. Redmayne Limited
The Old Mill, Warwick Bridge,
Carlisle CA4 0RR
Telephone 61661 (STD 0220)

Redmayne build expensive clothes at inexpensive prices

The Nora Organisation renowned for its excellent range of 'NORA' protective footwear and 'HAPPY FARMER' clothing offers the real opportunity of overall protection for any outdoor job. These superb ranges of clothing and footwear, specifically designed to suit your everyday requirements, are competitively priced, long lasting and easily obtainable through stockists all over Great Britain.

Contact us now for your local stockist's name

156

wonderful wellingtons

THE NORA ORGANISATION
Nora House, Forest Road,
Hainault, Ilford, Essex IG6 3HJ.
Telephone: 01-500 9091 Telex: 893256

Wiltsavon Leisure Ltd

**Welliwarmas**

The Workshop, Hankerton Priory,
Malmesbury, Wiltshire, SN16 9JY,
Tel: 06667 7120

Wisewear Waxproofs, C & D King Ltd
Unit 1, Church Street Workshops,
Church Street, Dorking, Surrey, RH4 1DJ

Ⓜ — **Wychwood Sportswear**
Wellesbourne House,, Wellesbourne,
Warwickshire, CV35 9JB, Tel: 0789 842330
Manufacturers of 'The Classic' shooting jacket

Hunters. Hand made in Britain for over 125 years

158

By appointment to
H R H. The Duke of Edinburgh.
Manufacturers of Waterproof Footwear,
Uniroyal Limited, Newbridge, Midlothian.

The best in the Field

UNIROYAL

COOL CALM AND PROTECTED

Cool comfort in warm weather and dry warmth in cold, wet weather. That's what you get with the specialist Classic shooting jacket (left).

The Classic is beautifully conceived using 100% waterproof Gore-Tex* fabric and warmth-without-bulk microfibre "Thinsulate" thermal insulation lining.

Ease of movement has been carefully considered resulting in a low level of body heat generation. Add to this the fact that both materials actually 'breathe' allowing perspiration vapour to escape and you will understand why the Classic is the perfect shooting garment whatever the weather.

To complete the protection all sewn seams are tape welded inside under heat and pressure so there's no chance of water penetration in those areas.

The Classic is just part of The Wychwood Range. There are other excellent garments from rugged waxproofs to PU nylons and Gore-Tex* fabrics and five standard sizes to choose from.

British made to combat the changeable British weather Wychwood have set new standards in outdoor wear.

If you would like the full facts send for our FREE full colour brochure or if you're in a hurry ring the warm line (0789) 842330 (24 hour answering).

(Gore-Tex* is a trade mark of W.L. Gore & Associates Inc.)
(3M and "Thinsulate" are trade marks.)

159

Wychwood Sportswear

To Peter Britton,
Wychwood Sportswear, Wellesbourne
House, Wellesbourne, Warwick
CV35 9JB
Tel: (0789) 842330
TLX: 338024 (prefix Britton)

ACCESS   VISA   AMERICAN EXPRESS

TRADE ENQUIRIES WELCOME

SSM INTERNATIONAL

TEDSTONE WAFRE NR. BROMYARD   HEREFORDSHIRE HR7 4PY   ENGLAND

SNIA BPD

TEL: 08867 646 & 284   TELEX: 336669

SOLE UK IMPORTERS & DISTRIBUTORS FOR SMI CARTRIDGES, SNIA POWDER & WADS

160

A CONTENTS

ACCESSORIES CONTENTS

193

CHRISTIE'S

Modern & Vintage Guns
Christopher Brunker
Antique Arms & Armour
Peter Hawkins
8 King Street, St. James's
London SW1
Tel: 01-839 9060

194
PROVINCIAL GUN AUCTIONS

Regular sales of:
Quality sporting guns,
antique arms, fishing
tackle, sporting sundries
and accessories.
Venues include:
Bromyard, Lutterworth,
Taunton and Knutsford.
No buyers premium.

Further details from
**28 Broad Street, Bromyard,
Herefordshire. Tel: 0885 83604**

WALLIS & WALLIS
197

THE SPECIALIST AUCTIONEERS OF ARMS & ARMOUR
1986 SALE DATES

308 JANUARY 8th	**312 JUNE 11th**
309 FEBRUARY 12th	**313 JULY 23rd**
310 MARCH 19th	**314 SEPTEMBER 3rd**
311 APRIL 30th	**315 OCTOBER 15th**
	316 NOVEMBER 26th

ILLUSTRATED CATALOGUES £2.00

WEST STREET AUCTION GALLERIES
Lewes, Sussex. BN7 2NJ. Tel: (0273) 473137.
Telex: 896691 TLX12G

AUCTIONS & AUCTIONEERS

Barber & Son, Shropshire/Mid Wales Gun Auctions
12 Shoplatch, Shrewsbury, Salop, Tel: 0743 613513

Banks & Silvers
Foregate Street, Worcester, Hereford & Worcester, Tel: 0905 23456

Barber & Son, Shropshire/Mid Wales Gun Auctions
12 Shoplatch, Shrewsbury, Salop, Tel: 0743 613513

Boot & Son
19 Wolverhampton Road, Cannock, Staffordshire, Tel: 054 35 5454

Buckland & Sons
Bridgewood, East Common Street, Gerrards Cross, Bucks

Christie, Manson & Woods Ltd
8 King Street, St James's, London, SW1Y 6QT, Tel: 01 839 9060

Dreweat Watson & Barton
Donnington Priory, Donnington, Newbury, Bucks, Tel: 0635 31234

Geoffrey Collings & Co
17 Blackfriars Street, King's Lynn, Norfolk, Tel: 0553 774135

John D Fleming & Co
No 4 & 8 Fore Street, Dulverton, Somerset, Tel: 0398 23597

Pearsons
Agriculture House, High Street, Stockbridge, Hampshire, Tel: 0264 81072
Annual sale of sporting guns, antique weapons etc

Phillips
7 Blenheim Street, New Bond Street, London, W1Y 0AS, Tel: 01 629 6602

Provincal Gun Auctions
28 Broad Street, Bromyard, Hereford, HR7 4BS, Tel: 0885 83604
Regular sales of all types of sporting guns, antique arms, fishing tackle, sundries and accessories. Sales venues include Bromyard, Lutterworth, Taunton and Knutsford

195
Sotheby's
Founded 1744

For expert advice on the sale,
insurance, valuation,
restoration and repair of sporting
guns and firearms
contact James Booth.

Sotheby's
34-35 New Bond Street,
London W1A 2AA. Telephone:
(01) 493 8080.
Telex: 24454 SPBLON G and at
Pulborough, Sussex
Tel: 07982 3831

Rennies
Newmarket Chambers, Lion Street, Abergavenny, Gwent, Tel: 0873 2327

Sotheby's
34/35 New Bond Street, London, W1A 2AA, Tel: 01 493 8080

Sotheby's

Tel: 07982 3831

Southam & Sons
Corn Exchange, Thrapston, Nr Kettering, Northamptonshire, Tel: 08012 4486
Auctioneers of modern sporting and trap shotguns, firearms, antique weapons, militaria, shooting equipment, sporting pictures and books. Sales March and September at the Corn Exchange Salerooms

R B Taylor & Sons
7 Cheap Street, Sherbourne, Somerset, Tel: 0935 23474, 0935 813577

Wallis & Wallis
West Street Auction Galleries, Lewes, East Sussex, BN7 2NJ, Tel: 0273 473137/8/9

Weller & Dufty Ltd
141 Bromsgrove Street, Birmingham, B5 6RQ, Tel: 021 692 1414
Major auctioneers of licensed weapons. Auctions held every five weeks

---

BLANK REVOLVERS

John Rothery(Wholesale) Ltd

John Rothery & Co. (Wholesale) Ltd

22 Stamshaw Road, Stamshaw, Portsmouth, Hants, Tel: 0705 667323

Phoenix Arms Company Ltd
Phoenix House, Churchdale, Eastbourne, East Sussex, Tel: 0323 645131

WELLER & DUFTY LTD
(ESTABLISHED 1835)
196
THE FINE ART SALEROOMS
141 BROMSGROVE STREET : BIRMINGHAM 5
Telephone: 021-692 1414/5   Telegrams: Fineart, Birmingham

Europe's Largest Arms Auctioneers

HOLD TEN 2 day sales each year
ACCURATE ILLUSTRATED CATALOGUE
FIRST DAY (MODERN) £2.25 (incl. post)
SECOND DAY (ANTIQUE) £2.25 (incl. post)
FREE COLLECTION SERVICE BY ARRANGEMENT

Modern....

....and Antique

AUCTION DATES FOR 1986

January 22/23	**July 16/17**
February 26/27	**August 20/21**
April 2/3	**October 2/3**
May 7/8	**November 5/6**
June 11/12	**December 10/11**

Scalemead Arms Co
3 Medway Buildings, Lower Road, Forest Row, Sussex, Tel: 034282 4433

CAPS

Buttstop Specialist Sportswear Ltd
Newcastle House (Business Centre) High Spen, Tyne & Wear, NE39 2BL, Tel: 0207 542484

Frank Dyke & Co Ltd
1/7 Ernest Avenue, West Norwood, London, SE27 0DG, Tel: 01 670 2224

John Male Ltd

Church Norton, Selsey, Chichester, PO20 9DS, Tel: 0243 603040

CARTRIDGE BAGS

Arnolds
1 Old Winch Hill Cottages, Winch Hill, Wandon End, Luton, Beds, Tel: 0582 34955

J Barbour & Sons Ltd
Simonside, South Shields , Tyne & Wear, NE34 9RD, Tel: 0632 552251

M Billingham & Co Ltd
Unit 3, Lye Valley Industrial Estate, Bromley St, Lye, Stourbridge, West Midlands, Tel: 038482 7035

Brady Brothers Ltd
Great Cornbow, Halesowen, Birmingham, Tel: 021 550 1784

Brettonbank Fieldsports
460 Cherryhinton Road, Cambridge, Tel: 0223 240368

Bryant (Gun Cases) Ltd

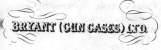

35 Astbury Road, London, SE15, Tel: 01 639 8311

David Bowman Leatherland Ltd
Lindridge Wood, Lindridge Lane, Desford, Leics, Tel: 04557 2298

David Nickerson (Tathwell) Ltd
The Old Vicarage, Tathwell, Louth, Lincolnshire, LN11 9ST, Tel: 0472 840536

Denton & Kennell
West Street, Somerton, Somerset, Tel: 0458 73732/72065

Gunmark Ltd
The Armoury, Fort Wallington, Fareham, Hants, LP016 8TT, Tel: 0329 231531

Leslie Hewett Ltd
Upton Cross, Liskeard, Cornwall, Tel: 0579 62319

Liddesdale Bag Co Ltd
Dalkeith House, Douglas Square, Newcastleton, Roxburghshire, Tel: 054121 616

Mediterranean Shooting Supplies Ltd
P O Box 7, Evesham, Worcs, WR11 6YT, Tel: 0386 3654

Oliver J Gower Ltd
Unit K1, Cherry Court Way, Stanbridge Road, Leighton Buzzard, Bedfordshire, LU7 8WH, Tel: 0525 377730

Outdoor Sport Supplies
24 Southam Road, Hall Green, Birmingham, B28 8DG, Tel: 021 777 1778

Pardoe Importers
Wychbold, Droitwich, Worcs, WR9 0BX, Tel: 052 786 517

Parker Hale Ltd
Golden Hillock Road, Birmingham, B11 2 PZ, Tel: 021 773 8481
'Fieldsman' and 'Arco' ranges

Partridge & Co Leathergoods Ltd
Highgate, Helpringham, Nr Sleaford, Lincolnshire, Tel: 0529 21207

Quality Gunslips Ltd

Regal Works, 402 Park Road, Biringham, B18, Tel: 021 554 6528

Ralph Grant & Son Ltd
Green Lane Road, Leicester, LE5 4 PD, Tel: 0533 767551

SSM International
Tedstone Wafre, Nr Bromyard, Herefordshire, Tel: 08867 646 & 284
Manufacturers of Pointer products, cartridge bags

William Powell & Son (Gunmakers) Ltd
35/37 Carrs Lane, Birmingham, B4 7 SX, Tel: 021 643 0689
Distributors of 'Siena' range of cartridge bags and belts

CARTRIDGE BELTS

Allen & Caswell Ltd
Regent Works, Cornwall Road, Kettering, Northants, Tel: 0536 512804

Arnolds
1 Winch Hill Cottages, Winch Hill, Wandon End, Luton, Beds, Tel: 0582 34955

J Barbour & Sons Ltd
Simonside, South Shields, Tyne & Wear, NE34 9RD, Tel: 0632 552251

Brady Bros Ltd
Great Cornbow, Halesowen, West Midlands, Tel: 021 550 1784

Brettonbank Fieldsports
460 Cherryhinton Road, Cambridge, Tel: 0223 240368

Bryant (Gun Cases) Ltd

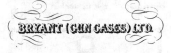

35 Astbury Road, London, SE15, Tel: 01 639 8311
Cartridge belts and cartridge magazines

C.C.A.W. Ltd
Gunhouse, Steeple, Bumpstead, Haverhill, Suffolk, Tel: 044 084 275
Suede leather waistcoats to carry 50 cartridges in closed loops. 20 over 30

Denton & Kennell
West Street, Somerton, Somerset, Tel: 0458 73732/72065

JCP Ivor Sound Ltd
Unit 1004, 80 Como Street,, Romford, Essex, RM7 7DT, Tel: 0708 755992 (Factory)

John Male Ltd

Church Norton, Selsey, Chichester, PO20 9DS, Tel: 0243 603040

John Rothery Wholesale Co Ltd

John Rothery & Co. (Wholesale) Ltd

22 Stamshaw Road, Stamshaw, Portsmouth, Hants, Tel: 0705 667323
Leather or vinyl 12 guage belts. Trade only

R S Lawson Firearms and Ammunition
Great Western Road, Martock Ind Est, Martock
Tel:[TL]0935 823201

L Le Personne & Co Ltd
Century House, Eley Estate, Angel Road, Edmonton, London, N18, Tel: 01 803 4266

Leslie Hewett Ltd
Upton Cross, Liskeard, Cornwall, Tel: 0579 62319

Liddlesdale Bag Co Ltd
Dalkeith House, Douglas Square, Newcastleton, Roxburghshire, Tel: 054121 616

Lupton Bros Ltd
P O Box 8, Accrington, Lancs, Tel: 0254 35011

Mediterranean Shooting Supplies Ltd
P O Box 7 , Evesham, Worcs, WR11 6YT, Tel: 0386 3654

Parker Hale Ltd
Golden Hillock Road,, Birmingham, B11 2PZ, Tel: 021 773 8481
'Fieldsman' belts and slings

Partridge & Co (Leathergoods) Ltd
Highgate, Helpringham, Nr Sleaford, Lincs, Tel: 0529 21207

Phoenix Arms Co Ltd
Churchdale Road, Eastbourne, East Sussex, Tel: 0323 645131

Price Western Leather Co Ltd
Ponsford Road, Minehead, Somerset, Tel: 0643 5071

Prodec Sports Ltd

Armstrong Buildings, 48 Kilton Road, Worksop, Notts, Tel: 0909 474093
Suppliers of fast loading, rot proof, 25 soft plastic clips - velcro fastening

Quality Gunslips Ltd
Regal Works, 402 Park Road, Birmingham, Tel: 021 554 6528

SSM International
Tedstone Wafre, Nr Bromyard, Herefordshire, Tel: 08867 646 & 284
Manufacturers of 'Pointer' products, cartridge belts

Sterling Armament Co Ltd
Sterling Industrial Estate, Rainham Road, South Dagenham, Essex, Tel: 01 595 2226
Canvas, leather and plastic

William Powell & Son (Gunmakers) Ltd
35/37 Carrs Lane, Birmingham, B4 7SX, Tel: 021 643 0689
Distributors of 'Siena' range of cartridge bags and belts

CARTRIDGES - BULK SUPPLIERS

Angus Gun Room & Fishing Tackle Centre
98 Ferry Road, Dundee, Tel: 0382 453668
All types of cartridges supplies. Quotes on request

Bloomfield (Gunmaker)

BLOOMFIELD Gunmaker

Hill Farm, Radlett, Herts, Tel: 09276 4639

The Cartridge
16 Smith Street, Warwick, Tel: 0926 491087

Chris Potter Guns
43 Camden Road, Tunbridge Wells, Kent, Tel: 0892 22208

Clay Shooters Supplies
32 St Mary's Road, Market Harborough, Leicester, Tel: 0858 66616
Sole distributors of Welland Royal Cartridges

Gentrys
32/34 Park View Road, Welling, Kent, Tel: 01 304 9922

C H Haygarth & Sons
The Cottage Gun Shop, Dunnet, Caithness, Scotland, Tel: 084785 602

A Kerr
213 High Street, Auchterarder

Paul DJ & M
Ivory Farmhouse, Burghclere, Newbury, Berkshire, Tel: 063 527 362
Maionchi, Winchester and Eley cartridges always in stock

Peter Coppin, Spinney Shooting Ground
Willoughby, Alford, Lincs, Tel: 0521 22357
Main agent for gamebore cartridges

Ralph Grant & Son Ltd
Green Lane Road, Leicester, Tel: 0533 767661/2

The Sportsman
7 Dartmouth Road, Paignton, Devon, TQ4 5AB, Tel: 0803 558142/551275

Wells A Sait, Wholesale Cartridge Suppliers
Weatherdfield Road, Sible Hedingham, Essex, Tel: 00787 61033

D Weatherhead Ltd
36 Kneesworth Street, Royston, SG8 5AB, Tel: 0763 42361

A & D Wheeler Guns
Weathersfield Road, Sible Hedingham, Essex, Tel: 0787 61033

The Wholesale Cartridge Co
P O Box 105, Dundee, DD1 9RL

CARTRIDGE DISPLAY CASES

Brettonbank Fieldsports
460 Cherryhinton Road, Cambridge, CB1 4EA, Tel: 0223 240368

CLAY TARGETS

CCI International Ltd
Priors Haw Road/Lammas Road, Corby, Northants, Tel: Corby 60933

Clay Targets (Peacocks)
Standalone House, Campton, Nr Shefford, Bedfordshire, Tel: 0462 813227
Specialists in manufacturing rabbits, battues and minis targets, all types and quantities of clays supplied

Coalite Fuels & Chemicals Ltd
The Refinery, P O Box 21, , Chesterfield, S44 6AB, Tel: 0246 822281

Eley
P O Box 705, Witton, Birmingham, B6 7UT, Tel: 021 356 8899

Esgee Clays
Normanton Lane, Bottesford, Nottinghamshire, NG13 0EL, Tel: 0949 43388

Hepworth Refractories Ltd
Hazlehead, Stockbridge, Sheffield, South Yorkshire, S30 5HG, Tel: 0226 763561

Leslie Hewett Ltd
Upton Cross, Liskeard, Cornwall, Tel: 0579 62319
Laporte targets. Sole distributors

Peacock's Clay Targets
Standalone House, Campton, Shefford, Beds, Tel: 0462 813227

Peter Coppin, Spinney Shooting Grounds
Willoughby, Alford, Lincs, Tel: 0521 22357
Sole distributor of CCI clays for Lincolnshire main agent Gamebore cartridges. Authorised Browning & Miroku dealers. Comprehensive range of shooting accessories. Buyers of wood pigeon and game in season.

Tranware Properties Ltd
Unit B, Normanton Lane Ind Estate, Bottesford, Notts, Tel: 0949 43388

CLAY TRAPS

KETTLEBURGH LODGE SHOOTING SCHOOL
FRAMLINGHAM, WOODBRIDGE, SUFFOLK
Tel: 0728 723523 | 166 |

Specialised trapping accessories and equipment, including a simple horizontal to vertical attachment and mobile folding protection trapper shield.

Please telephone for further information

Axe Vale Engineering Ltd
Western Road, Axminster, Devon, EX13 5PB, Tel: 0297 32038

W J Bowman (1984) Ltd
East Markham, Newark, Nottinghamshire, Tel: Tuxford 870243

Browning Traps Ltd
Arcall House, 1 Westminster Road, Wareham, Dorset, Tel: 09295 6451

C.C.I. International
Priors Haw Road, Corby, Northants, NN17 1JG, Tel: 05363 60933

Clay Sport Traps
Old Knebworth Forge Products, Park Lane, Old Knebworth, Herts, Tel: 0438 813576

Dan-Arms (UK) Ltd
8A Cannock Road, Burntwood, Staffs
Dan-Lack Traps

Farey Clay Pigeon Traps
Gulf Road, Guyhim. Nr Wisbech, Cambridgeshire, PE13 4ER, Tel: 094 575 273
Complete range of manual and fully automatic traps for sporting and I.S.U. regulations

Globe Engineering Ltd
Park Street, Thaxted, Essex, Tel: 0371 830884

Kettleburgh Lodge Shooting School
Framlington, Woodbridge, Suffolk, Tel: 0728 723523
Specialised trapping equipment and accessories. Horizontal to vertical attachment and mobile folding protection trapper shields

Leslie Hewett Ltd
Upton Cross, Liskeard Cornwall, Tel: 0579 62319
Leslie Hewett seat traps. Laporte competition traps

Newboult & Thorp Ltd
50/52 Bridgegate, Retford, Nottinghamshire, DN22 7XB, Tel: 0777 703508

Nottingham Gun Centre Ltd
155 Attenborough Road, Attenborough, Beeston, Nottingham, Tel: 0602 221233

Oliver J Gower Ltd
Unit K1, Cherry Court Way, Stanbridge Road, Leighton Buzzard, Bedfordshire, LU7 8WH, Tel: 0525 377730

Parker Hale Ltd
Golden Hillock Road, Birmingham, B11 2PZ, Tel: 021 773 8481

Rolls Sheet Metalwork
17B Whittle Road, Ferndown Industrial Estate, Wimborne, Dorset, Tel: 0202 892707

SSM International
Tedstone Wafre, Nr Bromyard, Herefordshire, Tel: 08867 646 & 284
Manufacturers of clay traps

Stuart Clay Traps

Stuart Clay Traps LIMITED

P O Box 14, Woodbridge, Suffolk, Tel: 03943 2600
Manufacturers of hand operated clay traps since 1969. Over 8,500 traps supplied to satisfied customers all over Europe and further afield. Traps to suit the beginner or advanced shooter

Tony Kennedy Guns
6 & 8 Church Street, Launceston, Cornwall, Tel: 0566 4465

Winchester UK Site 7

WINCHESTER.

Kidderminster Road, Cutnall Green, Hereford & Worcester, Tel: 029 923 461

CLAY TRAP - ACOUSTIC RELEASE UNITS

THE SYMBOL OF TOP QUALITY BRITISH MADE
CLAY ACOUSTIC RELEASE UNITS
for all types of layouts
ISU Skeet Random Timers, Relay Boxes and other accessories also available

THURLASTON INSTRUMENT SERVICES
Unit 9, St Mary's Mills, Leicester LE3 2BU

Tel: 0533 892444
for further details | 167 |
CPSA TRADE MEMBER

Thurlaston Instrument Services
Unit 9, St Marys Mills, Evelyn Drive, Leicester, LE3 2BU, Tel: 0533 892444
Manufacturers of acoustic release units for electrically operated clay pigeon traps. Full repair service including other makes. Please send for details

THINKING OF BUYING A CORDLESS PHONE. | 168 |
We are stockists for
SuperFone, Uniden, G.E.C. Etc.
CELLULAR CAR PHONES
Walkie Talkies, Ansering Machines, Intercoms, B.T Phones.
For Free Catalogue Contact:
D.W. SUPPLIES
P.O. Box 12, Petersfield, Hants
GU32 2AY
(0730) 67278

CORDLESS PHONES

D W Supplies
26 Osborne Road, Petersfield, Hampshire, Tel:[tn]0730 67278

CREDIT FINANCE

Lombard Acceptances Ltd
Lombard House, Baird Road, Enfield, Middlesex, EN1 1TP, :Tel: 01 804 8161

DECOY CALLS

Charles Henry Richards Ltd
84 Cardigan Street, Birmingham, Tel: 021 3595757

John Male Ltd

JOHN MALE LIMITED

Church Norton, Selsey, Chichester, PO20 9DS, Tel: 0243 603040

Parker Hale Ltd
Golden Hillock Road, Birmingham, B11 2PZ, Tel: 021 773 8481

Ralph Grant & Son Ltd
Green Lane Road, Leicester, Tel: 0533 767551

J Hudson & Co (Whistles Ltd)
Barr Street, Birmingham, B19 3AH, Tel: 021 554 2124

Shooting Developments
Valley Drive, Leslie, Fife, Tel: 0592 745029

West Dorset Nets
80 North Allington, Bridport, Dorset

DECOYS

Charles Henry Richards Ltd
84 Cardigan Street, Birmingham, Tel: 021 3595757

Deben Electronics Ltd
Wilford Bridge Road, Melton, Woodbridge, Suffolk, Tel: 03943 7762

Dick Brothers
23 St Thomas Road, Edinburgh, EH9 2LY, Tel: 031 667 3874
Full range of decoys and decoy calls.

East Anglian Shooting Products

East Anglian Shooting Products

The Street, Helhoughton, Fakenham, Norfolk, NR21 7BL, Tel: 048522 789
Manufacturers of Pigeon Flappers in plastic. Plastic decoys. Perching pigeon decoys, lofting poles etc

T H Grace
Redford House, Wiggonholt, Pulborough, West Sussex, RH20 2EP, Tel: 09066 2945

IJS Supplies
Apple Acre, Debden, Saffron Walden, Essex

James Decoy & Co
52 Moor Street, Gloucester
Super lofting pigeons, compact shell decoys, rous, magpies, oults. Inflatable ducks and pigeons (Pigeon, Mallard, Teal, Wigeon)

John Male Ltd

Church Norton, Selsey, Chichester, PO20 9DS, Tel: 0243 603040

R S Lawson Firearms and Ammunition
Great Western Road, Martock Ind Est, Martock
Tel:[TL]0935 823201
Lawson decoys. A full range of plastic decoys including pigeons, crows, ducks, magpies. Sole distributors.

Leslie Hewett Ltd
Upton Cross, Liskeard, Cornwall, Tel: 0579 62319
County decoys. Leslie Hewett pigeon decoys

Map Shooting Supplies
Unit 35, Gloucester Cattle Market, St Oswalds Road, Gloucester

Mediterranean Shooting Supplies Ltd
P O Box 7, Evesham, Worcs, WR11 6YT, Tel: 0386 3654
Full range of SPORTPLAST plastic decoys

E Parsons & Sons Ltd

Blackfriars Road, Nailsea, Bristol, Avon, BS19 2BU, Tel: 0272 854911
Manufacturers of Lofting poles and decoy pigeons and hide frames

Ralph Grant & Son
Green Lane Road, Leicester, Tel: 0533 767551
Distributors/Importers of duck, goose and pigeon decoys

Salter & Varge Ltd
Publicity House, 10a West Street, Southend, Essex, SS2 6HJ, Tel: 0702 332037
Sole UK factory for Sportplast Carrylite Decoys

Shooting Developments
Valley Drive, Leslie, Fife, Scotland, Tel: 0592 745029
Suppliers of Shell pigeon and goose decoys

West Dorset Nets
80 North Allington, Bridport, Dorset, Tel: 0308 23576

FERRETING EQUIPMENT

Arnolds

1 Old Winch Hill Cottages, Winch Hill, Wandon End, Luton, Beds, Tel: 0582 34955

Brady Brothers Ltd
Great Cornbow, Halesowen, Birmingham, Tel: 021 550 1784

Charles Henry Richards Ltd
84 Cardigan Street, Birmingham, Tel: 021 3595757

CTF Ltd
11 Langley Park Road, Sutton, Surrey, Tel: 01 642 5871

Deben Electronics Ltd
Wilford Bridge Road, Melton, Woodbridge, Suffolk, Tel 03943 7762
Manufacturers and suppliers of the FERRET FINDER electronic locator for ferret and terrier

Dick Brothers, Field Sports Equipment
23 St Thomas Road, Edinburgh, EH9 2LY, Tel: 031 667 3874
Trade suppliers of nylon and hemp purse nets, long nets and all ferreting equipment

John Male Ltd

Church Norton, Selsey, Chichester, PO20 9DS, Tel: 0243 603040
BASC

KP & S Nets

Castle Street, Axminster, Devon, Tel: 0297 33920
Ferret finders, ferret collars, muzzles, harness & lines. Largest stockists of D.I.Y. kits etc.

C & D King Ltd
27 Meadowbrook, Dorking, Surrey, Tel: 0306 883780

Nets & Sporting Supplies
P O Box 21, Dorchester, Dorset, DT2 9TE, Tel: 0305 67630

Norris Nets
2 Half Moon Cottages, Melpash, Bridport, Dorset

Redport Net Co Ltd
94 East Street, Bridport, Dorset, Tel: 0308 22592

West Dorset Nets 1985
80 North Allington, Bridport, Dorset, Tel: 0308 23576

S Young & Sons (Misterton) Ltd
Misterton, Crewkerne, Somerset, TA18 8NU, Tel: 0460 73461

FIELD GLASSES SPOTTING SCOPES

Bausch & Lomb (UK) Ltd
74 Oldfield Road, Hampton, Middlesex, TW12 2HR, Tel: 01 979 7788
Bushnell binoculars and telescopes

Carl Zeiss (Oberkochen) Ltd
P O Box 78, 17/20 Woodfield Road, , Welwyn Garden City, Herts, AL7 1LU, Tel: 0707 331144

Charles Frank Ltd
P O Box 5, Ronald Lane, Saxmundham, Suffolk, Tel: 0728 3506
Binoculars, telescopes

John R Gow & Sons Ltd
12 Union Street, Dundee, DD1 4BH
We can supply a range to suit all needs over a wide price range.

Hilton Gun Co Ltd
60 Station Road, Hatton, Derbys, Tel: 0283 814488

E Leitz (Instruments) Ltd
48 Park Street, Luton, Tel: 0582 413811

Arthur E S Matthews Ltd

Kowa Company. Ltd.

Epworth House, 25-35 City Road, London , EC1Y 1AR, Tel: 07373 50670
Agents for Kowa telescopes.

Monk Optics
Hewelsfield, Gloucestershire, GL15 6UU, Tel: 0594 530666
Specialists in all types of binoculars for the country sportsman, especially popular compact 8 x 24 monk petite, rubber armoured roof prism 7 x 42 monk sportsman - ideal hunting/ stalking.

Nikon UK Ltd
20 Fulham Broadway, London, SW6 1BA, Tel: 01 381 1551
Suppliers of Nikon Binoculars and spotting scopes

Opticon
Unit 6, Marlborough Trading Estate, 25 Lattimore Road, St Albans , Herts, Tel: 0727 56516
Spotting scopes

Optima Leisure Products Ltd

Gilnow Mill, Spa Road, Lancs, BL1 4LE, Tel: 0204 386899

Parker Hale Ltd
Golden Hillock Road, Birmingham, Tel: 021 773 8481
Nikko Stirling binoculars, Parker Hale spotting scopes

Pyser Ltd
Fircroft Way, Edenbridge, Kent, Tel: 0732 864111
Habicht Swarovski binoculars and telescopes; Swift binoculars and telescopes. Kahles telescopic rifle sights. Swarovski Habicht Nova telescopic rifle sights

Quiggs of Glasgow
94 Stockwell Street, Glasgow, Scotland, Tel: 041 552 6823

Viking Arms Ltd
Summerbridge, Harrogate, Yorks, Tel: 0423 780810

Webley & Scott Ltd

Frankley Industrial Park, Tay Road, Rubery, Rednal, B45 0PA, Tel: 021 453 1864

Distributors of Tasco binoculars, telescopic sights, spotting scopes

Wessexside Ltd

Bridge Works, Iver Lane, Uxbridge, Middlesex, Tel: 0895 36413

Binoculars and spotting scopes

GALLERIES & SPORTING ARTISTS

Ackermans

3 Old Bond Street, London, W1X 3TD, Tel: 01 493 3288

Addison - Ross Gallery

40 Eaton Terrace, London, SW1, Tel: 01 730 1536

Animals Unlimited, Animal Artist

Rosemarie Chambers, Herb House, Draycott, Moreton in Marsh, Glos, Tel: 0386 700453

Andrew Thomas
The Old Vicarage, West Pennard, Glastonbury, Somerset, Tel: 0458 32818

Berrisford Hill, Sporting & Wildlife Artist
Laurel Trees, West Coker, Yeovil, Somerset, BA22 9BG, Tel: 093586 3124

Brian Rawling
Woodray Cottage, New Alyth, By Blairgowrie, Perthshire, PH11 8NG

Brotherton Gallery Ltd
77 Walton Street, London, SW3, Tel: 01 589 6848

Burlington Gallery Ltd
10 Burlington Gardens, London, W1X 1LG, Tel: 01 734 9228
Fine prints

Clifford Gallery
11 Market Place, Woburn, MK17 9PZ

David Cemmick
Smithy House Farm, Great Smeaton, Northallerton, North Yorkshire, Tel: 0325 483271, Ext 144 & 060981 652
Professional wildlife artist. Specialising in field sketching and water colours.

Fores Gallery Ltd
Potterspury House, Potterspury, Towcester, Northamptonshire, Tel: 0908 543289

Geffrey Maund,
Purley Gallery Ltd, 927 Brighton Road, Purley, Surrey, Tel: 01 668 5217

W A Harris
Studio & Gallery, Berkeley House, Queen Street, Whittlesey, Peterborough, PE7 1AE, Tel: 0733 203356

Henry Brett Galleries
Halford House,Bourton on the Water, Gloucester, Tel: 0451 20443
Specialists in wildlife and sporting landscape art. Framers and restorers. Water colours, oils, etchings, bronzes, wood carvings and prints

Iona Antiques
5 Edwardes Square, London, W8 6HE, Tel: 01 602 6888

Jane Neville Gallery
Elm House, Abbey Lane, Aslockton, Nottinghamshire, Tel: 0949 50220
Specialises in wildlife, sporting and countryside pictures and prints

Jean Walker
Cannons, Tibberton,, Gloucestershire, GL19 3AB, Tel: 045 279 309

John Scott Adie
16 St John Street, Perth, Tayside, Scotland, PH1 5SP, Tel: 0738 25550

Keyser Gallery
The Quarry House, Corston, Malmesbury, Wilts, Tel: 06662 2429

Mrs L M Leich (Forstal Fine Arts)
Forstal, Lynford, Thetford, Norfolk, Tel: 084 287 246

Linda Heaton Harris
1 Upper Oakwood, Holney Lane, Selbourne, Nr Alton, Hants, Tel: 042 03 2356
Detailed individual. Ceramic game bird sculptures and miniatures

Lonsdale Art (Fine Art Publishers)
22 Clarence Street, Morecambe, Lancs, Tel: 0524 420198

Loquens Gallery
The Minories, Entrance corner Rother/Meer Street, Stratford Upon Avon, Warks, Tel: 0789 297706
Sporting, wildlife landscapes. Picture framing

Lower Nupend Gallery Ltd
Cradley, Nr Malvern, Worcs, WR13 5NP, Tel: 088684 334

Malcolm Innes Gallery
172 Walton Street, London, SW3, Tel: 01 584 0575

Malcolm Innes Gallery
67 George Street, Edinburgh, Scotland, Tel: 031 226 4151

Mandell's Gallery
Elm Hill, Norwich, Tel: 0603 626892/ 629180

The McEwan Gallery
Glengarden, Ballater, Grampian, Soctland, AB3 5UB

Michael Steward Galleries
61 Quarry Street, Guildford, Surrey, Tel: 0483 504359

Michael Webb Fine Paintings
Curlew Cottage, Weston, Pembridge, Leominster, Hereford & Worester, Tel: 054 47 477

Nigel Sweeting Galleries Ltd
Church Close, Ramsdell, Basingstoke, Hants, Tel: 0256 850616

Oliver Swann Galleries
117a Walton Street, London, SW3, Tel: 01 581 4229

Peter Hedley Gallery
6 South Street, Wareham, Dorset, Tel: 09295 51777

Pollyana Pickering
Brookvale House, Oaker, Matlock, Derbyshire, Tel: 0629 55851

R E & D J Dickerson
22 Philip Road, Blandford, Dorset, Tel: 0258 54426

Quorn Fine Art Co
46 Church Street, Loughborough, Leicestershire, LE11 1UE, Tel: 0509 213787

Richard Harrison
The Quarry Bungalow, Longburton, Sherbourne, Dorset, DT9 5NZ, Tel: 096 321502
Game bird artist. Paintings, prints, trays, table mats etc

Salley Mitchell Fine Arts
Thornlea, Askham, , Newark, Nottinghamshire, NG22 0RN, Tel: 0777 83234

Spink & Sons
5/7 King Street, St James's, London, SW1, Tel: 01 930 7888

Sutcliffe Galleries
Appletree House, Appletreewick, Nr Skipton, N Yorkshire, Tel: 075672 663

Thomas Lethbridge
Honeymead, Simonsbath, Minehead, Somerset, Tel: 064383 348

The Tyron & Moorland Gallery
23/24 Cork Street, London, W1, Tel: 01 734 6961/2256

Val Bennett Miniatures
Scethrog House, Brecon, Powys, Wales, LD3 7EQ, Tel: 087 487 255

Wildgoose Gallery
Silver Street, Fairburn, W Yorks, Tel: 0977 85089

Zara Fountain
Turpin Farm, Fillingham, Gainsborough, Lincs, Tel: 0427 788569

GAME BAGS & CARRIERS

Allen & Caswell Ltd
Regent Works, Cornwall Road, Kettering, Northants, Tel: 0536 512804

J Barbour & Sons Ltd
Simonside, South Shields, Tyne & Wear, NE34 9RD, Tel: 0632 552251

Brady Brothers Ltd
Great Cornbow, Halesowen, Birmingham, Tel: 021 550 1784

Brettonbank Fieldsports
460 Cherryhinton Road, Cambridge, Tel: 0223 240368

Bryant (Gun Cases) Ltd

35 Astbury Road, London, SE15, Tel: 01 639 8311

Charles Henry Richards Ltd
84 Cardigan Street, Birmingham, Tel: 021 3595757

Chilham Dart Products
Station Approach, Chilham, Canterbury, Kent, Tel: 0227 730310

Douglas Fraser & Sons (Manufacturing) Ltd
Friokheim, Angus, Scotland, Tel: 02412 341
Manufacturers of waterproof, washable game bags 'Perfectos' Brand.

East Anglian Shooting Products

East Anglian Shooting Products

The Street, Helhoughton, Fakenham, Kent., NR17 2BU, Tel: 048 522 789

Glenmuick Game Hook Co
Stroud, Gloucestershire, Tel: 028582 208

John Male Ltd

JOHN MALE
LIMITED

Church Norton, Selsey, Chichester, PO20 9DS, Tel: 0243 603040
BASC

John Rothery Wholesale

John Rothery & Co. (Wholesale) Ltd

22 Stamshaw Road, Portsmouth, Hants, Tel: 0705 667323

Liddlesdale Bag Co Ltd
Dalkeith House, Douglas Square, Newcastleton, Roxburghshire, Tel: 054121 616

Parker Hale Ltd
Golden Hillock Road, Birmingham, B11 2PZ, Tel: 021 773 8481

Quality Gunslips Ltd

quality gunslips

Regal Works, 402 Park Road,
Birmingham, Tel: 021 554 6528

Ralph Grant & Son Ltd
Green Lane Road, Leicester, LE5 4PD,
Tel: 0533 767551

SSM International
Tedstone Wafre, Nr Bromyard,
Herefordshire, Tel: 08867 646 284,
Telex: 336669
*Pointer products, game bags and game
carriers.*

Shooting Developments
Valley Drive, Leslie, Fife, Scotland,
Tel: 0592 745029
Bag for all season's game bag

**William Powell & Son
(Gunmakers) Ltd**
35/37 Carrs Lane, Birmingham, B4
7SX, Tel: 021 643 0689

GAME DEALERS

C Bambridge
Wayland Croft, Watton Green,
Thetford, Norfolk, Tel: 0953 881895

Band's of Perth Ltd
135 Glover Street, Perth, Scotland,
PH2 0JB, Tel: 0738 24222/3

The Boston Game Co
Hawks Farm, Dores Lane, Braishfield,
Nr Romsey, Hants, PO5 0QJ, Tel: 0794
68191

Brown's
21 High Street, Fordingbridge, Hants,
Tel: 0425 53125
Game dealer and fish smoker.

**George Campbell & Sons
(Fishmongers, poulterers &
gamedealers)**
18 Stafford Street, Edinburgh, EH3
7BE, Tel: 031 225 7507 Also at 168
South Street, Perth, PH28NY Tel:
0783 38454.

JJ Clendinning
High Street, New Galloway,
Kircudbrightshire

Dartmoor Game
Keepers Cottage, Modaoford Farm,
Okehampton, Devon & Whiteaway
Estate, Chudleigh, Devon

Davis R A Game Dealer
'Fairlawn' Back of Kingsdown Prd,
Coltham, Bristol, BS6 5TR, Tel: 0272
48313

Dickerson Game Dealers
Lynn Road, Swaffham, Norfolk, Tel:
0760 21271

**Duncan Fraser (Game Dealer)
Ltd**
17 Queensgate, Inverness, Highlands,
Scotland

Dunston Fish and Game Dealers
Dunstan Pig Farm, Bryn-Estyn,
Dunstan Lane, Burton, Wirral,
Cheshire, Tel: 051 336 3366

Empire Game Ltd, (Leo Naylor)

Tel: 0935 840042

Fentville Ltd
Royal Oak Game Centre, Farringdon,
Hants, Tel: 042058 239

Frans Buitelaar Game Ltd
New Hammond Beck Road,
Wyberton, Boston, Lincolnshire,
PE21 7JD, Tel: 0205 52020 Ext 36
& 37, Telex: 37364

Frans Buitelaar (Scotland) Ltd
Game and Salmon Processing
Factory, Dundee Street, Letham,
Angus, Scotland, Tel: 030781 458
& 676

Frost Game
Comon Lane, Brockdish, Nr Diss,
Norfolk, Tel: 037 975379

Gamekeepa Feeds Ltd
Southerly Park, Binton, Stratford
upon Avon, Warks, CV37 9IU, Tel:
0789 772429

D Daniel Garrett, Game Dealer
14 Sutton Street, Flore,
Northamptonshire, Tel: 0327 40672
Buy and sell all game in season.

Hampshire Game Farm Ltd
Clanville, Andover, Tel: 026 470 294

R T Harvey Ltd
8 Tambland, Norwich, Norfolk, Tel:
0603 21908

Hide n' Deecs
Pesterford Bridge, Stansted, Essex,
Tel: 0279 812638

James Burden Game Ltd
314/6 Central Markets, London, EC1,
Tel: 01 248 0121

**J E H Game Services Fresh n
Free**
Avilma, Wood Lane, Heskin, Nr
Chorley, Lancs, Tel: 0704 821807

John C Bain & Son
Duthie Road, Tarves, Ellon,
Aberdeenshire, Tel: 06515 284/452/675

Keevil & Keevil
221 Central Markets, Smithfield,
London, EC1, Tel: 01 236 0321

Ling J H
Eye Road, Hoxne, Diss, Norfolk, Tel:
0379 75 315

M & M Game
South Vale Factory, Kilham,, Driffield,
Yorks, Tel: 026282 615
*Require all game when in season. Top
prices paid.*

Marlborough Game Farm
Miletree Road, Heath & Reach,
Leighton Buzzard, Beds, LU7 9LA,
Tel: 052 523 563

Meer Booth Game Farm Ltd
Antons Gowt, Boston, Lincs, Tel: 0205
750306

Paul DJ & M
Ivory Farmhouse, Burghclere,
Newbury, Berks, Tel: 063 527 362,
Telex: 849141
*All game cartridge bought and sold.
Dog food and cartridges always in
stock.*

Whittlesey Gamedealers
2 Syers Lane, , Whittlesey, Tel: 0733
204294

Peter Howe Game Dealers
Sutton Camp Game Farm, Stoeke
Heath, Market Drayton, Shropshire,
Tel: 063083 236

David Ripper & Son
Pitt Street Mill, Macclesfield,
Cheshire, TE.el: 0625 25899
Game sausages and venison

Sproat & Harvey (Game) Ltd
10 St John Street, Smithfield, London,
EC1, Tel: 01 253 7733/2880

Sproat & Harvey (Factory)
Rylands Cottage, Blois Road, Steeple
Bumpstead, Haverhill, Suffolk, Tel:
04408 4639

Stamford Gun Room Ltd
8 St Marys Hill, Stamford, Lincs,
Tel: 0780 62796
*Always a good buyer of game in
season, especially venison.*

Sussex Game Group Ltd
Susses Game Farm, Kirkford, Nr
Billingshurst, Sussex, Tel: 040377 456

Test Valley Game Produce Ltd
North Houghton Manor, Stockbridge,
Hants, Tel: 0264 810526

West Country Game
The Old Silk Farm, Compton Park,
Sherbourne, Dorset, Tel: 0935 73247

West Lodge Game Farm

Whisby Moor, Lincoln, Lincs, Tel:
0522 681720
*Licensed Game Dealers. Also suppliers of
pheasant eggs, chicks, poults and
partridges.*

Warner & Hurst Ltd
The Waggon Way, Brunton Lane,
Newcastle, Tyne & Wear, Tel: 0632
366939

White Rabbits
Chalk Pit Farm, Whiteparish,
Salisbury, Wilts, Tel: 07948 205

Witham, Andrew
Winston Game, Gillingham, Beccles,
Suffolk, Tel: 0502 712260

Worbey, R Graveley Cold Store
42 High Street, Graveley, Nr Hitchin,
Herts, Tel: 0438 354134

GUN CABINETS &
SECURITY
EQUIPMENT

**21st Century Antique
Reproductions (TFCA Ltd)**
Florence House, High Street, Ripley,
Surrey, GU23 6AV, Tel: 0483 224884

Apollo Security Products
Heys Lane, Great Harwood, Blackburn,
Lancashire, BB6 7UA, Tel: 0254
885306

Armstrong Gun Cabinets
Bridge Farm, Slapton, Leighton
Buzzard, Beds, Tel: 0296 668731

Armstrong's Gunsmiths
360 Carlton Hill, Carlton,
Nottingham, Tel: 0602 873313
*Gun cabinets - made to order and from
stock.*

Ballistic Precision Ltd
PO Box 172, 31 Shadwell Street,
Birmingham, B4 6HE, Tel: 021 233
1640
*Manufacturers of Ballistic Precision
Security Cabinets.*

J R Clark & Co
4 Crondal Road, Exhall, Coventry, Tel:
0203 360516
Safety lock for shotguns.

Clay Shooters Supplies
32 St Marys Road, Market
Harborough, Leicestershire, Tel:
0858 62938/32189

Colin Gardner

Stone House, Cowgill, Dent, Nr Sedbergh, Cumbria, Tel: 05875 380
A small business which specialises in producing hand made gun cabinets and specially commissioned furniture. Main asset is the ability to discuss individual problems regarding size, style etc, and make the cabinet to suit. There are 2 standard styles and as well as metal lined and glass fronted cabinets, offer a style with removeable metal door for display purposes or to lock guns securely. [BASC]N

David Nickerson (Tathwell) Ltd
The Old Vicarage, Tathwell, Louth, Lincolnshire, LN11 9ST, Tel: 0472 840536

Dees Sports
7 Manor Road, Wallington, Surrey, SM6 0BZ, Tel: 01 647 7742

Derek T Hyatt
2 Welcome Stranger Cottages, Herstmonceux, East Sussex, Tel: 0323 832119 (evenings)
Security cabinets and furniture for firearms. Display cabinets a speciality.

Duglan & Cooper Ltd
14/16 Church Street, Dunstable, Bedfordshire, Tel: 0582 64649
Distributors of 'Gunsafe' security cabinets.

Halo Equipment Co Ltd
71a Newington Green Road, London, N1, Tel: 01 359 1340
The Halo Gun Cabinet

Haverburgh Engineering Ltd
Scotland Road, Market Harborough, Leicestershire, Tel: 0858 64411

Hovewell Ltd
15 St James Park, West Croydon, Surrey, Tel: 01 684 5383

JLS Arms Co Ltd
Scoltock House, Perry Street, Wednesbury, West Midlands, Tel: 021 556 9658, Telex: 336712 SHELTON G

John Male Ltd

Church Norton, Selsey, Chichester, PO20 9DS, Tel: 0243 603040

John Slough of London

John Slough of London

35 Church Street, Hereford, Tel: 0432 55416

James S. Kirkman
12d, Blackpool Old Road, Poulton-le-Flyde, Blackpool, Tel: Blackpool 882262
Suppliers of Intruder Alarm systems.

Leslie Hewett Ltd
Upton Cross, Liskeard, Cornwall, Tel: 0579 62319

Perimeter Security
30 Castle Gate, Newark, Notts, Tel: 0636 77404

Pinches Engineering Ltd
18 Tyla Teg, Whitchurch, Cardiff, CF4 6XL, Tel: 0222 618464

Precision Metalcraft Ltd

PRECISION METALCRAFT LTD.

Grovebury Road, Leighton Buzzard, Beds, Tel: 0525 373683
[BAC]N

PF & F Radcliffe
Pheonixworks, Booth Road, Littlelever, Nr Bolton, Lancs, Tel: 0204 793853

Sherdley Remec Ltd
Gorsey Lane, Clock Face, St Helens, Merseyside, WA9 5AP, Tel: 0744 816339

Shorrock Security Systems Ltd
Shadsworth Road, Blackburn, Lancashire, BB1 2PR, Tel: 0254 63644, Telex: 635151 SHOROK G

W Shuttleworth & Co Ltd
Shaw, Oldham, Lancs, Tel: 0706 845966

The Country Gun Shop,
Lilliesleaf, Melrose, Roxburghshire, TD6 9JD, Tel: 08357315

T H Thursby & Son
Sheep Street, Northampton, Tel: 00604 38225

Ward Metalwork Co Ltd
14 Morris Road, Leicester, Tel: 0533 704381

GUN CARE PRODUCTS

Abbey Supply Co
197 Great Knollys Street, Reading, Berks, RG1 7HA, Tel: 0734 584767

Baytree Arms
10 Baytree Hill, Liskeard, Cornwall, Tel: 0579 46636

Brady Bros Ltd
Great Carnbow, Halesowen, West Midlands, Tel: 021 550 1784
A range of cleaning equipment.

Casecraft Designs
The Old Telephone Exchange, Kingston Blount, Oxford, OX9 4RT, Tel: 0844 53614
Suppliers of the finest gun care accessories, casetools in ebony, horn and ivory.

CCL Traditional English Gun Products Ltd
Malt Mill Lane, Halesowen, West Midlands, Tel: 021 559 5717

Charles Henry Richards Ltd
84 Cardigan Street, Birmingham, Tel: 021 3595757

The Country Gunshop
Lilliesleaf, Roxburghshire, TD6 9JD, Tel:[TL]08357 315
Supplier of steel security cabinets.

David Nickerson (Tathwell) Ltd
The Old Vicarage, Tathwell, Louth, Lincolnshire, LN11 9ST, Tel: 0472 840536

Edgar Brothers
Catherine Street, Macclesfield, Cheshire, Tel: 0626 613177

Gamebore Cartridge Co
Great Union Street, Hull, North Humberside, Tel: 0482 22370

Guncraft
11 Woodcock Hill, Kenton, Harrow, Middlesex, HA3 0XP, Tel: 01 907 3651

Gunmark Ltd
The Armoury, Fort Wallington, Fareham, Hants, Tel: 0329 231531

Helston Gunsmiths
The Clies, Meneage Street, Helston, Cornwall, Tel: 032 65 3385

E R Howard Ltd
3-in-one Works, Creeting Road,, Stowmarket, Suffolk, IP14 5BB, Tel: 0449 615221

Leslie Hewett Ltd
Upton Cross, Liskeard, Cornwall, Tel: 0579 62319
Hoppes Gold crown gun oil.

NSRA
Lord Roberts House, Bisley Camp, Brookwood, Woking, Surrey, Tel: 04867 6969

Oliver J Gower
Unit K1, Cherrycourt Way, Stanbridge Road, Leighton Buzzard, Beds, LU7 8WH, Tel: 0525 377730

Parker Hale Ltd
Golden Hillock Road, Birmingham, B11 2PZ, Tel: 021 773 8481

Pat Walker Guns
143 Alexandra Road, Gateshead, Tyne & Wear, Tel: 0632 786736
Sole importers of I.M.I (Israeli Military Industries) boxed cleaning kits for pistols and rifles.

Ballistic Precision Ltd
P O Box 172, Shadwell Street, Birmingham, B4, Tel: 021 233 1640

Phillips Game Technology Ltd
Unit 16, Brandbridges Ind Estate, East Peckham, Tonbridge, Kent

Phoenix Arms Co Ltd
Phoenix House, Churchdale Road, Eastbourne, East Sussex, Tel: 0323 645131

SSM International
Testone Wafre, Nr Bromyard, Herefordshire, Tel: 08867 646 & 284
Manufacturers of gun cleaning equipment and gun care products. 'Pointer' brand.

Viking Arms Ltd
Summerbridge, Harrogate, North Yorkshire, Tel: 0423 780810

GUN CASES

ASI Alliance
Alliance House, Snape, Saxmundham, Suffolk , Tel: 072 888 555

Balblair Guns Ltd
West Street, Somerton, Somerset, Tel: 0458

Brady Brothers Ltd
Great Cornbow, Halesowen, Birmingham, Tel: 021 550 1784

Brettonbank Fieldsports
460 Cherryhinton Road, Cambridge, Tel: 0223 240368

Bryant (Gun Cases) Ltd

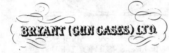

35 Astbury Road, London, SE15 2NL, Tel: 01 639 8311
Trade only. Repairs undertaken. Recoil pads-leather covered.

Casecraft Designs
The Old Telephone Exchange, Kingston Blount, Oxford, OX9 4RT, Tel: 0844 53614
Best quality oak and leather gun cases for shotguns, rifles and pistols. Also renovation service for old cases. Specialists in exotic hides. Brochure on request

David Nickerson (Tathwell) Ltd
The Old Vicarage, Tathwell, Louth, Lincolnshire, LN11 9ST, Tel: 0472 840536

East Anglian Shooting Products

East Anglian Shooting Products

The Street, Helhoughton, Fakenham, Norfolk, Tel: 048522 789

Edgar Brothers
Catherine Street, Macclesfield, Cheshire, Tel: 0625 613177

Fosters Countrysport
1 Cleveland Street, Darlington, Co Durham, Tel: 0325 51351

Gunmark Ltd
The Armoury, Fort Wallington, Fareham, Hants, PO16 8TT, Tel: 0329 231531

JLS Arms Co Ltd
Scoltock House, Perry Street, Wednesbury, West Midlands, Tel: 021 556 1322

John Male Ltd

JOHN MALE LIMITED

Church Norton, Selsey, Chichester, PO20 9DS, Tel: 0243 603040

L Le Personne & Co Ltd
Century House, Eley Estate, Angel Road, Edmonton, London, N18, Tel: 01 803 4266
Distributors of CBC Spanish cases

Liddesdale Bag Co Ltd
Dalkeith House, Douglas Square, Newcastleton, Roxburghshire, Tel: 054121 616

Mediterranean Shooting Supplies Ltd
P O Box 7, Evesham, Worcs, WR11 6YT, Tel: 0386 3654

Oliver J Gower Ltd
Unit K1, Cherry Court Way, Stanbridge Road, Leighton Buzzard, Bedfordshire , LU7 8WH, Tel: 0525 377730

Pardoe Importers
Wychbold, Droitwich, Worcs, WR9 0BX, Tel: 052 786 517

Parker Hale Ltd
Golden Hillock Road, Birmingham, B11 2PZ, Tel: 021 773 8481

Phoenix Arms Co Ltd
Churchdale Road, Eastbourne, East Sussex, Tel: 0323 645131

Precision Arms Co
Wheatfield House, Church Road, Paddock Wood, Kent, Tel: 089283 5730

Quality Gunslips Ltd

quality gunslips

Regal Works, 402 Park Road, , Birmingham, Tel: 021 554 6528

Ralph Grant & Sons Ltd
Green Lane Road, Leicester, LE5 4PD, Tel: 0533 767551

SSM International
Tedstone Wafre, Nr Bromyard,
Herefordshire, :Tel: 08867 646 &
284

Viking Arms Ltd
Summerbridge, Harrogate, North
Yorkshire, Tel: 0423 780810
*Viking and Safariland gun cases, holsters
and belts*

Ward Metalwork Co Ltd
14 Morris Road, Leicester, Tel:
0533 704381

**William Powell & Son
(Gunmakers) Ltd**
35/37 Carrs Lane, Birmingham, B4
7SX, Tel: 021 643 0689
*Distributors of 'Siena' range of gun
cases*

Winchester UK, Site 7

WINCHESTER.

Kidderminster Road, Cutnall Green,
Hereford & Worcester, Tel: 029
923 461

GUN ENGRAVERS

Blockside, D F
Lynwood, Worcester Road, Wychbold,
Nr Droitwich, Worcester, WR9 0DF,
Tel: 052786 453

Rose, P J L Firearms Engraver
'Homelea', Wallage Lane, Crawley
Down, West Sussex, Tel: 0342 714 757

F J Wiseman & Co Ltd
3 Price Street, Birmingham, B4 6JX,
Tel: 021 359 1256

GUN RACKS

Cab Parts & Accessories Ltd
Unit 4, Station Road, Thatcham,
Newbury, Berks, Tel: 0635 67697

Mill Accessory Group Ltd
Two Counties Mill, Eaton Bray, Nr
Dunstable, Tel: 0525 220671

Parker Hale Ltd
Golden Hillock Road, Birmingham,
B11 2PZ, Tel: 021 773 8481

Ralph Grant & Sons Ltd
Green Lane Road, Leicester, LE5 4PD,
Tel: 0533 767551

Tyler International
Bancroft House, 34 Bancroft, Hitchin,
Herts, Tel: 0462 35214

GUN SERVICING &
REPAIR

Alfred J Parker
348 Moseley Road, Birmingham, 12,
Tel: 021 440 1480

F A Anderson
12 East Street, Brighton, Sussex, Tel:
Brighton 23066

Armstrong Gunsmiths
360 Carlton Hill, Carlton, Notts,
Tel: 0602 873313
*Every type of gun, rifle and airweapon
repair*

Aylestone Gun Co
1-3 Paigle Road, Aylestone,
Leicester, Tel: 0533 832828
For specialist sales and service

Bailons Gunmakers Ltd
94/95 Bath Street, Birmingham, B4
6HG, Tel: 021 236 7593

Barbury Guns Ltd

BARBURY GUNS

44/45 High Street, Marlborough,
Wiltshire, SN8 1HQ, Tel: 0672
52862
*Full repair facilities for shotguns,
firearms and air weapons*

Benjamin Wild & Son
624 Bristol Road South, Northfield,
Birmingham, Tel: 021 477 4350

Bloomfield Gunmaker

BLOOMFIELD Gunmaker

Hill Farm, Radlett, Herts, Tel:
09276 4639

Boss & Co Ltd
13 Dover Street, London, W1, Tel: 01
493 1127

**A A Brown & Sons,
Gunmakers**
1 Snake Lane, Alvechurch,
Birmingham, B48 7NT, Tel: 021 445
5395

Bulmers Gunsmiths
1/7 Lord Mayors Walk, York, Tel:
0904 20788

Burton & Morgan (Gunsmiths)
The Old Bakery, Lower Icknield
Way, Chinnor Oxford, Tel: 0844
53655

Caer Urfa Guns and Ammo
399 Stanhope Road, South Shields,
Tyne and Wear, Tel: 0632 551045
*Gun servicing and repairs on just air
rifles.*

Carey (Gunmakers) Ltd
88 The Homend, Ledbury, Hereford,
HR8 1BX, Tel: 0531 2838

Catton Gunsmiths
Catton Hall, Burton-on-Trent, Staffs,
DE12 8LN, Tel: 028371 2447

Chambers & Co, Gunmakers
Ideal Gunworks, Northleach, Glos, Tel:
04516 372

B E Chaplin (Gunmakers) Ltd
6 Southgate Street, Winchester,
Hants, Tel: 0962 52935
*Shotguns and stalking rifles built to
order. Large selection of new and
second hand English and imported
guns. Over 150 held in stock*

The Chichester Armoury
20 Westgate, Chichester, Sussex,
PO19 3EU, Tel: 0243 774657

Country Gun Shop, The
Lilliesleaf, Melrose, Roxburghshire,
TD6 9JD, Tel: 08357 315
*Repairs and renovations to all types of
firearms and airweapons*

Chris Harding Guns
Cresswell Lane, Lea, Nr Malmesbury,
Wilts, Tel: 06662 2447

**Craig M Whitsey (Gunmakers)
Ltd**
Unit D, 10/12 Fitzalan Road,
Arundel, West Sussex, Tel: 0903
883102

K C Dawson
14 Meadow Road, Aldridge, Walsall,
West Midlands, WS9 0ST, Tel:
0922 51027
*Custom stock maker specialising in the
fitting of stocks to best quality guns
and rifles. Also general gunsmith. Gun
Trade Association Member.*

**Dorking Gun Company
(Gunmakers)**
243A High Street, Dorking, Surrey,
Tel: 0306 883451

R Drew Whurr
The Old Mill House, Helland Bridge,
Bodmin, Cornwall, PL30 4QR, Tel: St
Mabyn 206 (020 884)

Peter Dyson Ltd
29-31 Church Street, Honley,
Huddersfield, Tel: 0484 661062

Elvet Game Centre
8 New Elvet, Durham City, Durham,
Tel: 0385 46713

Empire Arms Co
14 Empire Parade, Great Cambridge
Road, Edmonton,London, N18
1AA, Tel: 01 807 3802
*Vintage and modern ammunition.
Lee, R.C.B.S. loading equipment.
Lyman, CCI primers, hard cast heads.
Manufacturers of ammunition
including 455; (Discounts on 1000).
D.P.M. and waterproofs. Repairs/
gunservicing by qualified gunsmith.*

John Ferguson Gunsmith
1 & 3 Fisher Street, Workington,
Cumbria, Tel: 0900 61559
*Over 100 weapons by leading makers,
English and Foreign in stock.
Clothing, cartridges, clays, traps, and
accessories for the game and clay
shooter. Repairs, overhauls and restocking.*

The Flintlock
17a High Street, Glastonbury,
Somerset, Tel: 0458 31525
Airgun specialists

Forest of Dean Armoury
'Canberra'
New Road, Coleford, Glos, Tel:
0594 33908
Specialist work for airguns

Forsyth Firearms
St Marys Street, Truro, Cornwall,
Tel; 0872 71744

Frank Richards (Gunsmiths)
25 Silver Street, Taunton, Tel: 0823
81487

Fosters Countrysport
1 Cleveland Street, Darlington, Co
Durham, Tel: 0325 51351

W W Greener Ltd
Belmont Row, Birmingham, Tel: 021
3595757

H S Greenfield & Son
4/5 Upper Bridge Street, Canterbury,
Kent, Tel: 0227 456959

Gloucester Rod & Gun Room
67 Alvin Street, Gloucester, Tel:
0452 410444

Gun & Sports
24 South Street, Wareham, Dorset,
BH20 4L, Tel: Wareham 3892
*Gun repairs and renovations. Re-
stocking. Good selection of walnut
blanks. Barrel blacking and
Browning. Stockists of Barbour,
Mascot and Keeper wear etc.*

Hartmann & Weiss Ltd
Folly Meadow, Hammersley Lane,
Penn, Bucks, Tel: 049481 2836

R E Heathcote Walker
Gunsmith to the Trade
The Cottage, Gomersal House,
Lower Lane, Gomersal, West
Yorkshire, BD19 4HY, Tel: 0274
877498
*Annual service, repairs, renovations,
re-blacking, stocking and customising.
New barrelling and sleeving service to
the trade.*

Hellis, Beesey and Watson
Gunmakers
33 South Parade, Mollison Way,
Edgware, Middlesex, Tel: 01 952 1579

Helston Gunsmiths
The Clies, Meneage Street, Helston,
Cornwall, Tel: 03265 3385

Hides n Deec's
Petersford Bridge, Stansted, Essex,
Tel: 0279 812638/813685

Hogan & Colbourne Ltd
Phoenix Works, Alscot Park, Stratford
upon Avon, Tel: 078 987 764

G C Holloway
63 Price Street, Birmingham, B46 JZ

Ian Tyrell Sports
5/7 Castle Street, Dumbarton,
Strathclyde, Tel: 0389 34438
*Trade work undertaken. All general
repairs, alterations and renovations for
firearms and air weapons*

E Jackson Gunsmith
9a Chester Road, Whitby, Ellesmere
Port, Wirral, L65 9BD, Tel: 051 356
2686

James Peter J (Gunsmith)
The Orchard Workshop, Gawcott,
Buckingham, MK18 4JE, Tel: 0280
814535

J K Angling & Guns
101 Mary Square, Laurieston,
Falkirk, Central, Tel: 0324 23156
Gun servicing undertaken.

John R Gow & Sons Ltd
12 Union Street, Dundee, DD1
4BH, Tel: 0382 25427
*All types of repair and overhaul
undertaken or arranged, also
reproofing.*

John Rigby & Co (Gunmakers)
Ltd
5 King Street, Covent Garden,
London, WC2E 8HN, Tel: 01 734
7611

John Slough of London

John Slough of London

35 Church Street, Hereford, Tel:
0432 55416

Kelly B (Gunsmith)
Unit FF5, New Buildings, 63 Price
Street, Birmingham, Tel: 021 359
1912
*Specialise in stocking, though service
repair and renovation of all types of
firearms and air weapons. Trade work
undertaken*

Knibbs, John Gillia
Blackfriars Lane, Bickenhill, West
Midlands, B37 7JE, Tel: 021 779
3391
*Repair service specialising in best
quality English shotguns. Spare parts
and mainspring for antique air rifles*

Lemon, Clive C Gunmaker
Malt Mill Lane, Halesowen, West
Midlands, B62 8JF, Tel: 021 559
5717

G E Lewis & Sons
32/33 Lower Loveday Street,
Birmingham, Tel: 021 359 2750

Lichfield Gun Co
13 Lyn Avenue, Lichfield, Tel: 054 32
22416

Limmex Field Sports
High Street & Wood Street, Old
Town, Swindon, Wilts, SN1 3ER, Tel:
0793 22056

Linsley Brothers Ltd
28 Kirkgate, Leeds, LE2 7DR, Tel:
0532 452790
*Repairers of all types of weapn,
specialists in English gun repairs,
fitting and alteration.*

Dave Lowrie Gunsmiths

Sevenoaks, Kent, Tel: 09592 2025

Lymm Sports Centre
8 The Cross, Lymm Cheshire, Tel:
092 575 3021
*Specialists in all target disciplines.
Gun repairs. Barclaycard and Access
welcome.*

Maskells Guns
18 Camp Road, Farnborough,
Hants, Tel: 0252 518062

Masters from
ChurchillGunmakers Ltd
Canon Works, Ockley Road, Beare
Green , Dorking, Surrey, RH5 4PU,
Tel: 0306 711435
*Best guns built to requirements, also
specialising in new barrels, stocks and
servicing work to Churchill, and all
other makes of guns*

Medway Gunrooms
115 Canterbury Street, Gillingham,
Kent, Tel: 0634 576332

Modern & Antique Firearms
147 Tuckton Road, Bournemouth,
BH6 3JZ, Tel: 0202 429369
*Specialists in custom made guns.
Servicing and repairs for all makes of
guns undertaken*

Moorlands Shotgun Supplies,
(Prop R M Blythe)
3 Lightoaks Level, Oakamoor, ST10
3AN

T O'Donnell
Chapel Cottage, Dark Lane,
Hollywood, Birmingham, B38 0HD,
Tel: 0564 823129
New barrels and sleeving a speciality

Philip Morris & Son
21 Widemarsh Street, Hereford, HR4
9EE, Tel: 0432 269501

K D Radcliffe Ltd
150 Hig Street, Colchester Essex, Tel:
0206 572758
Service shotguns, rifles and air weapons

W & C Scott (Gunmakers) Ltd
Premier Works, Tame Road, Witton,
Birmingham, B6 7HS, Tel➡ 021
3284107

C Smith & Sons (Newark) Ltd
Clinton House, Lombard Street,
Newark on Trent, NG24 1X, Tel: 0636
703839

Smith C H & Sons (Gunmakers) Ltd
63 Price Street, Birmingham, 4, Tel: 021 359 1680

Salisburys Gunsmiths

Salisbury's Gunsmiths

32a Lower Loveday Street, Birmingham, Tel: 021 359 7362
Specialising, restocking all grades best guns speciality. Overhauls, renovating and repairs, stock fitting. Ex W W Greener and Westley Richards.

W & C Scott (Gunmakers) Ltd
Premier Works, Tame Road, Witton, Birmingham, B6 7HS, Tel: 021 328 4107

J E Spalding
112 East Road, West Mersea, Essex, Tel: 020638 2477

The Sportsman
7 Dartmouth Road, Paignton, Devon, TQ4 5AB, Tel: 0803 558142/551275

The Stamford Gun Room Ltd
8 St Marys Hill, Stamford, Lincs, PE9 2DP, Tel: 0780 62796

Theoben Engineering
Stephenson Road, St Ives, Huntingdon, Cambs, PE17 4WJ, Tel: 0480 61718
Major stockists of Tasco scopes, silver jet pellets, air weapons and accessories. Repolishing and blacking on our own weapons to high standards, (must be completely disembled).

Victor Simmons
42 Manor Road, Streetly, Sutton Coldfield, W Midlands, Tel: 021 353 9795

R Watkins
17 High Street, Saffron Walden, Tel: 0799 23430

Westbury Guns
12 Edwardes Street, Westbury, Wilts, Tel: 0373 826081

A W Weale (Gunsmith)
Trebowen, Talgarth, Powys, Wales, LD3 0DB, Tel: 0874 711443
Restoration and repair of antique and modern sporting guns and appliances

Whitsey, Craig M
Unit D 10-12 Fitzalen Road, , Arundel, West Sussex, Tel: 0903 883102

William Powell & Sons (Gunmakers) Ltd
35/37 Carrs Lane, Birmingham, B4 7SX, Tel: 021 643 0689

Ian Wilson (Gunmaker)
53 Wide Bargate, Boston, Tel: 0205 65668

F J Wiseman & Co Ltd
3 Price Street, Birmingham, B4 6JX, Tel: 021 359 1256

Worcestershire Black Powder Supplies Ltd
Units 15-17 Brunel Craft Centre, Wribbenhalk, Bewdley, DY12 1BS

GUN SLIPS & COVERS

J Barbour & Sons Ltd
Simonside, South Shields, Tyne & Wear, NE34 9RD, Tel: 0632 552251

Baytree Arms
10 Baytree Hill, Liskeard, Cornwall, , Tel: 0579 46636

Brady Bros Ltd
Great Cornbow, Halesowen, West Midlands, Tel: 021 550 1784

Brettonbank Fieldsports
460 Cherryhinton Road, Cambridge, Tel: 0223 240368

Bryant (Gun Cases) Ltd

35 Astbury Road, London, SE15 2NL, Tel: 01 639 8311

Chilham Dart Products
Station Approach, Chilham, Canterbury, Kent, Tel: 0227 730310

East Anglian Shooting Products

The Street, Helhoughton, Fakenam, Norfolk, Tel: 048522 789

Martin J Hunt, Quality Gunslips
402 Park Road, Birmingham, B18 5ST

JCP Ivor Sound Ltd
Unit 1004, 80 Como Street, Romford, Essex, RM7 7DT, Tel: 0708 755992 (Factory)

JLS Arms Co Ltd
28 Market Place, Wednesbury, West Midlands, Tel: 021 556 1322

John Male Ltd

Church Norton, Selsey, Chichester, PO20 9DS, Tel: 0243 603040

John Rothery (Wholesale) Co Ltd

22 Stamshaw Road, Portsmouth, Hants, Tel: 0705 667323
The 'Universal' rifle cover

R S Lawson Firearms and Ammunition
Great Western Road, Martock Ind Est, Martock, Tel: 0935 823201

L Le Personne & Co Ltd
Century House, Eley Estate, Angel Road, Edmonton, London, N18, Tel: 01 803 4266
Distributors of CBC Spanish covers

Leslie Hewett Ltd
Upton Cross, Liskeard, Cornwall, Tel: 0579 62319

Liddesdale Bag Co Ltd
Dalkeith House, Douglas Square, Newcastleton, Roxburghshire, Tel: 054121 616

Mediterranean Shooting Supplies Ltd
P O Box 7, Evesham, Worcs, WR11 6YT, Tel: 0386 3654

Outdoor Sport Supplies
24 Southam Road, Hall Green, Birmingham, B28 8DG, Tel: 021 777 1778

Pardoe Importers
Wychbold,, Droitwich, Worcs, WR9 0BX, Tel: 052 786 517

Parker Hale Ltd
Golden Hillock Road, Birmingham, B11 2PZ, Tel: 021 773 8481
'Acro' and 'Fieldsman' gun covers

Phoenix Arms Co Ltd
Churchdale Road, Eastbourne, East Sussex, Tel: 0323 645131

Quality Gunslips Ltd

Regal Works, 402 Park Road, Birmingham, B18 5ST, Tel: 021 554 6528

Ralph Grant & Son Ltd
Green Lane Road, Leicester, LE5 4PD, Tel: 0533 767551

SSM International
Tedstone Wafre, Nr Bromyard, Herefordshire, Tel: 08867 646 & 284
Manufacturers of 'Pointer' products, gun covers and cases

Theoben Engineering
Stephenson Road, St Ives, Huntingdon, Cambs, PE17 4WJ, Tel: 0480 61718
High quality foam lined bags and gun slips bearing Theoben name and motif.

Tyler International
Bancroft House, 34 Bancroft, Hitchin, Herts, Tel: 0462 35214

Viking Arms Ltd
Summerbridge, Harrogate, North Yorkshire, Tel: 0423 780810

William Powell & Son (Gunmakers) Ltd
35/37 Carrs Lane, Birmingham, B4 7SX, Tel: 021 643 0689
Distributors of 'Siena' range of gun slips and covers

Winchester UK, Site 7

Kidderminster Road, Cutnall Green, Hereford & Worcester, Tel: 029 923 461

GUNSMITH TOOLS

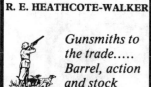

R. E. HEATHCOTE-WALKER

*Gunsmiths to the trade.....
Barrel, action and stock work.*

R.F.D. West Yorkshire D 291
R. E. HEATHCOTE-WALKER
The Cottage, Gomersal House,
Lower Lane, Gomersal,
West Yorks BD19 4HY
Telephone: 0274-877498 207

**Accuracy International
(Shooting Sports) Ltd**

43 Gladys Avenue, Northend,
Portsmouth, Hants, Tel: 0705
660371/2

**R E Heathcote Walker,
Gunsmiths to the Trade**
The Cottage, Gomersal House,
Lower Lane, Gomersal, West
Yorkshire, BD19 4HY, Tel: 0274
877498
*Manufacturer and distributor of
gunsmith tools, equipment and special
machinery*

Helson Gunsmiths
The Clies, Meneage Street, Helston,
Cornwall, Tel: 03265 3385

Newboult & Thorp Ltd
Bridgegate, Retford, Notts, DN22 7XB,
Tel: 0777 703508

Parker Hale Ltd
Golden Hillock Road, Birmingham,
B11 2PZ , Tel: 021 773 8481

F J Wiseman & Co Ltd
3 Price Street, Birmingham, Tel: 021
359 1256

GUNSTOCK BLANKS

C & R Gunstocks
5 Logan Mews, Logan Place, London,
W8, Tel: 01 373 6527

Charles Henry Richards Ltd
84 Cardigan Street, Birmingham,
Tel: 021 3595757

Fred Cross, Martins
Oxlynch, Stonehouse, Gloucester, GL1
3DG, Tel: 045 382 2876

Denton & Kennell
West Street, Somerton, Somerset,
Tel: 0458 73732/72065

T D Gray
Great Yeldham, Halstead, Essex

**R E Heathcote Walker,
Gunsmiths to the Trade**
The Cottage, Gomersal House,
Lower Lane, Gomersal, West
Yorkshire, BD19 4HY, Tel: 0274
877498

Helston Gunsmiths
The Clies, Meneage Street, Helston,
Tel: 03265 3385

**F J Wiseman & Co Ltd
(Wisemans of B'Ham)**
3 Price Street, Birmingham, B4 6JX,
Tel: 021 359 1256

HAND & BODY HEATERS

Mycoal Warm Packs Ltd
P O Box 43, London, SW10 9BZ,
Tel: 01 352 4056

HEARING PROTECTORS

AO Safety Products
Radlett Road, Watford, Herts, Tel:
0923 33522

Bilsom International Ltd
Fountain House, High Street, Oldham,
Nr Basingstoke, Hampshire, RG25 1LP,
Tel: 025 671 3581

British American Optical Co
Radlett Road, Watford, Herts, Tel:
0923 33522

Cabot Safety Ltd
First Avenue, Poynton, Stockport,
Cheshire, Tel: 0625 878320

Intergun
PO Box 1, Probus, Nr Truro,
Cornwall, TR2 4JJ, Tel: 087252 243

John Male Ltd

Church Norton, Selsey, Chichester,
PO20 9DS, Tel: 0243 603040

**John Rothery (Wholesale) Co
Ltd**

*John Rothery & Co.
(Wholesale) Ltd*

22 Stamshaw Road, Stamshaw,
Portsmouth, Hants, Tel: 0705
667323
*Distributors of Silenta hearing
protectors and Sole Distributors of
Sonic Ear Valves*

Leslie Hewett Ltd
Upton Cross, Liskeard, Cornwall,
Tel: 0579 62319

Matlock Inter
61/63 Smedley Street, aEast, , Matlock,
Derbyshire, Tel: 0629 3892
The Matlock Supersafe earmuff

MSA (Britain) Ltd
East Shawhead, Coatbridge, Soctland,
ML5 4TD, Tel: 0236 24966

**Neo Noise Control (Schort Ind
Ltd)**
Unit 5, Power Station Road, Rugeley,
Staffs, WS5 2JJ, Tel: 08894 3929

Oliver J Gower Ltd
Unit K1, Cherry Court Way,
Stanbridge Road, Leighton Buzzard,
Bedfordshire, LU7 8WH, Tel: 0525
377730

Pardoe Importers
Wychbold, , Droitwich, Worcs, WR9
0BX, Tel: 052 786 517

Parker Hale Ltd
Golden Hillock Road, Birmingham,
West Midlands, Tel: 021 773 8481

Racal Safety Ltd
Beresford Avenue, Wembley,
Middlesex, Tel: 01 902 8887

Silenta Hearing Protection Ltd
2 Tenter Road, Moulton Park
Industrial Estate, Northampton,
NN3 1PZ, Tel: 0604 499853
*Manufacturers of a complete range of
hearing protectors for shooters*

HIDES & CAMOUFLAGE NETS

Charles Henry Richards Ltd
84 Cardigan Street, Birmingham,
Tel: 021 3595757

Dick Brothers
23 St Thomas Road, Edinburgh,
EH9 2LY, Tel: 031 667 3874

John Male ltd

Church Norton, Selsey, Chichester,
PO20 9DS, Tel: 0243 603040

West Dorset Nets, 1985
80 North Allington, Bridport, Dorset,
Tel: 0308 23576

East Anglian Shooting Products

East Anglian Shooting Products

The Street, Helhoughton, Fakenham,
Norfolk, Tel: 048 522 789

Wm James & Co (Bridport) Ltd
The Court, Bridport, Dorset, Tel: 0303
56666

Jamie Wood Ltd
Cross Street, Polegate, E Sussex, Tel:
03212 3813

KP & S Nets

Castle Street, Axminster, Devon, Tel: 0297 33920
Nylon rabbit nets and hemp nets, gate and road nets, net game bags. Largest stockists of D.I.Y. kits etc.

Dick Brothers

FIELD SPORTS EQUIPMENT MANUFACTURERS & SUPPLIERS

Trade suppliers of nylon and hemp purse nets, long nets, rabbit, hare & fox snares, brass wire & eyelets, dog & slip leads, spring & cage traps & all ferreting equipment. CAMMO NETS, DECOYS AND CALLS A SPECIALITY

23 ST. THOMAS ROAD, EDINBURGH EH9 2LY.
031 - 667 3874

R S Lawson Firearms & Ammunition
Great Western Road, Martock, Tel: 0935 823201

Map Shooting Supplies
14 Harrington Drive, Cheltenham, Gloucestershire, GL51 6ER, Tel: 0242 2352

Nets & Sporting Supplies
PO Box 21, Dorchester, Dorset, Tel: 0305 67630

E Parsons & Sons Ltd

PARSONS

Blackfriars Road, Nailsea, Bristol, Tel: 0272 854911
Portable telescopic hide frames and camouflage hessian screens and nets

Ralph Grant & Son Ltd
Green Lane Road, Leicester, LE5 4PD, Tel: 0533 767551
Manufacturers, Portable hide frames and camouflage hessian screens and nets

Tarpaulin & Tent Mfg
101/3 Brixton Hill, London, SW21AA, Tel: 01 674 0121

West Dorset Nets
80 North Allington, Bridport, Dorset, Tel: 0308 23576

HOLSTERS & GUN LEATHER

Price Western Leather Co Ltd
Ponsford Road, Minehead, Somerset, Tel: 0643 5071

Parker Hale Ltd
Golden Hillock Road, Birmingham, B11 2PZ, Tel: 021 773 8481

Horseshoe Leather Products
132 Aberford Road, Woodlesford, Leeds, W Yorks, Tel: 0532 824790

Chilham Dart Products
Station Approach, Chilham, Canterbury, Kent, Tel: 0227 730310
Pistol covers and holders

Phoenix Arms Co Ltd
Phoenix House, Churchdale Road, Eastbourne, Sussex, Tel: 0323 645131

INSTANT FIELD MEALS

Hotcan Ltd
Mangham Road, Rotherham, South Yorkshire, Tel: 0709 69856

KNIVES

4 Shot Ltd

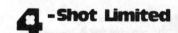
4-Shot Limited

Greenacre, Station Road, Beaconsfield, Bucks, Tel: 04946 2349

Battle Orders
71 Eastbourne Road, Lower Willingdon, Eastbourne, East Sussex, Tel: 032 12 7309
Fighting, hunting and survival knives, boot baggers, balisong martial arts knives. The latest ram bo survival knife. Over 100 to choose from.

Baytree Arms
10 Baytree Hill, Liskeard, Cornwall, Tel: 0579 46636

BSA Guns Ltd
Armoury Road, Birmingham, B11, Tel:
021 773 0845

Burton McCall Ltd
Samuel Street, Leicester, LE1 1RU,
Tel: 0533 538781
*Comprehensive range of sporting
knives including lock knives, sheath
knives and the Victorinox Swiss Army
knives*

David Nickerson (Tathwell) Ltd
The Old Vicarage, Tathwell, Louth,
Lincolnshire, LN11 9ST, Tel: 0472
840536
Distributors of Aitor knives

**Deer Management & Shooting
Sports**
Oxham School House, Jedburgh
Borders, Scotland, Tel: 08354 203

Finntrader Co
5 Verulam Avenue, Purley, Surrey,
CR2 3NR, Tel: 01 688 3905

Frank Dyke & Co Ltd
1/7 Ernest Avenue, West Norwood,
London, SE27, Tel: 01 670 2224

Gwynedd Firearms
99 High Street, Bangor, Gwynedd,
NL57 1NS

F Hall (Gunmakers) Ltd
Beetwell Street, Chesterfield,
Derbyshire, Tel: 0246 73133
*Special purpose knives made to order.
Large stock of knives from leading
makers*

Helston Gunsmiths
The Clies, Meneage Street, Helston,
Tel: 03265 3385

Intro Trading Ltd
The Coach House, Amberley, Stroud,
Gloucestershire, Tel: 045387 3633
*Sole UK importers of the Swedish Kniven
safety knife*

JLS Arms Co Ltd
Scoltock House, Perry Street,
Wednesbury, West Midlands, Tel:
021 556 1322

John R Gow & Sons Ltd
12 Union Street, Dundee, DD1
4BH, Tel: 0382 25427
*Retailers of sheath, hunting and
survival knives, lock knives, opinel
and swiss army knives.*

John Male Ltd

Church Norton, Selsey, Chichester,
PO20 9DS, Tel: 03243 603040

'Knifecraft', D Wise

304 Bexhill Road, St Leonards on
Sea, East Sussex, TN38 8AL, Tel:
0424 439168
*Hand crafted quality knives. Also,
knife making materials and
equipment supplies, including steels,
blades, with Sandvik C-27 special
knife steel-exotic hardwoods, brass
and nickel silver, plus hooks and knife
kits. Catalogue £1.*

Leslie Hewett Ltd
Upton Cross, Liskeard, Cornwall,
Tel: 0579 62319
Kershaw Knives. Normark Knives

Malcberry Ltd
366 Croydon Road, Beckenham, Kent,
Tel: 01 650 2255

**Mediterranean Shooting
Supplies Ltd**
P O Box 7, Evesham, Worcs, WR11
6YT, Tel: 0386 3654
*Sole Distributors of 'Fantoni' high
quality Hunting Knives.*

Keith Moorby
63 Cawdor Road, Sheffield, S Yorks,
Tel: 0742 651400
Hand crafted knives

Parker Hale Ltd
Golden Hillock Road, Birmingham,
West Midlands, Tel: 021 773 8481

Pat Walker Guns
143 Alexandra Road, Gateshead,
Tyne & Wear, Tel: 0632 786736
*Sole importers for I.M.I. (Israeli
Military Industries)*

Peter Henry & Son
332 Nine Mile Ride, Wokingham,
Berkshire, Tel: 0734 734475

Phoenix Arms Co Ltd
Churchdale Road, Eastbourne, East
Sussex, Tel: 0323 645131

Precision Arms Co Ltd
Wheatfield House, Church Road,
Paddock Wood, Kent, Tel: 089283
5730

Scalemead Arms Company
3 Medway Buildings, Lower Road,
Forest Row, Sussex, Tel: 034282 4433

**Springfield Firearms Company
Ltd**
8 Eastbourne Road, St Austell,
Cornwall, Tel: 0726 2733

Sterling Armament Co Ltd
Sterling Industrial Estate, Rainham
Road South, Dagenham, Essex, Tel: 01
595 2226

Viking Arms Ltd
Summerbridge, Harrogate, North
Yorkshire, HG3 4BW, Tel: 0423
780810

Whitby & Co
The Old Fire Station, Aynam Road,
Kendal, Cumbria, LA9 7DE, Tel: 0539
21032

**William Powell & Son
(Gunmakers) Ltd**
35/37 Carrs Lane, Birmingham, B4
7SX, Tel: 021 643 0689

Winchester UK, Site 7

WINCHESTER.

Kidderminster Road, Cutnall Green,
Hereford & Worcester, Tel: 029
923 461

KNIFE SHEATHS

Price Western Leather Co Ltd
Ponsford Road, Minehead, Somerset,
Tel: 0643 5071

4-Shot Ltd

4-Shot Limited

Beaconsfield, Bucks, Tel: 04946
2349

LAMPS

Accu Rest Design Products
Battle Lodge, North Trade Road,
Battle, East Sussex, Tel: 04246
2189
Solo Lamping System

Arnolds

1 Old Winch Hill Cottages, Winch
Hill, Wandon End, Luton, Beds, Tel:
0582 34955

Charles Henry Richards Ltd
84 Cardigan Street, Birmingham,
Tel: 021 3595757

Dan-Arms (UK) Ltd
8A Cannock Road, Burntwood,
Staffs
Maglite Torches

Deben Electronics
Wilford Bridge Road, Melton,,
Woodbridge, Suffolk, IP12 1RB,
Tel: 03943 7762
*Manufacturers and suppliers of a large
range of power packs, rechargeable
lights. UK distributors of the Optronics
lamp range, including the glare-free
'Blue Eye' range.*

Cluson Engineering Ltd
Unit 6, Bedford Road, Petersfield,
Hants, Tel: 0730 64672

John Male Ltd

Church Norton, Selsey, Chichester,
PO20 9DS, Tel: 0243 603040

C & D King Ltd
27 Meadowbrook, Dorking, Surrey,
Tel: 0306 883780

David Nickerson (Tathwell) Ltd
The Old Vicarage, Louth, Lincolnshire,
Tel: 0472 840536

Gunmark Ltd
The Armoury, Fort Wallington,
Fareham, Hants, Tel: 0329 231531
Kassnar and Wega recoil pads

L Le Personne & Co Ltd
Century House, Nobel Road, Eley
Estate, Angel Road, Edmonton,
London, N18, Tel: 01 803 4266

Parker Hale Ltd
Golden Hillock Road, Birmingham,
B11 2PZ, Tel: 021 773 8481

Phoenix Arms Co Ltd
Phoenix House, Churchdale Road,
Eastbourne, East Sussex, Tel: 0323
645131

Scalemead Arms Co
3 Medway Buildings, Lower Road,
Forest Row, Sussex, Tel: 034282 4433

Nets & Sporting Supplies
PO Box 21, Dorchester, Dorset, Tel:
0305 67630

Oliver J Gower Ltd
Unit K1 Cherry Court Way,
Stanbridge Road, Leighton Buzzard,
Beds, LU7 8WH, Tel: 0525 377730

Ralph Grant & Son Ltd
Green Lane Road, Leicester, LE5 4PD,
Tel: 0533 767551

West Dorset Nets 1985
80 North Allington, Bridport,
Dorset, Tel: 0308 23576
Suppliers of the Optronics lamprange

MAGAZINES

**Airgun World Burlington
Publishing Co Ltd**
10 Sheet Street, Windsor, Berks, Tel:
07535 56061

Countryside Monthly
Corry's, Roestock Lane, Colney Heath,
St Albans, Herts, Tel: 0707 371105

Countrysport Magazine
Unit 1, Pontiac Works, Fern Bank
Road, Ascot, Berks, SL5 8JH, Tel: 0344
884 222

Field, The
Carmalite House, Carmalite Street,
London, EC4Y 0JA, Tel: 01 353 6000

**Guns Review, Ravenhill
Publishing Co Ltd**
Standard House, Bonhill Street,
London, EC2A 4DA, Tel: 01 628 4741

Handgunner
7 Denton's Terrace, Wivenhoe,
Colchester, Essex, Tel: 020622 4635

**The Rifleman, National Small
Bore Rifle Association**
Lord Roberts House, Bisley Camp,
Brokwood, Woking, Surrey, Tel: 04867
6969

**Shooting Magazine, Burlington
Publishing Co Ltd**
10 Sheet Street, Windsor, Berkshire,
SL4 1BG, Tel: 07535 56061

Shooting News
Unit 25, Plymouth Road Industrial
Estate, Tavistock, Devon, PL19 9QN,
Tel: 0822 66460

**Shooting Times & Country
Magazine**
10 Sheet Street, Windsor, Berks, SL4
1BG, Tel: 07535 56061

**Sporting Air Rifle, Peterson
Publishing Co Ltd**
Peterson House, North Bank, Berryhill
Ind Estate, Droitwich, Worcs, Tel:
0905 775564

**Sporting Gun, Pursuit
Publishing Ltd, EMAP National
Publications**
Bretton Court, Bretton, Peterborough,
Cambridgeshire, PE3 8DZ, Tel: 0733
264666

**Tackle & Guns, Official Journal
of the Gun Trade Association**
9 The Shrubbery, Chatteris, Cambs,
Tel: 03543 3168

**Target Gun, Peterson Publishing
Co Ltd**
Peterson House, North Bank, Berryhill
Ind Estate, Droitwich, Worcs, Tel:
0905 775564

MILITARIA & REPRODUCTION WEAPONS

Antiques & Militaria
18 Pontefract Road, Castleford, W
Yorks, Tel: 0977 554339

Battle Orders
71 Eastbourne Road, Lower
Wallingdon, Eastbourne, East Sussex,
Tel: 032 12 7309
*Modern copies of medieval re-
enactment broadswords and rapiers.
Japanese samurai swords and historic
and modern replica firearms.*

British Sports
107 Praed Street, Paddington,
London, W2, Tel: 01 402 7511
*Stockists of all types of shotguns, rifles,
handguns, air guns, cartridges and
ammunition. Replica weapons and
clothing also available. Export
enquiries welcome. Open 9.00 - 6.00
Mon-Sat.*

A R Buckland

The Blue Barn, Stoke Holy Cross,
Norwich, Tel: 05086 3177
*We are full time gunsmiths to the trade
and public. We are also specialists in
military firearms, and cater for all
shooting enthusiasts, rifle, pistol or
shotgun.*

C.C.A.W. Ltd
Gunhouse, Steeple Bumpstead,
Haverhill, Suffolk, Tel: 044084 275

Phoenix Arms Co Ltd
Phoenix House, Churchdale Road,
Eastbourne, Sussex, Tel: 0323 645131

Uttings Tackle & Gun Shop
54 Bethel Street, Norwich, Norfolk,
NR2 1NR, Tel: 0603 621776

RECOIL PADS

Charles Henry Richards Ltd
84 Cardigan Street, Birmingham,
Tel: 021 3595757

RIFLESCOPES

**Accuracy International
(Shooting Sports) Ltd**

accuracy INTERNATIONAL

43 Gladys Avenue, North End,
Portsmouth, Hants, Tel: 0705
660371/2

Armalon Ltd
44 Harrowby Street, London, W1H
5HX, Tel: 01 262 1882

Armstrong's Gunsmiths
360 Carlton Hill, Carlton,
Nottingham, Tel: 0602 873313
*Habicht, Schmidt & Bender, Zeiss
Scopes, Zeiss Binoculars*

Arundel Sight Co
P O Box 56, Arundel, West Sussex,
Tel: 0903 883102
*Manufacturers of target sights and
scope mounts*

Bausch & Lomb (UK) Ltd
74 Oldfield Road, Hampton,
Middlesex, Tel: 01 979 7788
*Bushnell riflescopes, target scopes and
spotting scopes*

Caisson Supplies
91-95 Notting Hill Gate, London,
W11, Tel: 01 727 0530
*Suppliers of laserscopes and light
intensifying (80 000 :1)/night scopes.*

Carl Zeiss (Oberkochen) Ltd
P O Box 78, 17/20 Woodfield Road,
Welwyn Garden City, Herts, AL7
1LU, Tel: 0707 331144

The Country Gun Shop
Lilliesleaf, Melrose, Roxburghshire,
TD6 9JD, Tel: Lilliesleaf 0835 7315

Edgar Brothers
Catherine Street, Macclesfield,
Cheshire, Tel: 0625 613177
*Distributors of Weaver (USA) telescopic
sight mounts*

Gunmark Ltd
The Armoury, Fort Wallington,
Fareham, Hants, PO16 8TT, Tel: 0329
231531

Heron Optical
23/25 Kings Road, Brentwood, Essex,
CCM14 4ER, Tel: 0277 221259

Intergun
P O Box 1, Probus, Truro, Cornwall,
Tel: 087 252 243

Leslie Hewett Ltd
Upton Cross, Liskeard, Cornwall,
Tel: 0579 62319
Range of Leslie Hewett scopes

Hilton Gun Co Ltd
60 Station Road, Hatton, Derbys, Tel:
0283 814488

**John Rothery (Wholesale) Co
Ltd**

*John Rothery & Co.
(Wholesale) Ltd*

Portsmouth, Hants, Tel: 0705
667323
Distributors of Hunter riflescopes

Modern & Antique Firearms
147 Tuckton Road, Bournemouth,
Dorset, Tel: 0202 429369
*Importers of Leupold rifle and pistol
scopes*

Monk Optics
Hewelsfield, Glos, GL15 6UU, Tel:
0594 530666

Oliver J Gower Ltd
Unit K1, Cherrycourt Way, Stanbridge
Road, Leighton Buzzard, Beds, Tel:
0525 377730

Optima Leisure Products Ltd
Gilnow Mill, Spa Road, Bolton,
Lancs, BL1 4LF, Tel: 0204 386899

Parker Hale Ltd
Golden Hillock Road, Birmingham,
West Midlands, B11 2PZ, Tel: 021 773
8481

Pat Walker Guns
143 Alexandra Road, Gateshead,
Tyne & Wear, Tel: 0632 786736
*Sole importers of I.M.I. (Israeli
Military Industries) Nimrod rifle
scopes, night sights.*

Springfield Firearms Ltd
8 Eastbourne Road, St Austell,
Cornwall, Tel: 0726 2733

SSM International
Tedstone Whafre, Nr Bromyard,
Herefordshire, Tel: 08867 646/284

Theoben Engineering
Stephenson Road, St Ives,
Huntingdon, Cambs, PE17 4WJ,
Tel: 0480 61718
Stockist of Tasco scopes.

RIFLE SLINGS

Accuracy International Ltd
43 Gladys Avenue, Northend,
Portsmouth, Hants, PO2 9AZ, Tel:
0705 660371
Manufacturers of non slip rifle slings

Arnolds

1 Old Winch Hill Cottages, Winch
Hill, Wandon End, Luton, Beds, Tel:
0582 34955

JCP Ivor Sound Ltd
Unit 1004, 80 Como Street, Romford,
Essex, RM7 7DT, Tel: 0708 755992

John Male Ltd

Church Norton, Selsey, Chichester,
PO20 9DS, Tel: 0243 603040

Price Western Leather Co Ltd
Ponsford Road, Minehead, Somerset,
Tel: 0643 5071

SSM International
Tedstone Wafre, Nr Bromyard,
Herefordshire, Tel: 08867 646/284

Phoenix Arms Co Ltd
Churchdale Road, Eastbourne, East
Sussex, Tel: 0323 645131

Shooting Lodge Ltd
28/30 Victoria Street, Skipton, North
Yorks, Tel: 0756 5825

213

Pyser Ltd
Fircroft Way, Edenbridge, Kent, TN8
6HA, Tel: 0732 864111

SSM International
Tedstone Wafre, Nr Bromyard,
Herefordshire, Tel: TN08867 646/
284
Pointer riflescopes

Surrey Guns Ltd
9 Manor Road, Wallington, Surrey,
Tel: 01 647 0017

The Country Gun Shop
Lilliesleaf, Melrose, Roxburghshire,
TD6 9JD, Tel: 08357 315

Viking Arms Ltd
Summerbridge, Harrogate, North
Yorkshire, Tel: 0423 780810

**Weaver Scopes, Distributers
Winchester UK**

WINCHESTER.

Site 7, Kidderminster Road, Cutnall
Green, Hereford & Worcester, WR9
0NS, Tel: 029 923461

Webley & Scott Ltd
Frankley Industrial Park, Tay Road,
Rubery, Rednal, B45 0PA, Tel: 021
453 1864
Distributors of Tasco telescopic sights

ROLLER BLINDS

Colourspec Designs Ltd
Bridgeman Place Works, Salop
Street, Bolton, B12 1DD, Tel: 0204
397635

SHOOTING STICKS

4 Shot Ltd

4 -Shot Limited

Greenacre, Station Road,
Beaconsfield, Bucks, Tel: 04946
2349

Ballistic Precision Ltd
P O Box 172, Shadwell Street,
Birmingham, B4, Tel: 021 233 1640

Charles Henry Richards Ltd
84 Cardigan Street, Birmingham,
Tel: 021 3595757

Chilham Dart Products
Station Approach, Chilham,
Canterbury, Kent, Tel: 0227
730310

David Nickerson (Tathwell) Ltd
The Old Vicarage, Tathwell, Louth,
Lincolnshire, LN11 9ST, Tel: 0472
840536

**George Parker & Sons
(Saddlers) Ltd**
12 Upper St Martins Lane, London,
WC2, Tel: 01 836 1164

Hales HV & A (London) Ltd
2a Durants Road, Enfield. Middlesex,
Tel: 01 804 1911

John Male Ltd

Church Norton, Selsey, Chichester,
PO20 9DS, Tel: 0243 603040

John Slough of London

John Slough of London

35 Church Street, Hereford, Tel:
0432 55416

**The Leather Shop (Donald
Hanson) Ltd**
9 Swan Street, , Warwick, Tel: 0926
491571

Noirit Ltd
17/18 Hatherton Street, Walsall, Tel:
0922 25471
Manufacturers of Seat sticks

Normec (Manchester) Ltd
Smalley Street, Castleton, Rochdale,
Tel: 0706 32318

Prodec (Sports) Ltd

Armstrong Buildings, 48 Kilton
Road, Worksop, Notts

Quality Gunslips Ltd

quality gunslips

Birmingham, B18 5ST, Tel: 021
554 6528

Ralph Grant & Son Ltd
Green Lane Road, Leicester, Tel: 0533
767551

Ronnoco (Engineering) Ltd
Unit 7, Paddockholm North Ind
Estate, Kilbirnie, Ayrshire, Tel: 050 582
4559
Distributors of the 'T' seat

SSM International
Tedstone Wafre, Nr Bromyard,
Herefordshire, Tel: 08867 646/284

SHOTGUN CHOKE
GAUGES

JLS Arms Co Ltd
Scoltock House, Perry Street,
Wednesbury, West Midlands, Tel:
021 556 1322

Fosters Countrysport
1 Cleveland Street, Darlington, Co
Durham, Tel: 0325 51351

Helston Gunsmiths
The Clies, Meneage Street, Helston,
Cornwall, Tel: 032 65 3385

Parker Hale Ltd
Golden Hillock Road, Birmingham,
TEL: 021 773 8481

GUN CHOKES

F J Wiseman & Co
3 Price Street, Birmingham, B4 6JX,
Tel: 021 359 1256

SMOKING OVENS

Innes Walker Ltd
56-58 Queen Elizabeth Avenue,
Glasgow, G52 4NQ, Tel: 041 883
2139

SNAP CAPS

**Accuracy International
(Shooting Sports) Ltd**

43 Gladys Avenue, Northend,
Portsmouth, Hants, Tel: 0705
660371

Arnolds

1 Old Winch Hill Cottages, Winch
Hill, Wandon End, Luton, Beds, Tel:
0582 34955

Charles Henry Richards Ltd
84 Cardigan Street, Birmingham,
Tel: 021 3595757

Leslie Hewett Ltd
Upton Cross, Liskeard, Cornwall,
Tel: 0579 62319

Parker Hale Ltd
Golden Hillock Road, Birmingham,
Tel: 021 773 8481

Tonor Engineering Ltd
Ezekeil Lane, Short Heath, Willenhall,
West Midlands, Tel: 0922 75016

SPORTING BOOKS
SUPPLIERS &
PUBLISHERS

Anthony Atha Publishers Ltd
Weybread Lodge, Nr Diss, Norfolk,
Tel: 037 986 711
*Specialised publishers of fine limited
edition sporting books*

**Arms & Armour Press, Lionel
Leventhal Ltd**
2/6 Hampstead High Street, London,
NW3 1QQ, Tel: 01 794 0922

Blest P M
Little Canon Cottage, Wateringbury,
Maidstone, Kent, Tel: 0622 812940

Caisson Supplies
91-95 Notting Hill Gate, London,
W11, Tel: 01 727 0530
*Retailers of reloading manuals and
popular shooting titles. Restricted titles
also available to Military/Police
Officers.*

E Chalmers Hallam
Fernwood, Ringwood Road, Three
Legged Cross, Wimborne, Dorset, Tel:
0202 826700

Coleby R J W
Barrashead House, Lochmaben,
Dumfreisshire, DG11 1QF, Tel: 038
781 601

Fine Sporting Interests Ltd
Roundways High Street, Holt, Norfolk,
NR25 6BN

Grayling Books
Lyvennet Crosby, Ravensworth,
Penrith, Cumbria, CA10 3JP, Tel:
09315 282

Grosvenor Ltd
Station Works, Squires Gate Lane,
Blackpool, Lancashire, FY8 2SN, Tel:
0253 401402

Gwynedd Firearms
99 High Street, Bangor, Gwynedd,
NL57 1NS, Tel: 0248 351641

Hereward Books
32 High Street, Haddenham, Ely,
Cambridgeshire, CB 3XA

Hiller Airguns & Publications
92 Chorley Old Road, Whittle le
Woods, Chorley, Lancs, Tel: 02572
65489
*Publishers of the Collectors Guides to
Air Rifles, Air Pistols and other air
gun books. Send 60p for latest 34 page
catalogue.*

Jane Neville Fine Editions
Elm House, Abbey Lane, Aslockton,
Nottinghamshire, Tel: 0949 50220

John & Judith Head
The Barn Book Supply, 88 Crane
Street, Salisbury, Wilts, Tel: 0722
27767

John Male Ltd

Church Norton, Selsey, Chichester,
PO20 9DS, Tel: 0243 603040

Major Ian Grahame
Daws Hall, Lamarsh Bures, Suffolk,
CO8 5EX, Tel: 078729 213

Modern & Antique Firearms
147 Tuckton Road, Bournemouth,
Dorset, Tel: 0202 429369
*Suppliers of American magazines and
a wide range of sporting books*

Peterson Book Co
Peterson House, Northbank, Berryhill
Industrial Estate, Droitwich, Worcs,
WR9 9BL, Tel: 0905 775564

**Rowland Ward's at Holland &
Holland Ltd**
33 Bruton Street, London, W1X 8JS,
Tel: 01 499 4411

Nimrod Book Services
PO Box 1, Liss, Hants, GU33 7PR,
Tel: 0730 893541

B Shears & Sons Ltd
Homesteads Road, Basingstoke, Hants,
RG22 5RP, Tel: 0256 46777

The Sportsman's Press
5 King Charles Walk, London, SW19,
Tel: 01 789 0229

**Tideline Books Mail Order
Address**
PO Box 4, Rhyl, CLWYD, North
Wales,

Tideline Books
9 Kinmel Street, Rhyl, North Wales,
Tel: 0745 54919

Trotman, Ken
16 Hampstead High Street, London,
Tel: 01 794 3277

Way R E & GB Brettons
Burrough Gren, Newmarket, Suffolk,
CB8 9NA, Tel: 063 876 217

Willen Bookshop
Howard House, Howard Road,
London, E11, Tel: 01 556 776

STALKING EQUIPMENT

Armstrong's Gunsmiths
360 Carlton Hill, Carlton,
Nottingham, Tel: 0602 873313
*Stalking rifles, roe stacks, calls for
everything for the stalker. Agents for
'Arley' high seats*

4 Shot Ltd

4-Shot Limited

Beaconsfield, Bucks, Tel: 04946
2349

John R Gow & Sons Ltd
12 Union Street, Dundee, DD1
4BH, Tel: 0382 25427
*Most types of equipment available or
quickly obtained. Repairs undertaken.*

TARGET SHOOTING

**Leslie Bowler Ltd The Post
Office**
High Street, Little Bytham,
Grantham, Lincs, Tel: 078081 200
*Manufacturers of Bowlers Olympic
Grips, made to measure anatomical
target pistol grips*

Caisson Supplies Ltd
91-95 Notting Hill Gate, London ,
W11 , Tel: 01 727 0530

Guncraft
11 Woodcock Hill, Kenton, Harrold,
Middlesex, HA3 0XP, Tel: 01 907 3651
*Guncraft unique 100 rounds ammo boxes
.221r*

Accuracy International Ltd
43 Gladys Avenue, Northend,
Portsmouth, Hants, Tel: 0705
660371
*Distributors and manufacturers of all
target shooting accessories*

Surrey Guns Ltd
9 Manor Road, Wallington, Surrey,
Tel: 01 647 0017

SUNGLASSES

Accuracy International

43 Gladys Avenue, North End,
Portsmouth, Hants, Tel: 0705
660371/2
*Distributors of Junker Swiss shooting
glass frames*

Bausch & Lomb (UK) Ltd
74 Oldfield Road,
Hampton,Middlesex, Tel: 01 979
7788

Optix Cormorants Ltd
542 Fishponds Road, Bristol, BS16
3EX, Tel: 0272 650432
*Manufacturers of 'Optix' Cormorants
polarised sunglasses*

Solar Sunglasses Ltd
10 Belgrave Road, London, E11, Tel:
01 505 1580
*Manufacturers of unbreakable folding
sunglasses and Reactolite Rapide lenses*

Solar Sunglasses Ltd
154 Queens Road, Buckhurst Hill,
Essex

SURVIVAL AIDS

Survival Aids Ltd
Morland, Penrith, Cumbria, CA10
3AZ, Tel 09314 307

TARGET SYSTEMS

Abbey Supply Co
197 Great Knollys Street, Reading,
Berks, Tel: 0734 584767
*Manufacturers of knock-down field
targets. Life size. Distributors of Fieldskill,
knock out Head-Shot and Can-Shoot field
targets*

Dacle Products
109 Fermor Way, Crowborough,
Sussex

TAXIDERMISTS

A Allison
The Lodge, East Brackley, Kinross,
KY13 7LV, Tel: 0577 63115

Barry Williams, Taxidermist
Fleur de lys Cottage, Watling Street,
Cannock, Staffs, Tel: 0543 74247
*Birds, Mammals and fish artistically
mounted. Display cases and domes
available. Commission work and
specimens from stock*

Chris Campbell
3 Raleigh Court, Falkirk, Scotland,
Tel: 0324 29653
*Trohpy heads, gamebirds, fish casts.
Registered with DoE*

David Cemmick
Smithy House Farm, Great Smeaton,
North Allerton, North Yorkshire,
Tel:0325 483271 Ext 144 &
060981 652
*Professional work of the highest
standard. Attention to authentic
individual detail and natural
modelling a speciality.*

N Crewdson
Clayton Bank, Weasel Lane,
Tockholes, Tel: 0254 73632

C J Dennis
Sunnyside Farm, Breaton, Harrogate,
Tel: 0423 864707

Duncan Ferguson

64 Lauderdale Gardens, Hyndland,
Glasgow, Strathclyde, Scotland, Tel:
041 357 3929
Guild of Taxidermy member

C P Dunton, Taxidermist
The Firs,Chesham Road, Wigginton,
Tring, Herts, Tel: 024029 752

Christopher Elliott
51 Huntingdon Road, Thrapston, Tel:
08012 3022

D.Frampton

25 Durrant's Road,, Berkhampstead,
Herts., Tel: 04427 2840
Guild of Taxidermy member

M Gadd
18 Walton Road, Wetherby, West
Yorkshire, Tel: 0937 61285
Guild of Taxidermy member

M.R.Grace
3 Chapel Street, Camelford,
Cornwall, Tel: 0840 212289
*Bird, fish or mammals. Reg DOE.
Some specimen for sale.*

Hall A E
1 The Bourne, Cockshot Lane,
Dormston, Inkberrow, Hereford &
Worcester, Tel: 0386 792101

C A Horrocks Taxidermist
85 Higher Croft, Barton-upon-Irwell,
Peel Green, Eccles, Manchester, Tel:
061 707 6007

John C Metcalf
The Garden House, Noseley, Nr
Billesdon, Leicestershire, Tel: 0537
55604

Jamieson George
Cramond Tower, Cramond Glebe
Road, Edinburgh, Scotland, EH4
6NS, Tel: 031 336 1916
*George Jamieson is a registered
taxidermist with the DOE and
specialises in Scottish game. Stock
available for sale. Direct freighting
service to most parts of the world
including export licence.*

Jamieson George
Primrose Bank, 27 Primrose Bank
Road, Edinburgh, Tel: 031 552
2681
Guild of Taxidermy member

K L McDonald
Elmwood, Post Office Road,
Woodham, Mortimer Malden,
Danburyt, Tel: 024541 5378

Noahs Ark Taxidermy
35 Tankerville Street, Hartlepool,
Cleveland, Tel: 0429 74171
*The true artist. For details please ring
Kevin Wilmot or send SAE for price
list.*

North Devon Taxidermy
Lower Moor Copse, Atherington,
Umberleigh, Tel: 0769 60410

Partridge Taxidermy Studios
HIgh Street, Partridge Green,
W.Sussex, Tel: 0403 711204 or
0306 730939
*Anything birds, mammals, fish,
artistically mounted to high standard.
Glass domes a speciality.*

Peter O'Connor
136 High Street, Leagrave, Luton,
Bedfordshire, Tel: 0582 573158
*Taxidermist of Europe. Chairman of
Taxidermist Federation of Great
Britain and Ireland. Specialist in
trophy and museum work. Specimens
for sale. Red Star service to Luton.*

Pettitts Taxidermy Service
Camphill, Reedham, Norwich, Nr13
3UA, Tel: 0493 700132
*All types of taxidermy work
undertaken. Large selection always for
sale. Send SAE for details.*

Ronnie Sanderson
13 Westfield, Stainland, Halifax,
W.Yorks., Tel: 0422 78885
*Anything mounted in minimum time
possible-very competitive prices. Very
high quality craftsmanship. Distance
no object.*

Snowdonia Taxidermy Studios
Llanrwst, Gwynedd, Wales, Tel: 0492
640664

Tom Elliott
52 Eastfield Drive, Hanslope, Milton
Keynes, Buckinghamshire, Tel: 0908
510081

Windham Wright, M
Minard Farmhouse, Lerags, Oban,
Argyll, PA34 4SE, Tel: 0631 64936 &
54023

N R Wood
Coverside, The Soss, Misterton,
Doncaster, South Yorkshire, DN10
4DQ, Tel: 0427 890243
*Birds, mammals and fish mounted to
clients specifications. Specimens for sale*

TENTS

Fjallraven Ltd
Unit 5, Waterside, Hamm Moor
Lane, Weybridge, Surrey, KT15
5DN, Tel: 0932 57310

VIDEOS

Intervideo Publications Ltd
Bonnyton House, Inverarity,
Tayside, DD8 2JS, Tel: 030782 327
*Encompassing most aspects of field
sports.*

---

2 WHEEL DRIVE

NISSAN
Nissan UK Ltd
Nissan House, Columbria Drive,
Durrington, Worthing, E Sussex,
BN13 3HD, Tel: 0903 68561
PEUGEOT, 'Peugeot 505 Estate'

Talbot Motor Co
International House, Brickenhill Lane,
Marsden Lane, Birmingham, B37 7HZ,
Tel: 021 779 6565

SIERRA AND ESCORT ESTATES
**Ford Motor Company, Central
Office**
Eagle Way, Brentwood, Essex, CM13
3BW, Tel: 0277 253000
VOLVO 245

Aylmer Motor Works
2 St Georges Ind Estate, White Hart Lane, London, N22

Lex Mead Motor Co
Ariston House, London Road, Loudwater, High Wycombe, HP11 1HF, Tel: 0494 33460
SUBARU

Subaru UK (Ltd)
Ryder Street, West Bromwich, West Midlands, Tel: 021 557 6200

Volvo Concessionaires Ltd
Cressex Industrial estate, Lancaster REOAD, High Wycombe, HP12 3QE, Tel: 0494 33444

4 WHEEL DRIVE

AUDI QUATTRO RANGE
V.A.G. (UK) Ltd
Yeomans Drive, Buakelands, Milton Keynes, Bucks, MK14 5AW, Tel: 0908 679121

JEEP

Jeep (UK) Ltd
54 St James Street, London, SW1, Tel: 01 491 2599

MERCEDES

Mercedes Benz (UK) Ltd
Milton Keynes, Tel: 0908 668899

MITSUBISHI COLT,
MITSUBISHI SHOGUN

The Colt Car Company
Tel: 0285 5777

NISSAN
Nissan UK Ltd
Columbia Drive, Durrington, Worthing, West Sussex, Tel: 0903 68561

RANGE ROVER, LAND ROVER
Landrover Ltd
Lode Lane, Solihull, West Midlands, Tel: 021 743 4242

Advertiser's Index

General Index